Royal Zoological Society of Ireland

General Irish Natural History

Vol. V

Royal Zoological Society of Ireland

General Irish Natural History
Vol. V

ISBN/EAN: 9783744732154

Printed in Europe, USA, Canada, Australia, Japan

Cover: Foto ©ninafisch / pixelio.de

More available books at **www.hansebooks.com**

A Monthly Journal

OF

GENERAL IRISH NATURAL HISTORY,

THE OFFICIAL ORGAN OF

The Royal Zoological Society of Ireland; The Dublin Microscopical Club;
The Belfast Natural History and Philosophical Society;
The Belfast Naturalists' Field Club; The Dublin Naturalists' Field Club;
The Armagh Natural History and Philosophical Society;
The Cork Naturalists' Field Club; The Limerick Naturalists' Field Club.

EDITED BY

GEORGE H. CARPENTER, B.Sc., LOND.

AND

R. LLOYD PRAEGER, B.A., B.E., M.R.I.A.

VOL. V.

DUBLIN: EASON & SON, LIMITED,
85 MIDDLE ABBEY STREET, AND 40 LOWER SACKVILLE STREET.
BELFAST: 17 DONEGALL STREET.
LONDON: SIMPKIN, MARSHALL, HAMILTON, KENT & CO., LTD.

1896.

PRINTED BY ALEX. THOM & CO. (LIMITED), 87, 88, & 89, ABBEY-STREET, DUBLIN.

CONTRIBUTORS

TO THE PRESENT VOLUME.

—:o:—

G. E. H. BARRETT-HAMILTON, B.A., New Ross.
R. M. BARRINGTON, LL.B., F.L.S., Fassaroe, Bray.
W. B. BARRINGTON, Cork.
H. D. M. BARTON, Antrim.
J. BELLAS, Coleraine.
E. BLAKE-KNOX, Bray.
REV. S. A. BRENAN, B.A., Knocknacary, Co. Antrim.
HENRY W. BRÖLEMANN, Paris.
E. T. BROWNE, University College, London.
H. BULLOCK, Dundrum, Co. Dublin.
D. C. CAMPBELL, Londonderry.
GEO. H. CARPENTER, B.SC., F.E.S., Science & Art Museum, Dublin.
PROF. G. A. J. COLE, F.G.S., M.R.I.A., R. College of Science, Dublin.
NATHANIEL COLGAN, M.R.I.A., Dublin.
W. E. COLLINGE, F.Z.S., Mason College, Birmingham.
E. V. COOPER, Killanne, Co. Wexford.
R. H. CREIGHTON, M.B., Ballyshannon.
H. K. G. CUTHBERT, Blackrock, Co. Dublin.
J. H. DAVIES, Lisburn.
REV. A. H. DELAP, M.A., Strabane.
J. E. DUERDEN, A.R.C.SC., Kingston, Jamaica.
G. P. FARRAN, Templeogue, Co. Dublin.
PERCY E. FREKE, Borris, Co. Carlow.
REV. HILDERIC FRIEND, F.L.S., Ocker Hill, Staffordshire.
F. W. GAMBLE, M.SC., Owens College, Manchester.
REV. T. B. GIBSON, M.A., Ferns, Co. Wexford.
REV. W. S. GREEN, Dublin.
J. N. HALBERT, Science and Art Museum, Dublin.
W. A. HAMILTON, Ballyshannon.
G. V. HART, Q.C., LL.D., Dublin.
H. C. HART, B.A., F.L.S., Letterkenny.
MISS R. HENSMAN, Dublin.
R. F. HIBBERT, Scariff, Co. Clare.
C. B. HORSBRUGH.
J. HUNTER, Woodenbridge, Co. Wicklow.
C. HERBERT HURST, PH.D., Dublin.
H. LYSTER JAMESON, B.A., Castlebellingham.
PROF. T. JOHNSON, D.SC., F.L.S., Royal College of Science, Dublin.
REV. W. F. JOHNSON, M.A., F.E.S., Poyntzpass.
W. F. DE V. KANE, M.A., F.E.S., Drumreaske, Co. Monaghan.
C. LANGHAM, Enniskillen.

Rev. H. W. Lett, m.a., Loughbrickland, Co. Down.
H. C. Levinge, f.l.s., Knockdrin Castle, Mullingar.
C. J. Lilly, Larne.
Rev. E. F. Linton, m.a., f.l.s., Bournemouth.
F. W. Lockwood, Belfast.
W. Macmillan, Enniskillen.
E. A. Martel, Paris.
David M'Ardle, Royal Botanic Gardens, Glasnevin.
J. M. M'Bride, Westport.
Prof. E. J. McWeeney, m.a., m.d., Dublin.
C. B. Moffat, Ballyhyland, Co. Wexford.
Miss F. S. O'Connor, Ballycastle.
J. E. Palmer, Dublin.
R. A. Phillips, Ashburton, Co. Cork.
Greenwood Pim, m.a., f.l.s., Monkstown, Dublin.
R. Lloyd Praeger, b.a., b.e., m.r.i.a., Dublin.
P. Ralfe, Laxey, Isle of Man.
Rev. Canon C. D. Russell, m.a., Geashill, King's Co.
T. Ryan, Castlewellan, Co. Down.
R. F. Scharff, b.sc., ph.d., m.r.i.a., Dublin.
J. A. Scott, m.d., f.r.c.s.i., Dublin.
W. Sinclair, Strabane.
W. F. Sinclair, London.
R. Standen, Manchester.
S. A. Stewart, Belfast.
A. P. Swan, f.l.s., Bandon.
R. J. Ussher, j.p., Cappagh, Co. Waterford.
Rev. C. H. Waddell, b.d., Saintfield, Co. Down.
Miss A. Warren, Ballina.
Robert Warren, j.p., Ballina.
R. Welch, Belfast.
E. Williams, Dublin.
A. G. Wilson, Belfast.
Harry F. Witherby, f.z.s., London.

Acherontia atropos, 87, 191, 317.
Acrocephalus nævius, 191.
Aculeate Hymenoptera, 39, 294.
Adams' British Land and Freshwater Mollusca (Review), 285.
Alchemilla vulgaris, 296.
Algæ from Belfast Lough, 252.
Allis Shad, 191, 248.
Allium triquetrum, 167.
American Robin in Connaught, 214.
Andesitic volcanic tuff, 245.
Ascetta primordialis, 109.
Asperococcus compressus, 244.
Asteroscopus sphinx, 317.
Atypus in King's Co., 213.

Barrett-Hamilton, G. E. H.—Irish Hare going to ground, 119; Great Auk as an Irish Bird, 121.
Barrington, R. M.—Wasps catching flies on cattle, 272.
Barrington, W. B.—Bird-notes from Cork, 320.
Barton, H. D. M.—Razorbill on Lough Neagh, 214; Stock-dove in Co. Down, 214.
Belfast Club and its work, 209.
Belfast Natural History and Philosophical Society, 19, 82, 109.
Belfast Naturalists' Field Club, 20, 52, 82, 109, 138, 183, 209, 215, 245, 264, 295, 314.
Bellas, J.—Stray Snake near Coleraine, 168.
Bird-notes, 55, 191, 192.
Bird-notes from Co. Cork, 320.
Birds of Connemara, 1, 88, 299, 319.
Black Guillemots, nesting, 117.
Blake-Knox, E.—Wood-sandpiper in Co. Wicklow, 275.
Bone pins, 81.
Botanical Subdivision of Ireland, 29, 73.
Botany at Dublin University, 105.
Botany of Dublin School Playground, 277.
Brambling in Vale of Avoca, 28.
Brenan, S. A.—Irish Hawkweeds, 27; Notes from Cushendun, 166.
Brölemann, H. W.—Lithobius variegatus, 12.
Browne, E. T.—Medusæ of Valentia Harbour, 179.
Bullock, H.—Quail in Co. Dublin, 275.

Campbell, D. C.—Spring Migrants, 168; Crane at Inch, 214; Catocala fraxini at Londonderry, 318; Fork-tailed Petrel near Londonderry, 320.
Camptogramma bilineata, 74.
Canis vulpes melanogaster, 178.
Carabus clathratus, 191.
Carex teretiuscula, 270.
Carpenter, G. H.—Mingling of North and South, 57; Atypus in King's Co., 167; Spiders of Clonbrock, 225; Abundance of Acherontia atropos, 317.
Carrion Crow in Co. Antrim, 319.
Casuals in Co. Antrim, 309.
Catocala fraxini, 318.
Cavan, Field Clubs in, 193.
Cave, longest in British Islands, 276.
Cave at Westport, 320.
Caves, Irish, 123.
Caves in Co. Leitrim, 276.
Caves of Enniskillen and Mitchelstown, 93, 101.
Cephalozia Turneri, 136.
Chermes phaleratus, 215.
Chlorochytrium inclusum, 51.
Chromatium Okenii, 313.
Clonbrock, Flora and Fauna of, 217.
Coccidium oriforme, 53.
Cole, G. A. J.—Shell of Helix nemoralis, 47; Geological Studies in the North, 48; Oldhamia in America, 254; Alleged Eurite of Lisnamandra, 276.
Coleoptera of Clonbrock, 230.
Colgan, N.— Early flowering of Lathræa squamaria, 115; Scrophularia umbrosa, 182; Flora of Ox Mountains, 301.
Colliguaja odorifera, 51.
Collinge, W. E.—Slugs from N.W. Ireland, 144; Slugs of Ireland, 318.
Columba œnas, 192, 214.
Cooper, E. V.—Pinguicula grandiflora introduced in Co. Wexford, 212.
Copepoda, 27, 298.
Cork Cuvierian Society, 26.
Cork Naturalists' Field Club, 24, 84, 111, 164, 186, 216, 267, 317.
Cormorants in Co. Donegal, 214.

Corvus corone, 319.
Crane on Lough Swilly, 214.
Creighton, R. H.—Entomostraca, 89.
Crithmum maritimum, 297.
Crossbills, 28.
Curlews, 117.
Cuthbert, H. K. G.—Carabus clathratus in Co. Wicklow, 191.
Cyathus vernicosus, 55, 115.

Davies, J. H.—Carex teretiuscula in Co. Down, 270; Casuals in Co. Antrim, 309.
Death's Head Moth. 87, 191, 317.
Delap, A. H.—Lathræa squamaria 167; Formica rufa, 167.
Denudation of the Chalk, 56.
Dilsea edulis, 51.
Directory of Irish Naturalists, 107.
Dobson, G. E.—Obituary notice of, 73.
Donegal Plants, 298.
Dryas octopetala, 269.
Dublin Microscopical Club, 17, 50, 81, 108, 136, 183, 215, 244, 312.
Dublin Naturalists' Field Club, 23, 52, 83, 110, 141, 185, 216, 266, 295, 316.
Duck, Longtailed, in Co. Clare, 28.
Duerden, J. E.—Rock-pools of Bundoran, 153.

Early Emergence, 87.
Early Hawthorn, 143.
Earth-stars. 55.
Earthworms, 69; of Clonbrock, 222.
Entomological Notes from Poyntzpass, 190; from N. E. Ireland, 272.
Entomostraca, 89.
Eurite of Co. Cavan, 276.
Eurotium herbariorum, 183.

Farran, G. P.—Grasshopper Warbler in Co. Dublin, 191; Asteroscopus sphinx in Co. Dublin, 317.
Fauna of Belfast Lough, 271.
Fauna and Flora of Clonbrock, 217.
Feathered Pensioners, 118.
Field Clubs in Cavan, 193.
Field Club News, 26, 54, 86, 113, 142, 165, 181, 267, 300.
Flora of N. E. Ireland, 188; of Clonbrock, 217; of Lough Derg, 269; of Connemara Lakes, 292; of Ox Mountains, Co. Sligo, 301.
Flowering Plants and Vascular Cryptogams of Clonbrock, 239.
Formica rufa, 143, 167.

Freke, P. E.—Irish Hymenoptera Aculeata, 39, 294.
Freshwater Worms, 125, 189.
Friend, H.—Earthworms of Ireland, 69; Irish FreshwaterWorms, 125, 189; Earthworms of Clonbrock, 222.
Fringilla montifringilla, 28.
Fungi from Brackenstown, Co. Dublin, 6; of Clonbrock, 234; New Irish, 268; of Brittas Bay, 268.

Gamble, F. W.—Shore-collecting and dredging at Valentia, 124.
Geaster fimbriatus, 55.
Geological Studies in the North, 48.
Geology of the Curran, Larne, 120.
Gibson, T. B.—Botany of School Playground in Dublin, 277.
Glacial Geology, 255.
Gladiolus tristis, 108.
Gonepteryx rhamni, 87.
Grasshopper Warbler in Co. Dublin, 191.
Great Auk, 121.
Green, W. S.—Nesting of Black Guillemot, 118.
Grus communis, 214.
Gulls of Killala Bay, 169.

Halbert, J. N.—Insects from Lugnaquilla and Glenmalur, 210; Hemiptera of Clonbrock, 229; Coleoptera of Clonbrock, 230.
Hamilton, W. A.—Spring migrants, 144.
Hare, Irish, 119.
Harelda glacialis, 28.
Hart, G. V.—Gonepteryx rhamni in Queen's Co., 87; An early emergence, 87; Mixodia palustrana in Co. Wicklow, 318.
Hart, H. C.—Flora of N. E. Ireland, 188; Measurement of a Scotch Fir stump, 189.
Hawkweeds, 27.
Helix arbustorum, 213, 318; H. fusca, 318; H. nemoralis, 47.
Hemiptera of Clonbrock, 229.
Hensman, Miss, and Johnson, T.—Algæ from Belfast Lough, 252.
Hepaticæ of Co. Carlow, 200; of Clonbrock, 235.
Hibbert, R. F.—Longtailed Duck in Co. Clare, 28; Stock-dove in Co. Galway, 192.
Hornblende-Schist, 137.
Horsbrugh, C. B.—Night-heron in Co. Cork, 276.

Hottonia palustris, 115.
Hunter, J.—Brambling in Vale of Ovoca, 28; Crossbills in do., 28.
Hurst, C. H.—Fauna of Belfast Lough, 271.
Hydroids and Medusæ, 298.
Hyella nitida, 81.
Hymenoptera aculeata, Irish, 39, 116, 294.
Hypersthene, 18.

Iceland Gull, 192.
Insects of Lugnaquilla and Glenmalur, 210.
Irish Field Club Union, 215.
Island-Flora of Connemara Lakes, 292.
Isopods of Clonbrock, 225.
Ixodes marginatus, 17.

Jameson, H. L.—Caves of Enniskillen and Mitchelstown, 93; Caves in Co. Leitrim, 276.
Johnson, T., and Hensman, Miss—Algæ from north side of Belfast Lough, 252.
Johnson, W. F.—Irish Hymenoptera aculeata, 116; Draba verna at Poyntzpass, 188; Entomological Notes from Poyntzpass, 190; from N.E. Ireland, 273; Acherontia atropos at Bessbrook, 191; Spring Migrants at Poyntzpass, 191; Vespa norvegica at Omeath, 213.
Jungermannia exsecta, 245.

Kane, W. F. de V.—Pine Marten in Ireland, 28; Melanism in Camptogramma bilineata, 74.
Killala Bay Terns, 145; Gulls, 169; Skuas, 248.
Kingfisher in Co. Dublin, 318.

Land-locked Salmon, 16.
Land-planarians and Leeches of Clonbrock, 221.
Land-rail, 168.
Langham, C.—Iceland Gull on the Sligo Coast, 192.
Larus leucopterus, 192.
Lathræa squamaria, 115, 166, 167.
Lepidium Draba, 212.
Leptyphantes pallidus, 51.
Lett, H. W.—Lathræa squamaria, 156; Dryas octopetala in Co. Antrim, 269.
Levinge, H. C.—Plants of Westmeath, 44; Obituary notice of, 107.

Lilly, C. J.—Flora of Lough Derg, 269.
Limerick Naturalists' Field Club 25, 85.
Limosella aquatica, 297.
Linton, E. F.—Alchemilla vulgaris, 296.
Lithobius variegatus, 12.
Littorina obtusata, 248.
Lockwood, F. W.—Geology of the Curran, Larne, 120.
Loxia curvirostris, 28.

M'Ardle, D.—Co. Carlow Hepaticæ, 200; Mosses and Hepaticæ of Clonbrock, 235.
M'Bride, J. M.—Cave at Westport, 320.
Macmillan, W.—Globe-flower in Co. Fermanagh, 188; Quail in Co. Monaghan, 214.
M'Weeney, E. J.—Fungi from Brackenstown, 6; Fungi of Clonbrock, 234; New Irish Fungi, 268; Fungi of Brittas Bay, 268.
M'Weeney, E. J., and Praeger, R. Ll.—Fauna and Flora of Clonbrock, Prefatory Note, 217.
Magpie in Isle of Man, 168, 189.
Marine Mollusca of Co. Galway, 274
Martel, E. A.—Mitchelstown Cave, 101.
Martens, 28.
Matricaria discoidea, 290.
Medicago sylvestris, 249, 298.
Medusæ of Valentia Harbour, 179.
Melanism in Camptogramma bilineata, 74.
Melobesia confinis, 18; M. farinosa, 82.
Mercurialis perennis, 212.
Meyrick's British Lepidoptera (Review), 290.
Mildness of season, 87.
Mingling of North and South, 67, 116.
Mitchelstown Cave, 101.
Mixodia palustrana, 318.
Moffat, C. B.—Mingling of North and South, 116; Migration of Curlews, 117; Formica rufa in Co. Wexford, 143; Our introduced species, 189; Quail in Ireland, 203.
Mollusca of West of Ireland, 213. 248; of Cavan Excursion, 274; of Clonbrock, 223.
Molophilus ater, 137.
Moss Exchange Club, 55, 296.
Mosses and Hepatics of Clonbrock, 235.

Natural History Papers, Recent, 162.
Nectria aurantium, 136; N. sanguinea, 137.
Night-Heron in Co. Cork, 276.
Nitophyllum reptans, 51.

Obituary Notices.—G. E. Dobson, 73; H. C. Levinge, 107.
Oceanodroma leucorrhoa, 320.
O'Connor, Miss.—Spider carrying snail-shell, 299.
Oldhamia in America. 254.
Onesinda minutissima, 312.
Opal-bearing rhyolite, 137.
Ox Mountains, Flora of, 301.

Palmer, J. E.—Birds of Connemara, 88.
Peziza sclerotium, 313.
Phillips, R. A.—Ranunculus tripartitus, an addition to the Irish Flora, 166; Allium triquetrum in Co. Cork, 167.
Phonolite, 215.
Phyllactinia guttata, 51.
Phyllosiphon arisari, 137.
Pim, G.—Cyathus vernicosus, 115; Early Hawthorn, 143; Limosella aquatica in Clare, 297; Kingfisher in Co. Dublin, 318.
Pinguicula grandiflora, 212.
Plagiochila asplenioides, 51.
Plants of Westmeath, 44; Irish, 188; of Co. Down, 142; of Inismurray, 177.
Praeger, R. Ll.—Botanical Subdivision of Ireland, 29; Birds-nest Fungus new to Ireland, 55; Earth-stars in Co. Tipperary, 55; Directory of Irish Naturalists, 107; Early flowering of Hottonia palustris, 115; Raised Beach at Fort Stewart, 119; Irish Caves, 123; Submerged Pine-forest, 155; Plants of Inismurray, 177; Field Clubs in Cavan, 193; Teesdalia nudicaulis in Ireland, 212; Mercurialis perennis in Co. Monaghan, 212; Flora and Fauna of Clonbrock, 217, 239; Veronica peregrina in Ireland, 247; Scirpus parvulus, 247; Medicago sylvestris in Ireland, 249; in Scotland, 298; Island-flora of Connemara lakes, 292; Stachys Betonica in Antrim, 297; Matricaria discoidea at Howth, 298.
Praeger's Bibliography of Irish Glacial Geology (Review), 257.
Puccinia Lapsanæ, 136.

Quail in Cork, 192; in Ireland, 203; in Co. Monaghan, 214; in Co. Dublin, 275; in Co. Down, 299.

Ralfe, P.—Magpie in Isle of Man, 168.
Raised Beach at Fort Stewart, 119.
Ramulina, 81.
Ranunculus tripartitus, 166.
Razorbill, 214.
Reviews.—Geological Studies in the North, 48; Botany at Dublin University, 155; Witchell's Evolution of Bird-song, 160; Recent Natural History Papers, 162; Swann's Handbook of British Birds, 207; Proceedings of Belfast Naturalists' Field Club, 209; Sollas' Distribution of Eskers in Ireland, 255; Praeger's Bibliography of Irish Glacial and Post-Glacial Geology, 257; Adams' Manual of British Land and Freshwater Mollusca, 285; Tutt's British Butterflies, 287; Meyrick's British Lepidoptera, 290.
Riccardia latifrons, 18.
Rock-pools of Bundoran, 153.
Rooks, feathers of, 18.
Royal Irish Academy, 187.
Royal Zoological Society, 17, 50, 80, 108, 136, 164, 183, 215, 244, 263, 294, 312.
Russell, C. D.—Lathræa squamaria in King's Co., 167.
Ryan, T.—Lathræa squamaria in Co. Down, 142.

Salmon, supposed land-locked, 16.
Scapania compacta, 137; S. umbrosa, 183.
Scharff, R. F.—Supposed land-locked Salmon, 16; Canis vulpes melanogaster in Ireland, 178; Land planarians and Leeches of Clonbrock, 221; Land and Freshwater Mollusca of Clonbrock, 223; Isopods of Clonbrock, 225.
Sciæna aquila, 275.
Scirpus parvulus, 247.
Scotch Fir stump, 189.
Scott, J. A.—Death's-head Moth in Dublin, 87.
Scrophularia umbrosa, 182.
Seasonable Notes from Cushendun, 166.
Selaginella oregana 108.
Shade-fish, 275.

Sinclair, W.—Allis shad in Irish waters, 248.
Sinclair, W. F.—Submerged Peat-bogs in Co. Donegal, 192.
Sisyrinchium californicum, 269.
Skuas of Killala Bay, 268.
Slugs, 144, 318.
Snakes, 28, 168.
Sollas' Distribution of Eskers (Review), 255.
Song of Birds, 160.
Sphærostilbe flavoviridis, 215.
Sphagnum papillosum, 108.
Spiders of Clonbrock, 225.
Spider carrying snail-shell, 299.
Spirialis retroversus, 248.
Spring migrants, 144, 168, 191.
Stachys Betonica, 297.
Standen, R.—Carrion Crow in Co. Antrim, 319.
Stewart, S. A.—Crithmum maritimum in Co. Down, 297; Prof. R. Tate's visit to Belfast, 308.
Stockdoves, 28, 191, 214.
Submerged Peat-bogs 192.
Submerged Pine-forest, 155.
Swan, A. P.—Quail in Co. Cork, 192.
Swann's Handbook of British Birds (Review), 207.

Teesdalia nudicaulis, 212.
Terns of Killala Bay, 145.
Totanus glareola, 275.
Tribolium ferrugineum, 248.
Trichoniscus roseus, 213.
Trollius europœus, 188.

Trumbull, J.—Stockdoves in Co. Dublin, 28.
Tuberculina persicina, 18.
Turdus migratorius, 214.
Tutt's British Butterflies (Review), 287.

Ussher, R. J.—American Robin in Connaught, 214; Birds of Connemara, 319.

Veronica peregrina, 247.
Vespa norvegica, 213.
Volcanic bomb, 81.

Waddell, C. H.—Scarcity of Landrail, 168.
Warren, Miss—Spirialis retroversus in Killala Bay, 248.
Warren, R.—Terns of Killala Bay, 145; Gulls of Killala Bay, 169; Skuas of Killala Bay, 258.
Wasps catching flies on cattle, 272.
Welch, R.—Trichoniscus roseus, 213; Helix arbustorum, 213, 318; H. fusca, 318; Marine Mollusca of Co. Galway, 274; Mollusca of Cavan Excursion, 274.
White Swallow, 319.
Williams, E.—Irish Bird-notes, 55.
Wilson, A. G.—Quartzite, 56; Littorina obtusata at Bunowen, 248.
Witchell's Evolution of Bird-song (Review), 160.
Witherby, H. F.—Birds of Connemara, 1, 299.
Wood-sandpiper, 275.

PLATES AND ILLUSTRATIONS.

Ireland divided into Counties and Vice-Counties (Plate 1), To face p. 29
Mitchelstown Cave (Plate 2), ... To face p. 101
Section of glacial beds and submerged forest at Bray, . . p. 156
Section of post-glacial beds at Belfast, ... p. 157
Pardosa herbigrada (Plate 3), ... To face p. 227

ERRATA.

Page 51, lines 11 and 13, for " leaves " read " hairs."
 ,, 137, line 6, for " MARCH " read " APRIL."
 ,, 179, line 21, for " *H. allaria* " read " *H. alliaria.*"
 ,, 231, line 23, for " *Necordes* " read " *Necrodes.*"

TO THE BINDER.

Plate 2 (Mitchelstown Cave) was inserted in the number by error opposite page 100. It should face page 101.

The Irish Naturalist.

VOLUME V.

A FORTNIGHT WITH THE BIRDS OF CONNEMARA.

BY HARRY F. WITHERBY, F.Z.S.

On May 18th last, I arrived in the town of Galway intent on exploring Connemara. My sole object in so doing being to find out as far as possible what birds were there, and to note their habits and breeding-haunts.

It may be as well to say at once that the following record is very incomplete as regards inland birds, chiefly because, finding the country uninteresting and the birds few, I made my way as quickly as possible to the coast. Consequently this paper must not in any way be taken as a record of all the birds to be found in Connemara, but at the same time it is to be hoped that these few notes may be of some interest to Irish ornithologists.

Birds are fairly numerous round Galway town. Yellow Hammers, Blackbirds, Thrushes, Robins, Wheatears, Chaffinches, Willow Wrens, Cuckoos, Corncrakes, Jackdaws, and Magpies abound. All through Connemara I was struck by the numbers of Corncrakes and Jackdaws. The absence of the Whinchat, and more especially of the Stonechat, and the omnipresence of the Wheatear, are also remarkable.

After one day only in Galway I went on to Oughterard, but as I confined my attentions to Lough Corrib and its islands, which have already been explored by Mr. Ussher, there will be little important to say of my stay there. Of small birds I found the Reed, Common and Yellow Buntings, Chaffinches, and Blackbirds tolerably common on the islands, and Sedge-warblers especially so. A Reed-bunting's nest with eggs several feet up a tree was peculiar. Some of the islands boasted a pair of Magpies, while others literally swarmed with nesting Wood Pigeons. On one island I came across a

A

remarkable eccentricity, which has already been reported to the *Zoologist*.

"The island to which I refer was thickly wooded with small firs, oaks, willows, and other trees and shrubs. Round the edges of the wood there was a line of high heather. Wood Pigeons were breeding in considerable numbers in the wood; but as I was going round the edge of the island I almost stamped on a Wood Pigeon which rose from out of some high heather. Thinking that this was a curious place for the bird to be feeding, I looked down amongst the heather. In the midst of a thick clump of tall heather was a Pigeon's nest, composed of a few sticks placed literally on the ground. The nest contained one egg. This seemed very strange, but I thought it must be an accident. On the other side of the island, however, I flushed another Pigeon in the same way, and found another nest in exactly the same sort of position, but this nest contained quite a big young one. There seems no accounting for this curious fact. The birds must have nested in this position by deliberate intent. Yet there were plenty of good trees for their purpose, where other Pigeons were breeding."

As regards sea-birds on Lough Corrib—the Black-headed and Lesser Black-backed Gulls I found breeding on several islands, and the Merganser (*Mergus serrator*) was no doubt nesting, as I saw several pairs but found no eggs. This bird is locally known on Lough Corrib as the Shield-duck. A number of Dunlin, some of which were singing beautifully, were flying about in small flocks, and the Common Sandpiper was breeding fairly plentifully. A few Cormorants visit the lake every morning and evening to feed. The Wild Duck (*Anas boschas*) was breeding fairly numerously, but although I heard various rumours from the fishermen of Widgeon and Pochard I was unable to confirm them.

Recess, in the centre of Connemara, was my next stopping place. A more barren country for birds I never came across. The scarcity of birds is no doubt due to the scarcity of food. The mountains—the celebrated Twelve Pins—are stony and barren, and can support nothing. The rest of the country is a flat plateau of bog, studded with small lakes. One would expect to find the bog swarming with Snipe, but not a single one could be seen, and I was told that even in the hardest winters they were very scarce. A few pairs of Golden Plovers and innumerable Larks were nesting on this dreary expanse of miles and miles of flat bog, but beyond these, and now and then a Hawk sweeping by in the far distance, not a bird was visible. All the bird-life seemed to be concentrated in the lakes, every one of which has one or more islands, and, curious to say, in the midst of this treeless, shrubless waste, these islands are thickly covered with heather, willows, dwarfed oaks, and other trees. It would, no doubt, repay anyone who would take the trouble to explore these islands. It is, however, no easy matter to get out to them, as most of the lakes are too deep to wade, and hidden snags make swimming to them dangerous. An india-rubber boat would be valuable as a means of reaching the islands. With no such adjunct I was able to explore but a few out of a great number. The only birds I found were Wild Duck and Teal, but my guide told me that Hooded Crows and Herons used to nest on the islands. I began to believe that anything might be on the islands, which we could only view from a distance, as my guide's invariable answer to the question "Does such and such a bird breed here?" was, "It moight be on the island, sor, but faith I don't know!" Otters seem very plentiful here from the number of their tracks, and doubtless the many underground channels connecting the lakes are much to their liking. A Corncrake rattled incessantly all night just under my window.

At Clifden a fair absorbed my first day, and on the next I visited Cruagh and High Islands. I found a small colony of Great Black-backed Gulls on Cruagh, but nothing else of note. On High Island Black Guillemots were breeding, and I saw also a pair of both Peregine Falcons and Ravens. The latter had a young one, and a skirmish between the male Peregine and one of the Ravens was extremely interesting. The Peregine beat the Raven at all points, whirling up into the air and dashing down upon it like a stone. The Raven indeed only saved itself from the Falcon's savage onslaught by clinging closely to the cliff, and thus sneaking away. For a long time the Falcon flew round crying shrilly as a guinea pig, and whenever the Raven showed itself it made its life a burden. That Raven would do well to shift its quarters. On so small an island it must be difficult to keep the peace. It is the home of a good many Rabbits and Rock Doves, and they, no doubt, form good food for the Peregrine.

At this part of the coast, and north as far as Clare Island I think, there are no convenient nesting-ledges for Guillemots and Razorbills, consequently one misses these birds; but their genus is represented by the Black Guillemot, which is very fairly numerous. On both of these islands (High and Cruagh) I found a great number of dead birds. They chiefly consisted of Starlings, but there were also a good many Snipe and a few Curlew. Would the exceptional gales and hard weather of last winter account for this? Or may the birds have been driven out to the west by one of those inexplicable eruptive migration fevers only to return and die on the nearest land? On some of the low flat islands off Renvyle (my next stopping place), the Black Guillemots seemed to be laying their eggs under the large boulders scattered about. I saw several at different times fly out from amongst them, but could not reach the eggs. Another curious nesting habit I noted was, that the Oyster-catchers, which were numerous, invariably nested on the rocks or turf even on islands where there was shingle in every way suitable for them. This fact would seem to show that rock and not shingle is their original, or at all events their favourite nesting site, and yet one never finds their eggs without pebbles or some such substitute as rabbits' excrement, heads of Sea Campion, shells, or bits of wood underneath them. Terns, both Common and Arctic, were just commencing to lay on the lowest and smallest of the islands. It might be mentioned that off the west coast of Scotland, as here, the Terns seem to prefer the low islands for nesting. Cormorants and Shags, both young and old, were swarming everywhere.

On Inishturk I came across a large colony of Sparrows breeding in an ivy-covered cliff by the harbour. Had it not been so far west one would have expected these to have been *Passer montanus*, but they were all the homely *domesticus*, at least as far as I could see. It seems curious that there should be such a large colony of House Sparrows on this barren island containing but a score or so of houses, while throughout Connemara it is a comparatively uncommon bird. Indeed I saw more Sparrows in a day on Inishturk than I did in a fortnight in the rest of Connemara. On Inishturk the Wheatear and

Sedge-warbler were common, very far west for these migrants. Yellow Buntings and Twites were also present, and of course the Rock Pipit. I was surprised to find on the top of a small but fairly high island a little fresh-water lake, and still more surprised to find it inhabited by a Moorhen.

I will conclude these incomplete notes with an account of two interesting migrants which I found lingering in the south so late in the year. Curiously enough they were both on the same island (Inishdalla). The date of my visit to this island was May 30, and the two species I refer to were the Turnstone and the Purple Sandpiper. The first of these was represented by a small flock of six birds in nuptial dress. Since they are known to commence laying in the first part of June it seems strange that these birds should have been in a flock on May 30.

Before I landed on the island I had caught a glimpse of what I thought must be a Purple Sandpiper, and soon after landing I found two of them. Thinking that by some lucky chance they might be nesting on this island, I watched them for a long time, and then searched the whole island through, but without success. As I spent nearly the whole day in searching for their eggs, it is to be hoped that I shall be forgiven for shooting the birds. By this I was able to find that they were a pair, and that the ovaries of the female were fairly advanced. The presence of a pair of these birds in full breeding plumage in a place which was apparently in every way suitable for breeding purposes, seemed to me to be a hopeful sign that it might some day be added to the British list of breeding and resident birds. But this hope was damped when Mr. Harvie-Brown pointed out to me that in the Faroes this bird does not breed near the sea-level or on grassy holms, but on the tops of the highest hills. Therefore, if they do breed in Ireland, it would not probably be lower than 2,000 feet altitude.

Altogether Connemara is not in my opinion a tempting place for the ornithologist. Bird-life there is woefully scarce, both in species and numbers. Even the Hooded Crow and the Redshank seemed to be absent from Connemara.

FUNGI FROM BRACKENSTOWN, CO. DUBLIN.
BY E. J. M'WEENEY, M.A., M.D.

(Excursion of the Dublin Naturalists' Field Club, 5th October, 1895.)

WHEN, after many hours of sorting and dissecting and mounting and gazing down through the microscope, and measuring of spores and comparing of authorities, there confronted me at last the repulsive-looking list herewith presented, I conceived the idea of writing something which might render it intelligible to the large majority of Irish field-naturalists, and prevent it from remaining a useless monument of cacophonous terminology.

I am hardly entitled, however, to use the term cacophonous in connection with the first part of the list. For this comprises the Agaricini, the most highly organised of all the Fungi—the division which has been classified by the illustrious Swedish botanist, Elias Fries, who was certainly one of the most skilful inventors of well-sounding generic names the world has ever seen. Fries' classification of the mushroom-tribe is a triumph of ingenuity. Taking as his criterion the colour of the spores, he divided the hundreds of toadstool-species, which had hitherto lain inextricably jumbled, into five series:—

Those with white spores, or *Leucosporæ*.
Those with pink spores, or *Rhodosporæ*.
Those with brown spores, or *Ochrosporæ*.
Those with purple spores, or *Porphyrosporæ*, and
Those with black spores, or *Melanosporæ*.

What is very remarkable about this curious division is that the species in each group run parallel, or nearly so, to the homologous species in the other groups, and that, generally speaking, there is a gradual ascent in the evolution of the type from the lowest, least well-organized forms, which are in the black-spored series, to the highest best organized ones in the white-spored division. Fries places the majority of mushroom-like plants in the one great genus *Agaricus*, which he then divides, as above stated, into series, and each series is then further split up by certain characters into a number of sub-genera, the names of which are placed between brackets *after* the generic name *Agaricus* and *before* the name of the species. An example will serve to show how this plan works. Let us take an agaric with the gills free from (*i.e.* not touching) the stem. If such a specimen had white spores it would be in sub-genus *Lepiota*, if pink, then *Chamæota*, if brown, then *Pholiota*, if purple, then *Psalliota*. Again, an agaric with "sinuate" gills is, if white-spored, in *Tricholoma*, if pink, in *Entoloma*, if brown, in *Hebeloma*, and if purple, in *Hypholoma*. Neither character is represented in the black-spored series. Thus we have explained the names in brackets with which most Fungus-lists commence. In the present case the species of *Agaricus* and its allies are remarkably few, not a single specimen of the large genera *Russula*, *Lactarius*, and *Cortinarius* having been found. The reason would seem to be that the warm wet weather in August brought these great toadstools to maturity six weeks earlier than usual, and that they had already ripened their spores and died by the commencement of October. That this is not mere supposition is shown by the fact that in mid-August, whilst cycling through the beautiful wood near Glenealy, having been compelled to dismount and shelter from a tremendous downpour, I collected twenty species of the largest Agarics within the sheltered space under my own and a few neighbouring trees, as well as such a host of smaller sorts that all the available pieces of letters, envelope-backs, &c., which I had about me, were insufficient to write down the names. I emptied the contents of the tool-bag into my pockets and filled it with the smaller species. The hour and three quarters I spent under these trees was well employed.

Passing by *Agaricus* and its grimy poor relation *Coprinus*, a black-spored genus which, white and tender when placed in the vasculum, emerges from it next morning an inky mass of loathsome deliquescence—we come next to a couple of species of *Tremella*. Fungus-jelly they might be called, the first bright yellow, the second, as its name indicates, a dingy grey. We find them on dead branches, the tough bark of which they are able to crack, gelatinous as they are, in their efforts to expand. The puff-balls come next, *Lycoperdon* and *Scleroderma*. We found them in all stages, from a tiny nodule, not bigger than a pin's head, just emerging from the mycelial cord—fit research material for the student of development—

up to over-ripe specimens of *L. giganteum*, larger than one's head, and by this time fluffy, brown and dusty—very different to the creamy delicious specimens which some of us hoary-headed original members can still call to mind as they lay during a Club tea at the International Hotel in Bray. That was in 1886. I believe some enthusiastic mycophagist wanted to eat some then and there, and if my recollection serves me aright, our whilom Secretary, Mr. Pim, did actually remove the said specimens for the expressed purpose of feeding thereon. I have since repeated his experiment —on specimens found near Glensouthwell, and which were so big that my carrying them home on a Sunday afternoon excited comment —with most satisfactory results. The recipe for cooking them, however, I am under an honourable obligation to keep secret.

Next we come to the Rusts and their allies (Uredinei) which grow parasitically on flowering plants. These are anything but well represented, and with them we need not stay long, pausing, however, an instant to glance at the curious *Tuberculina*, a parasite of a parasite. It covers the Coltsfoot-Cluster-cup with its brownish-violet spore-beds. The Cluster-cup fungus is a parasite on the Coltsfoot, and the *Tuberculina* is a parasite on the Cluster-cup. At Brackenstown, however, we found it, not on the Cluster-cup, which had long since disappeared, but on its relative and successor the *Coleosporium*—a fact which deserves to be noted. *Synchytrium taraxaci*, next on the list, is also a parasite. It forms orange-red crusts on leaves of Dandelion, and is as far below those just named in point of structure as they are below the Agarics. The mysterious group Chytridieæ, to which it belongs, have not even got the length of forming a mycelium, and if we exclude the Myxomycetes and Bacteria, stand at the very bottom of known Fungi, whilst their strange sporangia and tiny, active, flagellate swarm-spores possess a deep interest for the microscopist, whose command of high powers permits him to trace the developmental cycle of these intra-cellular parasites. Four years ago, on Dalkey Hill, I found the first recorded Irish specimen of *S. taraxaci*, and to-day the species still remains the only one on our Irish list. Will any sharp-sighted reader find me the one on the Scabious ? or the species that inhabit Perennial Mercury, or Self-heal, or Chickweed?

We are now amongst the Mould-fungi, Hyphomycetes, and the very first we come to, *Oospora crustacea*, is only placed here provisionally, as the specimen does not quite agree with the description. It formed bright red patches the size of a pin's head on some old rotting cloth which I picked up and put in a bottle. The spots were not there when the specimen was collected, but developed whilst the contents of the bottle were awaiting examination. Several other strange organisms there were on this same old cloth, which I could not identify and whose development, from want of time, I had to leave untraced. *Bactridium flavum*—a new Irish record—puzzled me for long, and I had to appeal to the superior knowledge of my friend, Mr. Massee, of Kew, before finding a place for it. It has the largest spores of any fungus I have ever seen—about $\frac{1}{80}$-inch long, club-shaped, and divided by partitions into compartments. The fungus forms little yellow dots on rotten wood, and seems to be a speciality of this locality, for several members brought me specimens, including Mr. Jameson, who found it most abundantly on a fallen trunk in a swamp. The next species, *Monotospora sphærocephala*, is like a tiny round-headed black pin $\frac{1}{25}$ of an inch high. Hundreds of these stand up stiffly from the piece of rotten bark which they cover like bristles.

The moulds finished, we pass, with *Erysiphe*, over into the Ascomycetes—fungi that produce their spores in little sacs called asci. The species first mentioned, together with its ally the *Phyllactinia*, collected on Hazel by Mr. Jennings, are good examples of those forms that grow parasitically on green plants, and are called mildews. We hardly sympathize with a strong coarse weed like the Hog-weed (*Heracleum*) when it suffers from this disease; but many a cottage gardener has good reason to bewail the fate of his late peas when they fall victims to *E. Martii*. In early summer we see a sort of grey bloom overspreading the leaves. In autumn this is still there but covered with tiny black grains like gunpowder—the fruit of the fungus. These are like little brown spherical boxes, the wall of which is composed of hexagonal plates, and which are fastened on to the leaf by delicate mycelial threads which are often beautifully branched. Inside the boxes are the asci, each containing four to eight spores. The other ascomycetes must not delay us long. *Hymenoscypha* and *Mollisia* are small disc-shaped fungi, the former with a stalk, the latter without one. The next fungus is also a *Peziza*—as these disc-shaped species are called—and is a much prettier object, its blood-red disc being surrounded with a circlet of brown bristles. It grew at Brackenstown more abundantly than I had ever seen it previously, and was found on the fallen stumps by nearly every member of the party. The two *Ascoboli*, despite their lowly habitat, are also handsome objects. Their spores are large, violet, and adorned with a beautiful raised tracery, whilst there is besides the peculiar character that the ascus as well as the spores is ejected at maturity. The spore-bag, however, is not *quite* dislodged, but projects above the surface of the hymenium, and opens at the top by a dainty little lid, and so allows the spores to issue forth. Lastly, we have *Stemonitis*, a representative of that strange order intermediate between plants and animals, the Slime-fungi (Myxomycetes), which at one time appear as shapeless, creamy, or foamy masses of living jelly—pure undifferentiated protoplasm, the very naked and unadorned basis of life—whilst the next day they have turned into little spore-cases of various and distinct shapes. Sow the spores in a drop of water, and you will see them presently burst. A tiny, shapeless mass of jelly will crawl forth, and, meeting another such "amœba," the two will flow together, and others will then join the company until ultimately a large mass of protoplasm, quite easily seen, is the result. This crawls about, feeds, grows, becomes changed into spore cases, and thus the appointed cycle goes round.

Before concluding this little paper, in which I hope to have said something to clothe the dry bones of our Brackenstown fungus-list with a living interest, I must express my warmest thanks to my friend Prof. Johnson, whose liberality in giving me access to the fungus-literature at his disposal, has placed, me in a position to determine many of the species.

Agaricus (Collybia) radicatus, Relh.—One specimen had the stem 9 inches long, exclusive of the root, which was, unfortunately, broken off short. The pileus was 6 inches across.

A. (Clitocybe) infundibuliformis, Sch.
A. (Mycena) tintinnabulum, Fr.
A. (M.) corticola, Schum.
A. (M.) tenerrimus, Bk.
[Two other species of *Mycena* were collected, but not identified.]
A. (Pleurotus) corticatus, Fr.

A. (Flammula) lentus, Fr.—Short-stemmed form.
A. (Pholiota) aureus, Matt.—A smaller form, with stem very bulbous beneath.
A. (Hypholoma) velutinus, Pers.
A. (Psathyra) corrugis, Pers.
Coprinus plicatilis, Fr.
Tremella mesenterica, Retz.
T. indecorata, Schum.
Lycoperdon perlatum, Pers.
L. bovista, Linn.—Form *giganteum*.
L. pyriforme, Schaeff.
Scleroderma vulgare, Fr.
Puccinia veronicarum, DC.
Coleosporium sonchi, Pers.—On *Petasites*.
Tuberculina vinosa, Sacc.—On the last species.
Synchytrium taraxaci, De By.
Oospora crustacea, Sacc. ?—This curious red mould on old rotting cloth may prove distinct.
Cylindrium heteronemum, Sacc.—On Beech mast.
Cylindrium sp. ?—On hymenium of *Lachnea scutellata*.
Cylindrium.—Another sp. as yet unidentified.
Fusisporium sp.—Seemingly distinct.
Bactridium flavum, K. & S.
Monotospora sphærocephala, B. & Br.
Ramularia urticæ, Pers.
Torula expansa, Pers.
Pilobolus longipes, Van Tiegh.—Mr. Jameson—on rat's excrement.
Erysiphe umbelliferarum, Lév. (=*E. Martii* var. E.) On *Heracleum*.
Ascochyta graminicola, Sacc.
Septoria veronicæ, Desm.
Hymenoscypha tuba, Bolt.
Mollisia cinerea, Batsch.
Lachnea scutellata, Linn.
Ascobolus furfuraceus, Pers.
A. glaber, Pers.—In company with the last.
Diatrype disciformis, Hoffm.
Xylaria polymorpha, Grev.
Hypoxylon multiforme, Fr.
Stemonitis ferruginea, Ehrb.

Mr. Pim has kindly supplied me with the following additional species:—

Phyllactinia guttata, Lév.—On Ash leaves, plentiful, Mr. Jennings.
Lachnea stercorea, Fr.
Helotium citrinum, Hedw.
Sphæria canescens, P.
Valsa sp.—On beech mast.

LITHOBIUS VARIEGATUS, LEACH.

BY HENRY W. BROLEMANN.

Since Mr. R. I. Pocock's "Notes on some Irish Myriapoda" appeared in the *Irish Naturalist* (vol. ii., December, 1893) I do not know that any paper has been published on the matter, and the list, amounting to twenty-two species, given by him has not since been increased.[1]

Thanks to the extreme kindness of Prof. D'Arcy W. Thompson, of University College, Dundee, I have been enabled to examine the material collected by him in the County of Galway and was fortunate enough to find, amongst other species, four Myriapods, the presence of which in Ireland has not been mentioned, which brings the number of known Irish forms up to twenty-six.

Recapitulating briefly the species alluded to in Mr. Pocock's paper, I mark with a * the species which were not represented in Prof. Thompson's collection, and which I have not been able to examine, thus :—

Lithobius forficatus, L.
L. *variegatus*, Leach.
L. *melanops*, Newport.
*L. *microps*, Meinert.
Cryptops hortensis, Leach.
Geophilus longicornis, Leach.
G. *carpophagus*, Leach.
Scolioplanes crassipes, C. Koch.

S. *maritimus*, Leach.
Stigmatogaster subterraneus, Leach.
**Polyxenus lagurus*, L.
Glomeris marginata, Villiers.
Polydesmus complanatus, L.
P. *gallicus*, Latzel.
Brachydesmus superus, Latzel.

**Atractosoma polydesmoides*, Leach.
**Blaniulus fuscus*, Am-Stein.
Iulus britannicus, Verhoeff.
**I. pilosus*, Newport.
**I. albipes*, C. Koch.
I. *sabulosus*, L.

To these I add :—

Geophilus gracilis, Meinert,
G. *proximus*, C. Koch,

Blaniulus guttulatus, Bosc.
Iulus (*Leptoiulus*), sp. incerta.

---

[1] Since the present paper was written, there appeared in the special number of the "Irish Naturalist," vol. iv., No. 9, September, 1895, Mr. George H. Carpenter's list of the Myriapoda collected in Galway during the excursion of the Irish Field Club Union, where *Scolopendrella immaculata*, Newport, was recorded.

The following is to be observed in reference to the Myriapods here mentioned :—

Geophilus proximus, C. Koch.—One specimen has very short maxillipedes, which, when closed, do not reach the point of the head. Whether this is accidental or not, I have not been able to ascertain.

Polydesmus complanatus, L.—The males I examined belong to the variety named *angustus* by Dr. R. Latzel.

Polydesmus gallicus, Latzel.—The Irish specimens, though unmistakably belonging to Dr. Latzel's species, are much more narrow than the type of the south of France, with which I have compared them, the former measuring 2 mm. to 2·20 mm., while the latter reach 2·80 mm. to 3 mm.

Iulus britannicus, Verhoeff.—Certainly represents the form indicated by Mr. Pocock under the name of *Iulus luscus*, Meinert.

Iulus (Leptoiulus), sp. incerta.—Having seen no male, I do not risk a specific name for the female specimens of this form, owing to the difficulty of recognizing the species of this group, even when males are at hand. These probably belong to the same species which Mr. Pocock has called by Newport's name, *I. pilosus*; but as Newport's description can equally well be applied almost to any of the species of the *Leptoiulus* subgenus, his denomination has no meaning, and I find it unnecessary to retain it.

This paper, thus lacking in interest, would never have seen light, had it not been for the opportunity offered to me to examine specimens of *Lithobius variegatus*, Leach.

Described for the first time in 1817 by Leach[1] in a very abbreviated way, the species was mentioned afterwards by Newport and others, who added little to the knowledge we had of this, so far purely British form. Recently Mr. Pocock, in his above-mentioned pamphlet, reassuming the characters given by Leach, adds some particulars, but merely for the purpose of distinguishing it from the common species *Lithobius forficatus*, L., and omits the main point, which throws some light on the place this species has to occupy in the numerous list of congeneric forms, viz., the fact that the posterior angles of the seventh dorsal plate are produced, causing *L. variegatus* to belong to the group of *Lithobius* termed *Neolithobius* by Stuxberg. However, the obtuse shape of the angles might, to a certain extent, account for this omission.

---

[1] For bibliographical indications, see description of *L. variegatus*.

It is therefore advisable to publish a new description, which will read as follows :—

Genus, LITHOBIUS.
Subgenus, OLIGOBOTHRUS.
Lithobius variegatus, Leach, 1817.

Leach—The Zoological Miscellany, iii., London, xii., 1817, p. 40.
Do.—Edinburgh Encyclop:, vii., p. 409.
Gervais—Etudes p. servir à l'Hist. Nat. des Myriapodes—*Ann. d. Sci. Nat.* (2), vii., 1837, p. 49.
Lucas—Hist. Nat. des Animaux Articulés, i., Paris, 1840, p. 543.
Walker—Notes on Myriapoda.—*Newman's Entomol.*, January, 1842, p. 238.
Newport—A list of the species of Myriapoda, order Chilopoda, &c. *Ann. and Mag. Nat. Hist.* (1), xiii., 1844, p. 98.
Do.—Monograph of the Class Myriapoda, Order Chilopoda, &c. *Trans. Linn. Soc., London*, xix., 1845, p. 363.
Gervais —Hist. Nat. des Insectes Aptères, iv., Paris, 1847, p. 231.
Newport and Gray—Catalogue of the Myriapoda in the collection of the B. M., London, 1856, p. 15.
R. I. Pocock—Notes upon some Irish Myriapoda.—*Irish Naturalist*, vol. ii, 1893, p. 310.

Length and width nearly as in *L. forficatus.*

Robust, parallel-sided, flattened.

Cephalic plate rounded anteriorly, posterior angles blunt, surface not punctate, but bearing two distinct longitudinal furrows near the posterior margin. Ocelli condensed, numbering 16 or 17, disposed $1 + 4.5.4.3.$, the posterior ocellus very large, eliptical in shape, the three first ocelli of the upper row large, more or less rounded, the rows somewhat curved and irregular. Antennæ long, reaching the posterior border of the fifth dorsal plate, pilose, 36-42 jointed, the last joint alone as long as the two preceding joints, or even longer. Coxæ of maxillipedes with anterior margin wide, almost straight, slightly notched in the middle, armed with $6 + 7$ or $7 + 7$ black, small, blunt teeth; surface of coxæ punctate, the punctures well marked and dense towards the anterior margin, becoming scattered and gradually fading away posteriorly, medial sulcus deep.

Dorsal plates shiny, uneven in the sides; plates no. 3, 5, 8, 10. and 12, marked laterally with a transverse impression, almost equally distant from both angles, or nearer to the posterior angle; 14th dorsal plate with two rough impressions near the posterior angles, posterior margin somewhat concave. The above-mentioned sculpture or roughness having often been noticed on immature specimens of *L. forficatus*, cannot be considered as characteristic of *L. variegatus*.

The posterior angles of the 7th dorsal plate, though not much developed, project somewhat on the line of the posterior margin, and the posterior angles of the 9th, 11th, and 13th dorsal plates are acutely produced.

The two last pairs of legs are thin and long. The following details are to be observed as well on female as on male specimens, but are more marked on the 15th than on the 14th pair of legs. The superior inside edge of the third joint is hollowed longitudinally, the furrow being wider at the back end ; also the superior outside edge is sulcate, the furrow being only noticeable on the posterior two-thirds of the joint ; the superior surface is thus reduced to a rounded ridge. These two furrows are continued on the following joint, the fourth, being narrow and deep ; on the fifth joint, only the inside furrow is to be found, being much attenuated. On the inferior surface of the third joint a rounded ridge runs longitudinally between two furrows, the outer of which is often shortened.

The spines of the 1st, 14th, and 15th pairs of legs are disposed as follows :—

1st pair, $\frac{0.0.2.1-0.1-0.}{0.0.0.\quad 2.\quad\ \ 1.}$, double claw.

14th pair, $\frac{1.0.3.1.1.}{0.1.3.3.2.}$, double claw.

15th pair, $\frac{1.0.3.1.0.}{0.1.3.3.1.}$, single claw.

The spine of the fifth joint, below, occupies the medial position.

Female genitalia armed with 2 + 2 strong spines, the outer pair of which is the larger ; claw strong but narrow, with a blunt tooth on the inside edge.

Coxal pores large, circular, disposed on one line, numbering 6.5.5.5., 5.4.4.4.

This species much resembles *L. leptopus*, Latzel, from which it is easily distinguished by the arrangement and number of coxal pores.

A SUPPOSED LAND-LOCKED SALMON.
BY R. F. SCHARFF, PH.D.

ON the 21st of November last Mr. R. J. Ussher, of Cappagh, County Waterford, forwarded a fish to the Dublin Natural History Museum, which was found on the iron grating of a large sewer, through which flows the watercourse supplying his premises. On examination the fish proved to be a Salmon grilse twenty-three inches long and weighing 3lbs. 15oz. The prominent hook on the lower jaw indicated that it was a male fish in the breeding stage, and this was moreover proved by the condition of the reproductive organs, which were full of ripe milt. In colour it was trout-like, being covered with red spots and bars, a condition which has been observed, according to the late Dr. Day, in some of the land-locked Salmon raised at Howietoun, in Scotland. The question arises therefore whether we have in Mr. Ussher's fish a case of a true wild land-locked Salmon? To those who may not have heard of the interesting experiments which have been carried on at Howietoun by Sir James Maitland, the idea of a land-locked Salmon may seem an impossibility, but Dr. Day fully recognised the trustworthiness of these experiments, and says in his work on the British and Irish Salmonidæ, (p. 103) "They afford incontestible evidence that a sojourn in salt water is not necessary in order for a grilse to develop eggs, and that migratory Salmon are able to reproduce their kind in fresh water without migrating to the sea, thus removing one great obstacle which has stood in the way of ichthyologists admitting that a land-locked Salmon can beget a race of *Salmo salar*." He moreover refers to the following Irish case (p. 101):—
"Mr. Douglas Ogilby turned some Salmon smolts into Lough Ash (County Tyrone), which has no access to the sea, in 1881. In April, 1883, he captured a grilse 14½ inches long in this lake, where salmon had not previously been seen, and it was so distended with eggs that he considered it would have spawned very shortly." This specimen, according to Dr. Day, is now in the Natural History Museum, London, and is evidently a true *Salmo salar*. These are instances of the artificial production of land-locked Salmon. But Dr. Day states that Lake Wenern, in Sweden, is inhabited by a wild land-locked race of true Salmon, though Dr. Günther does not admit that the species is *S. salar*.

To return to Mr. Ussher's specimen, it would appear from information kindly given me by the discoverer, that during the usual condition of the small stream a Salmon ascending from the sea would be stopped not only by the grating referred to, but also by another equally formidable obstacle. The stream after leaving Mr. Ussher's premises sinks into a limestone cavern and runs underground for more than a mile, so that as he remarks "by no possibility could a fish come up this stream from the sea." During floods, however, it occasionally happens, that a separate communication is formed between the upper part of the small stream and the river Finisk into which it flows, so that fish could then come up, and Salmon peal[1] have actually been known to reach the glen above Mr. Ussher's house in this way. Several such fish were seen in a deep part of the stream about two years ago, and Mr. Ussher thinks the present specimen may be one of these, having being confined in the stream during that time.

Although this cannot be considered an undoubted instance of a Salmon reaching maturity in fresh water, I think the case deserves special mention, and its record may lead to continued observations on the habits of the salmon tribe in Ireland.

[1] Though a young Sea Trout is generally known as a "peal," the term is often indiscriminately applied to it as well as to young Salmon.

PROCEEDINGS OF IRISH SOCIETIES.

Royal Zoological Society.

A Sparrow-Hawk has been presented to the Gardens by J. Oglesby, Esq., and a large baboon deposited by M. J. Kerr, Esq. Three Angora Goats and six Shovellers have been purchased.

5,400 persons visited the Gardens in November.

Dublin Microscopical Club.

November 21st.—The Club met at Mr. G. H. Carpenter's, who showed specimens of *Ixodes marginatus*, Leach, which he had received from Dr. Scott, who reported that these ticks were so extremely abundant in the west of Ireland during the past summer as to be a serious annoyance, persons venturing to lie on heath in certain places becoming covered with them. These ticks are believed to live on plants of various kinds, but wherever opportunity offers, they attach themselves to an animal body, and suck blood voraciously. The mouth-organs, adapted for this purpose, consisting of a pair of maxillæ united to form a channeled rostrum with toothed edges, and a pair of retractile cheliceræ with complicated barbed processes at the extremity, were shown under a high power. Mr. A. D. Michael has kindly confirmed the identification.

Professor GRENVILLE COLE showed rhyolite-obsidian from Sandy Braes, Co. Antrim, containing a crystal of hypersthene. The minute structure of the glassy ground shows a delicate intermingling of little rods, each formed of a row of globular crystallites. These are excellent types of what Vogelsang called "margarites," from their resemblance to strings of pearls. In this slide a strongly pleochroic rhombic pyroxene (hypersthene) occurs. This mineral has not previously been recorded from the Antrim rhyolites, and has possibly in this case been picked up from a more basic lava.

Mr. GREENWOOD PIM exhibited *Tuberculina persicina*, a curious parasitic fungus growing on another fungus (*Coleosporium tussilaginis*) on leaves of *Tussilago* at Brackenstown, near Swords. It forms compact little cushions, surmounted by minute spores, and these cushions are seated on the *Coleosporium* pustules. In Plowright's book on the Uredines it is described as parasitic on the *Æcidium* which occurs very abundantly on *Tussilago* in spring, so that it also occurring on the *Coleosporium* is worth recording. The plant is very readily passed over as a specimen of the host fungus partially decayed.

Prof. T. JOHNSON exhibited *Melobesia confinis*, Grn., a calcareous red alga, growing on *Corallina officinalis*, on which, as also on limpet shells, it forms small slightly thickened hard swellings. A preparation showing the characteristic bisporous tetrasporangia and the vertically elongated thallus-cells was exhibited. The material was gathered by the exhibitor in 1891, at Frenchfort, Co. Mayo, when with Mr. Green in ss. "Harlequin" (R.D.S. Fishery Survey). *M. confinis* is recorded hitherto from the coast of Brittany only.

Mr. M'ARDLE exhibited a specimen of *Riccardia latifrons*, Lindberg, bearing the large perianth and capsule, with the androecium at the base of the perianth, showing the paroecious character of the plant. The specimens were collected in Lord Howth's demesne last March. This rare liverwort was first detected by Professor Lindberg, who collected it at O'Sullivan's Cascade, Killarney, in company with the late Dr. D. Moore, in 1873. It is an addition to the Co. Dublin list of Hepaticæ.

Mr. H. LYSTER JAMESON showed feathers from the base of beak of adult and immature Rooks, showing the frequent presence of unpigmented feathers in the young bird, and the aborted or abraded feathers in this region in adult Rooks, which gives the well-known appearance of a bare patch round the base of the bill. Mr. Jameson referred to the theory that these feathers are mechanically rubbed away by the Rook in digging for worms, which was urged by Weismann as a case of an acquired character which is not transmitted. The meaning of the unpigmented feathers in the young Rook was discussed. The presence of these white feathers was first observed by Mr. T. H. Gurney, of Norwich.

BELFAST NATURAL HISTORY AND PHILOSOPHICAL SOCIETY.

NOVEMBER 5th.—The opening meeting of the seventy-fifth session was held in the Museum. There was a large attendance of members and friends.

Mr. ROBERT LLOYD PATTERSON, F.L.S., President of the Society, in opening the proceedings, said his thanks were due to his fellow-members of the Council for electing him again their President.

The Honorary Secretary (Mr. R. M. YOUNG, B.A.), announced the receipt of several donations to the Museum, and a cordial vote of thanks was accorded the donors.

The PRESIDENT then proceeded to deliver an address on the Migration of Birds, which was effectively illustrated by a large series of special photo-lantern slides, shown by Mr. A. R. Hogg. Mr. Patterson commenced his paper by stating that of the large number of birds which have now—many of them, in his opinion, wrongly—been placed on the British list, some are mere accidental stragglers; and others, although met with regularly, do not occur with sufficient frequency to be called common; so that the number of different species of our well-known every-day birds is probably considerably below 200. Of these some occur only in summer, and others again only in winter, these two sub-divisions going to form the division of migratory birds; as compared with the other division, the permanent residents. The lecturer next proceeded to point out that even among our so-called permanently resident birds migration prevails to a large extent; and he illustrated this by reference to the habits of the Curlew, the Starling, the Skylark, and others. The questions of what began the migration movement and what leads to its continuance were next discussed at some length, and the theories of different authorities on the subject alluded to in detail. He next proceeded to give a comprehensive sketch of the great migratory movement —" the mystery of migration," as he not inaptly termed it—as observed in various places, paying a high compliment to Mr. Seebohm and Mr. Harvie-Brown for their investigations in this direction. Mr Seebohm he alluded to most particularly as having undertaken a journey of over 15,000 miles to the mouth of one of the great Siberian rivers—the Yenesay, falling into the Arctic Ocean—in his endeavours to track some of our migrants to their summer homes. The scenes witnessed by the intrepid travellers were graphically described, and were admirably illustrated by the lantern-slides. Migration in the United Kingdom, but in Ireland in particular, and in Continental Europe, was next alluded to, the lecturer concluding with a description of the wonderful migration which occurs in Heligoland, as recorded in a recently-published translation of the great work on the birds of that island by a veteran resident there, Mr. Gätke. The nesting habits of some of the birds were described, and views of some favourite nesting-places exhibited, these and the other views adding an artistic attraction to an interesting and instructive lecture, which was listened to with attention throughout by a most appreciative audience.

Dr. REDFERN had pleasure in moving a very hearty vote of thanks to the President. Mr. J. F. SHILLINGTON seconded the motion. Mr. PATTERSON pointed out that it was not their custom to pass votes of thanks to their own members, but he was very grateful for the kind, words used by Dr. Redfern and Mr. Shillington.

DECEMBER 3rd.—Mr. George Coffey, B.L., lectured to a large audience on the subject "From Egypt to Ireland; a chapter in the History of Ornament."

BELFAST NATURALISTS' FIELD CLUB.

NOVEMBER 19th.—The opening meeting was held, when the President (Mr. F. W. LOCKWOOD, C.E.), delivered his inaugural address. Mr. Lockwood took as his subject, "The Interdependence of the various Branches of the Club's Work." The address first touched upon the increasing prosperity of the Club, as indicated by the activity of the various sections, and though some of the older members had doubts as to the wisdom of the recent changes, Mr. Lockwood himself felt none. The President then referred to the different nature of the work done now to what was open to the students of thirty years ago, which necessitated sometimes a change in method. He then went on to show the dependence the various branches had upon each other. To take an instance, that pursuit which has brought the Club a very considerable reputation, microscopy, and more especially that branch so successfully pursued by Mr. Joseph Wright, the foraminifera, he (the President) thought it certain that Mr. Wright little considered his investigations into the white chalk powder in the flints would ultimately lead to discoveries necessitating careful reconsideration of the theories as to the origin of boulder clay. Mr. Lockwood then referred to the careful and minute work required in tracing out the erratic blocks to their parent formation. Broad questions of meteorology are well worth working at in order to help to solve such problems as why Greenland should be covered with an ice-cap and Siberia quite dry. The President next touched upon the engrossing subject of botany, and pointed out that although such work as that done by Messrs. Stewart, Corry, and Praeger cannot be done over again, very valuable results, indeed, could be obtained from the almost unknown deposits of plant-remains between the lava-flows of the upper and lower basalts. Good work also remains to be done in tabulating these outflows, such as the rhyolites and pitchstones. Referring to the work done by the Duke of Argyll, Starkie Gardner, and some of the Club's members, Mr. Lockwood suggested that the fauna be especially searched for in these old lake-bottoms. The Carboniferous period should also yield further results, from the Tyrone and Ballycastle coal-measures, and from the results of such exploration as this to form, perhaps, some idea of the ancient coast-lines, and whether or not the main continental outlines have ever been much as they are now. The next point considered was archæology, including ethnography and the Celtic department, and Mr. Lockwood suggested lines of work on the palæolithic remains and the ancient races of inhabitants of Ireland. Mr. Lockwood concluded by saying that he trusted he had said enough to show that there was plenty of work to do still, and that all the branches of the Club were mutually interdependent.

Mr. WRIGHT, F.G.S., in response to Mr. Lockwood, described his early experiences in searching for foraminifera, and concluded by criticising some of the arrangements with the Irish Field Club Union.

Mr. WM. GRAY, M.R.I.A., gave a report on the meeting of the British Association at Ipswich, to which he went as a delegate from the Club. Mr. Gray described the mode of arrangement of the various sections, and pointed out the value of minute and detailed work in all subjects, even temperatures, rainfalls, floods, and tides, also such work as the Club is now busily engaged in, in tracking down the erratic blocks in the boulder clay. He then spoke strongly against the all too prevalent custom of digging up rare plants, and thus destroying them, and especially entreated everyone not to buy the ferns offered for sale by the peasantry. Mr. Gray then referred to the excursions made to the deposits of the Red Crag at Ipswich, with its extraordinarily numerous fossils, of which a considerable number were on view, including the peculiar left-handed spiral so rare now, and apparently so common then in *Fusus*, and also the modern flint works at Brandon, from which Mr. Gray had brought a number of very beautiful copies of old axes, celts, spear-heads, and flakes made by the quarrymen.

Mr. LOCKWOOD briefly described some of his experiences in the Red Crag district, pointing out the layer of rolled fossils found below it, containing very numerous mammalian remains, and also the curious cutting down into the Crag by a recent stream, the bed of which is sometimes refilled with recent alluvium, forming a deceptive deposit unless carefully noticed.

DECEMBER 11th.—The Geological Section met, when Mr. F. W. LOCKWOOD contributed some notes on the Tarns of the Mourne Mountains. He first described the action of running water in canons and deep gorges, and then the modification caused by the action of frost on the sides of valleys. Running water and frost are the cutting instruments of nature, ice in the mass is a planing and smoothing instrument. Before the Glacial Epoch the hills were more rugged and the valleys deeper than at present. Four out of the five lakelets of the Mourne district are extremely small and shallow, the fifth, Lough Shannagh, is the only one of importance, but it also is small. They all lie upon ledges or shelves of rock a great height above the general level of the valleys, and have steep cliffs above them. There is no clear indication that they are true rock basins such as most of the tarns in Cumberland

and Westmoreland undoubtedly are, but Lough Shannagh may be in part. The others are probably formed by dams of boulder clay squeezed up on the side of the ice-stream of the main valleys. A most interesting feature is the rugged character of the hill-tops generally in the British Isles above a level of something about 2,500 feet, showing that the ice, from whatever source derived, did not rise above that level. The summits of Sca Fell, Helvellyn, Ben Nevis, and Slieve Donard are all a mass of large boulders apparently the result of sub-aerial weathering, the lower hills have all been swept bare. In the course of the subsequent discussion, Mr. J. O. CAMPBELL mentioned finding Ailsa Craig eurite as an erratic in the Spinkwee valley of the Mourne mountains, also an apparently Antrim flint on the Aran Islands. A portion of the British Association "Erratic Blocks" report, containing a reference to glacial work done by the Club, was followed by a paper on the Silurian rocks of Pomeroy, by Mr. R. BELL, who also contributed erratics from boulder clay at an elevation of 1,300 feet between Divis and Black Mountain, including Ailsa and Tormamoney eurite. Rock specimens were presented by the Hon. Sec.

NOVEMBER 30th.—The opening meeting of the new Botanical Section of the Club was held in the Club Rooms at the Museum, on Saturday afternoon. It was decided to meet on the last Saturday in each month at four o'clock, and to devote the first hour to structural botany and practical work with the microscope, and the remaining time to the study of the natural orders of British plants. Some notes were then given by Rev. C. H. Waddell, on protoplasm and chlorophyll. Papers and short notes have been promised on "Sedges," "Hieracia," "Alien plants," "Duckweeds," &c. The meetings are open to all who are interested in botany, and the names of any persons who wish to join should be sent in to the Secretary, Rev. C. H. Waddell, Saintfield.

DECEMBER 13th.—MICROSCOPICAL SECTION.—Dr. Lorrain Smith lectured on "The Study of Bacteriology."

DECEMBER 17th.—The President (Mr. F. W. Lockwood) in the chair. The PRESIDENT read a short note on the gravels at Larne, Co. Antrim, which will appear in our next issue.

Miss NORA STEEN contributed a short paper on Craiganogh cave, Co. Antrim, which we hope to publish shortly.

Mr. ROBERT BELL read a paper entitled "A Day among the Silurian Shales of Pomeroy." The paper dealt with the results of a visit in last July. These shales are very interesting, being the nearest place where those characteristic Palæozoic crustaceans, the trilobites, can be obtained. Mr. Bell's experience in expending half the time at his disposal in searching for the beds, in spite of full instructions kindly given by Mr. M'Henry, M.R.I.A., is one common to many geologists. The rough fossiliferous grits, with marks resembling sea-weeds and worm-tubes, lie south of the granite hill at Bardahessiagh; newer sandy beds have been deposited uncomformably upon them. The trilobites occur in a section cut by the river near Dickson's house and the slate quarry. The fossils found were on view during the evening.

Mr. ALEC G. WILSON described the geological features of the Galway Conference, illustrating his remarks by numerous fine lantern-slides from photographs taken on the excursion, by Messrs. Welch, Gray, and Fennell. A report on the geology of this excursion, by Miss S. M. Thompson, has already appeared in our September number.

Miss S. M. THOMPSON, Secretary of the Geological Section, read a report on the Geological excursions of the past season. We hope to comment upon this paper in our next issue. On the table there was a fine display of rocks, fossils, and glacial erratics, collected on the excursions referred to, and microscopic sections of rocks were also shown.

DUBLIN NATURALISTS' FIELD CLUB.

NOVEMBER 19.—The first business meeting was held. The PRESIDENT (Mr. G. H. CARPENTER) in the chair. The SECRETARY exhibited on behalf of Mrs. Ross a number of prize chrysanthemums. Professor JOHNSON exhibited a beautifully dried series of alpine plants prepared by Lady Rachel Saunderson. Mr. F. W. BURBIDGE and Mr. PRAEGER spoke in praise of the exquisite preservation of these specimens. The VICE-PRESIDENT (Professor COLE) having taken the chair, the PRESIDENT delivered an address on the subject, "The Mingling of the North and South." He first referred to the recent formation of the Irish Field Club Union, by means of which the members of the various Naturalists' Field Clubs were getting to know each other and to assist each other in their work. Reference was then made to the Field Club Conference held at Galway in July last, in which all the Irish Clubs and a number of English scientific societies took part. The districts visited on that occasion, it was pointed out, furnished a very remarkable mingling of northern and southern types of animal and plants. The various hypotheses that have been put forward to account for the strange overlapping of types were reviewed, and the evidence in support of various theories considered. The address, which was illustrated by zoological and botanical specimens and by many lantern slides of plants, animals, maps and scenery, will shortly appear in our pages. An interesting discussion on the paper ensued.

Prof. T. JOHNSON complimented the President on his address, and referred to the tradition that some of the Iberian plants had been introduced by the Spaniards. Mr. PRAEGER stated that he had been often struck by the way these western Irish species did *not* spread, in spite of their abundance in places, and the prevalence of strong winds. He thought this went against any theory of their introduction. Mr. M'ARDLE referred to the peculiar tropical distribution of a number of the south-west Irish liverworts. Mr. F. W. BURBIDGE also discussed the question of artificial introduction of species; and remarked that it did not appear correct to assume that an ice age would sweep all vegetation off the face of the country, since some of the species which flourish at sea-level in the west of Ireland had been found to grow up as far north as man has yet penetrated. Mr. H. LYSTER JAMESON referred to the importance of studying these questions of past and present distribution.

Mr. HALBERT remarked that as the late A. H. Haliday had not found *Otiorrhynchus auropunctatus*, it might be thought by some that that beetle had been recently introduced. Dr. C. H. HURST said that the success or failure of such attempts depended on a very large number of circumstances, and that there were many inter-relations between plants and animals that had important bearing on the question. Prof. COLE pointed out that in considering the possible ancient routes by which migration had taken place, it must not be forgotten that North-western Europe was really the ancient Europe, and was dry land while the more southern tracts were again and again submerged.

Mr. PRAEGER subsequently exhibited a number of additional photographs taken on the Galway excursion. The following were elected members of the Club:—Miss Lilias J. Aimers, B.A.; D. R. Alcock, J. J. Alcorn, F. H. R. Brady, Miss Ida Carolin, W. V. Coppinger, Alec Gray, M.A., C. Herbert Hurst, PH.D.; A. Vaughan Jennings, F.G.S.; Miss Laird, Geo. F. Mahon, Conolly Norman, F.R.C.P.I.; Kenneth C. Ogilvie, A. Ward, C.E.; and Rev. C. A. Williamson.

DECEMBER 10th.—Mr. WILLIAM GRAY, M.R.I.A., delegate from the Belfast Naturalists' Field Club, lectured on "The Physical Features and Scenery of County Antrim." The chair was occupied by the PRESIDENT (G. H. Carpenter, B. Sc.), and there was a crowded attendance. Some formal business having been transacted, Mr. GRAY proceeded with his lecture, which was illustrated by a magnificent set of lantern views. He first described the geology of the district, and dealt with the various formations in their order of succession. Special notice was taken of the basaltic rocks, which form the leading feature of Antrim geology and scenery. The Chalk, Greensand and Lias also came in for due attention. Afterwards the various headlands, bays and glens were described and illustrated. A vote of thanks to the lecturer was proposed by Prof. G. A. J. COLE, F.G.S., seconded by GREENWOOD PIM, M.A., and carried by acclamation. Frederick T. Eason and Wm. F. Henderson were elected members of the Club.

CORK NATURALISTS' FIELD CLUB.

NOVEMBER 28th.—A lecture was delivered by Mr. R. LLOYD PRAEGER, B.A., B.E., the President of the Club (Mr. W. H. Shaw, M.A.) in the chair. The lecture hall of the School of Science was crammed, and the lecture, which treated of the Galway Field Club Conference in 1895, and which was illustrated by an optical lantern, was followed with attention. Mr. Praeger first dealt with the visit of the members of the Conference, which included representatives from Belfast, Dublin, Cork, Limerick, and important centres in England, to Galway City, and pointed out the chief places of interest in that district. Connemara, Burren and the Aran Islands were duly described, and many views taken by members were shown. The peculiar flora of these districts was next described, and in conclusion the lecturer pointed out the important results of the Conference, and exhorted the members of the Cork Club to renewed exertions in their own sphere of work. At the close of the lecture a discussion took place, and seven new members joined the Club.

DECEMBER 13th.—Mr. WM. GRAY, M.R.I.A., of Belfast, delivered a lecture in the Ball Room, Imperial Hotel, to the members of the Cork Literary and Scientific Society, and the Cork Naturalists' Field Club on "The Physical Features and Scenery of the County Antrim." Mr. Wm. Lane, J.P., President of the Society, occupied the chair, and there was a full attendance of members. The lecturer, who is a prominent member of the Belfast Naturalists' Field Club, stated he attended under the auspices of the Naturalists' Field Clubs of Dublin, Belfast, Limerick, and Cork, as well as of the Literary and Scientific Society, to describe some portions of the field of investigation of their Club in Antrim. By means of lantern-slides the lecturer illustrated the geological strata of the county, and dwelt at length on the trap, Chalk, Greensand, Lias, and New Red Sandstone—giving their origin, their characteristic features, and their action of the various natural influences on them. He pointed out in detail the formation of the Giant's Causeway, which was of volcanic origin, and the columns of which were naturally formed by a process of cooling under pressure, and amongst the other principal natural phenomena treated of were the Cave Hill, the columns at Fair Head, and the sea-stacks to be found round the coast. The address was delivered in a more or less conversational style, and the interest of the audience was quickened by a copious supply of lantern-slides. The Chairman, at the conclusion, conveyed the warm thanks of the Society to the lecturer.

LIMERICK NATURALISTS' FIELD CLUB.

NOVEMBER 27th.—Mr. R. LLOYD PRAEGER delivered a lecture under the Field Club Union Scheme, his subject being "The Galway Field Club Conference, 1895, with notes on the Flora of the districts visited." Dr. Fogerty occupied the chair, and there was a good attendance. Mr. Praeger first touched on the history of the various Field Clubs of Ireland, and the formation of the Field Club Union. The excursions carried out during the Galway conference were next described, illustrated by a large series of lantern-slides from photographs of the districts visited taken by members. The peculiar flora of Connemara and Burren were considered, and a series of characteristic plants exhibited, and finally the part played by the Limerick Club was dwelt on, and the duty that rested with members of helping the growth and progress of their Club in every possible way.

DECEMBER 11th.—Mr. WILLIAM GRAY lectured on "The Physical Features and Scenery of County Antrim." He said he came as the representative of the Belfast Club, under the Field Club Union Scheme, to tell them of that part of the sphere of work of the Belfast Club which dealt with geology and physical geography. With the help of a large series of lantern-views, he described the structure of the county, and the characters and mode of origin of the Basalts, Chalk, Greensand, Lias, New Red Sandstone, and older rocks. The peculiar features of the Giants' Causeway were treated of in detail. The features of the coast were described, with numerous illustrations of the headlands, bays, and valleys.

FIELD CLUB NEWS.

An amusing incident occurred at a recent meeting of the Cork Field Club. A speaker referred to the Cork Cuverian Society, which did much good work in the middle of the century, as being "as extinct as the Irish Elk." Whereupon uprose a member of the said Society, to state that the Cork Cuverian Society was not dead, but hybernating; he had attended the last meeting which the Society held, some twenty years ago, which was adjourned *sine die*. He objected to be relegated to the Pleistocene period. As a consequence of the discussion which ensued there is talk of reviving the Cuverian Society, or of amalgamating it with the Cork Field Club.

Lectures under the Field Club Union Scheme are being energetically carried out. During the past month Mr. W. Gray, a veteran member of the Belfast Club, lectured before the Clubs at Dublin, Cork and Limerick, and in November Mr. Praeger, as representative of the Dublin Club, lectured at Cork and Limerick.

The Committee of the Dublin Club have nominated Professor Cole, F.G.S., as President for 1896, and Mr. N. Colgan as Vice-President. Mr. Colgan is well-known to Irish botanists by his papers on the flora of County Dublin.

A party composed chiefly of members of the Belfast and Dublin Field Clubs intend visiting Connemara next spring, with the object of investigating the kitchen-middens along the coast.

The Belfast Club do not intend to let the stimulus given to the study of geology and botany by the recent courses of lectures by Prof. Cole and Prof. Johnson die away for want of encouragement. The geological section is holding frequent meetings, both in the field and in the cosy workroom, and with regard to botany, a series of informal meetings is being held under the direction of Rev. C. H. Waddell, for practical botanical work.

The Rev. W. F. Johnson, so well known to all Irish naturalists through his work on the Coleoptera and other insects, has removed from Winderterrace, Armagh, to Acton Rectory, Poyntzpass, Newry. We have no doubt that Mr. Johnson's researches in this new field will largely add to our knowledge of Irish insects. Correspondents will please note the change of address.

Prof. Johnson, D.Sc., has kindly offered to give a course of practical work to serve as an introduction to the study of sea-weeds, for the benefit of members of the Dublin Club. The course would be held during the spring months.

The next undertaking of the Field Club Union will be a Directory of Irish Naturalists, the publication of which should do much to facilitate intercourse between Field Club members of similar tastes residing in different parts of the country. The preliminary steps are being now taken, and a printed form to be filled by persons wishing to be included in the Directory will be shortly sent to all Field Club members and subscribers to this Journal.

NOTES.

Col. G. T. Plunkett, R.E., has been appointed Director of the Science and Art Institutions in Ireland. He will therefore take up the late Dr. Ball's work in Leinster House, and also continue his former duties as Secretary to the Royal College of Science.

Prof. Sollas, F.R.S., of Dublin, will leave in March for Sydney, to take charge of an expedition that is being despatched to make deep borings in a coral atoll. The scheme, which is supported by a strong scientific committee, has been financed by the Royal Society to the extent of £800; and the Government are placing a gunboat at the disposal of the party, to convey them from Sydney to Funifuti, in the Central Pacific, which has been selected as the scene of operations.

BOTANY.

PHANEROGAMS.

Irish Hawkweeds, &c.—The following plants were collected by me during the summer of 1895, and verified by Mr. F. J. Hanbury:—

Hieracium Schmidtii, Tausch, Ballintoy, Co. Antrim; *H. murorum*, var. c., *microcladium*, Newtowncrommelin and Garvagh, Co. Derry; *H. iricum*, Fr., Lisoughter, near Recess, Co. Galway; *Carex Goodenovii* b. *juncella*, Fr., and *Scirpus rufus*, Schrad., Ballintoy, Co. Antrim.

S. A. BRENAN, Knocknacarry.

ZOOLOGY.

CRUSTACEA.

New Species of Copepoda from the South-west of Ireland.—In the *Ann. Mag. Nat. Hist.* for November, 1895, p. 359, &c., Messrs. T. and A. Scott describe with figures three new forms of parasitic crustaceans obtained at Valentia by Messrs. W. I. Beaumont and F. W. Gamble. Two of these, found on ascidians, are referred with some doubt to the genus *Enterocola* and named *E. hibernica* and *E. Beaumontii*. For the third, which was found as a parasite on the nudibranch *Lomanotus genii*, a new genus *Lomanoticola* is proposed, the species being designated *L. insolens*. This last form shows great degradation, there being no apparent segmentation of the fore-body, and the antennules, antennæ and mouth-organs being absent. Except for the hindmost segment of the abdomen with its two curious egg-sacs, the parasite was completely buried in the body of the nudibranch.

REPTILES.

A Stray Snake near Cork.—A recent issue of the *Cork Constitution* records the occurrence of a snake near Blarney. The reptile was encountered crossing a grass field and is said to have been at first mistaken for an eel! It was promptly knocked on the head, a fate which meets all the members of its order, which purposely or accidentally are let loose in Ireland.

BIRDS.

The Brambling (Fringilla montifringilla) in the Vale of Ovoca.—On December 8th, a specimen of this rare winter visitor was shot quite close to here by the Rev. J. M. Robinson, Rector of Ovoca, who kindly presented it to me; it is now with Messrs. Williams & Son of Dame-street for preservation.

J. HUNTER, Wooden Bridge.

Crossbills breeding in the Vale of Ovoca.—This year, 1895, Crossbills (*Loxia curvirostris*) bred in this neighbourhood. On April 1st I secured an old and young bird, which are in the collection of Mr. Barrington, Fassaroe, Bray.

J. HUNTER.

Crossbills in Queen's County.—The presence of a flock of these interesting birds in Queen's Co. is noted in the *Field* for November 16th.

Stock-Doves in Co. Dublin.—On the 19th of November, my brother shot two Stock-Doves (*Columba œnas*) at Carrick Hill near Malahide. They were first noticed in this district in November, 1893, when a flock of twelve remained for about a fortnight.

J. TRUMBULL, Malahide.

Longtailed Duck in Co. Clare.—I shot an immature Longtailed Duck (*Harelda glacialis*) on Lough Derg on Monday last, December 2nd. The bird was one of a pair. I also shot two more out of three (also immature birds) on the 27th December, 1890. These are the only two occasions on which I have seen them since I came here in 1888. As they are by no means common so far south (*vide* Seebohm) the fact seems worthy of record.

R. F. HIBBERT, Scariff, Co. Clare.

Long-tailed Duck in Co. Wexford,—Mr. H. R. Guiness records, in the *Field* of November 16th, an adult male of *Harelda glacialis*, shot on Tacumshin Lake.

MAMMALS.

Pine Martens recently taken in Ireland.—During the last twelve months I know of three specimens having been trapped or shot; as follows:—One last winter in Lord Clonbrock's Demesne, Co. Galway. One in the spring at Castle Taylor, Ardrahan, in the same county. One this autumn at Enniscor, on the shores of L. Conn, by the gamekeeper of Joseph Pratt, Esq., Co. Mayo.

WM. F. DE V. KANE, Monaghan.

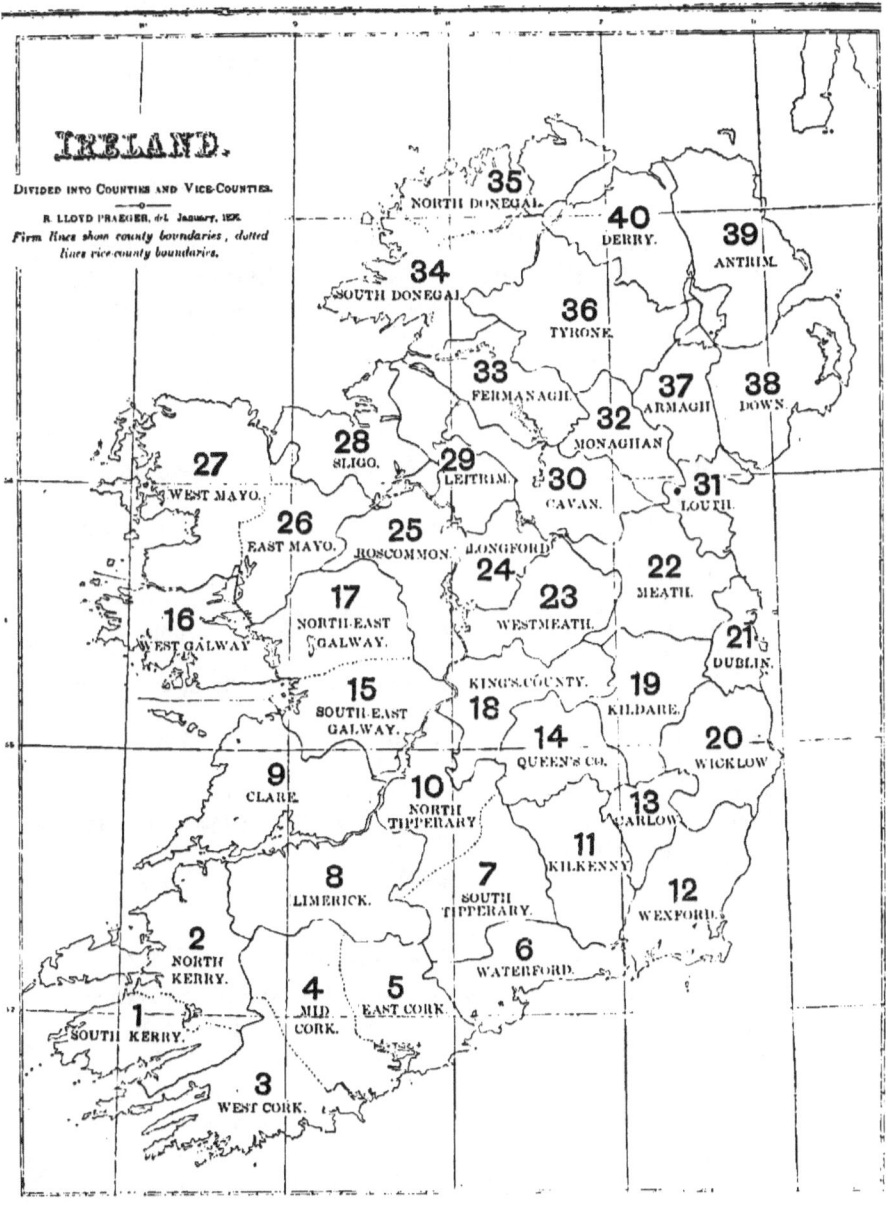

ON THE BOTANICAL SUBDIVISION OF IRELAND.
BY R. LLOYD PRAEGER, B.E.

(PLATE I.)

THIRTY-SEVEN years have now elapsed since, at a meeting of the Dublin University Zoological and Botanical Association, a paper by Charles C. Babington was read, entitled "Hints towards a Cybele Hibernica."[1] In this communication, the author put forward a scheme for the subdivision of Ireland into twelve provinces and thirty-seven counties and vice-counties, on the plan of Watson's *Cybele Britannica*; and as the paper is not readily accessible to most botanists, the suggested division may be reprinted here :—

XIX. SOUTH ATLANTIC.—113. South Kerry; 114. North Kerry; 115. South Cork.

XX. BLACKWATER.—116. North Cork; 117. Wexford; 118. South Tipperary.

XXI. BARROW.—119. Kilkenny; 120. Carlow; 121. Queen's Co.

XXII. LEINSTER COAST.—122. Wexford; 123. Wicklow.

XXIII. LIFFEY AND BOYNE.—124. Kildare; 125. Dublin; 126. Meath; 127. Louth.

XXIV. LOWER SHANNON.—128. Limerick; 129. Clare; 130. East Galway.

XXV. UPPER SHANNON.—131. North Tipperary; 132. King's Co.; 133. Westmeath; 134. Longford.

XXVI. NORTH ATLANTIC.—135. West Galway; 136. West Mayo.

XXVII. NORTH CONNAUGHT.—137. East Mayo; 138. Sligo; 139. Leitrim; 140. Roscommon.

XXVIII. ERNE.—141. Fermanagh; 142. Cavan; 143. Monaghan; 144. Tyrone; 145. Armagh.

XXIX. DONEGAL.—146. Donegal.

XXX. ULSTER COAST.—147. Down; 148. Antrim; 149. Derry.

Following Watson, Babington founded his twelve provinces as far as possible on the principal river-basins of the country. Ireland does not readily lend itself to such a plan of division. The Shannon valley occupies about one-sixth of the entire island, and other river-basins are small in comparison. Also, the mountain-chains being mostly near the coast, considerable areas are drained by small rivers only. The consequence was that in many cases river-basin provinces were not practicable, and this gave an opportunity for the using of

---

[1] *Nat. Hist. Review*, vi., pt. 2, 1859. *Proc. D. U. Zool. and Bot. Assoc.*, i.

natural botanical divisions, such as Kerry and South Cork, Connemara and West Mayo, and Donegal. So that, although the partition of Ireland by river-basins is not satisfactory, nevertheless Babington's twelve provinces appear to be as good as could have been selected.

Seven years after the publication of Babington's paper, *Cybele Hibernica* appeared, under the authorship of Dr. David Moore, and Mr. A. G. More. In this work the twelve provinces suggested by Babington were adopted, the only alteration being that they were called "Districts," and were numbered 1 to 12, instead of XIX to XXX.—of which more anon. In his *British Rubi*, published three years later (1869), Babington used the twelve provinces he proposed; indeed, it was for the purpose of showing the distribution of the *Rubi* that he first undertook the botanical division of Ireland; as he himself modestly says [1]—"I should not have intruded myself into a work which seems especially Irish, had it not become necessary for me to subdivide the country for the purpose of recording the distribution of the Irish *Rubi*, as a part of my projected, and to a considerable extent completed, treatise upon the *Rubi* of the United Kingdom." So much for the proposed twelve botanical divisions of Ireland; they have been adopted by the leaders of Irish botany, and the large amount of botanical survey work carried out since they were first suggested has not in any way shaken our faith in their scientific usefulness and practical convenience.

Next, as regards the second part of Babington's scheme— the subdivision into counties and vice-counties. We have not yet in Ireland got so far as a *Topographical Botany*; and, although the publication of *Cybele Hibernica* marked the commencement of a large amount of field-work, this was in most cases confined to small areas, and Babington's county list lay unused and apparently almost forgotten till 1884, when Prof. W. R. M'Nab read before the Royal Dublin Society, a "Short Note on the Botanical Topographical Divisions of Ireland" which is printed in their *Proceedings*.[2] This paper purports to be a revision and extension of Babington's scheme, but the suggestions put forward—the Roman numerals for

---

[1] Hints towards a Cybele Hibernica, *l. c.*
[2] *Sci. Proc. R.D.S.*, n.s., iv. 197 (1885).

the provinces, the use of the word "province" instead of "district" (which was used in *Cybele Hibernica*), the giving of names to the provinces, and the numbering of the vice-counties--all these had been already published in Babington's paper; and M'Nab's table of provinces and counties is identical with that of Babington, except that he commences the numbering of provinces and of counties with I., and that he does not subdivide the county of Kerry.

No further reference to or use of Babington's county-division scheme appears until the year 1895, when Messrs. Groves employed it in their valuable paper on "The Distribution of the *Characeæ* in Ireland,"[1] in which the distribution of the species and varieties is shown in list form, on the plan of Watson's *Topographical Botany*.

For some time past, a sense of the importance of commencing the large amount of field-work that must be carried out before an Irish *Topographical Botany* become a possibility, has been steadily growing in my mind; and this led me some months ago to go carefully into the question of the most advantageous subdivision of the country into counties and vice-counties. As regards about twenty-four out of the thirty-two Irish counties, I had the benefit of at least some personal knowledge, topographical and botanical; and regarding others, I have had the great advantage of the opinions of botanists whose special acquaintance with the flora of these counties is well known. The first result of my enquiry has been the conviction that the subdivision of the larger counties as proposed by Babington can be now improved upon; and indeed this is not a matter for surprise, when we consider the enormous advance made during the intervening period of thirty-seven years in our knowledge of Irish botanical topography (though that knowledge is yet very far from complete). I am also convinced that the order in which the counties and vice-counties are numbered in Babington's scheme is not the most convenient or useful one that can be devised: and in this view I am glad to have the support of several of the most practical Irish botanists. It is manifestly important that some scheme of county-division and county-numbering should be fixed once for all, according to which future records may

---

[1] *Irish Naturalist*, Jan. and Feb., 1895.

be systematically noted. This is especially desirable at the present time, when there appears to be a distinct increase of activity as regards Irish botany, as shown not only by the work which is being done by home workers, but also by the welcome visits which we have had during the past two seasons from quite a number of the leading field botanists of England. And if any alteration is to be made in the only county-division scheme that has been put forward, then the sooner it is made the better. Since they were proposed thirty-seven years ago, the only published paper in which Babington's county-numbers have been used is that of Messrs. Groves, already quoted. The scheme, in fact, has not been generally adopted, so that no great inconvenience can result from a revision of the county list : though if this scheme had already been used in a number of papers, it would be a question whether the inconvenience of any alteration of the county-numbering would not outweigh the advantages of an improved subdivision.

These considerations have led me to put forward without further delay the following revised scheme, not without a full enquiry as to the value of each of the alterations which is suggested, and careful consideration of its desirability. It will be most convenient to give the list first, and state the reason for the changes afterwards.—

1. South Kerry.
2. North Kerry.
3. West Cork.
4. Mid Cork.
5. East Cork.
6. Waterford.
7. South Tipperary.
8. Limerick.
9. Clare.
10. North Tipperary.
11. Kilkenny.
12. Wexford.
13. Carlow.
14. Queen's County.
15. South-east Galway.
16. West Galway.
17. North-east Galway.
18. King's County.
19. Kildare.
20. Wicklow.
21. Dublin.
22. Meath.
23. Westmeath.
24. Longford.
25. Roscommon.
26. East Mayo.
27. West Mayo.
28. Sligo.
29. Leitrim.
30. Cavan.
31. Louth.
32. Monaghan.
33. Fermanagh.
34. South Donegal.
35. North Donegal.
36. Tyrone.
37. Armagh.
38. Down.
39. Antrim.
40. Derry.

It may be stated at once that this arrangement differs from that of Babington, first, as regards the subdivision of the counties of Cork, Kerry, Galway, and Donegal; and secondly, in the renumbering of the counties and vice-counties according to a different plan. It will be seen that the figures ascend regularly from the extreme south-west of the country to the extreme north-east, the numbering following a backwards-and-forwards line, irrespective of the "province" boundaries.

In working out the above scheme, the following considerations influenced the subdivision of the larger counties:—

Natural Boundaries.—Where clearly-defined natural boundaries, botanical, geological, or physical, exist, it is manifestly advantageous that they should be followed; but it is not always possible to follow them, on account of other considerations. The convenience of county-divisions is so great, that except in the subdividing of a large county, it does not appear desirable to forsake county boundaries.

Equalization of Areas.—It is also desirable that, so far as possible, the country should be divided into portions of approximately equal area; but here again, the less the arrangement by counties is disturbed the better.

Utilization of past or future botanical Work.—It is manifestly desirable that the scheme as regards subdivision of counties should harmonize with the subdivisions used, or to be used, in published or future county or local floras; since this will save a large amount of labour, when it comes to working out the flora of each vice-county.

Nature of Boundaries.—Where a new boundary-line is required, it is desirable that it should be something conspicuous—a railway, road, or river—in order that it may be easily found in the field; an imaginary line, such as a straight line between two places, though it looks very well on a map, is often difficult to trace in the field.

Let me now take up in turn each of the cases in which the plan suggested differs from that proposed by Babington, explain the nature of the change, and give the reasons.

CORK.—Is now divided into three vice-counties (3, 4, 5), by two N.W. and S.E. lines. Babington divided it into two vice-counties, one much larger than the other, by the east and west course of the River Sullane and its continuation the River Lee. In that useful little flora, *The Flowering Plants and Ferns of the County Cork* (1883), the author, Rev.

Thomas Allin, departs from Babington's boundary, and adopts instead "a line drawn along the Killarney Junction Railway from the border of Co. Kerry to Millstreet, thence running across the country in a straight line to Macroom, thence in a similar line to Bandon and from that town, following the Bandon River, to the sea."[1] This line appears to have been wisely chosen, dividing the western mountainous portion of the county, with its Atlantic, Highland, and American plants, from the more level tract, with its calcicole and Germanic species. The latter district (1,747 square miles) being still considerably larger than the largest of the counties which it is not proposed to subdivide, is conveniently divided into two by the Great Southern and Western Railway from Charleville to Cork, and thence by the western shore of Cork Harbour to the ocean; this line forms approximately the western boundary of the Carboniferous limestone. The great county of Cork is thus divided into three parts of almost equal area, the size of each being about that of an average Irish county. As regards the division of Co. Cork, I have had the advantage of the hearty co-operation of Mr. R. A. Phillips, whose knowledge of the Cork flora is well-known, and who suggested to me the sub-division of the county adopted in this paper.

KERRY.—In Babington's scheme Kerry is divided into two vice-counties by a line following the River Flesk, the northern shore of the Lower Lake of Killarney, and the River Laune. Mr. R. W. Scully, F.L.S., whose researches in the Kerry flora readers of this Journal well know, has kindly favoured me with his views. He points out that the Dingle promontory, which Babington includes in North Kerry, belongs botanically to South Kerry; and this, indeed, Babington himself admits in his paper.[2] Mr. Scully also kindly informs me that when his forthcoming *Flora of Kerry* is published, the distribution of species will probably be shown by baronies; it will therefore be an advantage to use barony boundaries in fixing the Kerry vice-counties; and the best division is evidently a line separating the baronies of Magunihy and Trughanacmy on the one hand from Glanarought, Dunkerron, Iveragh, and Corkaguiny on the other; this forms roughly a N.W. and S.E. line, and divides the county into a mountainous south-western part, composed of Silurian and Devonian rocks, intersected by deep bays, and rich in alpine and Atlantic plants, and a more level and less maritime north-eastern portion, composed of Carboniferous limestone, and Coal-measures. Mr. Scully agrees as to this being the best division of Kerry into two vice-counties.

GALWAY.—Connemara forms a division in every way distinct, and Babington's line correctly cuts off the mountainous metamorphic maritime district lying west of Lough Corrib, with its peculiar flora, from the inland limestone plain of East Galway. The latter area is so very extensive (1,613 square miles, twice the size of an average county), that there can be no doubt as to the desirability of forming it into two vice-counties, and a convenient east and west dividing line is formed by

---

[1] *Op. cit.*, Introduction, p. xii.   [2] p. 536, line 1--3.

the Midland Great Western Railway from Oranmore, at the head of Galway Bay, to Ballinasloe on the River Suck, the eastern boundary of the county. It may be remarked here that the Aran Islands, though part of Co. Galway, belong botanically to Co. Clare, and are so treated in *Cybele Hibernica*; and that Inishbofin, formerly included in Co. Mayo, is now a part of West Galway, to which it naturally belongs.

DONEGAL.—This large county (1,870 square miles) should evidently form two vice-counties, in order to keep the variation of size of our ultimate divisions within reasonable limits, and thus ensure that a statement of the number of county-divisions in which a plant occurs in the country may be a tolerably correct indication of its area of distribution.

The boundary which I suggest is the roughly east and west line which separates the baronies of Inishowen and Kilmacrenan on the north from Raphoe and Boylagh on the south. This line crosses the Inishowen isthmus at its narrowest point, follows the shore of Lough Swilly, and then the River Swilly almost to its source, and descends to the western ocean along the course of the Gweedore River; and it divides the county into two almost equal parts.

The whole of Ireland, 32,513 square miles, is thus divided into 40 portions of as nearly equal size as conditions will permit, the average area of these portions being 813 square miles. This size is almost identical with the average size of Watson's 112 vice-counties of Great Britain, which is 804 square miles.

Next, as to the order in which the counties and vice-counties should be numbered. Watson numbered the British provinces I. to XVIII., commencing with S.W. England and ending with the extreme north of Scotland. The vice-counties he numbered in the same order, those included in Province I. being numbered 1 to 6, those of Province II. 7 to 14, and so on. Babington proposed a similar method for Ireland, but the result is not satisfactory. The Irish "provinces" are not numbered regularly from south to north, but the numbering runs first up the east coast, and then drops back into the south-west; and this absence of regular progression becomes accentuated if the vice-counties are numbered in the sequence of the provinces; when, for instance, we suddenly pass from Louth (127) 120 miles south-westward to Limerick (128). It will be generally admitted that the best scheme, and the most natural, is one which will show a regular progression from south to north—from a higher temperature to a lower: with such a system, the largeness or smallness of the numbers in the list showing the county-distribution of a species, will themselves be a key to the northward or southward range of the plant. Thus, if out of say 40 vice-counties we find the range of a plant is from 1 to 20, we shall immediately know that it is confined to the southern half of Ireland. It appears to me that the practical advantages of such a plan are much greater than those which arise from a consecutive numbering for the vice-counties of each "province;" and the scheme which I suggest therefore embodies this principle. A glance at the botanical map in *Cybele Hibernica* shows that the characteristic plants of Ireland are distributed according to lines which have a general trend north-west and south-east, rather than west and east; this is also the course followed by the isothermal lines of winter and spring; and I have adopted a system of numbering that follows these natural lines, and proceeds in a regular manner from the extreme south-west of the country to the extreme north-east. Such a plan does not prevent the vice-counties being grouped under the "provinces" if for any reason this is desired. We should then have the following table; for the "provinces" I give the numbering used by Moore and More in *Cybele Hibernica* :—

Province	No.	Vice-county
I. South Atlantic,	1.	South Kerry.
	2.	North Kerry.
	3.	West Cork.
II. Blackwater,	4.	Mid. Cork.
	5.	East Cork.
	6.	Waterford.
	7.	South Tipperary.
III. Barrow,	11.	Kilkenny.
	13.	Carlow.
	14.	Queen's County.
IV. Leinster Coast,	12.	Wexford.
	20.	Wicklow.
V. Liffey and Boyne,	19.	Kildare.
	21.	Dublin.
	22.	Meath.
	31.	Louth.
VI. Lower Shannon,	8.	Limerick.
	9.	Clare.
	15.	South-east Galway.
	17.	North-east Galway.
VII. Upper Shannon,	10.	North Tipperary.
	18.	King's County.
	23.	Westmeath.
	24.	Longford.

VIII. North Atlantic,		16.	West Galway.
		27.	West Mayo.
IX. North Connaught,		26.	East Mayo.
		28.	Sligo.
		29.	Leitrim.
		25.	Roscommon.
X. Erne,		33.	Fermanagh.
		30.	Cavan.
		32.	Monaghan.
		36.	Tyrone.
		37.	Armagh.
XI. Donegal,		34.	South Donegal.
		35.	North Donegal.
XII. Ulster Coast,		38.	Down
		39.	Antrim.
		40.	Derry.

Lastly, a word as to the numerals used to denote the districts and county-divisions. Babington numbered his first Irish province (South Atlantic) XIX, being the number following that of the last province of Great Britain (North Isles), and similarly numbered the first vice-county (South Kerry) 113; and the sequence involved in the latter has been used by Messrs. Groves in their recent paper on Irish *Characeæ*, their reason, as given in a friendly note to the writer, being that the British Isles form a natural botanical district, of which Ireland is a part. Quite so; but let us look more closely into this matter. According to Watson's arrangement, as first put forward in *Cybele Britannica*, and now universally adopted, the vice-county numbering in Great Britain commences in the Atlantic counties of Cornwall and Devon, which in all Britain have botanically the nearest affinity to the characteristic flora of Ireland; yet in the county list they are removed from the allied districts of Ireland by the whole length and breadth of England, Wales, and Scotland. The county-numbers in Great Britain led us gradually northward, from Cornwall right up to the Shetlands, and the largeness or smallness of the figures themselves thus afford a useful clue to the northern or southern range of a species; but, according to this scheme of continuous numbering, the moment we pass 112 we plunge from the almost Scandinavian flora of Shetland into the luxuriant southern flora of Killarney, thence to proceed by degrees to the more northern flora of Derry. A continuous numbering for the whole of the British Islands would be certainly a desideratum; but one which passes without a break or indication of a change from Shetland to Killarney is too unnatural to commend itself. Botanists will form their own opinions on this point; for my part, I prefer to follow the lead set by the careful and able authors of *Cybele Hibernica*, who numbered the Irish districts 1 to 12, not XIX to XXX; and I have numbered the counties and vice-counties of Ireland 1 to 40.

Another point requiring a passing notice is the use of the words "province" and "district." Babington, following Watson, called the twelve Irish botanical divisions "provinces";[1] the authors of *Cybele Hibernica* used the term "district" instead; M'Nab proposed to return to the word "province." Considering that Ireland is divided geographically into four provinces—Ulster, Munster, Leinster, and Connaught,—and that in Ireland the term "province" is invariably used in this sense only, I believe its use to signify the twelve botanical divisions of the country would lead to confusion; and I follow Moore and More, who (probably on the same consideration) called them "districts."

In conclusion, I wish to acknowledge the ready and willing assistance which I received from many Irish botanists in the inquiries made for the purposes of the present paper; and I would specially offer my thanks to Messrs. N. Colgan, M.R.I.A., R. A. Phillips, R. W. Scully, F.L.S., S. A. Stewart, F.B.S.E., and Rev. C. H. Waddell, B.D., for information and for useful criticism given in correspondence, or in conversation.

---

[1]. Babington's Irish "provinces" correspond in size and importance to Watson's "vice-provinces," rather than to his "provinces," and might preferably have been numbered XXXIX to L. in continuation of the last British vice-province (Shetland), rather than XIX to XXX.

A LIST OF IRISH HYMENOPTERA ACULEATA.
BY PERCY H. FREKE.

I OFFER the following paper on the Aculeate Hymenoptera of Ireland, not with any pretentions to its being a complete list of that part of our fauna, but as a first effort towards a more complete knowledge of the number and distribution of its members.

When taking up lately the study of this subject I found no list of our Irish Aculeate Hymenoptera to guide me with reference to occurrences or the distribution of such insects as I obtained, and it is with a view to establishing some such record, and inducing others to aid us with more complete information, that I now propose the following list as a basis on which to commence.

I regret that my notes cover but a part only of this country; from much of the western side of Ireland I have no records; and even the eastern side, with the exception of what might be termed the Dublin district, has hitherto been worked in a most casual manner. When others who have better opportunities than I have had, can be induced to record their captures, the number of species in my list will probably be very much increased, and many that I have met with but sparingly may be found abundant in other localities.

I must here offer my warmest thanks to Mr. Edward Saunders, for the patience and kindness he has shown me in naming insects which I have sent for his determination; to Mr. Carpenter and Mr. Halbert, of the Irish National Museum, for their unfailing kindness and courtesy in giving me on all occasions the benefit of their experience, and allowing me to inspect the insects in the National collection; and to my coadjutor, Mr. H. G. Cuthbert, in freely furnishing me with records of his many captures, and in largely adding to the material of my collection. I have also to thank the Flora and Fauna Committee of the Royal Irish Academy for the records of specimens collected under their auspices.

The letter (M) signifies that the specimen is in the Dublin Museum collection. The name of the collector or authority is added in all but the common species of general distribution.

FORMICIDÆ.

Formica rufa, Linn.—(Haliday, M.) Churchill, Co. Armagh (Rev. W. F. Johnson, M.)
F. fusca, Linn.—Common and generally distributed.
Lasius flavus, De Geer.—Very common everywhere.
L. fuliginosus, Latr.—Lismore (Halbert).
L. niger, Linn.—Common in suitable localities.
Leptothorax acervorum, Fab.—Carlingford (Rev. W. F. Johnson, M.); Oughterard (Carpenter).
Myrmica rubra, Linn.—
   Race *ruginodis*—Very common everywhere.
      lævinodis—Coolmore, Co. Donegal (Rev. W. F. Johnson, M.); Carrickmines, Lucan, Co. Dublin; Dingle (Halbert).
      scabrinodis—Less common than *ruginodis*; Castletown-Bere, Co. Cork (Carpenter, M.); Armagh (Rev. W. F. Johnson, M.); Greystones (M.); Dalkey (M.); Courtown, Co. Wexford, and Co. Dublin (Cuthbert).
      lobicornis—Armagh (Rev. W. F. Johnson, M.)

SPHEGIDÆ.

Pompilus rufipes, Linn.—I took three specimens at Courtown, Co. Wexford, last year. This season I have looked for them in the same place in vain.
P. plumbeus, Fab.—Very common in most sandy localities along the coast.
P. niger, Fab.—Glencullen, Co. Dublin (Cuthbert); Co. Kildare (Freke): common at Rosscarberry, Co. Cork (Cuthbert).
P. gibbus, Fab.—Common and generally distributed.
Salius fuscus, Linn.—(Haliday, M.); Armagh (Rev. W. F. Johnson. M.); Friarstown, Co. Dublin (Cuthbert).
S. exaltatus, Fab.—(Haliday, M.) (Dr. A. W. Foot, in *Proc. Nat. Hist. Soc. of Dublin*, vol. vi., pt. 1, p. 83).
Ceropales maculata, Fab.—Fairly common in suitable localities on the sea-coast.
Astatus boops, Schr.—Donabate, Co. Dublin (Cuthbert).
Tachytes pectinipes, Linn.—Very common in suitable localities on the sea-coast.
Ammophila hirsuta, Scop.—I took two specimens last season near Arklow, Co. Wicklow.
Spilomena troglodytes, V. de Lind.—(Haliday, M).
Pemphredon lugubris, Fab.—Monkstown, Co. Dublin, and Courtown, Co. Wexford (Cuthbert).
P. Shuckardi, Moraw.—Dundrum, Co. Dublin (Freke).
P. Wesmaeli, Moraw.—Monkstown, Co. Dublin (Cuthbert).
P. lethifer, Shuck.—Courtown, Co. Wexford, and Laytown, Co. Dublin (Cuthbert).
Passalœcus monilicornis, Dbm.—(Haliday, M.)
Mimesa unicolar, V. de Lind.—Laytown, Co. Dublin (Cuthbert).
Psen pallipes, Panz.—Monkstown, Co. Dublin (Cuthbert)
Gorytes mystaceus, Linn.—(Haliday, M.)
Nysson spinosus, Fab.—Glencullen, Co. Dublin (Freke).
Mellinus arvensis, Linn.—Common in suitable localities on the sea coast.

Oxybelus uniglumis, Linn.—Bundoran (Rev. W. F. Johnson, M.); Laytown, Co. Dublin; near Drogheda; and Roscarberry, Co. Cork (Cuthbert).

Crabro tibialis, Fab.—(Haliday, M.)

C. clavipes, Linn.—(Haliday, M.), Dundrum, Co. Dublin (Freke).

C. leucostomus, Linn.—Not uncommon.

C. palmipes, Linn.—Not uncommon. Portmarnock and Glencullen, Co. Dublin; Arklow, Co. Wicklow; and Courtown, Co. Wexford (Freke); Laytown, Co. Dublin (Cuthbert).

C. varius, Lep.—Not uncommon on sandhills on the east coast.

C. Wesmaeli, V. de Lind.—Dundrum, Co. Dublin (Freke); Laytown, Co. Dublin (Cuthbert).

C. quadri-maculatus, Fab.—Courtown, Co. Wexford (Freke), an unusual dark form.

C. dimidiatus, Fab.—Bruckless, Co. Donegal (Rev. W. F. Johnson); Sandyford, Co. Dublin (Cuthbert); Scalp, Co. Dublin (Freke); an unusual dark form.

C. cephalotes, Panz.—Not uncommon.

C. vagus, Linn.—Monkstown, Co. Dublin (Cuthbert).

C. peltarius, Schreb.—Common on sandhills on the sea-coast.

VESPIDÆ.

Vespa vulgaris, Linn.—Very common everywhere.

V. germanica, Fab.—Very common everywhere.

V. rufa, Linn.—Less common than the two preceding, but generally distributed, at least from Dublin southward.

V. austriaca, Panz.—Local and not very uncommon in the Dublin district. Females only recorded.

V. sylvestris, Scop.—Common.

V. norvegica, Fab.—Common.

Odynerus spinipes, Linn.—Killiney, Co. Dublin (Cuthbert).

O. parietum, Linn.—Not uncommon.

O. pictus, Curt.—Common.

O. trimarginatus, Zett.—(Haliday, M.); Courtown, Co. Wexford (Cuthbert), Rosscarberry, Co. Cork; a variety with spotted tibia (Cuthbert).

O. parietinus, Linn.—Common.

APIDÆ.

Colletes succincta, Linn.—(Haliday, M.); Rosscarberry, Co. Cork (Cuthbert).

C. fodiens, Kirb.—Courtown, Co. Wexford (Cuthbert).

C. picistigma, Thoms.—Common at Courtown, Co. Wexford (Freke).

C. daviesana, Sm.—Killiney, and Sandyford, and Laytown, Co. Dublin; Courtown, Co. Wexford; and Rosscarberry, Co. Cork (Cuthbert).

Prosopis confusa, Nyl.—(Haliday, M., as *punctatissima*); Glencullen, Co. Dublin (Cuthbert); Gorey, Co. Wexford (Freke).

Sphecodes gibbus, Linn.—Glencullen, Co. Dublin (Cuthbert and Freke).

S. subquadratus, Sm.—Rosscarberry, Co. Cork (Cuthbert).

S. spinulosus, Hag.—Kilkenny (Rev. T. B. Gibson, M.)

Sphecodes pilifrons, Thoms.—Kilkenny (Rev. T. B. Gibson, M.); Rosscarberry, Co. Cork (Cuthbert).

S. similis, Westm.—Glencullen, Co. Dublin, and Courtown, Co. Wexford (Freke).

S. variegatus, Hag.—Sandyford and Glencullen, Co. Dublin (Freke).

S. dimidiatus, Hag.—Sandyford, Co. Dublin (Cuthbert and Freke).

S. affinis, Hag.—Rosscarberry, Co. Cork (Cuthbert).

Halictus rubicundus, Chr.—Common everywhere.

H. sexnotatus, Kirb.—Saunders in his book on British Hymenoptera Aculeata, p. 214, states that it has been taken here by Haliday. I cannot trace the specimen in the Irish Nat. Museum.

H. cylindricus, Fab.—Common everywhere.

H. albipes, Kirb.—(Haliday, M.); Kilkenny (Rev. T. B. Gibson); Kildare (Freke); Lucan, Co. Dublin (Halbert).

H. subfasciatus, Nyl.—(Haliday, M.); Coolmore, Co. Donegal (Rev. W. F. Johnson); Kildare (Freke); Tallaght, Co. Dublin (Halbert).

H. villosulus, Kirb.—(Haliday, M.); Courtown, Co. Wexford, and Rosscarberry, Co. Cork (Cuthbert); common in Kildare (Freke); Killaloe (Halbert).

H. minutus, Kirb.—Courtown, Co. Wexford (Cuthbert).

H. nitidiusculus, Kirb.—(Haliday, M.); Dunsink, Co. Dublin (H. B. Rathborne, M.); Monkstown, Co. Dublin; Courtown, Co. Wexford; and Rosscarberry. Co. Cork (Cuthbert).

H. tumulorum, Linn.—(Haliday, M.); Golden Ball, Co. Dublin, and Courtown, Co. Wexford (Cuthbert); Dundrum, Co. Dublin (Freke); Lucan and Tallaght, Co. Dublin (Halbert).

H. smeathmanellus, Kirb.—Tallaght, Co. Dublin (Halbert).

H. morio, Fab.—Common.

H. leucopus, Kirb.—Dundrum, Co. Dublin (Freke).

Andrena albicans, Kirb.—Common everywhere.

A. atriceps, Kirb.—Kilkenny (Rev. T. B. Gibson, M.).

A. rosæ, var. **trimmerana,** Kirb.—Common everywhere.

A. cineraria, Linn.—Armagh (Rev. W. F. Johnson, M.); Rostrevor, Co. Down (W. Hooper, M.).

A. thoracica, Fab.—Armagh (Rev. W. F. Johnson, M.).

A. nitida, Fourc.—Kilkenny (Rev. T. B. Gibson, M.); Courtown, Co. Wexford (Cuthbert).

A. clarkella, Kirb.—"United Kingdom" (Smith, p. 40); "all over our islands" (Saunders, p. 242). I have not hitherto met with it myself.

A. nigroænea, Kirb.—Common.

A. gwynana, Kirb.—Not uncommon and generally distributed.

A. helveola, Linn.—Blanchardstown, Co. Dublin (Halbert).

A. fucata, Smith.—Skerries, Co. Dublin; and Courtown, Co. Wexford (Cuthbert); Portmarnock, Co. Dublin (Freke).

A. denticulata, Kirb.—Rosscarberry, Co. Cork (Cuthbert).

A. fulvicrus, Kirb.—Dunsink, Co. Dublin (Rathborne, M.); near Dublin (Cuthbert).

A. albicrus, Kirb.—Sandyford and Laytown, Co. Dublin (Cuthbert); Portmarnock, Co. Dublin (Freke).

A. analis, Panz.—Ireland (Smith, p. 65).

A. coitana, Kirb.—Limerick (Halbert).

A. minutula, Kirb.—Common and generally distributed.

Andrena nana, Kirb.—Rosscarberry, Co. Cork (Cuthbert).
A. afzeliella, Kirb.—Killiney, Co. Dublin (Cuthbert).
A. wilkella, Kirb.—Common and generally distributed; found stylopized by Cuthbert.
Nomada solidaginis, Panz.—(Haliday, M.)
N. succincta, Panz.—(Haliday, M.); Dunsink, Co. Dublin (Rathborne); Dundrum, Co. Dublin (Freke); Portmarnock, Co. Dublin (Halbert).
N. alternata, Kirb.—Very common and generally distributed.
N. ruficornis, Linn.—Common and generally distributed.
N. borealis, Zett.—(Haliday, M.); Stillorgan Park, Co. Dublin (Cuthbert).
N. bifida, Thoms.—Courtown, Co. Wexford, and Glencullen, Co. Dublin (Cuthbert); Dundrum, Co. Dublin (Freke).
N. ochrostoma, Kirb.—(Dr. A. W. Foot, *l.c.*); Stillorgan Park, Co. Dublin, and Rosscarberry, Co. Cork (Cuthbert); Howth, Santry, etc., Co. Dublin (Halbert).
N. obtusifrons, Nyl.—(Haliday, M.)
N. ferruginata, Kirb.—Glencullen, Co. Dublin (Cuthbert).
N. fabriciana, Linn.—(Haliday, M.)
N. flavoguttata, Kirb.—(Haliday, M.); Courtown, Co. Wexford, and Monkstown, Co. Dublin (Cuthbert); Glencullen, Co. Dublin (Freke); Santry and Tallaght, Co. Dublin (Halbert).
N. furva, Panz.—(Haliday, M.)
Cœlioxys elongata, Lep.—Not very uncommon. Fermoy, Co. Cork (Halbert); Monkstown, Co. Dublin, and Rosscarberry, Co. Cork (Cuthbert); Counties Wexford, Dublin, Kildare, and King's (Freke).
Megachile centuncularis, Linn.—Common and generally distributed.
Anthophora pilipes, Fab.—"United Kingdom" (Smith, p. 191, as *acervorum*).
Psithyrus rupestris, Fab.—Limerick (F. Neale, M.); Courtown, Co. Wexford (Freke); Rosscarberry, Co. Cork (Cuthbert).
P. vestalis, Fourc.—Dundrum and Tallaght, Co. Dublin, and Courtown, Co. Wexford (Freke); Sandyford, Co. Dublin, and Rosscarberry, Co. Cork (Cuthbert).
P. barbutellus, Kirb.—Dundrum, Co. Dublin (Freke); Rosscarberry, Co. Cork (Cuthbert).
P. campestris, Panz.—(Dr. A. W. Foot, *l.c.*); Rosscarberry, Co. Cork (Cuthbert); Ireland (Smith, p. 224).
Bombus cognatus, Steph.—Very common and generally distributed.
B. muscorum, Linn.—Very common and generally distributed.
B. latraeiliellus, var. **distinguendus,** Mor.—Courtown and Gorey, Co. Wexford, and Arklow, Co. Wicklow (Freke).
B. hortorum, Linn.—Common and generally distributed.
B. schrimshiranus, Kirb.—Carrickmines and Dundrum, Co. Dublin (Freke); Rosscarberry, Co. Cork (Cuthbert).
B. sylvarum, Linn.—Port Ballintrae, Co. Antrim (Rev. W. F. Johnson); Courtown, Co. Wexford, and Rosscarberry, Co. Cork (Cuthbert).
B. derhamellus, Kirb.—Coolmore, Co. Donegal (Rev. W. F. Johnson).
B. lapidarius, Linn.—Very common and generally distributed.
B. terrestris, Linn.—Both forms *lucorum* and *virginalis* are very common and generally distributed.

THE PLANTS OF WESTMEATH.

BY H. C. LEVINGE, D.L.

DURING the past season a considerable number of species and varieties of plants not previously recorded from this county, or from District VII. of *Cybele Hibernica*, have been discovered, almost altogether by my friends the Revds. E. F. Linton, W. R. Linton, and E. S. Marshall, who paid me a visit in July last, and to whom I am indebted for much valuable information kindly afforded.

Among the *Rubi* especially, as might be expected in a country which had not previously been examined for the genus in any but the most casual manner, many interesting discoveries were made by the Messrs. Linton, so much so indeed that several of the species collected have not as yet been finally determined.

LIST OF SPECIES.

Caltha palustris, L., var. **procumbens,** Beck (VII.) *fide* Ar. Bennett.—Shores of Brittas Lake, Knock Drin. This plant appears to be very near *C. radicans*, Forster, rooting at the nodes of the branches, and with deltoid toothed leaves.

Aquilegia vulgaris, L.—Shore of L. Derevaragh near Knock Body. This plant has been already recorded from the county; but in the present locality it has every appearance of being indigenous, whereas in those previously mentioned it is doubtfully so.]

Papaver dubium, L., var. **Lecoqii,** Lamotte (VII.)—Shore of L. Derevaragh at Lake House.

Viola Reichenbachiana, Bor. (VII.)—Knock Ross.

Vicia cracca, L., var. **incana,** Thuill. (VII.)—N.W. end of L. Owel.

Prunus insititia, Huds. (VII.)—Roadside hedge, Gararee, Knock Drin.

P. cerasus, L. (VII.)—Knock Drin wood.

Rubus Idæus, L., var. **asperrimus,** Lees (VII.). Growing with the type, Knock Drin wood.

R. plicatus, W. and N., form with pink petals.—Drinmore and Crooked Wood—rather plentiful in the latter locality.

R. opacus, Focke (VII.)—Crooked Wood.

R. carpinifolius, W. and N. (VII.)—Crooked Wood.

R. villicaulis, Koehl., var. **Selmeri,** Lindeb. (VII.)—Clonave; N.W. end of L. Derevaragh, also in boundary hedge between Ballynegall and Loughanstown.

R. hirtifolius, Muell. and Wirtz., hairy form (VII.)—Knock Drin.
    var. **danicus,** Focke (VII.)—Knock Drin woods.

R. leucostachys, Schleich (VII.), form with spreading sepals.—Crooked Wood and Knock Ross.

[**R. Drejeri,** G. Jansen, included previously among the Westmeath plants (*Irish Naturalist* for May, 1894, p. 98), must now be struck out of the list. It has been excluded from the 9th edition of the London Catalogue, *R. Leyanus,* Rogers, having taken its place; but careful examination of the Westmeath plant has satisfied Mr. Rogers that it is not his *R. Leyanus,* and it must, for the present, remain undetermined.]

R. radula, Weihe, form tending towards var. **echanitoides** (VII.)—Knock Drin.—Var. **echinitoides,** Rogers (VII.)—Knock Body.

R. oligoclados, Muell and Lefv., var. **Newboldii,** Bab. (VII.)-Crooked Wood, a somewhat less glandular form than the type; but otherwise not differing from it.

R. scaber, W. and N. (VII.)—Crooked Wood, Knock Ross, and Knock Drin.

R. fuscus, W. and N., var. **macrostachys,** P. J. Muell (VII.)—Knock Ross.

R. fuscus x incurvatus.—Crooked Wood. A well-marked hybrid.

R. thyrsiger, Bab. (VII.)—Knock Drin. Mr. Rogers remarks that this differs from the type in the want of hairy clothing, and in the slightly less irregular serrature of the leaves, and rather less armature.

R. rosaceus, W. and N., var. **silvestris,** R. P. Murray (VII.)—Knock Drin; this is considered to be only a shade-grown form of *R. hystrix.*

N.B.—Besides the above-mentioned *Rubi,* about a dozen species were collected last summer in the neighbourhood of the Lakes, and at Knock Drin, including several of the *hirtus-viridis* group, which have not as yet been finally determined.

Potentilla procumbens, Sibth.—Shore of L. Derevaragh near Knock Body wood. Not previously definitely recorded from this county; but found in the Co. Longford (Dist. VII.) by Messrs. Barrington and Vowell.

P. procumbens x sylvestris (VII.)—Same locality as, and growing with, the last.

Rosa sepium, Thuill. (VII.)—Shores of L. Derevaragh at Knock Eyon and Knock Body; rather plentiful.

R. canina, L., var. **urbica,** Leman (VII.)—Shore of L. Derevaragh at Knock Body.

R. canina, L., var. **dumalis** (Bechst.) (VII.)—Near the plantation at Clonave. Shore of L. Derevaragh.

[**Lythrum Salicaria,** L.—Shore of L. Owel at Clonhugh, all three forms—*i.e.,* with long, short, and intermediate length style—were collected, growing together.]

Epilobium obscurum x palustre (VII.)—Bog of Lynn.

Apium nodiflorum, Reichb. fil., var. **ochreatum,** Bab. (VII.)—Shore of L. Owel at Clonhugh—and shore of L. Derevaragh at Donore. Not uncommon.

Galium palustre, L., var. **Witheringii,** Sm. (VII.)—Bog of Lynn and shore of Brittas L., Knock Drin. Not previously definitely reported from the county; but said to be common about L. Ree (Barrington and Vowell).

Leontodon hispidus, L.—Shores of L. Derevaragh at Knock Eyon and Donore—new localities. Previously reported from Creggan Lough, near L. Ree, by Messrs. Barrington and Vowell.

Taraxicum officinale, Web., var. **udum,** Jord. (VII.)—Knock Drin

Scrophularia aquatica, L., var. **cinerea,** Dum. (VII.)—Shore of L. Derevaragh at Donore.

Veronica anagallis-aquatica, L., var. **anagalliformis,** Bor (VII.)—Knock Drin, and Scraw Bog, Loughanstown.

Euphrasia officinalis, L., var. **Rostkoviana,** Hayne (VII.)—Bog of Lynn.

Rhinanthus Crista-Galli, L., var. **fallax,** Wimm. and Grat. (VII.) —Bog of Lynn.

Melampyrum pratense, L., *forma* **latifolia,** Bab.—Knock Eyon. This is given as a variety in the London Catalogue; but it appears to run into the type.

Utricularia Intermedia, Hayne (VII.)—Tullaghan Bog—a very interesting discovery by Mr. E. F. Linton.

Chenopodium rubrum, L. (VII.)—Shore of L. Derevaragh near the mouth of the Yellow River, and shore of L. Drin.

Polygonum maculatum, Trim. and Dyer (VII.)—Shore of L. Derevaragh near Knock Body.

Rumex crispus x obtusifolius (*R. acutus,* L.) (VII.)—Knock Drin —*vide* remarks in *Cybele Hibernica,* p. 252.

*****Humulus lupulus,** L.—Naturalized and well established in hedges near Mayne—Lady Katherine Pakenham.

Salix triandra, L. (VII.)—Roadside, Quarry Bog, Knock Drin.

S. cinerea, L., var. **oleifolia,** Sm. (VII.)—Bog of Lynn.

S. aurita x cinerea (*S. lutescens,* A. Kern.) (VII.)—Near the mouth of the Yellow River, at L. Derevaragh.

S. aurita x caprea (*S. capreola,* J. Keon) (VII.)—Shore of L. Derevaragh at Donore.

S. aurita x repens (*S. ambigua,* Ehrh.) (VII.)—Scraw Bog, Loughanstown.

[*****S. nigricans,** Sm. (VII.),
*****S. phylicifolia,** L. (VII.),
*****S. aurita x nigricans** (VII.),
*****S. nigricans x phylicifolia** (VII.)]

Near the mouth of the Yellow River, L. Derevaragh. Were introduced by the Earl of Longford when planting a strip of the foreshore of the lake after it was lowered. This fact is mentioned here for the information of any botanists who may hereafter meet with these plants in this locality, and consider them to be indigenous]

S. viminalis x caprea (*S. Smithiana*, Willd.)—Roadside, Quarry Bog, near Mullingar.
Epipactis media, Fries. (VII.)—Knock Drin wood.
Orchis incarnata, L. (VII.)—Bog of Lynn; *vide* remarks regarding this plant in the *Cyb. Hib.*, p. 281.
Sparganium ramosum, Huds., var. **microcarpum**, Newm. (VII.)—Quarry and Tullaghan Bogs.
Potamogeton rufescens, Schrad.—Drain from L. Drin. A new locality for this uncommon Westmeath plant. It is recorded from L. Ennel (Belvedere Lake) in the *Cyb. Hib.*—and was again found there this year; also from near L. Ree by Messrs. Barrington and Vowell.
P. decipiens, Nolte. (= *P. lucens x perfoliatus*) (VII.)—L. Derevaragh.
P. Friesii, Rupr. (VII.)—In a dense mass in Lord Longford's boat harbour at L. Derevaragh; also at L. Ennel.
Carex divulsa (Good.) (VII.)—Knock Ross.
C. Goodenovii, J. Gay., var. **juncella**, T. M. Fries (VII.)—Bog of Lynn.
Agrostis canina, L., *forma* **mutica**, Doll. (VII.)—Drinmore.
Phragmites communis, Trin., var. **nigricans**, Gren. and Godr. (VII.)—N.W. end of L. Owel.
Poa pratensis, L., *forma* **subcœrulea**, Sm. (VII.)—Bog of Lynn.
Glycerea plicata, Fr. (VII.)—In drains, Knock Drin.
Athyrium Filix-fœmina, Roth., var. **convexum**, Newman (VII.)—Knock Drin.
Lastrea Filix-mas, Presl., var. **affinis**, Bab. (VII.)—Knock Drin.
    var. **paleacea**, Moore (VII.)—Knock Drin.
Chara vulgaris, L., var. **longibracteata**, Kuetz. (VII.)—L. Ennel.

CORRESPONDENCE.

The Shell of Helix nemoralis.

Sir,—In the admirable issue of the *Irish Naturalist* for September, 1895, Mr. R. Standen describes (p. 270) the shells of the sub-fossil *Helix nemoralis* of Dog's Bay as being "not calcareous as in recent examples, but more of the nature of aragonite." We have passed out of the days, let us hope, when shells were commonly said to consist of "lime"; but the above statement is so surprising that it should not remain without comment. What is aragonite if it is not calcareous? And how can a substance be "more of the nature of" a well defined mineral species? I presume that the shell of *Helix nemoralis* has been proved to consist of calcite in fresh specimens.

Grenville A. J. Cole.

GEOLOGICAL STUDIES IN THE NORTH.

MESSRS. R. Tate, Wm. Gray, Swanston, Wright, and Stewart, have always been known to their brother-geologists by their active researches in the field; but the meeting of the Belfast Naturalists' Field Club held on December 17th, 1895, deserves special comment, as affording so remarkable a proof of the spread of geological observation in the north. Miss Steen described the contents of a newly opened cave; Mr. Robert Bell gave the results of his patient search among the Silurian shales of Pomeroy; and Mr. A. G. Wilson detailed the geological features seen on the great Galway excursion. But the paper requiring separate attention is that by Miss S. M. Thompson, secretary of the geological section of the Club, in which the series of excursions held by that section were described, with the accompaniment of critical notes upon the districts studied.

The area covered by the field-work of the section, from Annalong to Ballycastle, enabled the fourteen or fifteen excursions in themselves to form an admirable *précis* of geology. As one reads the report, one sighs to think of the hundreds of students to whom the subject is still one of diagrams and text-books, and who have to study in regions far removed from the enthusiastic guidance of Miss Thompson. On March 23rd, glacial and marine post-Pliocene beds were visited, in a new sea-swept exposure, at Ballyholme. The numerical work of the boulder-recorders was continued; and the submerged peat, intermediate in age between the glacial and the "estuarine" clays, was found exposed on a second visit. This study of "post-Pliocene diastrophism," as our Californian friends term it, was completed by an excursion to the fossiliferous boulder-clay on Divis, some 1,350 ft. above the sea. It is typical of the energy of these northern workers that one unsuccessful visit was made to this mountain-plateau during a storm, and was followed six weeks later by a fruitful one under the guidance of Mr. Stewart, the veteran discoverer of the deposit. Miss Thompson comments on the abundance of chalk boulders at these high levels, far above their parent masses. One would be glad to know how far the former chalk surface spread to eastward; was the eurite of Ailsa Craig intruded into a highland of Cretaceous rocks, on the lower and western slopes of which the basalt vents had already opened? The hardened chalk and northern igneous rocks might then have come rolling down these slopes in glacial times, to become mingled in the boulder-clays on the denuded surface of the basalts. The frequent discovery of large blocks of the Ailsa rock in Co. Down and Co. Antrim points to its having at one time formed a mountainous and snow-covered mass comparable to the Mournes themselves. There is always the possibility, however, that some of the riebeckite-rocks have been derived from those in Skye; and the Belfast geological section should endeavour to obtain from the Survey Office in London a sample of the more northern variety, which should be kept, with a section, for purposes of close identification. As to the Upper and Middle Lias fossils, however, which form one of the most brilliant discoveries of Prof. Sollas and Mr. Praeger at Kill-o'-the-Grange near Dublin, I feel by no means "driven to the Hebridean islands"[1] for their source; there seems no reason why higher Liassic beds should not have existed in Co. Antrim, and even, with a capping of Cretaceous strata, in Co. Dublin. We often lose sight of the fact that every fragment of detrital material found in one spot means that so much has vanished away from another spot; occasionally, as in the case of the Inch conglomerate near Dingle and the diamonds of Golconda, it is only the detritus that remains.

On Easter Tuesday, the geological section visited Tardree, and this interesting rhyolitic area has been subsequently attacked several times. Mr. J. J. Phillips's photographs of the quarries vie with the best successes of Mr. Welch as scientific works of art. Miss Thompson, in her paper, reviewed the controversy as to the relative ages of the rhyolites and the basalts. On Oct. 26th, an expedition was made to Templepatrick quarry, to follow out the observations of Mr. M'Henry,[2] and a number of photographs were taken, Miss M. K. Andrews securing a series of four, illustrating the whole north face. Changes at the east end were noted, due to quarrying since the date (1888) of Mr. M'Henry's drawing. Miss Thompson showed how the surface of the Chalk falls northward, and allows the overlying rhyolite to thicken in that direction. The well to which she referred is, however, west, not north of the quarry, and the fact that the rhyolite is intrusive—in part, at any rate—may give it a very variable lower boundary with the Chalk. Miss Thompson was able, in perfect fairness, to communicate the analysis of the rhyolite of Cloughwater, near Ballymena, made by Mr. A. P. Hoskins, F.I.C., as one of the outcomes of the geological activity of the Belfast Field Club. From the determination of species of fossil foraminifera to original chemical work, it is clear that the geological section will soon be competent to form a "bureau" for the survey of the county. It is not often that government offices, for special purposes, are so well equipped with specialists.

Another excursion described was that to Coalpit Bay, near Donaghadee, where Mr. Swanston worked in the earlier days of field-club enterprise. Graptolites fortunately rewarded the expedition. The beautiful little sections in Jurassic and Cretaceous rocks at Woodburn, where the Greensand is so green that the term can be no longer scoffed at, occupied another good May day. On June 8th, the glacial beds near Ballycastle were examined; on the 22nd, Liassic fossils were being unearthed at Island Magee; and the week spent in the north of Ireland by the Geologists' Association owed much of its organisation and success to the experience of the geological section. The dykes of the Mourne coast were visited on August 31st, and Miss Thompson made some interesting notes on intrusive rocks at Castlewellan.

Now that so much experience as to general geological features has been obtained, may I suggest, as an addition to the winter work, the collecting and, where necessary, the abstracting, of all papers relating to or bearing closely on the geology of Co. Antrim, so that this literature may

---

[1] *Irish Naturalist*, Dec., 1895, p. 328.   [2] *Geological Magazine*, June, 1895.

be permanently accessible to the Club? Chronological order need not be observed, provided that each pamphlet receives a number, and a triple index, arranged according to date, authors, and subjects, be kept going. Thus Jean François Berger's papers in the early Transactions of the Geological Society of London—containing, by-the-by, the best account hitherto published of the rocks of Sandy Braes—the works of Sir A. Geikie on Tertiary volcanic activity in our islands, Prof. Judd's three papers on the Secondary rocks of Scotland, and separate copies of geological papers in the Field Club's own Proceedings, should be collected whenever opportunity occurs. Second-hand catalogues will help, in the case of authors who are no longer living or who are unable to spare copies of their papers. The Geological Section has now established its position ; every field-worker in our islands will be happy to assist in observations so brightly and energetically carried out.

GRENVILLE A. J. COLE.

PROCEEDINGS OF IRISH SOCIETIES.

ROYAL ZOOLOGICAL SOCIETY.

Recent donations comprise a Squirrel and a Plover from Master Despard ; a pair of Wolves and a pair of Storks have been purchased.

3,170 persons visited the Gardens in December.

DUBLIN MICROSCOPICAL CLUB.

DECEMBER 19th.—The Club met at Mr. MATTHEW HEDLEY'S, who exhibited a section of the intestine of a Lamb in which the presence of a large number of coccidia was evident. Coccidiosis or psorospermosis of the liver of the domestic Rabbit is comparatively common, and the disease is not rare among wild Rabbits. In that form in which the liver is attacked, the parasite has been designated *Coccidium oviforme*. Besides this there is another form, which attacks both Pheasants and Rabbits almost identical, and which invades the intestinal epithelium, named *Coccidium perforans*. It is probable that the Lamb, in the instance under discussion, was affected by the *C. perforans*. The *Coccidia* belong to the class Sporozoa, and like the others of that class are reproduced by spores; there is an absence of flagella, cilia or suckers. They are parasitic in habit, and in the adult stage possess a capsule or shell. Mr. Hedley laid on the table a large number of transparencies which illustrated the characteristics and life history, so far as such is known, of this interesting division of Sporozoa. For these transparencies and slides he expressed indebtedness to Professor M'Fadyean, of London.

Mr G. H. CARPENTER showed a female spider, *Leptyphantes pallidus*, Cb., collected in the Mitchelstown cave in July last by Mr. H. L. Jameson. It is an addition to the Irish fauna. Although possessing well-developed eyes, this spider is stated by M. Simon to be, in France, an inhabitant of caves. It has been found in similar situations in Bavaria. Mr. Cambridge took the type specimen at roots of Heather in Dorset.

Mr. MOORE exhibited root-hairs of a plant which had been received at Glasnevin, as *Colliguaja odorifera*, but which was not this species. The plant produced slender green stems, bearing rather fleshy leaves. From the epidermal tissue around these leaves a dense cushion of unicellular delicate white root-leaves were produced, and later on from this cushion, in the axil of the leaves, an adventitious root was developed. The appearance of this cushion of fine leaves was very remarkable. The hairs had protoplasmic contents.

Mr. GREENWOOD PIM showed *Phyllactinia guttata*, Lev., an interesting mildew which occurred in great abundance on Ash leaves at Brackenstown.

PROF. T. JOHNSON exhibited a section of *Dilsea edulis*, Stackh., a red alga to be found at low water all round the Irish and English coasts. The section showed growing, in the *Dilsea* thallus, a small green alga, *Chlorochytrium inclusum*, Kjell., and, on its surface, a red alga *Nitophyllum reptans*, Crn., which creeps over the *Dilsea* thallus, clinging to it by short multicellular crampons (sucker-like bodies). The endophyte, *C. inclusum*, and the epiphyte, *N. reptans*, are additions to the Irish marine flora. Both are recorded from the south coast of England, and *N. reptans* from the east coast of Scotland. The specimens (of which spirit material was also exhibited), were gathered in September, 1895, on the west coast of Sherkin Island (Co. Cork). Judging from Kjellman's remarks ("Algæ of the Arctic Seas"), *C. inclusum* should be found wherever *D. edulis* occurs. *C. inclusum* is a good illustration of a 'raum-parasite.' *N. reptans* was also found on *Laminaria* stalk, its more usual anchorage.

Mr. M'ARDLE exhibited the reproductive organs of *Plagiochila asplenioides*, L., which he collected recently in Howth demesne. This widely distributed liverwort is rarely found in fruiting condition. One specimen under the microscope showed the fully grown perianth, cut longitudinally and folded back, exposing several unfertilised archegonia at the base. The antheridia exhibited were large, obovate to sphærical in shape, with a well-marked hyaline marginal ring, stalks or pseudopodia as long as the antheridia, of which there were three enclosed in the saccate base of each altered leaf, the whole amentæ is formed of from four to seven pairs, situated at the apex of each stem, which becomes incurved during growth in a remarkable manner. The male plant is much smaller than the female, and was growing apart from it, this may account in some measure for the scarcity of the fruit, although it has been reported to be found with both organs on the one plant (monœcious).

BELFAST NATURALISTS' FIELD CLUB.

JANUARY 8th.—The Geological section met, when Alec G. Wilson, Hon. Sec. of the Club, gave some notes on a recent visit to Dungiven. The Cretaceous rocks exposed there are specially interesting, being believed to represent a higher zone than is found in County Antrim; and are noted for the numerous gastropods which they contain. A series of fossils obtained during the visit was exhibited. Much interest was aroused by some specimens of the porphyritic Rhyolite which occurs near Hillsborough, exhibited by Mr. Wilson, who succeeded in obtaining this rock, which is rather difficult to discover or obtain, as the quarry is flooded and no longer worked, and consequently overgrown with herbage. Extracts from an important pamphlet by P. F. Kendall, F.G.S., on the Glacial Geology of the Isle of Man, were also read. Rock specimens were presented by A. G. Wilson and R. Bell, who also presented a rock section for the microscope of the dyke of basaltic Andesite found by him at Ballygomartin.

JANUARY 21st.—The President (Mr. F. W. LOCKWOOD) in the chair. Mr. G. H. CARPENTER, delegate from the Dublin Naturalists' Field Club, lectured on "Our Plants and Animals: Old Inhabitants and New Arrivals.' The lecture, illustrated by lantern slides of specimens and scenery, dealt with the problems of geographical distribution, and covered much the same ground as the address to the Dublin Club to be printed in full in our next issue.

The PRESIDENT expressed the pleasure it had given the Belfast Club to hear Mr. Carpenter's views on such an interesting subject.

Mr. W. GRAY was sure that Mr. Carpenter had not put forward his theories in a dogmatic spirit, but with a view to stimulate research. It was possible that the absence of records of a species from a certain district meant only that no one had looked for it there.

Prof. SYMINGTON said that no laboratory worker could disparage the labours of a systematic or faunistic naturalist, with the example of Darwin in view.

Mr. CARPENTER, in reply, thanked the Club for their kind reception. He quite agreed with Mr. Gray that there was need for caution, and remarked that such speculations as he had put forward, must rest on the records of animals and plants whose range had been fairly ascertained.

DUBLIN NATURALISTS' FIELD CLUB.

JANUARY 14th.—The Annual General Meeting was held at the Royal Irish Academy House. The President (G. H. CARPENTER, B.Sc.) occupied the chair, and there was a good attendance of members. The SECRETARY, in response to a call from the chair, read the Annual Report, which showed that during the year the membership had risen from 158 to 194. Reference was made to the decease of two original members of Committee—Dr. V. Ball and Mr. A. G. More. During the year six business meetings and seven excursions were held, and a conversazione in addition. Special reference was made to the good work done on the excursions, the results including many species of plants and animals not hitherto found in Ireland. The most important event of the year was the week's Conference and Excursion of all the Irish Field Clubs, held at Galway in July, which has been fully reported in the *Irish Naturalist*. Under the Field Club Union an interchange of lecturers between the different Clubs was carried out. The Committee voted a sum of money towards defraying the expenses of the Union, and propose an addition to the Rules of the Club which will render membership of the different Clubs interchangeable. The Report of the Flora Committee showed good progress during the year. The Committee recommended a grant of £5 to the *Irish Naturalist*. The Treasurer (Prof. T. JOHNSON, D.Sc.) next submitted his report, which showed an increase of £13 in the balance on hand, and a thoroughly sound financial condition. The adoption of the report and accounts was moved by Prof. HADDON and seconded by Mr. W. F. DE V. KANE, and passed after a discussion in which Mr. J. J. Dowling, the President, Secretary, and Treasurer took part. In accordance with the Rules, the following officers for 1896 were declared elected—President, Prof. G. A. J. Cole, F.G.S.; Vice-President, N. Colgan M.R.I.A.; Treasurer, Prof. T. Johnson, D.Sc.; Secretary, R. Lloyd Praeger, B.A., B.E.; Committee, G. H. Carpenter, B.Sc., H. K. G. Cuthbert, J. J. Dowling, Rev. T. B. Gibson, M.A., Mrs. W. S. Green, Miss Hensman, H. Lyster Jameson, Miss E. J. Kelsall, D. M'Ardle, E. J. M'Weeney, M.A., M.D., Greenwood Pim, M.A., Mrs. J. T. Tatlow. PROF. COLE having taken the chair, a hearty vote of thanks to Mr. Carpenter for his care and attention during the two years of his Presidency was passed, on the motion of Mr. H. C. Ramage, seconded by H. Lyster Jameson. The Secretary moved an addition to Rule V., providing "that Members of other Irish Field Clubs residing temporarily or permanently in or near Dublin may be enrolled members of the Club without election or entrance fee on production of a voucher of membership of another Club, and without subscription for the current year on production of a receipt showing that such subscription has been paid to another Club. Failing the production of such receipt, the usual subscription for the current year to be paid to the Treasurer on enrolment. The names of members so admitted to the Club to be published with the notice of meeting following the date of their enrolment." Mr. Carpenter seconded the motion, which was passed after a short discussion. The thanks of the Club were voted to the Council of the Royal Irish Academy for the use of the rooms, and to the press for their kindness in reporting the proceedings. A general discussion ensued on the improvement of the Club, next Summer's excursions, and other matters. Prof. Haddon subsequently addressed the meeting on the importance of studying the fresh-water fauna of Ireland, pointing out the interesting discoveries that have already been made, and the large field open for future research. The Secretary exhibited, on behalf of Mrs Lawrenson, a number of beautiful Christmas Roses of her own raising, which were much admired. Mr. H. Roycroft was elected a member of the Club.

FIELD CLUB NEWS.

THE accounts of the Galway Conference are only now finally closed. They show a turn-over of over £500 during the week, and, all charges being paid, a balance of just 16s. remains in the Secretary's hands. A still closer cut was made in the case of the Dublin Club's Excursion account for the past year, which, with a total turn-over of £210, shows a balance on hands of 2d.!

The Cork Field Club purpose holding a Conversazione on March 10th, in conjunction with the Literary and Scientific Society. Arrangements are being made whereby all the Irish Field Clubs will be represented personally or by exhibits.

When, two years ago, the Belfast Club decided to make a collection of specimens of the rocks of their district, a hope was expressed that microscopic sections of many of the rocks would also be presented. Mr. Robert Bell has given the first section as yet received, being a portion of the dyke of basaltic andesite which he recently discovered at Ballygomartin, and other members have intimated their intention of bestowing similar gifts. The possession of a representative collection of rocks of their district will probably commend itself to all our Clubs, whose members recall the great advantage which they experienced during the Galway Conference in seeing the fine collection of local specimens in the Queen's College Museum.

Arrangements are now complete for the course of lectures on Sea-weeds by Professor T. Johnson, D.SC., which we mentioned in our last issue. The lectures will be given on Wednesday and Saturday afternoons, commencing, on Saturday, March 7th, and several will take the form of excursions for the study of Sea-weeds in their native haunts. Inquiries about the course (the fee for which is only 10s. for the twelve lectures) should be addressed to Professor Johnson at the College of Science, Stephen's Green.

Professor J. W. Carr, M.A., lectured to a large audience of the Nottingham Naturalists' Society on January 14th, on the Field Club Union Excursion to Galway last July. The President (W. Stafford, M.B.) occupied the chair. The lecture was illustrated by the beautiful series of lantern views of the excursion by Mr. R. Welch, which most of our readers have already had an opportunity of seeing, and by a fine set of plants collected on the trip. The lecture was followed with deep interest, and very high praise was bestowed on the slides by experts who were present.

Dr. R. F. Scharff has contributed to the *Mémoires* of the *Société Zoologique de France* a most valuable paper, *Etude sur les Mammifères de la Région Holarctique et leurs Relations avec ceux des Régions voisines*, for which the Czar's prize was awarded at the Moscow International Zoological Congress. The present and past distribution of each animal is dealt with in turn, and conclusions are drawn therefrom regarding the geological history of Europe during Tertiary times.

NOTES.
BOTANY.
FUNGI.

A Bird's-nest Fungus new to Ireland.—Some few years ago, and again last month, I received from Mr. James Thompson, Macedon, Belfast, specimens of a small Bird's-nest Fungus, which Dr. M'Weeney has identified for me as *Cyathus vernicosus*, DC., of which, he remarks, he has no previous record from Ireland. Miss S. M. Thompson has kindly supplied particulars about its occurrence. The fungus comes up year by year in pots of *Crassula*, *Petunia*, Carnation, &c., in a cold house at Macedon; and its occurrence there has been noticed for more than twenty years. As some interest attaches to this very curious group of Fungi, I have deposited the specimens in the Herbarium at the Science and Art Museum, where they may be examined.

R. LLOYD PRAEGER.

Earth-Stars in Co. Tipperary.—Last month Rev. J. W. ffrench Sheppard, M.A., sent me from Rodeen, Borrisokane, three specimens of one of the strange-looking Earth-stars. They were found in a fir-wood. The specific characters of this group of Fungi appear to be somewhat slight, but Mr. Greenwood Pim, who has kindly examined the specimens, has little hesitation in referring them to *Geaster fimbriatus*, Fries.

R. LLOYD PRAEGER.

MUSCINEÆ.

Moss Exchange Club.—It is proposed to form an Exchange Club for Mosses and Hepaticæ somewhat on the lines of those at present in existence for exchanging and recording Phanerogams. Any persons interested in Bryology who would wish to become members are invited to send in their names to Rev. C. H. Waddell, Saintfield, Co. Down.

ZOOLOGY.
BIRDS.

Irish Bird Notes.—GREEN SANDPIPER (*Totanus ochropus*).—During the month of August several specimens of this bird have been obtained in different parts of Ireland, one so early as August 8th, shot at Kinnegad, Co. Meath, one on the 20th at Broadford, Co. Clare, and a third obtained at Mount Charles, Donegal.

BLACKTAILED GODWIT (*Limosa ægocephala*).—Have been very numerous this autumn. A small flock frequented Baldoyle Estuary the latter end of September, but I failed to obtain a specimen; one shot on 27th August, Rathangan, another at Clare Castle; several, Rosslare, Wexford, 24th August.

BARTAILED GODWIT (*Limosa lapponica*).—An individual of this species shot at Dundalk, September 7, retaining a good deal of the red summer plumage.

AVOCET (*Recurvirostra avocetta*).—A specimen of this exceedingly rare visitor to Ireland was obtained by Mr. Gibbon, junr., at Rosslare, Wexford, on the 27th August; it was a young bird of the year.

HOOPOE (*Upupa epops*).—One from Rosslea, Co. Fermanagh, 19th September, a very curious date for the occurrence of this bird, as it is generally on the spring migration and usually in the south of Ireland that it occurs.

RICHARDSON'S SKUA (*Stercorarius crepidatus*).—All the specimens of this bird I have met this autumn belonged to the dark form; one obtained Rathangan, 13th August, a good many from Cliffoney, Sligo, during September; amongst them a curious variety with patches of pure white on wings and breast.

POMATORHINE SKUA (*Stercorarius pomatorhinus*).—One from Killarney, October 10th, one on 14th, Ballinfull, Sligo, and another captured whilst eating a good-sized chicken at Ballinastragh, Gorey, Co. Wexford.

SQUACCO HERON (*Ardea ralloides*).—A beautiful specimen of this bird was shot at Waterville, Co. Kerry, 17th September, a young male in second year's plumage; the stomach was filled with remains of small crustacea; I have heard of another shot in Co. Cork same time, but have not particulars.

GREAT NORTHERN DIVER (*Colymbus glacialis*).—In full summer plumage, obtained so late as 16th October, without a trace of the winter moult, Kylemore, Connemara.

A variety of the BALD COOT (*Fulica atra*), with almost half the plumage pure white was obtained near Enniskillen, and a ROCK PIPIT (*Anthus obscurus*) with head, wings, and part of breast white, was shot near Bray.

EDWARD WILLIAMS, Dublin.

GEOLOGY.

Quartzite.—It might, perhaps, be worth mentioning that on the occasion of the Belfast Naturalists' Field Club excursion to Co. Donegal last year, I secured in the quartzite specimens of suncracks, ripple-marks, and raindrop marks, the two first being especially characteristic. All three are small hand-specimens chipped off large slabs of the formation, and were obtained in or close to the Seven Arches Cave, Portsalon. Should they be thought of sufficient interest either Mr. Watts or Mr. Kinahan are very welcome to examine them. Their general appearance, excepting, of course, the material, is wonderfully like the Triassic sandstones of Scrabo, near Newtownards, Co. Down, as the markings seem to occur chiefly on thin fine-grained bands, which are of mud, in the Triassic stones. A lucky chance might even hit on a fossil in some of these less altered deposits.

ALEC. G. WILSON, Belfast.

The Denudation of the Chalk.—Prof. Cole contributes a paper on this subject to the *Geological Magazine* for December, 1895. Particular reference is made to the startling photograph, by Mr. R. Welch, showing the condition of White Park Bay, Co. Antrim, after the great storm of December, 1894—a chaotic expanse of great blocks of Chalk, resting on a floor of Lias, where on the previous day, and for years previously, an uninterrupted expanse of smooth sand had stretched.

THE MINGLING OF THE NORTH AND THE SOUTH.
BY GEORGE H. CARPENTER, B.SC.

(Presidential Address to Dublin Naturalists' Field Club, Dec. 10th, 1895).

THE last few years have been noteworthy in the annals of natural science in Ireland. Signs of renewed interest among the people in the studies which we hold dear, and the steady progress of zoological, botanical, and geological research in the country have combined to cheer us; though we feel deeply how much more of this western land of scientific promise still remains to be possessed. But the one feature which helps to make the last two years memorable, is the realisation of fellowship among our workers in different parts of the country which has culminated in the establishment of the Irish Field Club Union. It is a hopeful sign that the differences, which in Ireland array province against province and race against race, have no power to hinder the mingling of the naturalists of the north with their brethren of the south. Mr. Praeger's series of papers on the Irish Field Clubs[1] taught those societies each other's histories, and in his concluding remarks he presaged the foundation of the Union which this year has seen accomplished. In his history of our own Club, he reminded us how on several occasions we had enjoyed the privilege of a joint excursion with our elder sister of Belfast. Last year[2], however, saw not only a most successful reunion of these two Clubs (and of a contingent of the North Staffordshire Club) at Drogheda, but a highly satisfactory gathering of the Dublin, Cork, and Limerick Clubs at Fermoy, where the Union was first proposed. During last winter, the Committees of all four Irish Clubs definitely constituted it by each appointing its President and Secretary to serve on a central Committee; and this year[3] has seen the first conference of the federated Clubs held at Galway, the meeting being rich both in edifying discussion and good practical work in the field. The pleasure and profit of the gathering were enhanced by the presence of many naturalists from England. How heartily they joined with us in exploring the natural treasures of the far west, and what results followed from the united labours of our harmo-

---
[1] *Irish Naturalist*, vol. iii., 1894.   [2] 1894.   [3] 1895.

A

nious party have been fully recorded.' Among the noteworthy utterances at that conference, I would recall and heartily wish fulfilment to the hope expressed by the Hon. R. E. Dillon—whose recent remarkable discoveries among the lepidoptera will be fresh in all our minds—that Galway may soon have a Field Club of its own. And I would also venture to echo Mr. F. J. Bigger's hope that the Union may be the means of knitting the various Clubs even closer together, until there shall be but one Naturalists' Society for the entire country. The mingling of the north and the south in the west, last July will, we trust, have far-reaching and beneficial effects. None could be present at such a gathering without realising the unity which binds together the naturalists of the country, cheers them for renewed effort, and makes them feel that all are working towards the same great end.

But is the end which field naturalists set before themselves indeed great? Who is the better or the wiser for knowing that some weed or beetle has been found in a county—or an island—where it had not been found before? Or for being able to decide whether the particles in a lump of clay were dropped from an ice-berg, left by a glacier, or carried by a current? In a recent charming book² one of our most eminent English entomologists has expressed the wish that more field naturalists would leave their records of "parochial distribution" and turn their attention to life-histories. It cannot be denied that such a rebuke is timely; and yet it is not the study of parochial distribution, but the study of distribution in a parochial spirit that deserves rebuke. The result obtained by the man who, after years of patient research with scalpel and microscope, calls up for us, from the vanished ages of the past, the image of the ancestor of the vertebrates or the arthropods "in fashion as he lived," appeals to the dullest mind as a veritable "fairy-tale of science." But can this be said of the product of the worker whose years of toil are rewarded by a list of long Latin names, meaningless to nine-tenths of the people who glance at them? If the list were the end, perhaps not. But each worker however humble, at the flora or fauna of a district however small, may realise,

---

[1] *Irish Naturalist*, vol. iv. (Sept. 1895).
[2] L. C. Miall.—*Natural History of Aquatic Insects*. London, 1895.

if he will, that the list is not the end: that each step towards a more complete knowledge of the geographical distribution of animals or plants is a step towards a more complete knowledge of the past history of the species he has studied, of their original home, their emigrations and immigrations, their advances and retreats; a more complete knowledge of the nature and positions of the old lands over which they passed, of the old seas, lakes, or rivers by whose margins they wandered. These are the problems which the combined work of the systematic and distributional naturalist and of the field geologist—may they ever work side by side—must help to solve. And when the problems have been solved, we shall see not only the hypothetical ancestor; we shall restore in imagination the sunken continent wherein he lived, and the severed isthmuses which his descendants crossed.

The members of our Galway Conference might have furnished material to the ethnographist for an interesting study. Gathered in that old western city were men and women representing varying types of race, and speaking with differing accents their common English tongue. A true Irishman whose ancestors have lived in the land since the days of the mythical heroes of the old folk-tales; an Ulsterman whose name is evidence that his forbears came from the "land of the mountain and the flood"; a member of one of those old Anglo-Norman families whose long sojourn in this island is said to have made them "more Irish than the Irish"; a Dubliner, settled since a few generations on Irish soil, though his name and sympathies mark him for a Teuton; an unmistakably English immigrant, who seems nevertheless to have come here to stay; another Englishman who will return to his own country when the Conference ends:—all these types might have been noted by the Connemara roadside or on the deck of the *Duras*. And the thoughtful naturalist could not fail to consider how this mixed assembly was typical of the fauna and flora of Ireland, made up as they are of varying elements which have entered the country at different times and by different roads—at what times and by what roads it is our business to find out.' We might present each of these typical naturalists with an appropriate animal or plant, whose

---

' C. Kingsley—"On Bio-Geology" (1871) in "Scientific Lectures and Essays." London, 1880.

place of origin roughly resembles his own, but whose age of family vastly exceeds his. The true Irish native who believes he came from Spain will be suited with St. Patrick's Cabbage ; the Ulsterman with the Varying Hare ; the Anglo-Norman with *Trifolium repens*—clover in England, but shamrock in Ireland. To the settler from England of some generations' standing, the Common Frog (if we are to trust tradition) would be a happy zoological partner. The English immigrant who has recently come to stay may be compared to the Magpie, and the visitor who will flit back straightway across St. George's Channel to the solitary Nightingale that once was seen on Irish soil—only that visitor was shot.

This recognition of distributional types among Irish animals and plants calls us to remember famous men. We have this year mourned the loss of two naturalists who did much for Irish science. Of the value of Alexander G. More's work there is no need for me to speak, but it would be ungracious not to recall the philosophical spirit in which he approached the study of distribution, and the importance of his work in applying Watson's botanical distributional types[1] to two groups of animals, the Birds[2] and the Butterflies.[3] The name of Valentine Ball I would mention, not only as that of a hearty friend and original member of our Club, but as a direct link with the naturalists of a past generation. His father's house was the meeting-place of a group of men whose brilliant labours threw a halo round British science in the first half of this century. Prominent among these men was Edward Forbes, and no one who takes up this subject of distribution can afford to neglect his classical paper[4] in which the special features of the Irish flora are treated with so masterly a hand. Into the labours of such men—Forbes and Thompson, Haliday and Jukes, we have entered. May we be worthy of our trust.

Of the various problems presented by the distribution of animals and plants in Ireland, I wish to dwell on the remarkable mingling of northern and southern forms, so well typified by the mingling of the northern and southern Clubs of the new Union. This mingling has been often alluded to

---

[1] H. C. Watson—"Cybele Britannica." London, 1847.
[2] *Ibis* (2), vol. i., 1865.   [3] *Zoologist*, vol. xvi., 1858, p. 6018.
[4] *Mem. Geol. Surv. Gt. Brit.*, vol. i., 1846.

by the originator of this Club, Prof. Haddon,[1] as characteristic of the marine invertebrates of the west coast, and, as I have remarked in a recent paper,[2] the southern forms often range northwards up the coast as far as Donegal, the northern ones southwards as far as Cork. Within the last few months has been issued by the Royal Dublin Society the full report by Messrs. Holt and Calderwood[3] on the rare fish found during the survey of the western fishing grounds in 1890-1. The mingling of the north and the south is most markedly shown here, so that the vertebrate and invertebrate marine faunas are seen to present similar characters.

Such a mingling of northern and southern species is to be noted also among the land animals and plants, especially in the west. The wonderful assemblage of Pyrenean and Spanish plants, found in Cork, Kerry, and Galway, and nowhere else in the British Isles—the Saxifrages, the Arbutus, the peculiar Connemara Heaths are doubtless familiar to us all. Mingled with such southern forms as these, our Galway party noticed growing on Gentian Hill and elsewhere, hardly above sea-level, such characteristically arctic and alpine species as *Dryas octopetala*, *Arctostaphylos uva-ursi*, and *Lobelia dortmanna*. And it is well known that in the western counties are also to be found a few plants of North American origin—*Eriocaulon septangulare*, *Naias flexilis*, *Sisyrinchium anceps*, *Spiranthes romanzoviana*, the two latter unknown elsewhere in Europe, the first-named occurring also in Skye and other isles of the Hebrides, and the second in Perthshire. Discoveries within the last few years by Mr. Praeger and Mrs. Leebody have extended the range of the *Spiranthes* northwards to Armagh[4] and Derry.[5]

It will be of interest to see how Irish animals can be referred to distributional types corresponding with those of the plants just mentioned. Only this year has the assembly of North-American plants been matched among animals by Dr. Hanitsch's researches into our Freshwater Sponges,[6] showing that lakes in the west of Ireland possess three North-American sponges hitherto unknown in Europe.

---

[1] *Proc. R.I.A.* (3), vol. i., p. 42.   [2] *Irish Nat.*, vol. iv., 1895, p. 297.
[3] *Sci. Trans. R. D. Soc.* (2), vol. v., 1895, pp. 361-512.
[4] *Irish Nat.*, vol. ii., 1893, p. 159.   [5] *l.c.*, p. 228.
[6] *Irish Naturalist*, vol. iv., 1895, p. 122.

Turning to the group of southern or Pyrenean plants we find a corresponding group of animals. The Kerry slug—*Geomalacus maculosus*, confined to a few square miles in the south-west and only known elsewhere from Portugal; *Mesites Tardyi*, a beetle of a Mediterranean and Atlantic Island genus, distributed nearly all over Ireland, and occurring also at a few points in the west of Great Britain; the house-spider (*Tegenaria hibernica*) of Dublin and Cork—unknown in Great Britain and closely related to a Pyrenean species; and the new British weevil (*Otiorrhynchus auropunctatus*) also a Pyrenean species, discovered by Messrs. Halbert and Cuthbert along the coast north of Dublin, are a few examples of this group. Striking additions to it have lately been made by Mr. Pocock's record of the millipede *Polydesmus gallicus*,[1] and Mr. Friend's discovery of two Mediterranean earthworms, *Allolobophora veneta* and *A. Georgii* in Ireland.[2] It is remarkable and puzzling, however, that while the Pyrenean plants keep strictly to the west of Ireland, most of these animals range to the east and some are not found in the west at all. There is a western species, however, which I have no doubt should be reckoned as belonging to this southern group. Last year a former member of this Club—Rev. R. M'Clean—took on a mountain behind Sligo a specimen of *Erebia epiphron*—a butterfly unknown in Ireland since Birchall took it thirty years ago on Croagh Patrick. As this is a Scottish and north of England insect, it has been believed that it came into Ireland from the north. But when we consider that it is confined to the mountains of southern Europe: Pyrenees, Alps, Vosges, &c., and is unknown in Scandinavia, we must believe that it came to us with the Pyrenean flora and passed northward from us into Scotland.

But there is another and very distinct southern fauna in western Ireland. In a study of the distribution of British butterflies on which I am now engaged, I find that all the species of southern range in Great Britain have a southern *or western* range in Ireland. Our collections made in Galway furnish some striking parallels in other groups to this observation. The Rose-chafer (*Cetonia aurata*) which we found in numbers on Inishmore might not be seen in a walk of two hundred miles across Ireland. It seems only to be at all plen-

---

[1] *Irish Nat.*, vol. ii., 1893, p. 309. [2] See pp. 70 and 72 of current number.

tiful along the south and south-west coasts. Yet on Aran, this insect—characteristic of the well-wooded and highly cultivated south of England—was abundant. On Aran too we got three species of *Attidæ* or jumping-spiders—a family which in tropical countries outnumbers all other spiders—though but seven species are, as yet, known in Ireland. Most striking of all however is the fact that some of the western Irish animals have a south-eastern range in Great Britain, and would be confidently referred to Watson's Germanic type of distribution. Such are some of Mr. Dillon's most startling Clonbrock lepidoptera[1]—*Zeuzera pyrina, Macrogaster castaneæ,* and *Limacodes testudo.* And it is possible that two of the most conspicuous animals which attracted our attention around Galway—the large grasshopper *Mecostethus grossus*, and the great wolf-spider *Dolomedes fimbriatus*—must be reckoned as corresponding to these, though their continental range might indicate a northern origin. With little doubt we may place alongside them the Lough Corrib jumping-spider—*Attus floricola*—perhaps the most remarkable zoological find of the excursion, a German species, possibly occurring in France, but unknown in Great Britain. And here also belongs a discovery made by Messrs. F. Neale and J. N. Halbert near Limerick this year: *Panagæus crux-major*, a handsome ground beetle confined in Great Britain to south-eastern England, and ranging over Europe into the south of Siberia.

So much for the south. What had the Galway excursion to tell us of northern animals? On the summit of Ben Lettery, it was my good fortune to take a specimen of the rare alpine ground-beetle, *Leistus montanus*, not occurring in Great Britain south of Cumberland. By Lough Corrib shore, Mr. Halbert found another mountain beetle of the same family—*Carabus clathratus*—which inhabits various localities in Scotland, is unknown in England, Wales, or eastern Ireland, but is found on the mountains of the west as far south as Bantry Bay. But most striking of all was another ground-beetle which Mr. Halbert took on Lough Corrib shore: *Pelophila borealis.* By many an Irish lake is this beetle to be found, from Killarney to Armagh and Donegal. On the mainland of Great Britain it is quite unknown; but it reappears in the Orkneys, and

---

[1] *Entom.*, 1894.

occurs all through the northern, sub-arctic regions of Europe and Siberia, another species of the genus being found in Alaska. This beetle yields in interest to no member of our fauna, and the occurrence of such a practically arctic animal within a few yards of *Mesites Tardyi* or *Geomalacus maculosus* is as striking an instance as can be found of the mingling of the north and the south which Ireland presents.

In our excursions of the year nearer home, we have also found examples of the mingling. The Braganstown expedition in August will be remembered by us, not only because of Mr. Garstin's kind hospitality to our party, but on account of Dr. M'Weeney's discovery of *Stysanus ulmariæ*, a new species of fungus whose nearest relation is to be found in Ceylon. This recalls to mind the remarkable tropical affinities of many of the Irish mosses and liverworts' with which Mr. M'Ardle has made us familiar. And, on this same Braganstown excursion, Mr. Halbert added to the Irish list of Hemiptera *Teratocoris Saundersii*, a Russian and Scandinavian species, which in Great Britain is known only from Aberdeen, Norfolk, and Kent. The continental range of this bug recalls that of the sedge *Carex rhynchophysa*, which Mr. Praeger in his investigation of the flora of Co. Armagh[2] added to the British flora three years ago.

Such are some of the facts which ask for an explanation from us, students of the natural history of Ireland. Is it wise, as yet, to attempt to explain them? Not if our explanation be dogmatic, but surely research will be stimulated by our endeavours to get an inkling of how these things have come to be. Let us theorise, and then test our theories by the light of the fresh facts with which the labours of years to come will surely supply us.

In the classical work of Forbes, to which reference has already been made, the group of southern plants characteristic of western and south-western Ireland was considered the oldest group in our flora, and was explained by the supposition of a Miocene Atlantic continent reaching to beyond the Azores. The boreal and alpine flora was believed to be a

---

[1] A. R. Wallace—"Island Life," 2nd Ed. (p. 366). London, 1892.
[2] *Irish Naturalist*, vol. ii., 1893, p. 184.

remnant of the Ice Age. The plants of Watson's British, English, and Germanic types were all referred by Forbes to one great Germanic invasion which, after the Ice Age, overspread most of our islands. To decide the time of the incoming of the various groups of our animals and plants is however very difficult. Mr. A. G. More[1] considers our entire flora, including the Pyrenean species, to have come in since the Pleistocene cold period, while Dr. Scharff[2] believes that the whole of our fauna entered Ireland in Pliocene times.

Forbes' theory of an Atlantis is now generally held to be beset with insuperable difficulties, though there is a very general belief in the former extension of the European continent to the 100 fathom line to the west of our present Atlantic shore. Whatever view may be held as to the absolute ages of the three groups of our flora which I have mentioned, the comparative ages assigned to them by Forbes are highly probable. Let us see how they work with the corresponding groups of animals. It seems very likely that the Pyrenean animals are the oldest members of the British fauna, because they have been driven so far westwards, being almost confined to Ireland, a few occurring in the west of Great Britain. Most of the alpine and northern animals are less characteristically Irish than Scotch, and seem to have entered this country from Scotland. An apparent exception to the first of these statements we have seen in *Erebia epiphron*, a southern insect which, not rare in Scotland, is almost extinct in Ireland through which it must have passed northwards; and to the second in *Pelophila borealis*, an arctic beetle not rare in Ireland, but apparently extinct in Scotland through which it passed southwards.

If, as I consider well-nigh certain, the Pyrenean fauna at least must be supposed to have come to us from a time before the Ice Age, we are met with the question: how did the animals (and plants) survive? It may be that they did not survive in any part of the present Irish area, but in some old land tract to the south or west where the conditions were less severe. But it must be remembered that in the highest north which explorers have reached an abundance of life marks the short summer.[3]

---

[1] *Journ. of Botany*, vol. xxxi., 1893, p. 299.
[2] *Proc. R.I.A.* (3) iii., 1894, p. 479; *Mem. Soc. Zool. France*, 1895, pp. 436-474.
[3] See also G. W. Bulman in *Nat. Science*, vol. iii., p. 261.

In arranging a small museum case to show the comparative distribution of British animals,[1] I have applied the term Celtic to the combined older Northern and Pyrenean faunas, and Teutonic to the animals characteristic of eastern and south-eastern England, while recognising a general British fauna of more extended range over our islands, presumably older than the Teutonic, but more recent than the Celtic group. That this general British fauna was later than the Pyrenean or the Northern is admitted on all hands, as the existence of the older faunas in western districts, only or chiefly, is probably due to the pressure of new invaders having exterminated them in regions further to the east which there can be little doubt they once held. This consideration also gives us a clue to the mingling of the old northern and southern faunas in Ireland only. It seems to me that no peculiar climatic conditions are needed to explain how this can be. Both are with us because the eastern invasion was so largely kept out of Ireland by the breaking down of the land connection to our south-east. In North America Dr. Hart Merriam[2] has mapped the areas occupied by the Boreal and Sonoran faunas with a transition zone 300 miles wide in which they overlap. I would conceive of a time when a somewhat similar state of things prevailed in Western Europe, when all along the tract to the south of the glaciated area there was such a mingling of the north and the south as we have only in Ireland to-day. The great eastern invasion then came in and drove like a wedge between the two. Over most of the common area which the two old faunas once occupied together, they were exterminated; the one was driven to the north and to the Alps, the other to the south, while both were pushed to the west, where in Ireland they found something of a protected area to which only part of the incoming host was able to pursue them. This thought suggests a return to our ethnographical illustration, for have not successive races of men been driven to north, south, and west by invaders from the east? Dun Aengus, that last stronghold of a vanished people on the ocean cliff of Inishmore, has a lesson for the naturalist as well as for the antiquarian.

---

[1] *Rep. Museums Assoc.*, 1894; also *Irish Nat.*, 1895, p. 215.
[2] *Proc. Biol. Soc. Washington*, vol. vii., 1891.

There remains to be considered the newer southern fauna which we saw to be so unexpectedly represented round Galway, those animals of English or Germanic type which seem so strangely out of place in the west of Ireland. Forbes, as has been said, considered the plants of the British, English, and Germanic types of Watson to form but one great flora; and though many of our British animals have a range readily referable to one of these three types, others show a gradual transition from Germanic to English or from English to British. There is much reason therefore for considering these three types to be all sections of one great Central European fauna, some of which have attained in the British Isles a wider predominance than others.

Most of the animals of the British type of distribution, being found all over Ireland, may be presumed to have come in from the east across the valley which now forms St. George's Channel. But this assemblage of animals we are specially considering, of English or Germanic type in Great Britain, are not found in the east of Ireland. It seems a general rule that members of this newer fauna which are confined to the south of Britain are confined to the south or west of Ireland. It should be remembered that Forbes separated, as distinct from the Germanic flora, a small group of plants characteristic of the Chalk districts of south-eastern England, thinking them much older, older indeed than the Northern flora. But even if we compare with these the western Irish animals that we are discussing, we must hold them to be more recent than the Pyrenean group.

The explanation of the facts, which I now suggest, is that this section of the newer fauna broke through the line of the older, and, in the west of Ireland, was able to take the country of the latter in the rear, and spread from west to east. It will be generally admitted that the anilmas of this fauna would spread more rapidly over plains and along valleys than among hills. And the line of least resistance in our area was the wide-spreading valley which must at some time have led westward along the present area of the English Channel and to the south of Ireland. Down this valley, I suggest that this migration passed, and arrived at the south-west corner of

A 4

the present Irish area; thence a limestone plain stretched west and north-west as far as the present 100-fathom line of the Atlantic. Established in this plain the colony invaded our present Ireland from the west. And so we have around Galway, Limerick, and Cork these animals, which are unknown near Dublin, where we might rather expect to find them. The Aran Isles are the remnants of the former extension of the limestone plain, and preserve for us some survivors of this colony which made so gallant an invasion of the far west.

I must, in conclusion, ask your pardon for having put before you at such length these tentative speculations. If they have done anything to indicate the great questions which lie behind the work of the humblest field naturalist, I shall be satisfied. We doubtless all recall the noble passage at the close of the "Origin of Species," in which Darwin dwells on the intense interest of some bank, covered with tangled vegetation, peopled with singing birds, hovering insects, and crawling worms, in the light of the descent of all these from "the few forms or one into which life was first breathed." Looking back to a past, distant though less remote, we may regard our animals and plants as travellers which at different times and by various roads have come to the spot where we now find them; as members of armies whose battles for the possession of our fair land have been fought through ages, compared with whose length the duration of the struggle of Teuton with Celt has been but as a day.

THE EARTHWORMS OF IRELAND.
BY REV. HILDERIC FRIEND, F.L.S.

DURING the past year we have witnessed the publication of a work on Oligochaeta which is of the first importance. Much fragmentary matter previously existed in sundry magazines and journals, but for a systematic treatment of the Order it was necessary for the student to consult the Continental memoirs of Rosa, Vejdovsky, or Vaillant. And even these did not attempt to cover all the ground. Now, however, the collector can consult Beddard's "Monograph of the Order OLIGOCHAETA"[1]—a work which merits the warmest commendation.

It will naturally be asked—What does the latest work on the subject say on the question of Irish Earthworms? I will endeavour to answer. Though I have received sundry specimens from Ireland which belong to other genera than *Lumbricus*, *Allolobophora*, or *Allurus*, these have never been described, because the specimens were either solitary or immature, and science gains nothing by the rash publication of imperfect matter. Consequently to the three genera above-named alone we have to look for information. It is rather curious to find (p. 723) that *Lumbricus papillosus*, Friend, is still entirely unknown outside of Ireland. Mr. Beddard gives it an undisputed place in his list. His definition, quoted from my original account, is—

"Length, 100 mm.; diameter, 8 mm.; number of segments, 130; colour, ruddy brown; clitellum, xxxiii.-xxxvii.; tubercula pubertatis, xxxiv., xxxv., xxxvi., xxxvii.; first dorsal pore, ix.-x. Hab.—Ireland."

The most interesting point about this species is the fact that it exactly fills a gap in the graduated series based upon the numbers of the segments which bear the tubercula pubertatis. This is the only species of *Lumbricus* peculiar to Ireland.

The number of species of *Allolobophora* recorded by Beddard is fifty-two, as against seven of *Lumbricus*. Among these one only calls for special notice, namely, *Allolobophora veneta*, Rosa, p. 713. It will, perhaps, be well to transcribe the whole account, which is prefaced by a list of synonyms.

---
[1] Oxford, Clarendon Press, 1895.

"**A. veneta,** Rosa, *Boll. Mus. Zool. Torino*, 1886, No. 3."

" *A. subrubicunda*, forma *hortensis*, Michaelsen, *J. B. Hamb. Wiss. Anst.*, vii., 1890, p. 15.

" *A. (Notogama) veneta*, Rosa, *Boll. Mus. Zool. Torino*, 1893, No. 160, p. 2.

" *A. hibernica*, Friend, *P. R. Irish Acad.*, 1893, p. 402.

" Definition. Length, 70 mm.; breadth, 5 mm.; number of segments, 153; clitellum, xxvi., xxvii.-xxxii., xxxiii. Setæ paired, but not strictly, the setæ of ventral pair more separated than those of dorsal pairs. Tubercula pubertatis on xxx., xxxi. Spermathecæ, two pairs in ix., x., opening posteriorly. Habitat—Venice; Argentina; Portugal; Palestine.

" This species comes very near to *A. fœtida*, with which it agrees absolutely in colour. It is to be distinguished by the position of the tubercula pubertatis. The spermathecæ open close to the dorsal middle line, as in the species mentioned. The Portuguese specimens form a variety which is marked by its smaller size, and by the more strictly paired setæ. This same variety is found in Liguria and in the Argentine (whither it has been probably accidentally imported). It is not certain whether *A. submontana* of Vejdovsky is really different. The clitellum seems to have a different position (*i.e.*, xxiv.-xxxiii.), but the structure of the worm is not fully known."

It will be observed that no allusion is made to its Irish habitat. Is this a pure oversight, or did the author not wish to commit himself to an opinion respecting its indigenous or imported character?[1] I must point out that whatever may be said of Rosa's original specimens, those which he sent to me in spirits, and those which I received alive from Ireland, bore no colour-resemblance to *A. fœtida* whatever, so that the strong affirmation of Beddard is misleading.

Turning now to *Allurus*, we find ourselves on debateable ground, owing to the fact that the different species which have at various times been recorded are insufficiently described and figured. After discussing the views of Michaelsen and Rosa the author adds (p. 696) :—

" Friend has added three other species, viz., *A. tetragonurus, A. flavus*, and *A. macrurus*. Pending further information, *A. macrurus* seems to be a valid species, on account of the very forward position of the clitellum (xv.-xxii.). *A. tetragonurus* is probably, as Rosa thinks, merely a form of *Tetragonurus pupa*."

The difficulty arises from the fact that both *A. macrurus* and *A. tetragonurus* are based upon solitary specimens. I have not the least doubt about the genuineness of *A. macrurus*;

---

[1] In studying the " Monograph " more carefully I find that, by an unfortunate oversight, Beddard has not been made aware of the publication of my researches in the *Irish Naturalist*. Hence the absence of all allusion to Irish worms not recorded in the *Proc. R.I.A.*

A. flavus is probably only a variety of *A. tetraedrus*, while Rosa's supposition may or may not be correct respecting *A. tetragonurus*.

On page 3 the writer calls attention to the "remarkable extension backwards of the prostomium (in *Allolobophora chlorotica*), which reaches as far as the end of the fourth segment," to which I drew attention in *Nature*[1] on the strength of material received from Ireland.

It may be well in conclusion to supply an amended list of Irish Worms[2] so far as known at the end of 1895, following the nomenclature adopted by Beddard, with such modifications as my judgment leads me to think necessary.

Allurus tetraedrus (Savigny).—Tipperary. Also var. *flavus* (not noted by Beddard) from the same locality; also found in Mitchelstown Cave.

A. macrurus, Friend.—Dublin.

Allolobophora calignosa, (Savigny).

A. turgida, Eisen.

I cannot but think Mr. Beddard ill-advised in putting the two very distinct species formerly known as *trapezoides* and *turgida* under one heading *(A. calignosa)*. I have examined many hundreds of specimens from all parts of the country, and could tell at a glance the one from the other. The author makes a point of Michaelsen's discovery of an "intermediate form which showed on one side of the body the character of one species, and on the other the character of the other species." I have often observed the same thing, and wonder it has not occurred to Mr. Beddard to ask what bearing such facts have on the question of hybridity—a question which, though treated by Rosa and myself, seems to have been entirely overlooked in the present memoir.

A. terrestris (Savigny).—Takes the place of the old *A. longa*, Ude. It is, however, not given by Beddard as an Irish species. I have received it from Cork, Tipperary, and elsewhere.

A. fœtida (Savigny).—Cork and Valencia.

A. chlorotica (Savigny).—Cork and Tipperary.

A. Eiseni (Levinsen).—Takes the place of *Dendrobaena Eiseni*. Found in Dublin. The author has done well for the present, no doubt, to sink several of the generic terms which had been adopted by various authors, for this and other species. I think, however, that the genus will bear division into three or four sub-genera.

A. subrubicunda, Eisen.—Tipperary.

---

[1] Vol. xlvii., p. 316.   [2] See *Irish Nat.*, vol. ii., 1893.

A. profuga, Rosa.—Not even entered as British by Beddard. I have recorded it for several English counties, and for North Wales. It is abundant in my garden in Cumberland, and I had specimens from Malahide in 1893, as well as written descriptions. I believe the Irish form differs from the continental in some particulars, but there is no doubt about the worm being Irish and English.

A. veneta, Rosa.—Dublin and Louth. Not entered as British by Beddard, though he records my paper in *Proc. R.I.A.*

A. rosea (Savigny).—Formerly entered as *A. mucosa.* Tipperary and Malahide.

A. Georgii, Mich.—Co. Clare.[1] (Not recorded as British by Beddard).

Lumbricus rubellus, Hoffmeister.—Cork, Kerry, Tipperary.

L. castaneus (Savigny).—Same as *L. purpureus.* Cork, Kerry, Antrim, Tipperary.

L. papillosus, Friend.—Unknown at present out of Ireland. Received first from co. Dublin. Later from Cork with spermatophores, Kerry and Tipperary.

L. herculeus (Savigny).—Takes the place of *L. terrestris.* Received from Cork, Tipperary, and Kerry.

Ireland, therefore, at present possesses seventeen well defined species of Earthworm, and I am convinced that at least two or three other species could be found if those parts of the country from which specimens have never yet been received were carefully worked.

I have received specimens from the Mitchelstown Cave, but while it was easy to identify *Allurus,* the others were too small and immature for determination, though there did not seem to be any ground for supposing them to represent new species.

From time to time there have reached me, among the many interesting consignments which I have received from a large band of willing co-workers, a number of specimens not usually classed as Earthworms, but still belonging to the great oligochaet order. The publication of Mr. Beddard's monograph having necessitated the searching up of old notes, records, and specimens, I have found some facts which have never yet been published relating to these lesser species of Worms. It is my wish and purpose, therefore, to work out this material, and I shall be grateful if collectors will supply me with specimens as before. They are to be found in the ooze of rivers, ponds, lakes, and ditches, in wells, reservoirs, and tanks, among decaying matter and debris, and generally distributed where there is moisture enough to enable them to live. They vary

---

[1] *Irish Nat.*, vol. iii., 1894, p. 39.

in colour from white and cream to yellow, red, green, and dirty brown, and from a quarter of an inch to three or four inches in length, generally no larger round than a thread. They may be sent in wide mouthed bottles or tins with damp moss, but should not be packed in earth, as they are too delicate to endure the battering which results from their transit when so dispatched. If the specimens are decidedly aquatic, the moss may be well saturated with water when a well corked bottle is used. Here is an entirely new field for working naturalists, and one may reasonably hope that the present year will add many interesting species to the Irish fauna.

OBITUARY.

George Edward Dobson, M.D., F.R.S.

We regret that pressure on our space has so long delayed reference to the death of this distinguished zoologist of Irish birth, who passed away on November 26th, 1895, at the age of fifty-one. After an exceptionally brilliant course in arts, natural science, and medicine at Trinity College, Dublin, he entered the Army Medical Service in 1868, and after twenty years' activity, mostly spent in India, was obliged to retire on account of ill-health, with the rank of Surgeon-Major. He was the highest British authority on the small Mammals:—Rodents, Insectivores, and Bats In 1876 he published a monograph of the Asiatic Cheiroptera, and two years later the British Museum Catalogue of that order. He projected a magnificent monograph of the Insectivora in which anatomical and systematic studies were to be combined, but, to the great loss of science, only the first two parts ever appeared (in 1882-3). Some years ago he presented some of his most valuable type specimens of Insectivores and Bats to the Dublin Museum.

THE BOTANICAL SUB-DIVISION OF IRELAND.

Mr. Praeger wishes it known that he has retained the block from which the map of Ireland divided into vice-counties was printed in our last issue, as it may be useful to naturalists working out the distribution of plants or animals in Ireland; and he will be glad to arrange for supplying any number of copies to those desiring them.

OBSERVATIONS ON THE DEVELOPMENT OF MELANISM IN CAMPTOGRAMMA BILINEATA.

BY WILLIAM F. DE V. KANE, M.A., F.E.S.

[Report to the R.I.A. Flora and Fauna Committee].

MANY species of Lepidoptera are polymorphic, and exhibit an instability of character in the imaginal stage which appears to arise from constitutional tendencies rather than immediate environmental influence. Their varieties are not restricted to locality, but occur in the same brood with the type, and in wide distribution. *Luperina testacea* and *Apamea didyma* may be cited as typical examples of this heterogeneous polymorphism.

There are other species, however, which, while showing considerable instability of coloration and pattern in most localities, apparently respond more or less directly to external influences, and produce topomorphic varieties. These last offer peculiar opportunities for studying the influence of environment and natural selection in stereotyping aberrations into local races, or eliciting new forms. The Geometer *Camptogramma bilineata* is a notable example in point. It is one of the most widely spread and numerous of our common species. Feeding on low plants and grasses, it is in no way restricted to locality by the necessities of food supply, and its constitution apparently enables it to acclimatise itself over a wide distributional range, being found in North Scandinavia, as well as in Syria and Siberia. In almost every British locality the yellow ground-colour is variable in strength of tint in different specimens, and the pattern of dark waved lines is sometimes distinctly marked, but often almost obsolete, producing a rather unicolorous form. Similarly the white waved lines are sometimes strongly represented, and often quite absent. The median band often present, especially in the females, is also very variable in strength, and a well known aberration occurs in which its exterior edge is darkly shaded, and defined sharply externally but suffused internally. The inner margin of the band in some examples is also similarly shaded. This form with its various phases I shall call the "banded aberration." It occurs very widely, but is usually somewhat scarce.

A second form which I took some years ago at Dursey Island and Ballinskelligs Bay, Co. Kerry, has the whole ground-colour of the fore-wings, and in a less degree that of the hind wings darkened, closely approximating to suffused specimens described by the late Mr. Jenner Weir from Unst, one of the Shetland Islands, but more melanic. This I shall call ab. *infuscata*. Mr. G. H. Carpenter in a subsequent year got another specimen also at Dursey Island which confirms its localisation there, and indicates that my specimens were not the result of any particular seasonal influence. In the year 1892, however, on the same coast I got 20 examples of a most remarkable local variety, with all four wings of a uniform sooty black, a trace of yellowish being perceivable on the hind wings of one or two only. No typical or intermediate forms were seen, and subsequent searches have proved that this melanic form has wholly superseded the type in that locality. It may be described as follows:

Var. *isolata*.—With all the wings of a sooty black, upon which the waved strigæ and median band are marked in darker tone. The hind wings in some instances are shot with a yellowish tone. The body and underside of the wings are also of a sooty black. The size is above the average, being in many examples $1\frac{3}{8}$ inches from tip to tip, which is a proof that the blackening is not a result of dwarfing or diseased conditions.

In 1893 I secured about forty examples, but in the following summer very few were to be had, but I got a batch of ova from some females. The larvæ were healthy and fed freely on grass and I left them in the care of a friend, but most unfortunately the experiment was not conducted to a successful issue, and no moths were bred. Through this misfortune I fear the opportunity of procuring good specimens has been lost, as the race seems to have come to an untimely end. The place of their occurrence is a small rock-islet off the coast of Kerry. Formerly there were considerable tracts of sward between the rocky heights, and *Silene maritima* as well as a limited number of other maritime plants were to be found in the crevices and ledges. But the winter of 1893-4 was fearfully stormy in those parts, and all the headlands of Kerry were perpetually swept by enormous Atlantic waves, which breaking on the cliffs dashed floods of water high into the air; the salt brine was carried by the fierce gales over heights 100 feet above the sea-level in some instances, so that the islet in question must have been continuously soaked by the deluge of sea-water, and a hot dry season succeeding in 1894, the thrift and grass became brown and dead, and the *Silene* showed no signs of life. By careful searching only a few *C. bilineata* were to be found on the rocks, from some of which I secured ova, the fate of which I have already narrated. At the end of June, 1895, I could find no specimens; and only in one sheltered nook a little grass had sprung up. Some *Silene*, however, had sprouted again from the roots and produced foliage and flowers, and a little Sea Camomile and other small sea-plants had also survived. It is therefore to be feared that this interesting race has been extirpated, unless perhaps a few individuals may have survived the famine by feeding on the plants above-mentioned. There is also a chance that on other larger islands the variety may exist. It now remains for me to analyse the circumstances and environment which have given rise to this extreme case of melanism. The cliffs and islands which are found on this part of the coasts of Cork and Kerry are of a dark slate formation, and in some cases of dark conglomerate. I have taken a considerable series of *Camptogramma bilineata* from various points of this coast-line, and find the ordinary bright yellow type frequent, but among them unusual numbers of the banded form, and also numerous specimens with the dark scaling of the waved lines much increased, and an evident tendency toward darkened suffusion, producing a great variety of dingy and dark striated aberrations.

The deepest mainland form, that of ab. *infuscata*, is rare, and occurs with the rest, and not isolated, at Ballinskelligs Bay and Dursey Island. This shows a further advance toward melanism, and is in excess of any previously noted in the British Islands, as stated (*in litt.*) by Mr. Barrett, to whom I sent the first specimen taken. In it the yellow forewings of the type are darkened throughout by the mixture of dark scales, giving them a dark yellowish brown hue, with the central band and outer margin more darkly shaded; the hind wings being either a dingy brown or dull yellow. In all the transitional aberrations taken (i.e., between the type and the v. *isolata*), the hind wings were variable and apparently responded partially only in a small number of instances to the melanic tendency. I have specimens from Unst which are similar to some of the Kerry coast forms, but are not so dark as ab. *infuscata*. No remarkable aberrations occur inland at Killarney or Kenmare, but on the shores of Dingle Bay, about Dingle and Slea Head, a large proportion of very striking banded and suffused forms are to be found. On the coast of Donegal and at Killary Bay clouded forms occur also. It would therefore appear that a tendency to dark suffusion shows itself in the vicinity of the dark rocky shores of the south-west, from Bantry Bay to Valentia on the mainland; and when isolated the phenomenon becomes accentuated to an extreme degree, and a stable melanic variety arises and wholly supersedes the type. It is not difficult to imagine the stress of the environment in an island such as I have described. The herbage is sparse and the turf close-shaven by the wind, affording little or no shelter for moths to hide in, and small in comparison with the rock-surface. It is haunted by bats and insectivorous birds such as Rock Pipits, Wheatears, and the smaller gulls, which are most active in pursuit of insects, both larvæ and imagines. These no doubt thinned out the paler immigrants from time to time as they were conspicuous on the dark rocks, the darkest escaping in greater proportion, and surviving to continue the progeny. Probably also similar catastrophes to that of 1893, perhaps in less degree, occurred, by which the stock was almost eliminated, so that a close in-and-in breeding resulted in the selected race. The conclusion, therefore, I have arrived at is, that on the rocky portions of the mainland this species is acquiring a melanic tendency as a protective adaptation, and that isolation on a small area out at sea, and a severe struggle to maintain their existence has brought about the survival of the most melanic forms. On the pale grey limestone tracts of the Co. Clare forming the shore of Galway Bay, and in the Aran Islands I noticed that this species had assumed a very washed-out and patternless form, a protective adaptation in the opposite direction. Those who lay much stress on moisture as a factor in the production of melanism, over and above its influence in temporarily darkening rock and tree surfaces, will doubtless be inclined to point to the great rainfall for which Kerry is notorious. And indeed no more crucial test could be produced than the results observable on the lepidopterous fauna of that county. Yet I found on the east slope of Mangerton, where the recorded annual rainfall often considerably exceeds 60 in. as against about 46 in Co. Cork and 41 in Co. Sligo, that the normal typical coloration prevailed, and likewise at Killarney ; while darkly clouded forms seem to be strictly localised on the coast, which militates strongly against the theory in respect of this unstable species. If we accept the view I have put forward as to the selective agencies at work in producing these melanic forms, the inquiry suggests itself whether in similar localities the same influences have affected other species in like manner.

Owing to the dangers and difficulties which beset the collector in such rugged and inaccessible spots I have not very much evidence to produce. But remarkable examples are not wanting. We should remember however that the Geometridæ from their habit of resting with outspread wings on rock faces are likely to be more pliable than Noctuæ in assuming protective coloration, and of these I have been unable to secure any examples on the islands on the south-west coast, except a few *Melanippe fluctuata* from Dursey, dark forms, but not numerous enough to be accepted as evidence. Probably very few immigrants would be able to survive the selective ordeal. Dursey Island is easily accessible, but being separated from the mainland by only a narrow sound, and being some three miles in length, and having a large proportion of grass and herbage in comparison to cliff and rock, does not afford a field in which the selective agencies referred to exercise a very severe test. If it were possible to explore carefully the fauna of such places as Sherkin Island off Baltimore, The Cow, The Bull, the two Hogs off Kenmare Bay, The Skelligs, Puffin Island, Inish-na-bro, Inishtearaght, Inishvickillaune, etc., the result would, I am sure, prove of the utmost scientific interest. I append a few results of my attempts in this direction on three of them. *Agrotis lucernea* is extremely black. *Hadena oleracea*, darker than usual, with the stigma reduced in size and dark yellow, and the white subterminal line attenuated. *Dianthœcia cæsia*, very dark, but *D. nana* (one specimen only taken) typical. *Dianthœcia capsophila*, however, shows remarkable melanism in the three examples captured. The ground-colour is very black, with the usual white pattern obliterated excepting pale outlines round the stigmata, and greyish discontinuous traces on the costa, subterminal band, and nervures, not however inclining to ochreous as in *D. carpophaga*. This is a form of great interest, as in all my experience of this species hitherto I have found it but slightly variable in colour and markings round the Irish coast. That a purely maritime species (in Great Britain), maintaining a fairly constant character in its distribution over all varieties of our rock-formations and climatic conditions, should here develop well-marked melanism would suggest the operation of some special local influence. But on the cliffs of the mainland opposite, of similar rock, a few miles distant only, I have taken specimens of the type. Isolation therefore, as in the case of *Camptogramma bilineata*, seems to be the chief probable factor at work. *Xylophasia monoglypha* also offers remarkable testimony in the same direction. Hitherto I have been unable to detect any topomorphism in the occurrence of the varieties of this polymorphic species. But on two of these islands I found no pale forms among over forty examples secured. Most belonged to the v. *brunnea*, Tutt, and varied to black forms. A few were of paler brown with the whitish markings usually present in the commonest forms reproduced in paler tone of the ground colour. The melanochroism is most apparent in the absence from this series of any grey marked specimens.

Camptogramma bilineata shows a tendency to develop dark scaling not only on the cliffs of Kerry, but also in the vast tracts of bog and moor of Connemara. It is not found in the wet swamps, but occurs on the broken banks of cut-out peat, and on dry heather slopes of rising ground. Near Aasleagh and Glendalough the varieties of the banded form with black edges are very striking and numerous, and with them clouded and black striated forms are frequent, similar to those of Unst. A parallel phenomenon is presented by the dark variety *scotica* of *Melitæa aurinia*, which, in Ireland, I have only noticed to occur on the margins of heathery bogs of ample extent; while the very brightly coloured v. *præclara* affects green marshes and wet pastures. It therefore seems probable that a proportion of the variable species that occur in any dark moorland district (if we exclude from our consideration such as are strickly confined to heathery habitats) may be expected to assume dark characters for protection, as I have noticed is the case with *Cidaria immanata.* If this prove to be so, it would in part account for the greater abundance of clouded forms in Scotland, as compared with England (exclusive of smoke-stained districts).

PROCEEDINGS OF IRISH SOCIETIES.

ROYAL ZOOLOGICAL SOCIETY.

Recent donations include a pair of Polecats from A. H. Cocks, Esq., a Tawny Owl from J. Boland, Esq., a monkey from Miss Meldon, a Kestrel from H. K. Richardson, Esq. 4,129 persons visited the Gardens in January.

JANUARY 28th.—The Annual meeting was held at the Royal College of Physicians, when the Report and accounts for the past year were submitted. The financial condition of the Society is satisfactory, the income for 1895 being larger than that for any year since 1882. Reference is made to the loss sustained by the Society in the death of Dr. V. Ball, who acted for so many years as honorary secretary, and a hearty tribute is paid to the work which he did in improving the Gardens. During the year two islands have been built in the lake; these will afford a welcome nesting-place for the water-fowl. In the excavation left on the lake shore by the removal of material for these islands, a rockery and goat-house is to be formed. But one litter of Lion cubs (two males and a female) were born in the Gardens in 1895, but these are thriving. Ten Puma cubs, in three litters, were born during the year; of these, five have died and two are weakly, but the last litter (of three) are doing very well. The fine Burchell's Zebra, which had lived twenty-one years in the Gardens, died of old age in October. Another serious loss is that of the female Ostrich, which died of a ruptured aorta. Anthropoid Apes are at present represented by a fine male Chimpanzee and a male Gibbon (*Hylobates hacnarus*). The latter is an exceptionally rare and valuable animal, no European having ever studied it in its native haunts. A white-tailed Gnu, one of the most interesting of South African Antelopes, has been obtained by exchange from the London Gardens. The appendix to the Report contains some valuable suggestions for the further improvement of the Gardens, such as the enlargement and ventilation of the Anthropoid house and the removal of the reptiles now housed there to new quarters in the Aquarium. A new paddock for Marsupials and another for Llamas and Camels are also contemplated at some future time.

DUBLIN MICROSCOPICAL CLUB.

JANUARY 16th.—The Club met at Dr. FRAZER'S, who exhibited microscopic sections made from bone pins of large size found in a fragmentary state and bearing evidences of exposure to strong heat causing charring. They were obtained by E. Crofton Rotheram, Esq., in recent explorations of cairn R^2 at Slieve na Calliagh, Co. Meath. Some of these portions of bone are figured in the *Journal of the Royal Society of Antiquaries of Ireland*, vol. v., 1895, p. 313, by Mr. Rotheram. The bone implements had sharp points and blunt semi-conical heads, and may have been used for pins. Fragments of similar objects (three in number) were obtained by Colonel Wood-Martin some years since from a cairn in Co. Sligo, and are figured in his work on the "Rude Stone Monuments of Sligo." Dr. Frazer had examined these, and was induced to believe they were of Cetacean origin, but the re-examination of his former preparations and sections made from the Co. Meath find demonstrated that they were all obtained from the antlers of the Red Deer, once so widely distributed in all parts of the country, and now almost extinct. Dr. Frazer likewise exhibited careful drawings of all the fragments obtained in Sligo and Meath. No less than eleven of the bone implements were found at Lough Crew cairn judging by that number of the blunt semicircular top portions discovered amongst the fragments.

PROF. G. A. J. COLE showed a section of a remarkably unaltered and scoriaceous volcanic bomb from the Silurian tuffs north of Clogher Head in the Dingle promontory. In this region a handsome series of bombs occurs, precisely resembling those of the Petit Puy-de-Dôme, in Auvergne; they have been preserved without infilling of their cavities, and present a remarkable contrast to the other volcanic rocks interstratified with them.

PROF. T. JOHNSON exhibited *Hyella nitida*, Batt. *in litt.*, a shell-perforating alga, new to science, found on the Merrion strand this last December, after the storm which caused the Kingstown life-boat disaster. The *Hyella nitida* was shown accompanied by *Conchocelis rosea*, Batt., both of which were gnawing away the Razor-shell. The differences between the two species were pointed out.

MR. A. VAUGHAN JENNINGS showed a specimen of the Foraminiferal genus *Ramulina* growing within a chamber of the large Foraminifer *Carpenteria rhaphidodendron* Möbius. The slide was from the collection of the late Dr. W. B. Carpenter, and had in 1880 been the subject of a paper in the *Journal of the Royal Microscopic Society* by the late Dr. Martin Duncan, who described the *Ramulina* as a calcareous sponge and gave to it the name of *Mobiusispongia parasitica*. The specimen might be regarded as raising the question whether any of the Foraminifera have the power of boring through calcareous shells; but in the case in question it is more probable that the *Ramulina* was at first growing on the outside of the *Carpenteria* and was subsequently enclosed by the rapid growth of the latter. A note on the subject was communicated to the Linnean Society in June, 1895.

Dr. C. HERBERT HURST showed preparations of the auditory organ situated in the swollen basal joint of the antenna of the gnat (*Culex*) which he described and figured in the *Trans. Manchester Micros. Soc.*, 1890.

PROF. A. C. HADDON showed preparations illustrating the nauplius and cypris stages in the development of *Balanus balanoides*.

MR. R. J. MITCHELL exhibited a microscopic preparation and microphotograph of *Melobesia farinosa* ? The distinction of some of the species of *Melobesia* is based on minute characters in the structure of the thallus; the use of microphotographs in indicating these microscopic differences was noted.

BELFAST NATURAL HISTORY AND PHILOSOPHICAL SOCIETY.

JANUARY 7th.—Mr. JOSEPH BARCROFT lectured on "The Properties of the Surface of Liquids."

FEBRUARY 4th.—Mr. S. F. MILLIGAN lectured on "Antiquities, Social Customs, and Folk-lore of Tory, Inismurray, and the South Islands of Aran."

BELFAST NATURALISTS' FIELD CLUB.

JANUARY 25th, BOTANICAL SECTION.—The proceedings commenced with an account of the vascular structure of plants by Rev. C. H. WADDELL, who showed how the various forms of vessels formed the skeleton of plants, while at the same time serving as a system of circulation.

Mr. R. LLOYD PRAEGER then gave a very complete account of the various species of British ferns, illustrated by a fine set of mounted plants, which were handed round. He pointed out the means of distinguishing some of the closely allied species which are often mistaken by amateurs. Among the most interesting were some plants of Adder's-tongue with several fertile spikes, and some fronds of *Hymenophyllum* grown under glass, which had produced several years' innovations from the ends of the old fronds instead of dying down as usual.

GEOLOGICAL SECTION.—Mr. PRAEGER gave an address upon "The Glacial Series at Belfast and Dublin—A Contrast." The subject was of special interest, as the Club is investigating the glacial geology of the district, whilst Professor Sollas and Mr. Praeger are working out the Dublin drift deposits. Mr. Praeger described the beds in Wexford as being of late Pliocene age, the ancient sea-beach at Ballyrudder being our earliest glacial beds, being overlaid by lower boulder clays. Marine shells are much more abundant in the Dublin series than in the north; fossils, derived from Lias, being also singularly plentiful in beds at Kill-o'-the-Grange. The splendid series of sands and gravels about Dublin were described, which overlie, and are intercalated with boulder clay, Mr. Praeger suggesting their being probably represented in the North by the sands and gravels of Neill's Hill and the Dundonald Valley, which, he thought, should be thoroughly investigated. The existence of an upper boulder clay, less hard and more sandy and earthy, with plentiful marine shells in places, was mentioned as being now accepted in the metropolitan district, although local geologists fail to find such a distinction in the Belfast neighbourhood. This clay contains fewer large boulders than the lower boulder clay beds. Mr. Praeger concluded by referring to an investigation into the historical succession of our northern fauna, which indicated an almost arctic climate, ameliorating slightly in the boulder clays, and showing a distinctly southern facies in the estuarine clays and raised beaches, whilst dredgings in this century show a recurrence of colder conditions.

In the subsequent discussion Mr. Praeger mentioned that although perfect shells with the valves still united had been found near Dublin as well as in the north, yet they are very rare, the usual condition being much broken and worn. Specimens were handed round for inspection, as well as a selection of rocks found in the glacial beds about Dublin, which Mr. Praeger subsequently presented to the Club. Amongst them were a Cushendall rock and the well-known Ailsa Craig rock. Miss S. M. THOMPSON expressed a hope that rocks with riebeckite might even yet be found in Co. Down, as a series of very diverse-looking erratics recently submitted to Prof. Cole all proved to contain that mineral; some of these fragments were found in the bed of boulder-clay in the banks of the stream between Divis and Black Mountain, mentioned in the January number of the *Irish Naturalist*, whose elevation is found not to be as much as was at first supposed (1,300 feet), but whose precise height has yet to be determined. Mr. L. M. BELL drew attention to the great difference between the boulder-clays in Antrim and Down, the latter being much looser in texture, resembling the upper boulder-clay described by Mr. Praeger. A collection of rock-specimens was presented by Miss M. K. Andrews.

JANUARY 31st.—A special meeting was held in the Museum—the President (Mr. F. W. LOCKWOOD, C.E.) in the chair, when Mr. W. GRAY, M.R.I.A., delivered his lecture, "To Galway by Sea and Land," being an account of the Excursion last summer of the Irish Field Clubs and the Royal Society of Antiquaries to Galway.

FEBRUARY 18th.—The President in the Chair. Mr. W. H. PATTERSON read a Paper on "Gaelic Charms, Incantations, and Curses."

DUBLIN NATURALISTS' FIELD CLUB.

FEBRUARY 10th.—The Chair was taken by the President (Prof. G. A. J. Cole, F.G.S.) There was a large attendance of members and friends. After the signing of the minutes, the Vice-President (Mr. N. COLGAN) took the Chair, while Prof. COLE delivered his address on "Some Problems in the Geology of Co. Dublin and Co. Wicklow." He said that by indicating how many points of interest still remained unsettled in the geology of Co. Dublin and Co. Wicklow, he hoped to attract some of the energy of the Club towards the study of these matters in the field. He dwelt on the possibility of the discovery of fragmental, but serviceable, organic remains in the slates of Bray or Howth ; on the dubious position of *Oldhamia* ; on the desirability of checking and adding to the old determinations of species from the Ordovician limestone of Portrane; and on the paucity of graptolites hitherto discovered in the associated shales. The minerals of the contact-zone along the flanks of the Leinster granite may attract other observers; and the suggestion, made by Prof. Sollas, that the granite is a laccolitic mass overlying the Howth and Bray series, requires further investigation. The zones in the Carboniferous Limestone have yet to be indicated by a study of the fossils on various horizons; and attention was called to the blocks of older rocks found embedded in the limestone; finally, the author referred to the difficulties raised by the abundant shelly gravels associated with the glacial epoch. He himself was inclined again to urge, as he had done in an early number of the *Irish Naturalist*, that the shells in these gravels represent a late Pliocene (Astian) submergence, and that they were brought into their present positions by the action of glacial and other streams during the cold period that succeeded.

REV. MAXWELL H. CLOSE, in a happy and effective speech, reviewed the history of many of the controversies that had been touched on by the President. He described the interesting discovery of well-rounded quartzite and granite boulders in the Carboniferous Limestone at Stillorgan, during the making of the reservoir there, the other records being granite boulders on the south of Dublin, and pieces of Ordovician schist, unrounded, at Blackrock. Mr. Close described himself as a sceptic, in the true sense of the word, with regard to the causes which had laid down the shelly gravels as we now find them. He was quite unconvinced, however, by Prof. Carvill Lewis, who urged, when in the field with him at Ballyedmonduff, that the gravels had been pushed uphill before a gigantic glacier. Mr. COLGAN and Mr. PRAEGER also discussed the paper, after which Prof. COLE replied.

MR. H. LYSTER JAMESON then read his account of his explorations of the caves at Mitchelstown and Enniskillen, undertaken on behalf of the Royal Irish Academy Fauna and Flora Committee. The paper, which was of much interest, and will shortly be published *in extenso* in our pages, was prefaced by some remarks on the animals obtained, by Mr. G. H. Carpenter; the subject-matter of his communication will appear in Mr. Jameson's paper. A short discussion ensued. The following were declared elected members of the Club:—Miss Dixon, Rev. C. W. Follis, B.A., Joseph Maguire, B.L., Miss Sweeny.

CORK NATURALISTS' FIELD CLUB.

FEBRUARY 10th.—The President (W. H. SHAW) in the chair. A very interesting paper was read by Mr. WM. MILLER—"The Climate of Cork," and a lively discussion followed.

PROFESSOR HARTOG read a note on Mr. Rousselet's method of preserving Rotifera. He pointed out the need of keeping specimens for comparison of microscopic organisms, as is done for larger animals and plants, in order to avoid the doubt due to imperfect descriptions and sketches. As examples he cited the cases of *Hexarthra*, a Rotifer with six articulated limbs, so described by Schmarda as to render it impossible to say whether it is or is not identical with Hudson's genus *Pedalion*, and of *Plœsoma*, a genus founded by Herrick twelve years ago, and since described under no less than *five* other new generic names! The first requisite is to stupefy the active animals; this is conveniently done by first fishing them out into clean water, and then adding drop by drop the following solution of cocain :—

    A. Cocaine Hydrochlorate, 1 gram.
       Water, 50 cc.
       Methylated spirit (without petroleum), 12 cc.
    This solution keeps indefinitely.
    B. Solution A, 4 cc.
       Water, 6 cc.
    To be made as required.

The solution must be added gradually at intervals of a few minutes. When the animals are sufficiently sluggish the addition of a drop or two of osmic acid solution $\frac{1}{4}$ per cent. fixes them. They must then be removed by a medicine dropper to clean water, and thence to a cell containing a 2 to $2\frac{1}{2}$ per cent. solution of commercial formalin (also called "formol" and "formal"=a solution of 40 per cent. formic aldehyde in water; or equal volumes of $\frac{1}{10}$ per cent. mercuric chloride and $\frac{1}{5}$ per cent. sodium chloride). The cells used are the hollowed glass slides to be obtained from any optician. The cover is sealed down with Miller's caoutchouc cement, and finished with a ring of asphaltum, &c. (See Journal of the Quekett Microscopic Club, vol. v., ser. ii., March, 1895). Five slides of Mr. Rousselet's preparation were shown:—*Asplanchna Brightwellii, Synchæta tavina, Cyrtonia tuba, Pedalion mirum,* and *Plœsoma Hudsoni.*

The SECRETARY called members' attention to Mr. Praeger's article in current number of the *Irish Naturalist,* and hoped it would prove a stimulus to the botanists in the coming year, and also gave particulars regarding the conversazione, arrangements for which are progressing rapidly. Four new members joined the Club, which has received substantial increase since the lectures under the auspices of the Field Club Union.

LIMERICK NATURALISTS' FIELD CLUB.

JANUARY 23rd.—The annual meeting unanimously adopted a suggestion of the Committee, recommending that the Club should cease to hold its meetings in a private room, and admit the public to membership, with the result that an immediate increase of ten members took place, and at least as many more are likely to be added by next meeting, which is to be held in the Board Room of the City Library, kindly given to the Club, free of all charges, for its future gatherings, by the Corporation Library Committee. The Club now numbers upwards of sixty members, and under its new conditions should be capable of doing good work in its hitherto almost virgin locality.

The report of Committee for 1895, mentioned the occurrence of several interesting records, amongst them being a male specimen of the large Footman (*Gnophria quadra*) from Adare, an example of a ground beetle (*Panagæus crux-major*) from Finlough, Co. Clare, this insect being an addition to the Irish list; a Red Squirrel (*Sciurus vulgaris*) from Cratloe Wood; and amongst Lepidoptera the Secretary reported having taken the Holly Blue (*Lycæna argiolus*) for the first time in May, 1895.

FIELD CLUB NEWS.

Mr. R. Welch, of the Belfast Field Club, sends us a second supplement to his Catalogue of Geological Photographs. We have had the advantage of examining this beautiful series, and can say that it includes many views of the highest interest and importance. First come some illustrations of coast denudation, including the remarkable scene in White Park Bay, described by Professor Cole in the *Geological Magazine* for Dec., 1895. Then follow photographs of raised beaches, and of Palæozoic and Mesozoic strata. The Roundstone kitchen-middens come next, and finally we have the beautiful series of mountain views taken in Connemara and Clare on the Field Club Union Excursion, which most of our readers have already seen and admired.

The arrangements for the Cork Field Club Conversazione on March 10th, are rapidly progressing, and the function promises to be a very interesting one. A number of new members have lately joined this Club, which appears to have now firmly taken root, and to have a successful future before it.

In a course of five lectures on Ireland, at the Dublin Coffee Palace last month, three members of the Dublin Field Club have taken part. Dr. M'Weeney lectured on "Invisible Natives"—bacteria; Professor Cole on "The Land and the Landscape," and Mr. Carpenter on "Wild Life in Ireland." The other lectures of the course were "Ancient Irish Crosses" by Rev. D. Murphy; and "The People of Ireland" by Rev. Canon Carmichael.

In the Royal Dublin Society's course of afternoon lectures, Natural Science is represented by "The Bath Sponge" (Prof. Sollas), "The Glaciers of the Alps" (Rev. Monsignor Molloy), "Irish Animals Old and New" (G. H. Carpenter), "The Food of Plants" and "The Making of Timber" (Prof. T. Johnson).

The Limerick Field Club has now felt strong enough to forsake the protecting wing of the Young Men's Christian Association, and to start on an independent career. The result of this action is to throw the benefits of the Club open to all sections of the public, and as a consequence an immediate rise of membership has taken place. The Corporation Library Committee has generously placed the Board-room of the City Library at the disposal of the Club for its future meetings, free of charge. We have no doubt that on this wider basis the Club will continue to prosper, and will increase in numbers and in activity.

The Geological section of the Belfast Club are arranging for a continuous week's study of geology during the month of March under Professor Cole, F.G.S. The forenoons are to be devoted to field geology, and each evening a class for the study of petrography will meet in the Club's rooms at the Belfast Museum. This new scheme should prove highly valuable, as geological students are well aware of the difficulty of recognising rocks in the field with which they are perfectly familiar in museum collections. This is the third year in which the Club have had the great advantage of studying under Professor Cole.

NOTES.

Mildness of the Season.—Many reports reach us illustrating the remarkable mildness of the present season. Mr. R. A. Praeger reports a Blackbird's nest with two eggs found at Holywood, Co. Down, on 29th January; at the same date the Rooks at Cultra rookery were busily engaged in building their nests. *Vespa germanica* was observed on the wing at Limerick, as early as 11th February, a specimen having been taken on that date by the Secretary of the Limerick Club. The weather had been very fine and mild for some days previously. Among several reports of early flowers, we may mention that on 2nd February the Scurvy-grass (*Cochlearia officinalis*) was flowering abundantly on Howth, the blossoms set in luxuriant tufts of succulent glossy foliage.

ZOOLOGY.

INSECTS.

Death's Head Moth in Dublin.—A dead but perfect specimen, except for the antennæ, of the Death's Head Moth (*Acherontia atropos*) was found by the children of the caretaker of the now disused Carmichael College of Medicine, Aungier St., Dublin. It lay on the floor of the former dissecting room, and from inquiries as to the dates on which the room was swept, &c., I believe that earlier in this or last year it sought shelter in some cranny and was recently dislodged by the strong winds prevailing about Christmas. The windows are generally open, and in summer the room is much frequented by the children looking for flies, bees, wasps, &c., constantly to be found there dead. Their father, a pensioner, who used to collect butterflies, &c., in the tropics when on service, recognised the specimen and saved it from destruction.

J. ALFRED SCOTT, Dublin.

Gonepteryx rhamni in Queen's County.—Miss Bewley captured a fine specimen of this butterfly about the end of August last at Dunmore in the Queen's County, which appears to be a new locality, as Mr. Kane in his catalogue only gives Kerry, Galway, and an island in Lough Ree, Co. Longford (*Entomologist*, vol. xxvi., p. 120). Another specimen is said to have been seen on the wing at the same time and place. This discovery is interesting, as the Queen's County has been known as a habitat for this insect's food-plant, the Buckthorn (*Rhamnus catharticus*), which grows on the banks of the Barrow.

GEORGE V. HART, Dublin.

An Early Emergence.—A specimen of *Phlogophora meticulosa* emerged at Howth on the 1st January. The pupa was in a flowerpot in the open air. This bears witness to the mildness of the season.

GEORGE V. HART.

BIRDS.

Birds of Connemara.—In Mr. Witherby's account of Connemara birds in the January issue of the *Irish Naturalist* he states that "a number of Dunlin, some of which were singing beautifully, were flying about in small flocks" on Lough Corrib. I should like to ask Mr. Witherby whether it was beyond doubt the Dunlin (*Tringa alpina*) that he refers to, and not the Ringed Plover (*Ægialitis hiaticula*), which is locally called the Dunlin in some parts of England. The islands of Lough Corrib are hardly the kind of habitat for the Dunlin during the nesting season. Several years ago I spent two days on Lough Corrib and its islands for ornithological purposes at the middle of May, and I saw no Dunlins; but on every island that had any shingly shore—and I landed on about sixteen or eighteen such—there was at least one pair of Ringed Plovers. Mr. Witherby's other observations relating to Lough Corrib coincide with mine to a remarkable degree; and as the Ringed Plover is fairly plentiful on the islands during the nesting season he can hardly have failed to observe it, as he has noted nearly all the other birds to be expected; but he makes no mention whatever of it. Many who know the pleasing whistling notes of the Ringed Plover will probably agree that "singing beautifully" seems a not inappropriate description of them. Altogether it rather looks as though it was the Ringed Plover Mr. Witherby referred to, not the Dunlin; but should it prove to be the latter, it would of course be an occurrence of interest to Irish ornithologists.

Mr. Witherby also states that "on some of the low flat islands of Renvyle the Black Guillemots *seemed* to be laying their eggs under the large boulders scattered about," and that he "saw several at different times fly out from amongst them, but could not reach their eggs." It is well known that various birds occasionally nest in situations very different from the sites usually chosen; and it would be interesting to know whether Black Guillemots were really nesting in the situation described. Can Mr. Witherby or anyone else throw further light on the question? Mr. Witherby says: "Another curious nesting habit I noted was, that the Oystercatchers, which were numerous, invariably nested on the rocks or turf even on islands where there was shingle in every way suitable for them." Perhaps West of Ireland Oystercatchers may have found that it is not always safe to nest on the shingle within possible reach of an unusually high Atlantic wave, and have consequently gone to higher and safer situations. At all events the site mentioned hardly seems an unusual one with these birds in the West of Ireland. In 1894, during the first week of July, on Inishkeeragh—the island between North Inishkea and Inishgloria—off the west coast of Co. Mayo, I found two Oystercatchers' nests containing young birds on small patches of turf among the rocks, near where Arctic Terns were nesting. I identified the nests and young as Oystercatchers by the broken fragments of egg shells about the nests.

J. E. PALMER, Dublin.

NOTES ON COLLECTING ENTOMOSTRACA,
WITH A LIST OF THE IRISH SPECIES OF CLADOCERA KNOWN AT PRESENT.

BY R. H. CREIGHTON, M.B.

Entomostraca are found everywhere; they are especially abundant in marshes, the weedy pools on the outskirts of a bog, and in the bed of weeds which exists in most lakes where the deep and shallow waters meet. In the centre of the larger lakes a regular pelagic fauna exists; it has been little studied in the United Kingdom, as it is impossible to collect it without the aid of a boat. The best time to obtain these pelagic forms is at night, when they crowd to the surface in large numbers, even in the middle of winter.

For collecting in the smaller pools, the ordinary muslin net and glass bottle at the end of a stick about four feet long answer well. In larger ponds and in lakes of course they are of no use; here I find Professor Birge's cone dredge (8) a great comfort, as the cone keeps out weeds, insects, larvæ, &c. "It consists of four parts, the body, the cone, the net, and the screw-top. The body is a cylinder of stout tin, strengthened by a wire at each end, four inches long, and four inches in diameter. On top of this is placed a cone of brass netting, five inches high; this is attached below to a circle of tin so that it fits into the top of the body like the cover of a tin pail. The bail of the body is of stout brass wire, the ends passed through the side of the body and enlarged, and the loop of wire shaped so as to fit within the cone and project through a hole in its top, with an eye into which the dredge-line can be fastened. Two cones are provided, one of one-tenth inch mesh and one of one-twentieth inch. The net is of fine cheese-cloth, eighteen to twenty-two inches long, conical, large enough at the base to slip over the dredge-body to which it is tied. It is faced with stout muslin for a distance of two or three inches at each end. At the smaller end it is small enough to fit the screw-top, a tin cylinder one inch in diameter and one inch and a quarter long, with a wire in one end, and on the other a zinc screw-top such as is used on paraffin cans." This dredge can be thrown easily twenty yards from the shore and hauled in by the line, thus collecting much more extensively than it is possible to do with the ordinary hand-net. It can be pulled through weeds, and can strain a large quantity of water without getting filled with vegetable debris. When used as a surface net the cone is removed.

Entomostraca are best examined alive in a drop of water, either in a hollow-ground slide or on an ordinary slide, the pressure of the coverglass being taken off by a pellet of wax, or as Professor Hartog suggests, a frond of Duckweed. If unable to examine them at once, remember that they live much longer if kept in the dark.

Mounting permanent specimens is very troublesome. I get the best results by killing with osmic acid, bleaching carefully with chlorate of potash and hydrochloric acid, grading through alcohol, staining with tincture of cochineal or with hæmatoxylin (the latter is very liable to overstain), and mounting in Canada balsam. Prof. Herman Fol advises killing with tincture of iron (steel drops) added to a small quantity of water in which the animal is swimming, and subsequent staining with gallic acid. I have not had much success with this method. Sometimes, more especially with the smaller Cladocera, the osmic acid alone gives sufficient differentiation. Kleinenberg's picro-sulphuric acid is useful for killing, and has the great advantage of being cheap. If you use it, remember to wash out with dilute alcohol, not water.

For preserving specimens for future study glycerine does well for Copepods; the following is a good formula :—glycerine one ounce, proof spirit two ounces, water one ounce, liquefied carbolic acid one dram, mix. They can be examined in this solution without staining, and can be mounted out of it in glycerine jelly. Cladocera are much harder to deal with; I get the best results by killing with osmic acid and grading carefully through 30, 50, 70 and 90 per cent. alcohol; but it is much better, in fact almost essential, to examine specimens of this group alive.

In the following list I have endeavoured to collect all the species recorded from Ireland; they number only 23! In a synopsis of the British Cladocera published in the *Journal* of the Birmingham N. H. Society in February, 1895, Mr. Hodgson gives a list of 64 British species, of which 31 have been found within 15 miles of Birmingham. In all probability the whole 64, if not more, are to be found in Ireland.

Mr. J. D. Scourfield has given me great aid by kindly naming some of the more difficult species for me. Where no reference follows a locality in this list, the species has been taken there by myself.

IRISH CLADOCERA.

Sida crystallina, O. F. Muller. This is by far the most widely distributed and abundant Entomostracan in the lakes and ponds of the N. of Ireland; I have found it in all I have examined except those which are liable to be completely dried up in hot weather. My experience is thus directly opposed to Baird's observations in England, viz :—" They do not seem to be numerous in the localities in which I have found them, and indeed are of rare occurrence." (1); Scourfield has recently confirmed Baird's statement in researches conducted at Wanstead Park (2) and in Wales (3). Irish localities are L. Corrib (4), L. Erne (5), L. Melvin, lakes of Donegal, and near Galway (6).

Daphnia pulex, Müller. Common in small ponds, ditches, and wells; also near the shore in lakes; L. Erne (5), Donegal, &c.

D. longispina, Müller. Near Galway (6); lakes of Fermanagh and Donegal.

D. obtusa, Kurz. Common in a pond in the townland of Dunmuckrim, near Ballyshannon.

D. galeata, Sars. Only in L. Erne (5) and L. Melvin in this locality; near Galway (6).

Ceriodaphnia reticulata, Jurine. Scarce. L. Unshin, near Ballyshannon.

C. pulchella, Sars. Mr. Scourfield kindly identified this species for me; it resembles *C. quadrangula*, Müller, very closely. I have found it only in L. Nabrackalan, near Ballyshannon.

C. megalops, Sars. Near Galway (6).

Scapholeberis mucronata, O. F. Müller. L. Corrib (4).

Simocephalus vetulus, O. F. Müller. Common in ponds everywhere.

Bosmina coregoni, Baird. Upper L. Erne (5).

B. longirostris, O. F. Müller. Clonhugh Lake, near Mullingar (4).

B. longispina, Leydig. L. Bollard, Connemara (7). L. Melvin.

Lathonura rectirostris, Müller. L. Bollard, Connemara (7).

Macrothrix laticornis, Leydig. Near Belfast, W. Thompson (7).

M. rosea, Jurine. Lakes of Connemara (7).

Acantholeberis curvirostris, Müller. Bog pools near L. Corrib (4); Connemara (7); near Columbkille Lake, Ballyshannon.

Drepanothrix hamata, Sars. L. Bollard, Connemara (7).

Eurycercus lamellatus, Müller.   Common everywhere in weedy ponds.
Acroperus harpa, Baird.   Near Galway (6).
Alonopsis elongata, Sars. L. Corrib and L. Clonhugh (4); Connemara (7).
Lynceus costatus, Sars.   Connemara (7).
L. testudinarius, Fischer.   Connemara (7).
L. nanus, Baird.   Connemara (7).
L. affinis, Kurz.   Near Galway (6).
Graptoleberis testudinaria, Fischer.   Near Galway (6).
Alonella nana, Baird.   Near Galway (6).
Pleuroxus trigonellus, Müller.   Near Galway (6).
Chydorus sphæricus, Müller.   Common all over Ireland.
C. globosus, Baird.   Connemara (7).
Polyphemus pediculus, De Geer.   L. Corrib and L. Bay (4) ; Lough Columbkille, near Ballyshannon.   This species is very local; it appears to swim in shoals usually within a few yards of the shore.
Bythotrephes longimanus, Lilljeborg.   Very plentiful in Upper L. Erne in 1886-7-8 (5).   Rare in L. Melvin, and the individuals are smaller than in L. Erne.
Leptodora hyalina, Lilljeborg.   Common in Upper L. Erne (5); neighbourhood of Galway (6).

REFERENCES.

1.	Baird, W.	Nat. Hist. of Brit. Entomost.; *Ray Society*, 1850.
2.	Scourfield, D. J.,	Entomost. of Wanstead Park. *Journal of the Q. Micro. Club,* Ser. 2, Vol. v.
3.	,,	Prelim. Account of the Entomost. of N. Wales, *Journal of Q. Micro. Club,* Ser. 2, Vol. vi.
4.	Andrews, A.	*Irish Naturalist,* Vol. ii., page 24.
5.	Creighton, R. H.	*Irish Naturalist,* Vol. ii., page 24.
6.	Hodgson, T. V.	*Irish Naturalist,* Vol. iv., page 190.
7.	Norman & Brady.	*A Monograph of British Entomost.,* London, 1867.
8.	Birge, E. A.	List of Cladocera from Madison, Winsconsin. *Trans. of Winsconsin Acad. of Sc., &c.,* Vol. viii., page 397.

ON THE EXPLORATION OF THE CAVES OF ENNISKILLEN AND MITCHELSTOWN FOR THE R.I.A. FLORA AND FAUNA COMMITTEE.

BY H. LYSTER JAMESON.

(Read before the Dublin Naturalists' Field Club, Feb. 10th, 1896.)

Early in 1895 Dr. Scharff informed me that Mr. E. A. Martel, the celebrated French explorer of caves, had determined to visit Ireland in July, with a view to investigating some of the numerous caverns with which our Carboniferous limestone is in places riddled.

I at once expressed myself anxious to join him in his explorations, and in due time was informed that the Fauna and Flora Committee of the Royal Irish Academy had done me the honour of making a grant to me for the purpose of further investigating the cave-fauna, already discovered at Mitchelstown by Dr. Wright and Mr. Haliday, and so ably described by Mr. Carpenter in his most interesting paper on the "Animals found in the Mitchelstown Cave" (*Irish Naturalist*, February, 1895).

On July 10th I left Dundalk for Enniskillen, where I hoped to meet Mr. Martel, whose investigations were to commence in that district. At Enniskillen I was met by Mr. Thomas Plunkett, M.R.I.A., who kindly made me his guest while I was there, and whose intimate knowledge of the geology and physical features of the district was of very great assistance to me in my work.

On July 11th I set off for Bohoe, where I was met by the Rev. A. Knight, who acted as my guide.

We first proceeded to investigate the underground river-bed at Bohoe, a winding subterranean watercourse. Beside the outlet was a dry cavern which presumably was once connected with the present river-bed, and has for some reason become cut off. It was only accessible for a short distance, large angular blocks, falling from the roof and walls, having formed an impassable barrier. This grotto must have been inhabited by numerous bats, as the floor was strewn with their fæces, and also with the rejected wings of insects. The rivercourse itself, though at the time of my visit dry, is after heavy rains traversed by a mountain torrent, which evidently floods right up to the roof, as debris of all kinds, branches of trees, sods of turf, &c., were jammed into all crevices, even in the roof. Consequently no animals of the typical cave-fauna were to be found.

We entered at the end of the cave where the stream discharges itself, and noticed that just inside the exit, where exposure to weather had enlarged the calibre of the cave, there were two colonies of Daubenton's Bat (*Vespertilio Daubentonii*), clustered together in crevices in the roof like swarms of bees. I captured five specimens with some difficulty; they were all males, and two of them can now be seen in the Science and Art Museum, Dublin.

The invertebrates found in this cave had evidently been accidentally brought in by floods, with the exception of two large spiders, *Meta Menardii* and *Meta Meriana*, which Mr. Carpenter, who has kindly identified the invertebrates collected, tells me often inhabit the entrances to caves. The other invertebrates were a water-bug, *Velia currens*, and two flies belonging to the genera *Erioptera* and *Molophilus*.

On leaving this cave Mr. Knight invited me to lunch at the Rectory, and, when there, showed me a Bat that he had killed in his room on the previous night. This proved to be the Whiskered Bat (*Vespertilio mystacinus*), another of our rarer Irish species. This specimen, a male, is now in the Science and Art Museum, Dublin. Some time after I left Enniskillen Mr. Knight sent me a specimen of the Hairy-armed Bat (*Vesperugo Leisleri*) taken in his house, a female Daubenton's Bat, and a Long-Eared Bat (*Plecotus auritus*) captured in the dry cavern to which I have already referred.

After lunch we explored Coolarkin, a cave of considerable dimensions, and one which must once have been traversed by a river of large size. All that now remains of the river is a small stream that sinks into the floor of the cave close to the entrance, meeting no doubt some watercourse at a greater depth. But, from the presence of flood-rubbish further in, I infer that in floods a stream of some kind traverses it, though the greater part is always dry. Any stream rising in the neighbourhood could occupy but a small part of the vast capacity of this cave, which is in places fully forty feet high, and fifteen or twenty feet wide. Unfortunately a couple of hundred yards from the entrance further progress was prevented by a heap of fallen debris which completely blocked the way. At the inner end of the passage, where the heap of boulders stopped us, was a burrow, possibly belonging to a Badger, and Mr. Knight's dogs which had accompanied us showed by their excitement that the animal was within. This further supports my belief that this cave is in great part dry at all seasons.

The Invertebrates I found here are all species which occur above ground; they are—a spider, *Porrhoma microphthalma*, which Mr. Carpenter tells me has been found in a coal-pit, occurring also above ground; *Brachydesmus superus*, a blind millipede, which also occurs above ground; *Iulus pilosus*, a typical millipede; *Tomocerus tridentiferus*, a collembolan, found at Mitchelstown by Wright and Haliday; recorded by Packard from North American caves, occurs under stones above ground;[1] *Velia currens*, the water-bug found at Bohoe; a fungus-midge, *Sciara Thomæ*; and four beetles, *Bembidium rufescens, Ancyrophorus omalinus, Helodes marginata*, and *Coprophilus striatulus*; the last, Mr. Halbert tells me, has not hitherto been recorded as Irish. All these beetles inhabit moist, marshy places, and were probably washed into the cave.

After leaving Coolarkin cave we visited Bohoe church, where Mr. Knight informed me there was an immense colony of bats. We found a number of young Pipistrelles (*Vesperugo pipistrellus*) from a few days old to half-grown individuals, crawling about the floor of the church, having fallen through a hole in the ceiling. There must have been an immense colony in the roof, but unfortunately there was not a ladder at hand to enable me to inspect it. Having collected a number of these young bats I returned to Enniskillen, as darkness was already coming on.

On July 12th, next day, I drove to the Marble Arch, at Florence-Court, and, after collecting a few invertebrates about the grounds, I was met by Mr. Bowles, the keeper, who accom-

---

[1] For this and other information respecting the invertebrates found I am indebted to Mr. Carpenter.

panied me to the caves. In the Marble Arch cave, which is a favourite resort for tourists, I collected a few invertebrates which, like those collected on the previous day, were species which occur above ground.

This cave is, I may here remark, in its upper part dry, the river that has carved it out having found a passage on a lower level, and appearing as a spring some distance in. Here I took *Porrhoma microphthalma, Brachydesmus supcrus, Tomocerus tridentiferus*, and *Clivina fossor*, a carabidous beetle.

None of the other Florence Court caves were accessible without Mr. Martel's exploring apparatus, so I had to defer my visits to them till his arrival.

On the 15th Mr. and Mrs. Martel and I drove to the Arch Spring, and Noon's Hole, bringing with us in a cart Mr. Martel's copious equipment of cave-exploring apparatus. This consisted of a canvas boat, some hundreds of feet of rope-ladders, a light portable folding wooden ladder, ropes, axes, compass, barometer, telephone, maps, &c.

We first proceeded to Noon's Hole, which is a vertical shaft or swallow-hole down which a stream precipitates itself. Mr. Martel sounded the shaft with a lead-line and found the depth to be 150 feet. The rope ladders were then got ready and Mr. Martel began his descent; he could not, however, descend more than about 60 feet, as the falling water, which at the time was unusually high, broke over the ladder and rendered further progress impossible. The descent of this chasm would be made possible if the stream could be for a time deflected.

We also explored Poolaneffaran, a pit formed partly by the falling in of the roof of an underground river-bed.

The streams traversing Noon's Hole and Poolaneffaran converge to form the Arch spring, where they discharge themselves through a beautiful grotto, and form a waterfall. In the Arch spring I found *Meta Merianæ*.

On the 16th we visited the Marble Arch, bringing the same equipment. Here we were met by Mr. Bowles and his son, who accompanied us to the caves. Several streams, meeting underground, flow out at the source, under the "Marble Arch," a beautiful natural archway, cut off from the cave.

The first cavern we explored we gained access to by means of an entrance at the bottom of a pit, formed evidently by the falling in of a part of the roof. After exploring several dry galleries and a vertical swallow-hole opening on the hill above us, we found on a lower level the river itself. Further progress was impossible without the boat, as a large and deep pool, an expansion of the underground stream, barred our way. The boat was brought into the cave, its constituent parts filling two large canvas bags, and was put together; by this means we were able to investigate this hitherto unexplored river. A detailed account of this "voyage" would occupy too much space, and no doubt it will in due time be fully described by Mr. Martel. The stream was "navigable" for about 300 yards.

We afterwards investigated some small swallow-holes which mark above ground the course of these streams. The chief stream, the Monaster, as it is called, enters upon its subterranean course at Poolawaddy.

Above this its course is through a deep narrow gorge, which ends in a cliff, into a cavern in which the stream falls. I was informed that in heavy floods the volume of water in this gorge is so much greater than the cave can quickly drain off that the valley becomes a deep lake.

This day's work completed our Enniskillen explorations.

From the 22nd to the 25th of July I was engaged exploring Mitchelstown Cave. I will not attempt any description of this underground labyrinth, as it has now been completely mapped by Mr. Martel, who is publishing in this number of the *Irish Naturalist* a description and plan of it. It was discovered some sixty years ago by the grandfather of the present tenant of the land on which is the entrance; he broke into one of the obstructed swallow-holes when quarrying. This is the only known opening. The so-called "river" is only a little pool of water in a basin of rock. I fully explored it, crossing over to the opposite side of it. I found that its high-water line is marked all round by a calcareous deposit, and, when it is flooded up to this, it empties itself by a small opening, about a foot in diameter, into some deeper and unexplored chamber.

A 3

Although no opening is known except the artificial one by which we entered, the presence of a number of specimens of an above-ground staphylinid beetle, *Ancyrophorus omalinus*, all dead, and floating on the surface of another small pool of water (about eight or ten feet in diameter and a foot deep) points to the fact that water has access from the outer world otherwise than by infiltration.

In the passage called the "Mud Cave," which is the deepest part, is a vertical shaft, the walls of which are thickly coated with fine red extremely sticky mud, so that descent without ropes would be impossible; I tried to get down, but the mud, sticking to my boots in large masses, threatened to pull me down more rapidly than would have been pleasant, so I had to leave it. This shaft has never been explored, but as it is in the deepest known part of the cave I feel pretty certain that if it could be followed it would be found to lead into some deeper passages, and perhaps to the bed of the river that must in former times have drained the cave. Mr. Martel, however, does not attach much importance to this pit, but he has very generously made me an offer that, if I wish to carry out further explorations, he will lend me some of his ladders. About four or five hundred yards west of the entrance is a swallow-hole, which opens on the side of a hill overlooking the valley north of the caves. This the guide informed me has once or twice been partly explored, but he could tell me nothing about it, except that he believed there was a river in some of the passages. It is not known to communicate with the other cave. The man who drove me from Mitchelstown to the caves informed me that there was a large spring a couple of miles south of the cave, but I could get no further information about it. The dip of the strata is towards the south.

The invertebrates I collected at Mitchelstown have all been identified by Mr. Carpenter; they are—

MITES.

Gamasus attenuatus; found in several parts of the cave, chiefly under paper and other refuse left by tourists.

SPIDERS.

Porrhoma myops; discovered by Mr. Carpenter in 1894 and recorded in his paper.

Leptyphantes pallidus; new to the Irish fauna; Mr. Carpenter tells me it is a rare species which has been found by Pickard-Cambridge in Dorsetshire, at roots of heather; also in caves in France and Bavaria; unlike the former species it has large eyes. Both these species occurred in the driest parts of the cave, under stones, and one or two specimens (? species) in webs among the boulders.

MYRIAPODA.

Brachydesmus superus; found also in some of the Enniskillen caves.

COLLEMBOLA.

Tomocerus tridentiferus; see remarks on this species under Coolarkin Cave.

Sinella cavernicola; occurred everywhere; on the whole I found this species frequenting drier spots than the *Lipura.* Mr. Carpenter tells me that my series of *Sinella* shows the species to be very variable in its antennal joints.

Lipura Wrightii; in almost every nook and corner of the cave, dry or damp, outnumbering all the other species.

BEETLES.

Ancyrophorus omalinus; mentioned before, probably washed in.

Trechus micros; taken alive under stones.

Besides these "natives" of the cave, as with the exception of *Ancyrophorus* they may all more or less be called, I found a frog, a specimen of *Pterostichus vulgaris* (beetle), and a fungus midge belonging to the genus *Sciara*; these had evidently wandered in, and got lost in the darkness.

A small mollusc, taken in some numbers, has been identified by Dr. Scharff as *Hyalina contracta,* this is the second British record; first found at Killarney by Dr. Scharff; occurs in Sweden, Germany, France, and Switzerland; all the members of this genus live in concealed localities.

When an attempt is made to group together the various animals collected at Enniskillen and Mitchelstown, in relation to the physical conditions of the caves they were found in, it appears that they fall into several divisions.

(i.) Species inhabiting the entrances to caves, near the light, using the cave as a convenient hiding-place; such are the two species of *Meta*, perhaps *Leptyphantes pallidus*, and the bats.

(ii.) Species which have wandered into the caves, accidentally, perhaps, or have been washed in by floods, and are so to speak "fish out of water;" examples of such are the water-bugs and crane-flies from Bohoe; *Iulus, Velia, Sciara* and the beetles from Coolarkin; *Clivina fossor* from the Marble Arch; and the frog, *Pterostichus, Sciara*, and *Ancyrophorus* from Mitchelstown.

(iii.) The *Troglodytes*; only found in Mitchelstown, *e.g.* *Lipura, Sinella* and *Porrhoma myops*.

(iv.) Those species which do not fall under any of these three groups seem to me to form a division intermediate in position between the last two, and in most cases inhabiting caves which present conditions intermediate between Bohoe and Mitchelstown caves, which I may safely take as the extremes of my series. Such are *Tomocerus tridentiferus, Brachydesmus superus*, and *Porrhoma microphthalma*, which seem to be equally at home above ground and underground. These creatures seemed quite at home in Coolarkin, and the dry part of the Marble Arch cave, and I see no reason to doubt that *Brachydesmus* and his companions in darkness may have lived and multiplied there for many generations, undisturbed by any such catastrophes as the floods that characterize Bohoe cave.

While fully aware of the great gap that exists between a cave-fauna of this type and that of Mitchelstown, I see no reason to doubt that at one time the Mitchelstown fauna was one somewhat of this type, consisting of a few unwary animals which got into the cave and had to make the best of it; the isolation and probably much greater age of the Mitchelstown fauna may account for their specialization; and if so, provided that among the many unexplored caves of Ireland we can find some presenting conditions intermediate between those we find in Coolarkin and in Mitchelstown, we may almost hope to fill up some of the gaps in the history of the evolution of cave-faunas.

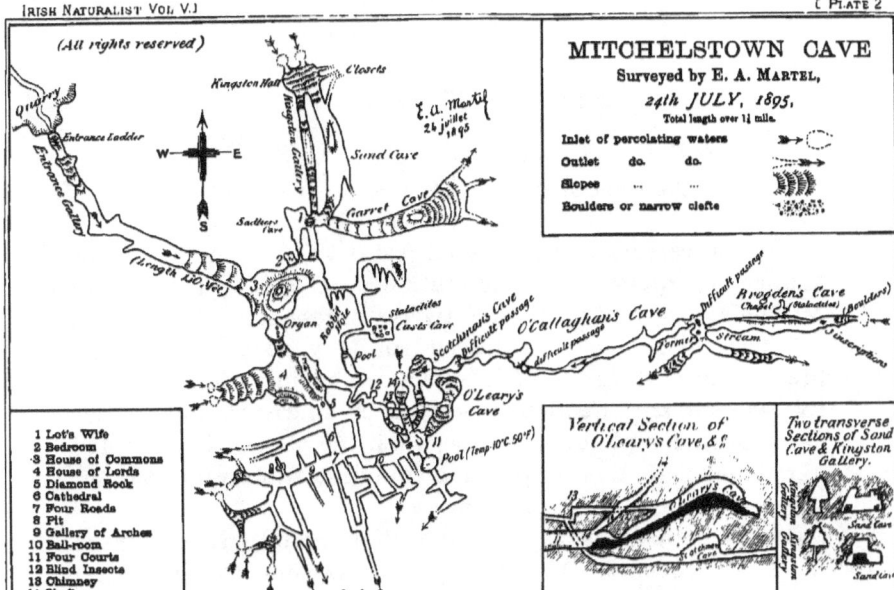

MITCHELSTOWN CAVE.

BY E. A. MARTEL,
President of the Société Spéléologique, Paris.

PLATE 2.

THE most celebrated and the largest cave in Ireland is in the county of Tipperary, in the south of the island; it is that of Mitchelstown, and is situated twelve miles east of this town.

It was discovered on the 2nd of May, 1833, by a stone-breaker, named Cowden : it is referred to in various descriptive works, and frequently visited by tourists; but it has never been completely described, and the plan of it remained unfinished.[1] It was supposed to contain a subterranean river, and many unexplored passages.

On the 24th of July, 1895, I spent six hours visiting all the accessible corners, and drawing out the short topographical survey here given, which will prevent the necessity of a long analysis. My survey does not offer any new peculiarity, and I will confine myself to a brief indication of the principal features. Hollowed out under a hill which overlooks the surrounding plains, this cave does not seem to be in connection with any actual river.

The cave of Mitchelstown has been formed, like others, by the drainage of superficial waters, at an epoch when they were much more abundant than they are in our days. In the interior the galleries offer two different aspects; some of them, the largest, have served and serve still as swallow-holes for the waters from without; they are—1st, the Entrance Gallery, which is the highest, being 13 yards in altitude at the mouth ; the orifice of this gallery was discovered, by chance, in the working of a quarry ; 2nd, the double avenue, with parallel branches, of the Kingston Gallery and Sand Cave,[2] where the effects of the erosion and corrosion have produced the most curious sections (see the two transverse cuts of Sand Cave);

---

[1] Apjohn : *Journal Geological Soc. of Dublin*, vol. i., 1833, pages 103–111.
Rev. Canon Courtenay Moore : *Journal of the Cork Historical and Archæol. Soc.*, January, 1894.
Dublin Penny Journal, 27 Dec., 1834.

[2] Eighty yards long, and not forty-one, as stated by Rev. Courtenay Moore.

3rd, the west side of the hall called the House of Lords ; 4th, the long eastern corridor which retains, clearly marked, the traces of the passage of a subterranean stream (O'Callaghan's Cave and Brogden's Cave); 5th, and lastly, several fissures situated at the south-west angle, and near O'Leary's Cave. Each of these parts is terminated by an ascending slope, ruins of vaults, or rubbish washed in from the exterior, which obstruct them completely, as I have already seen in the ancient draining passages, now stopped up, of Bramabiau, France, of Adelsberg, Austria, etc. They are filled-up swallow-holes. The other fissures, generally narrower, and situated in the lower parts of the cave, have conducted these waters no one knows where, either to some undetermined and distant outlet, or even into the depths of the terrestrial shell; they are rendered impenetrable sometimes by broken pieces of stone, as at the extremity of Garret Cave, sometimes by the narrowness of the clefts, which become more and more contracted in the southern part of the cave; this last disposition is exactly like that of the large grotto of Cro de Grandville, or of Miremont, in the Dordogne (see "Les Abimes,"[1] chap. xx.), and we ask ourselves if, like the latter, the cave of Mitchelstown has not served as a receptacle for some great lake of ancient times, which has emptied itself into it. The lowest part of the cave is, at most, thirty-three yards below the level of the entrance, and not one hundred yards as is stated in the guide book.

The checkered disposition of the *diaclases* (upright joints, generally perpendicular to the joints of stratification) is remarkable in the southern portion (see plan); three sets of fissures perpendicular to each other have there cut out large polyhedrons of rock, often quite cubic, the right-angled interstices of which have let out the waters that have gradually widened them out; in depth they get more contracted the more they branch out; besides they have been in a great measure coagulated by the clay, which comes either from the outside or from the chemical decomposition of the interior rock which has become corroded.

The Well (No. 8) marked in the Gallery of Distaffs is impracticable on account of the glutinous mud with which it is covered.

---

[1] E. A. Martel: *Les Abimes*, Paris: Delagrave, 1894, in 4to, 570 pp., 100 engravings, 200 plans, and 20 plates.

The rock, according to Mr. Kinahan, is the same (Carboniferous) as at Cong, where the actual waters probably circulate in a network of crevices of this kind. We comprehend why the galleries of absorption are nearly all in the southern part of the grotto (except Garret Cave) when we remark that such is the general direction of the dip (at 40°) of the calcareous strata.

Certain diaclases have been widened out into distaff shape and communicate with each other under the low strata which have not been carried away, as at the source of Marble Arch cave near Enniskillen, County Fermanagh.

There are no longer any traces of running water in Mitchelstown Cave, at least in summer; the so-called "river" is a pool of stagnant water ten yards long by half a yard or one yard in depth and width, which has taken refuge in an impervious hollow; there is another basin near the hall of the Four Courts; both are produced by infiltration; their temperature is 10° Cent., the air of the grotto being (in two different points) 10·5° Cent.

One will remark on the plan, and on the vertical section of O'Leary's Cave, the indescribable entanglement of three stories of superposed galleries; they communicate by a very narrow "chimney." The subterranean waters have accomplished there a singularly complicated work of mining.

From a picturesque point of view the cave of Mitchelstown is much inferior to those of Adelsberg, Dargilon, Padirac, Han-sur-Lesse, etc. Its highest vault is only ten yards high; the galleries of Kingston, Sand Cave, and the Cathedral are nevertheless very remarkable in form. The most part of the calcareous concretions do not deserve the attention that the guide-book demands for them; and unfortunately, the prettiest stalactites, which would look well in any cavern, are situated in Brogden's Cave, the access to which being very difficult, is quite impracticable to tourists. At the cross-way marked on the plan "*difficult passage*," the local guide who alone accompanied me, and who had only been there once, when a child, twenty-five years before, completely lost his way; we were obliged to have recourse to the compass and to the plan I had drawn out, to find the passage again. It is a great pity, for the little lateral chamber in Brogden's Cave which I name "the Chapel," is a real gem, provided with the thinnest of curtains, and the finest needles of brilliant white carbonate of lime. In spite of the restricted dimensions, there is a marvellous corner there, which has not its equal in all the rest of the cave, even in the hall called "Cust's Cave," which is also pretty well ornamented. It was supposed that this gallery of the ancient stream (O'Callaghan's and Brogden's Caves) had never been explored to the end: this is not correct. I found, at a few steps from the extremity, on a ledge of the vault, three inscriptions: "Raymond, May, 1840"; "Brogden (whose name has been given to the last corridor), 5th October, 1868"; the third was illegible. So that all the grotto was known (except some little clefts in the south-west, into which I crawled with great trouble and without any result). But it is very possible that the talus of broken stones which blocks up the end of Brogden's Cave, is not a real end, but that a partial falling in of the vault has only obstructed the gallery; it would be very interesting to make a clearing there to seek if there does not exist a prolongation of the beautiful gallery of the dried-up stream.

To sum up, three things are remarkable in Mitchelstown Cave:—

1st. Its ramification in every direction, and the infinite subdivisions of its central part.

2nd. Its extent, which attains and even exceeds, including all the passages, one mile and a quarter; this must be the longest cave, yet known, in the British Isles.

3rd. Its blind fauna. It is the only grotto in England, Scotland, or Ireland, where, up to the present time, there have been found animals peculiar only to caverns.[1] Mr. H. Lyster Jameson occupied himself during several days in the month of July, 1895, in collecting specimens, and he has the intention of making a further study of them.

The cave of Mitchelstown, even in the parts that are shown to the public, is not at all easy to go through; the Chimney and all the parts round about it (O'Leary's Cave) are nearly impracticable to ladies.

---

[1] See G. H. Carpenter: Animals found in Mitchelstown Cave, *Irish Naturalist*, February, 1895, Dublin; and *Bulletin de la Société de Spéléologie*, No. 1, 1895, p. 44.

It appears that there have never been found in it any bones of animals no longer existing, and this fact is explained by remarking the absence of any known large natural opening. This is plausible; nevertheless, for want of serious excavations the question cannot be considered as decided.

Peasants told Mr. Jameson, that on a hill, situated at about 400 yards from the entrance of the cave, there exists a natural well (abyss), which had only been insufficiently explored, but where, nevertheless, a current of water had been met with. It would be a good thing to verify and complete this indication.

Finally, the cave of Mitchelstown may still be considered as a worthy object for interesting future work and research.

BOTANY AT DUBLIN UNIVERSITY.

Notes from the Botanical School of Trinity College, Dublin: No. 1, February, 1896. Printed at the University Press.

In this brochure of thirty-four pages we have cheering evidence of the vitality of botanical studies in Trinity College. Two of the three items of which these *Notes* are made up are contributed by Mr. H. H. Dixon, B.A., Assistant to the Professor of Botany, and deal with some points of vegetable physiology which the author has made the subject of observation in the botanical laboratory of the College. The value of these contributions, entitled: "On the Chromosomes of *Lilium longiflorum*," and "On the Nuclei of the Endosperm of *Fritillaria imperialis*," can only be appreciated by the advanced student who is skilled in tracing those mysterious stirrings of life which go on within the narrow confines of the vegetable cell. The third item in the *Notes*, entitled: "The Herbarium of Trinity College: a Retrospect" is from the pen of Dr. E. P. Wright, University Professor of Botany. In this we find a strong human element: for the retrospect deals with the lives and labours of some three generations of Irish botanists, in so far, at least, as these lives and labours were effective in bringing together the important collection of dried plants now preserved in the Trinity College Herbarium. After all, the lives of men, as Mr. Dixon himself will cheerfully admit, stir us more deeply than the lives of vegetable cells; so that even a biologist may be excused for taking a warmer interest in the *Retrospect* than in the laboratory observations.

In the compass of a few pages Dr. Wright traces the history of the Herbarium and the Botanical School for upwards of a century, from the institution of the botanical professorship in 1785, to the foundation of the laboratory in 1893. The most prominent figures brought before us in this rapid survey are Dr. Edward Hill, first professor of the Botanical School; Dr. William Allman, one of the earliest teachers of the Natural System in the Three Kingdoms; James T. Mackay, the well-known author of *Flora Hibernica*; Dr. Thomas Coulter, who made botanical explorations in California and Central Mexico; and, last and most illustrious of all, Dr. William H. Harvey, *facile princeps* amongst British botanists of the century in knowledge of the sea-weeds of the globe. Harvey's indefatigable zeal in building up the Trinity College Herbarium is well shown by some extracts given by Dr. Wright from the memoir published in 1869. No one can read this admirable memoir, almost entirely made up of selections from his wide correspondence, without conceiving a strong esteem, not to say affection, for the gifted Quaker botanist who has done so much to illustrate by his pencil no less than his pen, the flowering plants of the Cape and the marine algæ of Australia and the South Seas.

It would appear from an extract given us by Dr. Wright from Harvey's evidence before the Dublin University Commission of 1853, that the College herbarium then contained upwards of 45,000 species. Since that date the collection has grown considerably and still continues to grow; but as lack of funds and consequent lack of skilled assistance has prevented the thorough arrangement of the herbarium, its actual extent can only be surmised. It is satisfactory to learn, however, that the department of algæ contains all, or almost all the species described by Harvey in his classical works, *Phycologia Britannica*, *Nereis Americana*, *Nereis Australis* and *Phycologia Australis*, and that the large collection of specimens brought together for the preparation of his *Flora Capensis* is in fairly good order. It is now thirty years since Harvey's death brought the *Cape Flora* to an abrupt close, at the end of the *Compositæ*. Is there no rich and patriotic South African to provide the funds for the completion of this work, which it seems hopeless to expect either the imperial or the colonial government to take in hand? The extent of the General Herbarium of Phanerogams in Trinity College is well shown in the rough geographical index given by Dr. Wright. Almost all quarters of the globe appear to be represented in the collection, the only striking blank being Siberia.

In a future number of these Notes we trust that we may find a brief history of the College Botanic Garden at Ball's Bridge.

OBITUARY.

HARRY CORBYN LEVINGE.

The late Mr. H. C. Levinge, D.L., J.P., who died at his residence, Knockdrin Castle, Mullingar, on March 11th, in his 68th year, was the ninth and youngest son of Sir Richard Levinge, 6th Baronet, and a member of an old Westmeath family, who have been identified with that county for over two hundred years. Though but a comparatively recent recruit to the ranks of Irish botanists, Mr. Levinge did much to further our knowledge of the distribution of the flowering plants of this country. His three papers on the plants of Westmeath in this Journal, the last of which appeared so lately as last February, form highly important contributions to the flora of that beautiful and interesting county, previously almost unexplored; and his wise encouragement of that remarkable self-taught botanist, Mr. P. B. O'Kelly, of Ballyvaughan, resulted in the publication of two plants new to Ireland—*Potamogeton lanceolatus* and *Limosella aquatica*—the discovery of both of which was due to Mr. O'Kelly's keen eye. To the *Journal of Botany* he also contributed occasional notes of Irish plants, his most important paper being that on "*Neotinea intacta* in County Clare," published in 1892. Among those who had the privilege of exchanging botanical specimens with him, Mr. Levinge's plants were famous for the beauty and perfection of the drying, and his herbarium of British plants, to which he devoted much time, was a model of what such a collection should be. Mr. Levinge's devotion to Irish botany, which commenced but a comparatively few years ago, on his return to Ireland after a long period of labour in the Indian Civil Service, was, we believe largely due to the unobtrusive influence and enthusiasm of his friend, A. G. More, who did so much to quicken the activities of a whole generation of Irish botanists.

Directory of Irish Naturalists.—A number of members of Irish Field Clubs well qualified for insertion in the new *Directory* have not yet returned the forms issued with the February number of the *I.N.* They are requested to fill them in and return them without delay, as the list will shortly close. Extra forms may be obtained from the undersigned.

R. LLOYD PRAEGER,
Sec. Irish Field Club Union

PROCEEDINGS OF IRISH SOCIETIES.

ROYAL ZOOLOGICAL SOCIETY.

Recent donations comprise a Peregrine Falcon from J. C. Carter, Esq. Two Black-backed Jackal cubs have been born in the Gardens. Seven Monkeys, two Turkey Vultures, twelve Pekin Nightingales, a pair of Penguins, a pair of Rose Cockatoos, a pair of Brazilian Caracars, a pair of Visachas, and a Coypu have been purchased.

6,335 persons visited the Gardens in February.

DUBLIN MICROSCOPICAL CLUB.

FEBRUARY 20th.—The Club met at Mr. ARTHUR ANDREWS'.

Mr. GREENWOOD PIM showed a leaf of *Gladiolus tristis*. The transverse section is, in form, an almost perfectly symmetrical Maltese cross. The tips of the cross, which are somewhat convex, are covered with a thick layer of sclerenchyma, beneath which are one large and two much smaller vascular bundles; other small bundles are found in the parenchymatous tissue of the leaf. The cuticle of the arms is covered with numerous wartlike processes. Towards the base, the leaf gradually expands, and becomes more flattened. This form of leaf if not unique is at any rate extremely rare, although some of the Irises exhibit a distant resemblance, being quadrangular with angles more or less marked. The plant is figured in *Bot. Mag.* I., 578, under name of *G. recurvus*, syn. *G. tristis*.

Prof. T. JOHNSON showed a section of the stem of *Selaginella oregana*, cut lengthwise. Vessels were pointed out, present in the xylem (wood) of the vascular tissue, in addition to the tracheïdes. *S. oregana* and *S. rupestris* are two species in which Harvey Gibson has recently, in the course of an anatomical revision of the genus *Selaginella*, discovered vessels (cell-fusions), the characteristic elements in the wood of Dicotyledons, and until his discovery not known to be represented in the wood of Ferns and their allies (except in a few cases), where tracheïdes are the normal elements. The section was made by Miss Sollas from material of a specimen grown in the Royal Botanic Gardens, Glasnevin.

Mr. McARDLE exhibited the leaf cells of *Sphagnum papillosum*, Lindb., var. *confertum*, from plants which he gathered on Connor-hill, near Dingle, Co. Kerry, in July, 1894. It was very scarce, and grew on damp peat amongst rocks in short, dense tufts. Specimens were identified by Dr. Braithwaite. The inner cell-walls are furnished in a remarkable manner with rows of conical papillæ; in this way and by its large size it approaches closely the rare *S. Austini*, Sullivant, leaf-cells of which were also exhibited from specimens collected by Mr. McArdle on Ard bog, King's County, in September, 1890, and kindly verified by Dr. Braithwaite. The papillæ in *Austini* are larger, extending for some distance into the cells, forming pectinate rows. A drawing of the cells showing the papillæ of both plants highly magnified and specimens of the plants with their peculiar branching were also shown.

Dr. C. HERBERT HURST exhibited a pocket microscope made by Swift, with an addition by Aylward. The instrument is contained in a case measuring 6¾ inches by 2⅞ inches by 2½ inches outside, and weighs, with the case, 1 lb. 9 oz. When set up inclined for use with a zoophyte-trough its area of support is a triangle, the sides of which measure 5 inches, 5 inches, and 6 inches respectively, and the height being only 7½ inches, it possesses extraordinary stability and is particularly well adapted for use at sea. Aylward's addition is a folding foot with an equilateral triangular area of support, each side of which measures 4½ inches, fitting the instrument for use in a vertical position for examining objects in a watch-glass or on a slide. The fine adjustment screw is good, and the instrument works well with powers from 4-inch to $\frac{1}{12}$-inch.

Dr. HURST also showed *Ascetta primordialis*, Hæckel, a specimen taken with the dredge in Rhoscolyn Bay, Holy Island, Anglesey, May 25, 1890. This exceedingly simple calcareous sponge, like another specimen taken the same day, was found attached to the base of a tuft of *Antennularia antennina*.

Mr. MOORE exhibited a pseudo-bulb of a species of *Anguloa* which had been attacked by a Fungus. The Fungus had not yet been identified, and the exhibit was to show the manner in which the pseudo-bulb was attacked and destroyed. The inner tissues were gradually disrupted, and at certain spots the hard epidermal tissues were burst outwards, small irregular yellow masses of fungoid growth coming through the openings.

Corrigendum.—In report of December meeting, p. 51, lines 11 and 13, for "leaves" read "hairs."

BELFAST NATURAL HISTORY AND PHILOSOPHICAL SOCIETY.

March 3.—The President in the Chair. Mr. CONWAY SCOTT, C.E., lectured on "The Production of Ability."

BELFAST NATURALISTS' FIELD CLUB.

FEBRUARY 26.—GEOLOGICAL SECTION.— Mr. F. W. LOCKWOOD (*President*) in the Chair. Mr. J. O. CAMPBELL, B.E., gave an address on the polarisation of light, and its application to micro-petrography. After a short preliminary explanation of the undulating theory of light, the lecturer described the construction of the polariscope and the manner in which the phenomena of polarisation arise. The methods employed by petrologists to utilise polarised light in examining and determining minerals was illustrated by blackboard diagrams, and the practical application of the method to the study of crystals in rock sections was explained. The paper was especially useful in anticipation of Professor Cole's approaching course on field geology, when the evenings will be devoted to a course on the study of rock-sections. Rock-specimens were presented by Messrs. L. M. Bell, R. Bell, J. O. Campbell, and the Honorary Secretary.

FEBRUARY 29.—BOTANICAL SECTION.—Rev. C. H. WADDELL, described the dermal tissues of plants and the various kinds of hairs and glands. A number of spring flowers illustrating various genera which the members had brought in were then examined.

MARCH 5.—MICROSCOPICAL SECTION.—The President of the section, Rev. JOHN ANDREW, opened the meeting by a few remarks dealing with the practical work connected with microscopy. Mr. Andrew introduced a practical lesson on the making of rock-sections for the microscope by a short paper, the points of which were illustrated by specimens of chips in the various stages of preparation. The paper and the practical illustrations of how to proceed were instructive, and may encourage some of our microscopists among the geologists to try their hand. After some conversational remarks, the President called upon Mr. W. B. DRUMMOND, M.B., C.M., to read a short paper, entitled "Hints on collecting marine zoological specimens." Marine field work naturally divides itself into three sections, viz.—The study of the littoral fauna, by shore-hunting; of the surface fauna, by tow-netting; of the fauna of the sea-bottom, by dredging or trawling. The tow-net, dredge, and trawl, and their uses, were described. Also the processes of killing, fixing, hardening, staining, and mounting. In preparing delicate specimens the process of fixing is particularly important, as, if not resorted to, changes in the microscopic appearances occur very rapidly. Less delicate specimens, such as the copepods, may be simply hardened in dilute spirit and mounted in glycerine jelly. The technique of mounting and staining will be found very fully described in Bolles Lee's "Microtomist's Vade Mecum." After the reading of the papers, the members present examined some fine rock-sections of Mr. Charles Elcock, shown by different instruments, but the centre of attraction was around the microscopes of Messrs. James Stelfox and W. S. M'Kee, who were showing working specimens of that very beautiful and interesting little artisan, the *Melicerta*, and other living organisms.

DUBLIN NATURALISTS' FIELD CLUB.

MARCH 9.—The PRESIDENT (Prof. GRENVILLE COLE) in the chair.

Mr. R. LL. PRAEGER described a pine forest buried below marine clay on the foreshore near Bray.

On the top of the Boulder-clay and glacial gravels is a bed of coarse grey sand, without marine organisms. Overlying this is the old forest bed, a peaty deposit about a foot thick, full of trunks, branches, and roots of the Scotch Fir, and yielding its cones in hundreds. Overlying this is fine blue clay full of marine shells such as are found on muddy shores between tide-marks. This clay is in one place over six feet deep. Above all is the coarse shingle of the existing beach. The various changes of level and conditions, which this series proves, were pointed out, and specimens of the different beds exhibited. The paper will shortly appear in our pages.

A discussion ensued in which Mr. H. L. Jameson, Prof. Johnson, Mr. N. Colgan, and Prof. Cole took part.

Mr. GREENWOOD PIM, M.A., then exhibited an attachment for taking photographs of objects vertically under or over the camera. Prof. T. JOHNSON showed slides illustrating Parasitic Flowering Plants. Mr. R LLOYD PRAEGER exhibited a calcareous deposit from Brackenstown River. Mr. H. J. SEYMOUR showed a micro-section of nepheline phonolite from Blackball Head, Bantry Bay; and Mr. GREENWOOD PIM exhibited a remarkably fine specimen of *Pinguicula caudata*, a Mexican Butterwort; Mrs. ROSS exhibited named varieties of Daffodils, grown by Miss Curry, Lismore.

CORK NATURALISTS' FIELD CLUB.
CONVERSAZIONE.

IN the Ball Room of the Imperial Hotel an agreeable re-union, jointly promoted by the Cork Historical and Archæological Society and the Cork Naturalists' Field Club, took place on the evening of March 10th. The attendance was large, both bodies being influentially represented, while there were several visitors, including some from the Dublin Naturalists' Field Club. A musical programme was a feature of the Conversazione. Tea was served between 7 and 8.

An excellent and varied series of exhibits occupied the walls and table of the hall. They included the following items:—

Professor G. A. J. Cole, F.G.S.—1. Rhyolitic Lavas, including Natural Glass from the Volcano of Tardree, Co. Antrim; 2. Enlarged photographs of the higher Alps, by the late W. F. Donkin. Professor T. Johnston, D. Sc., Dublin N.F.C.—1. Alpine flowers, prepared by Lady Rachel Saunderson; 2. Coloured drawings of Freshwater Algæ, by M. C. Cooke; 3. Rare Irish seaweeds. G. H. Carpenter, B. Sc., Dublin N.F.C.—1. Set of Irish moths, illustrating variation; 2. Insects, illustrating protective coloration and mimicry. R. Lloyd Praeger—1. Flowering plants, Galway excursion, 1895; 2. Rare Irish flowering plants. W. H. Phillips, Belfast N.F.C.—Nature prints of rare varieties of British ferns. Robert Welch, Belfast N.F.C.—Photographs of Galway Field Club Conference and Excursion, 1895. Professor M. Hartog, M.A., D. Sc. Queen's College—Type specimens of Rotifers, prepared by C. Rousselet, F.R.M.S.; 2. Live objects illustrating pond life. Miss H. A. Martin—Siamese flowers, pressed, mounted and named by Mrs. G. H. Grindrod, Bangkok. R. A. Phillips—1. Rare and characteristic plants of Co. Cork; 2. Land and fresh-water shells. J. J. Wolfe, Skibbereen—Some British moths and butterflies. The Misses Chillingworth and Lester—Fifty botanical specimens from Crosshaven, pressed and mounted. W. B. Barrington—Some sea-birds' and waders' eggs. Mrs. J. H. Thompson—Microscopes—live objects. H. Lund—Photographic transparencies—Snapshots on the Field Club. F. R. Rohu—Rare specimens—Black rat, Squacco Heron, white Shrew, &c. T. Farrington, M.A.—Some geological specimens. Telescopic speculums made in Cork in the last century. F. Neale, hon. sec. Limerick N.F.C.—Specimens of *Gnophria quadra, Gonopteryx rhamni, Dolomedes fimbriata*, &c. Robert Day, F.S.A.—The flags of the Cork Volunteers, with the medals and regimental decorations of the Irish Volunteers of 1782 and 1796, and other exhibits. Herbert Webb Gillman, V.P., C.H. & A. Society—Colours of the Muskerry cavalry (lent by the owner, Captain

R. Tonson Rye, of Rye Court)—Orderly book of the same corps, 1822-44 (lent by Sir Augustus Warren, Bart., of Warren's Court), and other exhibits. J. P. Dalton—Statue of William III (formerly in the Mansion House, Cork). Allan P. Swan, F.L.S.—Photographs of Micro-fungi, including salmon disease. The Franciscan Fathers—The chalices of the Franciscan Abbeys of Shandon, Timoleague, Buttevant, and Ardfert. A ciborium of Shandon Abbey. The Dominican Fathers—The chalice of the Dominican Abbey of Youghal. W. B. Haynes—Coat of an Irish Volunteer. J. H. Bennett—Galway rent-roll *temp.* Elizabeth; petition of Kinsale fishermen *temp.* Charles I. Miss Hutchens, Bantry—Local Shells, &c. Cecil Words—Rare Books. Greenwood Pim, M.A., Dublin N.F.C.—1. Facsimile of the Book of Kells; 2. Illustrations of British Fungi by General Bland. The Munster Camera Club—Frames of photographic transparencies exhibited by Messrs. W. R. Atkins, J. Bennett, F. Scott, H. Schroter, and C. H. Pearne.

At eight o'clock,

Mr. ROBERT DAY ascended the platform, and formally opened the conversazione amidst applause. He said by the very merest accident of birth his name had been placed first upon the programme, and that because the society over which he had the honour to preside was a little older than its twin sister, the Field Club (laughter). He took no credit whatever to himself for the happy union of that evening, as he was away from Cork when all the arrangements were made, and when the idea was conceived by Mr. Copeman. On his having informed him of what had been done, his only regret was that the conversazione could not have been continued upon the second day, so that a larger number of the country members of both societies would have been afforded an opportunity of seeing the various collections which have been so generously lent to us for the occasion. In Belfast a Field Club had flourished for a quarter of a century. He was a member of it for quite that period, and he alluded to it because it embraced from its inception archæology and the study of Irish antiquities. What that club had done for the North their dual clubs should do for the South. He feared that the name and claims of the Archæological Society were not so attractive to the general public as were those of the Naturalists' Field Club. He knew a little of the enjoyment of the naturalist, the pleasure of the botanist, the patient study of the student of geology, and the fascination and delight that centred in the revelations of the microscope. But he could claim for the so-called dry subject of antiquities that the objects embraced by it were quite as varied and equally enjoyable. He trusted that the conversazione would be the forerunner of similar yearly gatherings, and that the Cork Historical and Archæological Society and the Cork Naturalists' Field Club might travel hand-in-hand together for many years to come. He would now make way for one who was a master in the domain of science and natural history, Mr. William H. Shaw, President of the Cork Field Club.

Mr. W. H. SHAW, B.E., President of the Cork Naturalists' Field Club, followed in an interesting speech, during the course of which he pointed out that owing to its peculiar position this district possessed a flora and fauna of unique interest, and presented opportunities of research which should be more thoroughly availed of. He mentioned that the flora had been thoroughly gone into by Mr. Phillips, who was second to none in local botanical knowledge and the fauna had also interested him greatly, but the speaker was sorry to say with reference to the physical geography of the district that very little was being done. In conclusion he hoped that further interest would be manifested in the operations of the Cork Naturalists' Field Club, and with reference to the union of the various Field Clubs—Cork, Limerick, Galway, Dublin, and Belfast—mentioned that there were present that evening three visitors from Dublin—Professor Cole, President, Dublin N.F.C., and Messrs. Pim and Praeger.

Professor COLE also spoke, pointing out that large membership of Field Clubs was not so desirable as activity, and directing attention to the splendid field possessed by the Cork Club. Indeed, they in Ireland had several advantages over their brethren in England, where, owing to the large population, everything was practically worked out. In Ireland the Field Clubs had a future, and with added active members their work would become more valuable. With Messrs. Pim and Praeger he was proud to be there that night to represent the Dublin Club, and in the name of that club he greeted the members of the Cork club, and in the name of that club also he should sincerely thank them.

Mr. SHAW then declared the Conversazione open.

FIELD CLUB NEWS.

The Conversazione organized by the Cork Field Club, of which a report appears on another page, was a pleasant and highly successful function, and one well tended to increase the popularity of the Club. No trouble was spared to ensure success, and the spirit of enterprise which caused the electric light to be specially laid on for the occasion, producing brilliant illumination not only by means of large arc lights in the ceiling, but by numerous portable incandescent lamps among the exhibits on the tables, is deserving of the highest commendation.

It is with feelings of much pleasure that we publish an account of the proceedings which took place at the recent Annual Meeting of the Geological Society of London, when Mr. Joseph Wright, of Belfast, was awarded a moiety of the proceeds of the Barlow-Jameson fund "in recognition of the valuable services he has rendered to palæontology." This honourable recognition of his industry and scientific attainments will cause gratification to Mr. Wright's large circle of scientific friends, and to his fellow-members of the Belfast Field Club, in whose *Proceedings* many of his most important papers have appeared.

The practical course on Irish seaweeds recently undertaken by Prof. T. Johnson is well attended, the class of thirteen being mostly members of the Dublin Field Club. The first excursion took place on March 17th when, in a steady downpour, a party of nine did "shore-hunting" between Skerries and Balbriggan. The most interesting find was *Prasiola stipitata* in quantity and in full reproduction.

The Committee of the Dublin Field Club have arranged their summer excursion programme as follows:—April 25, Bray and Killiney (geological half-day); May 30, Lambay Island; June 20, Bective and the Boyne; July 10, 11, and 13, Cavan; August 12, Kelly's Glen (half-day); September 5, Brittas Bay, Co. Wicklow; September 20, Woodlands (fungus foray, half-day). The excursion to Cavan, when three days will be spent exploring the many lakes, rivers, and woods of that beautiful county, should prove especially productive, as the district is one almost unworked by the naturalist. The Dublin Club have invited their brethren of Belfast to join forces with them on this occasion, thus providing an opportunity for the renewing of many acquaintances formed last year at Galway.

We extract the following from the official report of the Annual General Meeting of the Geological Society of London, held on February 21st:—

"In handing a moiety of the Barlow-Jameson fund to Dr. G. J. Hinde, F.G.S. (for transmission to Mr. Joseph Wright, F.G.S., of Belfast), the President (Dr. Henry Woodward, F.R.S.), addressed him as follows:—Dr. Hinde, the council have awarded the sum of twenty pounds from the Barlow-Jameson fund to Mr. Joseph Wright, in recognition of the valuable services he has rendered to the palæontology, not only of the Carboniferous rocks in the South, but of the Cretaceous and Post-Tertiary deposits in the North of Ireland, and the glacial deposits there and in Scotland. Mr. Wright is the author of numerous papers in the transactions of the Belfast Naturalists' Field Club on the Irish Liassic and Cretaceous foraminifera and other microzoa; he has also prepared and published many lists of foraminifera from the Scottish and Irish boulder-clay and other post-tertiary deposits. He has done much good work, extending over many years, when resident in the South of Ireland, in connection with the fossils of the Carboniferous limestone, and, both as regards these and the newer deposits of the North, his specimens have been always available to anyone engaged in writing on the fossils. To Davidson, Rupert Jones, Holl, Brady, myself, and others Joseph Wright's cabinet was ever accessible, and his specimens freely lent for study. I trust that this award will serve to express to Mr. Wright our appreciation of his services, and will act as an incentive to him to continue his useful geological work.

Mr. Hinde replied as follows:—Mr. President, it gives me great satisfaction to receive this award on behalf of my friend Mr. Joseph Wright. He is unfortunately unable to be present, and has sent the following letter for communication to you:—I desire to express my sincere thanks for the honour conferred upon me by the council of our society in recognition of my past work, and for their assistance in the further prosecution of my researches. Working so remote from the head-quarters of the society causes this award to be the more appreciated. I regret I am prevented from being present to receive it in person, but I hope the council will accept this expression of my feelings regarding their approval of my work in a somewhat neglected field. For some time past nearly all my spare time has been spent in microscopically examining the glacial clays for foraminifera. My anticipation as to the occurrence of these organisms in clays laid down under glacial conditions has been fully confirmed, both as regards our local deposits and other British clays, and I cannot avoid thinking that this fact must more or less influence our views on the origin of these drifts."

NOTES.

BOTANY.

FUNGI.

Cyathus vernicosus—a correction.—The note in the February number of the *Irish Naturalist* on this subject is scarcely accurate, inasmuch as the plant will be found in the list of Fungi in the Handbook prepared for the meeting of the British Association in 1878. It occurred in a greenhouse in Dublin, and it is interesting to note that Mr. Praeger's specimens were found in a similar situation. This curious little plant may be an addition to the Mycologic Flora of the North of Ireland, as it is not mentioned in Mr. Lett's list published by the Belfast N. F. Club some years ago.

GREENWOOD PIM, Dublin.

PHANEROGAMS.

Early flowering of Lathræa squamaria.—On the 12th of last month (March) I received from Miss M. Chearnley, of Cappoquin, Co. Waterford, some flowering plants of the Toothwort, which she had discovered the day before growing under a yew tree in the grounds of Tourin, near Cappoquin. Even allowing for the southern position of the station, this appears to be an exceptionally early record for the species, which in Ireland rarely flowers before mid-April. Miss Chearnley's specimens were quite mature, showing well formed capsules on some of the spikes.

N. COLGAN, Dublin.

Early Flowering of Hottonia palustris.—In a pond in a garden at Dundrum, Co. Dublin, *Hottonia palustris* is already in flower (March 22nd). This is a remarkable case of early blooming. The plants are self-sown, from stock introduced two years ago from the North of Ireland.

R. LLOYD PRAEGER.

ZOOLOGY.

"Mingling of North and South."—On reading the extremely interesting address of the ex-President of the Dublin Naturalists' Field Club published last month, I feel constrained to question the strict appropriateness of one of the animals selected for special dedication to "typical" members of the Galway Conference as reminders of their respective types of origin. I will not quarrel with the allocation of the Common Frog to the "settler of some generations standing," inasmuch as the historical introduction of the Frog by Dr. Guithers was perpetrated as far back as 1696. But is it not inconsistent in the next sentence to compare "the English immigrant who has *recently* come to stay" to the Magpie, a bird which, "if tradition is to be trusted," came to our coast to stay in the year 1670, and which was certainly a spreading though still scarce member of our avifauna in 1700, while in 1743 it had grown so common that war was waged upon it by Irish Statute Law? I would suggest that a fitter ornithological partner for the recently arrived Britisher might be found in the Missel-thrush—"believed to have settled in Ireland (says Mr. More's invaluable List) since 1800," first authenticated as an Irish bird by Templeton in 1808, and unknown (as such) by sight to Thompson till a specimen was sent him from Fermanagh in 1832. While on this subject I would add that in the Isle of Man, the fauna of which much resembles that of Ireland, both the Frog and the Missel-thrush are, as in Ireland, held to be introduced or recently settled, species; but I have never heard that the Magpie is so regarded there.

C. B. MOFFAT, Dublin.

INSECTS.

Irish Hymenoptera Aculeata.—I was much pleased to see Mr. Freke's paper on our native Aculeate Hymenoptera in the February number of the *Irish Naturalist*. His list will form a most useful basis for future work, and it is to be hoped will induce collectors to attend to these interesting insects.

I am able to add two species to the Irish list, and a few additional localities.

The species new to Ireland are *Cœlioxys acuminata*, Nyl., and *Bombus soroensis*, Fabr. The former I took in my garden in Armagh on July 6th at blossoms of *Geranium pratense*, and the latter in Mullinure in May. The following are additional localities for the species named:—

Myrmica lœvinodis.—Armagh, and Scotstown, Co. Monaghan.
Mellinus arvensis, Linn.—Tynan, Co. Armagh, on the canal bank.
Halicitus albipes, Kirby.—Armagh and Loughgall, Co. Armagh.
Andrena clarkella, Kirby.—Armagh, in Mullinure and at Lowry's Lough, fairly common at Sallows in April.
A. fucata, Smith.—Armagh.
Nomada borealis, Zett.—Armagh.

As regards *Formica rufa*, L., I do not think that it is indigenous at Churchill, for as far as I can find out it was imported there some fifty years ago, possibly more. It has however taken most kindly to the place and multiplied to an extraordinary extent. I was standing one day looking at them when I noticed a curious crackling sound. After several vain endeavours to discover the source of the noise I found it to be caused by the myriads of ants running over the dry pine needles. This will give some idea of their immense numbers. I should very much like to know if these ants are to be found elsewhere in Ireland and whether they are indigenous or imported.

W. F. JOHNSON, Poyntzpass.

BIRDS.

Migration of Curlews.—The wails of the host of curlews which passed over Dublin on the night of the 11th inst. (March) must have greeted the ears of a large number of the residents. The night was warm and wet, and the curlews cried in chorus with but little intermission from about 9 P.M. until midnight, and probably for some hours longer. For several years I have taken notice of these nocturnal outbursts of curlew music over our city, and I find that March is the month in which they most generally occur. For instance a very striking "rush" took place in March, 1892, on the nights of the 23rd, 24th, and 25th, as reported by me at the time in the natural history column of the *Irish Sportsman*. On that occasion the wild cries of the birds were not the only evidence given of their passage, for at least one curlew was picked up dead in Sackville-street, having flown with violence against the telegraph wires; and simultaneously with these occurrences notes showing a general migration-movement of curlews were forwarded from Limerick, Liverpool, and other places. Again, in March, 1893, the nights of the 18th and 19th were signalised by similar demonstrations, noticed in Dublin by my brother and myself and doubtless by many others. On all the nights referred to the sky was thickly overclouded,—indeed, I have several times remarked that the breaking up of the clouds has put an end to the clamour, probably because on bright nights the birds fly too high to be easily heard; for in the stillness of the country—and, for that matter, of the Phœnix Park—I have heard them in clear starlight, calling to one another from apparently a very great elevation.

C. B. MOFFAT Dublin.

Nesting of Black Guillemots.—Mr Palmer in the current number of the *Irish Naturalist*, asks whether any one else can throw further light on Mr. Witherby's observation of Black Guillemots nesting "under large boulders scattered about."

When I was in the Lofoden Islands some summers ago, where the Black Guillemot goes by the name of *Testhe* and is particularly common, breeding in large communities instead of in single pairs, as is so much the case on our western coasts, I invariably found their nests under boulders with which the low islets off the main islands were strewn. The high boulder-beaches were the favourite places, and in seeking the eggs, which we had to do from a commissariat point of view, we found it necessary to reach in arm's length between the boulders before reaching their nests.

W. S. GREEN, Dublin.

Feathered Pensioners.—Wintry weather with its accompaniments of frost and snow always brings the needs of our birds specially to our notice, and a few notes upon our feathered pensioners and their ways ways may perhaps prove worth recording. The winter of 1894-95 was more trying upon our birds than any year since the bitter frost of 1878-9, when Blackbirds, a Gold-crest, and many Titmice came into our bedrooms, in addition to the Robin who habitually frequented the room, eating groats from a dish on the chimney-piece, and drinking out of the water-jug. Those long snowy weeks were very fatal to the songsters, and the diminution in Blackbirds and Song-thrushes was noticeable for years afterwards; Rooks turned carnivorous, and were seen to attack and devour the smaller birds at Carnlough, and about Lisburn; an old nurse who had spent many years in America, saw what she believed to be a "Snowbird." Another day we saw a strange bird with a scarlet crest, which it could erect and depress at will, feeding on the balcony; it may have been an escaped Cardinal-bird. The general rejoicing when at last the thaw came, and green grass was revealed once more, was wonderful, Curlews coming and feeding on our lawn, which no doubt was more rapidly cleared owing to the close proximity of the sea. Opposite our diningroom stands a Laburnum-tree covered with pods, the favourite winter resort of the Finches and Titmice; that winter it was frequented by a handsome Mountain-finch, or Brambling (*Fringilla montifringilla*) who remained for a couple of days only, but last winter we again had one or two of these beautiful birds feeding there for several days. I remember that bitter winter counting seventy Starlings crowded on the tree, shelling the pods, with a watchful eye on our windows, and a firm determination not to lose a moment in attacking any contributions from our table—for Starlings are more than a little greedy! It is very interesting to split a cocoa-nut, and fastening it to the railing of a balcony watch the Coal Tits, Blue Tits, and Greater Tits hammering away at its contents. After some years the Robins ventured to try the unwonted food, and now Sparrows and Blackbirds dig away contentedly, also. We always provide plenty of groats and hemp, but the most interesting study is to put out some new kind of food, and see in what order the birds attack it. Some years ago a whole loaf was tossed upon the snow, and it was ludicrous to watch the famishing Sparrows hopping anxiously round it, with outstretched necks and eager glances, doubtful whether some trap were not intended, whilst the Rooks cawed questioningly and sidled cautiously towards it, anxious to be assured that all was right. Down came a brisk Blue Titmouse, spied the loaf, and without a moment's hesitation alighted upon it directly and commenced joyfully to attack the abundant supply! I think when the next "Glacial Period" descends upon our northern shores that *Parus cœruleus* will be the last bird to be starved out of its present familiar haunts.

S. M. THOMPSON, Belfast.

MAMMALS.

Irish Hare going to Ground.—A discussion on the subject of Hares going to ground has recently been going on in the pages of the *Field* newspaper, and among other interesting notes is the following,[1] which altough appearing over an anonymous signature ("Aquarius") I can well believe to be true:—"On many Irish mountains the Hares take to natural fissures in the rocks, or to natural water-courses, called by the natives water-brakes, formed by the percolation of the water through the peaty formation overlying the rock or other hard subsoil, often to a depth of several feet. In many localities, as for instance, in the Bannermore[2] chain in Donegal, where there is little covert, the Hares become nearly as subterranean in their habits as Rabbits. In these holes or crevices they seek safely from their enemies or shelter from bad weather, coming to the entrances of their "burrows," if such they may be termed, to bask in the sun, their "seats," as they are termed, being clearly marked. It is supposed that the Hares took to this habit to escape from their chief enemies, the eagles, formerly abundant in these mountains, but now pretty nearly extinct." It has not been my good fortune to have any experience of Hares in an open country like that described by "Aquarius," but my knowledge of them in wooded and cultivated districts, and of what has previously been written on the subject (*vide* Thompson's *Natural History of Ireland*, vol. iv., p. 29, *Field* for Jan. 14, 1882, July 18, 1891, and more recent numbers, and for Scotland, Mr. William Evans' remarks in the *Annals of Scottish Natural History*, Oct., 91, p. 267), leads me to believe that the above remarks are perfectly true. It would be interesting, however, if some reader of the *Irish Naturalist* could confirm them from his own experience.

G. E. H. BARRETT-HAMILTON, London.

GEOLOGY.

The Raised Beach at Fort Stewart, Lough Swilly.—A further examination of material from this raised beach shows the presence of the following shells, additional to those recorded in my paper on "The Raised Beaches of Inishowen," in the *I.N.* for October, 1895 (vol. iii., pp. 278-285):—*Trochus umbilicatus, Littorina rudis, Rissoa membranacea, R. striata, Hydrobia ulvæ, Fusus antiquus.*

Geology of the Curran, Larne.—On the 12th December, 1895, Miss S. Thompson, Mr. R. Bell, and the writer visited the new bauxite works at Larne, to investigate the report that some of their foundations were sunk below the lower beds of the estuarine clays and gravels examined and reported upon by a Committee of the Field Club during the Session 1889-90. This report we found misleading. The new siding to the works has been cut through, and the works themselves have been built, mainly upon a raised bank of boulder clay about 300 yards northwest of the Larne Harbour railway station. The boulder clay is of a particularly hard, stiff nature, full of large and beautifully striated and polished boulders mostly of basalt, and is covered by a layer of water-rolled pebbles and coarse stratified sand, almost three feet thick, upon which is a natural land surface with trees apparently from 50 to 100 years old. The altitude of the surface of this bank is at a somewhat higher level than the beds on the Curran, from which it is separated by the two lines of broad and narrow gauge railway and the public road. Although the pebbles and sand are in all reasonable probability of the same age as the raised beach upon the Curran, yet, owing to the separation mentioned above, their exact continuity cannot be absolutely traced, nor their precise position in the series definitely fixed, though in all probability the boulder clay was partly denuded before the gravels were laid down, and the portions of gravels, &c., at the bauxite works represent the shoreward end of the series, deposited against and partly over the boulder clay. The works are now approaching completion, and no exact record has been kept of the deeper foundations such as the tall chimney for instance, but we saw a pit sunk for part of the machinery, at which place the boulder clay is about 11 ft. to 12 ft. deep.

A boring for a well is in progress, and has now reached a depth of 130 feet. On being interrogated, the workmen regretted that a more accurate record of the strata passed through had not been kept, but they reported verbally as follows, in the order of descent:—

1. Gravel with shells.
2. Black clay (qy. Lias?).
3. Limestone (qy. a boulder?).
4. White alabaster and clay. ⎫
5. Red clay. ⎬ Keuper marls.
6. Blue clay. ⎭

We obtained a sample of the boring at 130 feet depth, and it is clearly a portion of the blue Triassic Keuper marl, a clay with gypsum veins.

From the above noted results we may reasonably infer that the Field Club has had no very serious loss from not having had an earlier opportunity of inspecting the excavations at these works.

F. W. LOCKWOOD, Belfast.

[Miss Thompson writes that "shells" from the black clay (bed No. 2 above) gathered by the workmen, have been sent up by Mr. Close, the architect, and they turn out to be Lias fossils, including fine specimens of *Gryphæa incurva* obtained eight feet down in the black mud; showing that Mr. Lockwood's supposition is correct.—EDS.]

THE GREAT AUK (ALCA IMPENNIS) AS AN IRISH BIRD.

BY G. E. H. BARRETT-HAMILTON, B.A.

So little is known of the past occurrences or status in Ireland of the Great Auk, that I think no apology is needed for bringing to the notice of readers of the *Irish Naturalist* the statement of Mr. W. J. Knowles in his " Third Report on the Pre-historic Remains from the Sandhills of the Coasts of Ireland"[1] that he had obtained on the Antrim coast bones which had been identified by Mr. E. T. Newton, of the Geological Survey, as those of the Great Auk. These bones were obtained in the sandhills of Whitepark Bay, Co. Antrim, in conjunction with human remains which Mr. Knowles believes to be those of the earliest Neolithic inhabitants of Ireland. In accumulations of the same age were found bones of the Horse, and of the Dog or Wolf (whether wild or domesticated is uncertain), as well as remains of geese, ducks, and gulls. Mr. Knowles remarks that "from the number of bones [of the Great Auk] which have been found, it must have been a common inhabitant of the North of Ireland at the time when the people of the Stone Age occupied Whitepark Bay and other parts of the coast." In a previous paper[2] Mr. Knowles recorded the finding, in the same locality, of two humeri of the Great Auk, besides bones of *Bos longifrons, Cervus elaphus,* Sheep or Goat, Fox, Pig, a small goose, a small gull, and cod. This statement is of such great interest, not only to Irish ornithologists, but to ornithologists in general, that it is a pity that it should be hidden away in a paper which deals with a subject other than natural history.

The only localities given by Professor Newton[3] where bones of the Great Auk have been found are in the kitchen-middens of Denmark, and in similar deposits in Caithness and Oronsay, and in a cave on the coast of Durham. The Irish locality, therefore, makes an interesting addition to our knowledge of the distribution of this bird in past times. Mr. Knowles points out that the " old surfaces of the sandhills, with their shells, broken bones, and implements, are really kitchen-

---

[1] *Proc. R.I.A.* (3), vol. iii., No. 4, pp. 650-663 (Dec., 1895).

[2] *Proc. R.I.A.* (3), vol. i., No. 5 (1891).

[3] " Dictionary of Birds," article " Extermination," p. 220.

middens, and of the same nature as those of the continent, e.g., in Portugal, and also at various parts along the coast of France, as well as in Denmark. The fauna of the sandhills is wonderfully in line with that of the kitchen-middens of Denmark, and the finding of the Great Auk, which is now extinct in Europe, among the Irish remains, makes the likeness more complete."

As regards the occurrence of this bird on the Irish coasts in modern times, the last authenticated British example[1], and the last but two which is known to have lived, was taken alive near the entrance of Waterford Harbour, in May, 1834, by a fisherman named Kirby. It was kept alive for some little time by Mr. Jacob Gough of Horetown, in Co. Wexford, but eventually came into the hands of Dr. Burkitt of Waterford, and it is now in the museum of Trinity College, Dublin. The details of the capture of this bird, and of its subsequent history, as given by Thompson[2], appear to have been somewhat inaccurate, and have been corrected by Mr. J. H. Gurney, jun.,[3] on the authority of Dr. Burkitt. It was afterwards ascertained by Mr. Davies that a second specimen was procured on the Waterford coast at about the same time, but was not preserved.

Besides the above, details of three other occurrences are given by Thompson[4], but in no case was a specimen forthcoming. One of these specimens was stated, in a note communicated by Rev. Joseph Stopford, in February, 1844, to Dr. Harvey of Cork, no date being mentioned, to have been "obtained on the long strand of Castle Freke (in the west of the County of Cork); having been water-soaked in a storm." In the other case Thompson believed that two birds described to him by H. Bell, a wild-fowl shooter, as having been seen in Belfast Bay, on September 23rd, 1845, were of this species.[5]

---

[1] Newton, *Op. cit.*, p. 220.
[2] *Proc. Zool. Soc., Lond.*, 1835, p. 79; and "Nat. Hist. of Ireland," III., p. 238.
[3] *Zoologist*, 1868, pp. 1449-1453.
[4] *Op. cit.*, p. 239; *Zoologist*, 1868, pp. 1442-1453; 1869, pp. 1039-1043.
[5] The statement in Sampson's "Survey of Londonderry" (1802) that the *Alca Impennis*, Penguin, "frequents the rocks of that county and of Donegal," evidently refers to the Razorbill, which bird is not mentioned in his list. It is curious that Dr. Pocock describes "the Razorbill or Auk, as big as a Pheasant, with a parrot bill," as breeding at Horn Head in 1752—*vide* Dr. Stokes' edition of Pocock's "Tour in Ireland in 1752," p. 59.

IRISH CAVES.

BY R. LLOYD PRAEGER, B.E.

In his "Notes on the Irish Caves" (*I.N.*, iv., pp. 57-59, 1895), Dr. Scharff expressed a hope that readers of this Journal would add to the list of caves which he then published, and some additions were promptly made by Mr. Ussher and Mr. James Coleman (*ibid.*, p. 94). And in the last issue of the *Irish Naturalist*, Mr. Jameson has mentioned one or two others. In looking up the literature of this and kindred subjects recently, I met with some further references to caves, which are now given, arranged according to the plan adopted by Dr. Scharff. Only those caves are named which have not been mentioned in the papers quoted. I have not thought it necessary to give many additional references to caves which one or other of the writers named has already referred to.

Co. CLARE.
    Cave at Kiltannon near Tulla.
      White, Rev. P., "History of Clare," Dublin, 1893, p. 2.
    Caves of Kilcorney.
      Foot, F. J., *Geol. Survey Memoir to sheets* 114, 122, 123, 1863, p. 18.

Co. CORK.
    Cave at Cloyne.
      Brash, R. R., "Antiquities of Cloyne." *Journ. Kilkenny and S.E. of Ireland Archæol Soc.*, n.s. II. 1858-59, p. 258.
    Cave at Ballybronock near Castlemartyr.
      Croker, T. C., "Researches in the South of Ireland." 1824.
      Ussher, R. J., in "Second Report of the Committee . . . appointed for the Purpose of exploring the Caves of the South of Ireland." *Brit. Assoc. Report for* 1881, pp. 218-221.
    Cave at Carrigower.
      Ussher, R. J., in First Report, ditto, ditto. *Brit. Assoc. Report for* 1880, pp. 209-211; and *Geol. Mag.* (2) VII., 1880, pp. 512-514.

Co. GALWAY.
    The Pigeon Hole, Cong.
      Nolan, J., *Geol. Survey Memoir to sheet* 70, 1877, p. 10, &c., &c.
    Pollduagh and cavern of Beagh River.
      Kinahan, G. H., *Geol. Survey Memoir to sheets* 124 *and* 125, 1863, p. 7.
    Many caves about Coole, most of them still occupied by streams.
      Kinahan, C. H., *loc. cit.*, pp. 7-9.

Co. LEITRIM.
    Templepatrick, in upper part of Glencar.
    Dermod and Graunia's Bed, Glenarriff.
      Wynne, A. B., *Geol. Survey Memoir to sheets* 42 *and* 43, 1885, p. 28.

Co. MAYO.
  Caves of Aille.
    Symes, R. G., *Geol. Survey Memoir to sheet* 75, 1872, p. 9.
Co. MONAGHAN.
  Rock House, Carrickmacross, &c.
    Nolan, J., *Geol. Survey Memoir to sheet* 70, 1877, p. 10.
Co. SLIGO.
  Keishcorran and others.
    Cruise, R. J., *Geol. Survey Memoir to sheets* 66 and 67, 1878, p. 13.
  Caves on Ben Bulben.
  Caves at Lissadill.
    Wynne, A. B., *Geol. Survey Memoir to sheets* 42 and 43, 1885, p. 28.
  Kesh Caves.
  Gleniffe Caves.
    Hardman, E. T., "Limestone Caves of Sligo," in Wood-Martin's "History of Sligo," First vol., 1882, appendix A.
Co. WATERFORD.
  Cave at Nicholastown.
    Brownrigg, W. B., and Theodore Cooke, "Geological Description of the District extending from Dungarvan to Annestown, County of Waterford." *Journ. Geol. Soc. Dublin*, IX., 1860, pp. 8-12.

The caves at Anna-Clogh Mullon, Co. Cork, mentioned by Mr. Coleman, *loc. cit.*, are artificial, and should not therefore be included in the list of Irish caves.

In certain districts in Ireland caves are so numerous that any attempt to list them would be futile. Such, for instance, is portion of Co. Fermanagh, concerning which Mr. Thomas Plunkett, in reply to a query, stated that the hills around Enniskillen are riddled with caves, and that he could not attempt a list of them. So also in Cos. Mayo and Galway, in the district that stretches along the eastern shore of Lough Corrib from Cong to Galway, and in portions of Co. Clare, subterranean passages abound, so that the streams are continually disappearing into the earth and re-appearing at other places. But these caverns, being still occupied by the waters by which they were formed, are of course not so interesting to the student of either past or present cave-faunas as the older passages, long since deserted by the streams which excavated them, and subsequently tenanted by troglodytic insects, or roving beasts of prey, or pre-historic man.

IRISH FRESHWATER WORMS.
BY REV. HILDERIC FRIEND, F.L.S.

ALL true worms may be divided into two great classes or groups, based on the relative number of their bristles or setæ. If they are very numerous they are known as polychætous worms or Polychæta; if few, they are called oligochætous worms or Oligochæta. It is true that the rule has exceptions, and some worms belonging to the Oligochæta have more setæ than are to be found in some species belonging to the Polychæta; but then there are other considerations. As a rule the worms with many bristles are marine, and being specially adapted for life in the ocean are quite distinct in form from those belonging to the land and fresh water. Hence generally speaking the Oligochæta are terrestrial, the Polychæta marine. Of the Polychæta I shall for the present have nothing to say, further than this, that very rarely the Polychæta and Oligochæta meet, as one might expect in estuarine and salt-marsh habitats. The true Oligochæta again are separable into two very distinct groups, and the order contains the terrestrial forms and those which are found either in or near fresh water. The terrestrial forms or true earthworms have received considerable notice in these pages, and while we still hope to add a few further species to the Irish list, it may be said roughly that the earthworms of Ireland are well known. Of the limicolous and aquatic species, however, we have heretofore been in absolute ignorance. They are small, not easily discovered, and when found are very difficult to determine, so that one need not wonder that they have been little studied. Now, however, thanks to the labours of Mr. Beddard, we have a Monograph[1] which contains much information for the guidance of the student, and it is to be hoped that before long the aquatic worms of Ireland will be as completely understood as the larger species are.

Thanks to the kindness of my indefatigable correspondent, Mr. Trumbull of Malahide, I have already been able to make a start with the study, and I send a first instalment in order if possible to secure the interest and aid of the large and ready band of co-workers who so generously supplied me with

---

[1] F. E. Beddard, "Monograph of the Oligochæta." Oxford, 1895.

materials for my former studies. To these and to any new workers who would like to send me material, a few hints may be permitted. Where, it may be asked, shall specimens be sought? We answer, everywhere! The smaller worms are ubiquitous. Being in the neighbourhood of a village in Cumberland the other day, I saw a little gutter flowing on to a piece of waste land. Here some dirty straw and vegetable matter was being saturated with the ooze, a handful of which I picked up, wrapped in paper, and carried home. To my surprise I found that the dirty straws were crowded with a beautiful little red worm new to science, hundreds of which crawled forth from their hiding-place or hunting-ground when the material was laid upon an old dish. The ooze on the margins of ponds, ditches, lakes, and estuaries should be examined, also the roots of grasses and plants in and near the water's edge, the moss and plants on damp rocks or dripping ledges, or wherever there is moisture. Mr. Trumbull has sent me a species, which is probably new to science, from a decaying elm tree, and I have found other species in decaying leaves, among debris, manure, and even in water-tanks, springs and wells. They are usually small, and may be easily overlooked, but a little practice will make collecting easy.

Most specimens may be sent with a small quantity of the earth, or water, moss, leaves, or debris among which they are found, and should either be placed in tubes, bottles, or tin boxes with damp moss. Care should be taken so to pack them that they will not be subject to battering in transit, or the delicate creatures will probably arrive quite dead and unrecognizable. It is of the utmost importance that as many species as possible should be studied in a living condition, as it is only by this means that many of the difficulties relating to the aquatic species can be cleared up.

I will now give an account of those worms which, through the kindness of Mr. Trumbull, I have been able to examine. They were collected at Malahide, April 1st, 1896, and it is important to note the date when collections are made because all worms do not mature at the same time, and we are anxious to ascertain what season of the year yields the best results in the matter of adult forms. Take for example—

Lumbriculus variegatus, Müller.—I have never yet seen this in its adult stage, and Beddard says that the reproductive organs have not yet been properly described, though the worm has long been under observation. This species is, among the aquatics, pretty much what *Lumbricus terrestris* formerly was among the earthworms. If a water-worm was found it was formerly customary to call it *Lumbriculus*, and there was an end of the matter. Beddard gives but this one species, though I am certain we have at least two if not three species already discovered in Great Britain. I have no doubt about the Irish species belonging to Beddard's form (Monograph, p. 214). I had the good fortune to see one of the specimens throw off its tail, just as a crab or lobster will cast a claw, when in danger or irritated, and the question of its regeneration has been the subject of special study by more than one biologist. The *Lumbriculus* is one of the largest and most active of our aquatic worms, being two or three inches long, and as large round as a piece of grocer's twine or a large pin. It wriggles violently if captured, and may be frequently met with in weedy ponds and lakes or wide ditches. It is quite aquatic in habit, and has the setæ in four pairs on each segment. The most beautiful and striking feature is the blind contractile appendages to the blood-vessels, which can be readily seen through the transparent integument. Mr. Beddard (p. 209) gives a figure after Claparède. The pharynx occupies the second, third, and fourth segments, then follows the œsophagus in the fifth and sixth segments, the intestine commencing in the seventh. The intestine can at once be recognized by the presence of special (chloragogen) cells. The body usually appears of a greenish brown hue, and there are as many as 200 segments. In England a second species, nearly allied to this, but I believe as yet unnamed, is found under the strong growths of moss and waterweed which choke the streamlets flowing into our Cumberland lakes. I mention this in the hope that some one living near the lakes of Ireland may be induced to examine similar localities with a view to adding other species to the list.

Limnodrilus Udekemianus, Clap.—I am in doubt about the actual identity of this worm owing to the fact that Beddard's account is meagre, and I am unable to consult the original memoirs of Claparède and Vaillant. It may yet prove a new species, and I therefore give my observations without reference to Beddard's account. Unfortunately an accident with my specimens resulted in their being destroyed before I had completed my study or mounted a specimen for further reference. The setæ, five or six (even up to eight) in each bundle of the anterior segments, are seated on papillæ. About four setæ in the posterior bundles, bifid, the outer tooth being much the larger of the two. Blood-vessel springing from segment 12, dilating in segment 9 (sometimes going back to segment 10 when the worm is in motion). I observed here and there a constriction of the large blood-vessel near the dilatations as if for a valve. Penial setæ wanting. The trumpet-shaped chitinous penis (or penis-sheath) not more than four times as long as broad (resembling that of my new species, *Limnodrilus Wordsworthianus*). Dark chloragogen cells beginning immediately behind segment 5. Spermathecæ with short, uncoiled tubes, little, if any, longer than the chamber. Should this eventually prove to be a new species I shall supply figures when I submit the account to the Royal Irish Academy.

Hemitubifex Benedii (D'Ud.).—Here again, owing to the imperfect state of our knowledge, and the number of synonyms, I am somewhat in doubt. This is just the worm which I should have named *Tubifex papillosus*, and such is the name given to a species by Claparède which Beddard (p. 261) places under the above heading. It is a wonderfully interesting worm, with capilliform and forked setæ, length about one inch, the first third of the body being about three times as thick as the posterior part. Head very small compared with the segments containing the organs of generation; about 70 segments in all. The body entirely covered with papillæ. Beddard says the papillæ are wanting on the clitellum of *H. Benedii*. I could not, however, find a girdle on my specimens, and as we find setæ wanting on the girdle of many worms when they are adult which possess them invariably in a younger stage, possibly the girdle of this worm discards its papillæ when it becomes adult. This is a point for further observation. The capilliform and forked setæ alike extend through the whole extremity of the worm's body, the capilliform setæ being in the dorsal bundles only. As many as nine or ten capilliform setæ in the anterior bundles, but six or eight is the most usual number, gradually decreasing till at the posterior extremity there is usually only one. Dilating hearts in segments 7 and 8; the dark cells of the œsophagus beginning in segment 5. The forked setæ of the under-side sigmoid, much curved, the outer tooth being smaller than the inner one. While the outer tooth goes almost straight forward, the inner tooth is greatly curved. Blood red; body-segments composed of prominent annuli, three or more to each segment.

In addition to the foregoing I found among the gleanings part of a very pretty lumbriculid about two inches in length, but as the head and important segments were missing I cannot be sure of the species. A later consignment included a white worm found in an old decaying elm tree, which I have no doubt is a new species of *Fridericia*. The brain, spermathecæ, and setæ are all so well-marked and characteristic that I propose to describe it for the Irish Academy under the name of *Fridericia ulmicola*. These preliminary remarks will, I trust, suffice to show how interesting a field lies open here for any one who wishes to pursue a new course of investigations.

NOTES ON A ZOOLOGICAL EXPEDITION TO VALENCIA ISLAND, CO. KERRY.

SHORE-COLLECTING AND DREDGING,

BY F. W. GAMBLE, M.SC.,

Demonstrator and Assistant Lecturer in Zoology, Owens College, Manchester.

AT the beginning of April, 1895, Mr. E. T. Browne (Univ. Coll., London), Mr. W. I. Beaumont, and the author paid a visit to Valencia Island for the purpose of making further observations on certain groups of marine invertebrate animals, which we had severally investigated at Professor Herdman's Laboratory, Port Erin, Isle of Man, and also at the Marine Biological Association's Laboratory at Plymouth.

Mr. Browne's object was to examine the composition and seasonal changes of the floating fauna by the aid of the tow-net. The present article is, however, confined to a record of the forms obtained by Mr. Beaumont and myself, by means of shore-collecting and shallow-water dredging in Valencia Harbour and the immediate neighbourhood during April and May of last year. The groups referred to are, chiefly, the Hydroids, Nemertea, Turbellaria, Gephyrea, Nudibranchiate Mollusca, and the Pycnogonida or "Sea-spiders." Since these groups are, for the most part, composed of small and soft-bodied animals, requiring careful observation for their detection, and microscopical methods for their determination, we resolved if possible to fit up a temporary laboratory in which we could examine our captures at leisure, and keep them under observation for some time. We were fortunately able to carry out this resolve successfully.

It is to Prof. A. C. Haddon that we are indebted for suggesting Valencia Island as the base of operations. The advantages which it offers are, a rich fauna close at hand; a well-sheltered harbour, enabling us to dredge under conditions of weather that would have rendered the use of a small boat in a more exposed situation out of the question; and finally it is now easily accessible by the Great Southern and Western Railway. We were also greatly aided in discovering the most favourable localities, and in many other ways, by the vicar of Valencia (the Rev. A. Delap) and his family, who contributed so largely in making our visit as successful as it was enjoyable.

Accepting Professor Haddon's suggestion, we landed on Valencia Island last April, bringing sufficient apparatus, chemicals, and instruments to stock a small laboratory. Soon after our arrival we obtained the use of the greater part of a conveniently situated house close to the beach. One large room we forthwith fitted up as our laboratory; in another room we stored our tackle and gear; and in a third we laid out the results of the day's dredging and shore-collecting in enamelled dishes. Dredging was carried on almost exclusively in the harbour itself from a small rowing boat. We hope on a future occasion to investigate the fauna of the deeper water outside.

Valencia Island (5 miles long and 2 wide) is bounded by the Port Magee Sound on the south, by the extensive shallow harbour on the north and east, and is open to the Atlantic on the west. About 12 miles out to sea, in a south-westerly direction, lie the fine Greater and Lesser Skellig Rocks. The former is well-known on account of the intactness of the cells, once occupied by the anchorites of the 8th and 9th centuries, which occur upon it: the latter from the fact of its being the chief nesting-place of Gannets in the neighbourhood.

The upper reaches of the harbour, especially that part known as Lough Mark, appear to be largely composed of submerged peat-bog. The harbour itself is shallow, having a depth of 8 or 9 fathoms only in certain spots. The bottom is chiefly mud, and with here and there collections of shells, but it becomes more sandy or gravelly as the mouth is approached. Church Island lies between the harbour and Lough Kay to the north, and we found the shore of this island to be the most prolific locality for shore-work. Indeed at low springs, Valencia Harbour is an exceedingly favourable district for the study of littoral animals.

I will first give a description of the fauna between tide-marks according to the localities we examined, and will then proceed to detail the results obtained by dredging. In considering these notes it must be remembered that our visit followed upon an exceedingly severe winter, the effects of which could scarcely fail to thin the numbers of certain groups ; and secondly, that though we explored a portion of the district very carefully, a number of localities were either not examined, or insufficiently searched.

Beyond the quay opposite our laboratory, a sandy spit is exposed at low tides. In the immediate neighbourhood of the quay and on this spit, *Clava squamata* occurred, the ova of which, at first pinkish in colour, become purple or bright blue when mature. *Coryne vaginata* (with gonophores) was found here, and generally from this point westward to the light-house at the harbour-mouth. *Eolis papillosa* was breeding on the spit itself, and was accompanied by *Elysia viridis*; the Turbellaria, *Leptoplana tremellaris*, *Fecampia erythrocephala*, *Plagiostoma Girardi*; the Nemertea, *Lineus obscurus*, *L. longissimus*, *Amphiporus lactifloreus*, *Carinella annulata*; and lastly, *Dinophilus tæniatus*.

Westwards from the spit lies a long strip of collecting ground in the direction of Glanleam, terminating for practical purposes just beyond some pools, in which the purple burrowing sea-urchin (*Strongylocentrotus lividus*) occurs in numbers. At low spring tides, *Zostera*-beds are here uncovered, and on these and under the loose boulders the following fauna was obtained :—*Actinia equina*, *Anemonia cereus*, *Actinoloba dianthus*, *Sagartia bellis*, *S. troglodytes*, *S. venusta*, *S. nivea*, *Tealia crassicornis*, *Bunodes gemmaceus*, *Corynactis viridis*, and *Cereanthus Lloydii*. The Hydroids were not abundant, and had apparently suffered from the severity of the preceding winter. We obtained, however, on this ground small colonies of a species of *Rhizogeton* very similar to *R. fusiformis*, Agassiz, a genus new to British seas, and hitherto only described from Massachusetts Bay. A number of the commoner species of *Campanularia* and *Sertularia* occurred here, together with *Coryne pusilla* and *C. vaginata*. In the "lividus" pools the creeping medusa *Clavatella prolifera* was obtained, with young budding off from it. The Polyclad Turbellaria, probably abundant here in a good season, were represented by *Stylochoplana maculata*, *Leptoplana tremellaris*, *Stylostomum variabile*, and *Cycloporus papillosus*: the Rhabdocœlida by *Proxenetes flabellifer*, *Promesostoma marmoratum*, *Macrorhynchus Nægelii*, *Monotus fuscus*, and *M. lineatus*. Several species of the Nemertine genus *Tetrastemna* were found, including *T. dorsale*, *T. candidum*, *T. vermiculatum*, and *T. melanocephalum* (var. *diadema*). The Annelids were extensively represented on this ground, and *Siphonostoma diplochætos*, *Halosydna gelatinosa*, and a form, apparently *Myrianida maculata* (Clap.) (= *Myrianida pennigera* of Montagu), were noted, the last bearing a chain of buds at its hinder end. A Gephyrean, *Phymosoma papillosum*, Thompson, was dug out of the tide-pools. It has been previously taken by Dr. Kinahan from the coast of Clare, by Dr. Norman in Birterbuy bay, and from Polperro by Laughrin. The Nudibranch Molluscs were abundant. *Archidoris tuberculata* was spawning, *Acanthodoris pilosa* (several varieties), *Goniodoris nodosa* and *Jorunna Johnstoni*, *Polycera quadrilineata*, *Triopa claviger*, *Ægirus punctilucens*, *Eolis papillosa*, a form identical with *E. Peachii*, A. and H., *Æolidella glauca*, *Facelina coronata*, *Favorinus albus*, *Coryphella gracilis*, and perhaps best of all *Antiopa hyalina*, occurred here. The last species has not, I believe, been previously recorded from this coast. In addition, *Limapontia nigra*, *Actæonia corrugata* and *Elysia viridis*, *Pleurobranchus plumula*, and very small *Aplysia punctata*, form the list of Opisthobranchiate molluscs. Of the Pycnogonida, the most interesting form on this shore was *Anoplodactylus virescens*, Hodge, apparently a new species for Ireland, as Mr. G. H. Carpenter, who has kindly examined the collection of Pycnogonida, informs me. *Ammothea echinata*, and *Pycnogonum littorale* also occurred in this locality.

Below Glanleam, the seat of the Knight of Kerry, is a shore composed of boulders imbedded in sand. This, although not so prolific a locality as the last, yielded the following, in addition to many of the foregoing species. NEMERTEA:—*Nemertes Neesii*, *Micrura fasciolata*, *Lineus longissimus*; NUDIBRANCHIA:— *Facelina punctata*. A Decapod (*Xantho rivulosa*) is abundant here, and Kinahan found it when collecting at Valencia. (*Nat. Hist. Review*, 1857, vol. iv).

A short walk across the headland bounding the entrance to the harbour on the south, brings one near Murreagh Point to a bay, which at low water affords good collecting. *Myriothela phrygia* and *Corynactis viridis* are the most striking Cœlentera, while *Coryphella gracilis* and *Æolidella glauca* are the most characteristic Nudibranchs. Church Island, however, is the best locality for shore-collecting, particularly at the lowest spring tides. *Myriothela* is again abundant, *Haliclystus auricula* clusters on the *Zostera*-beds, and *Caryophyllia Smithii* occurs under stones. The Polyclad Turbellaria occurring on the opposite side of the harbour are here also, and in greater numbers, together with *Nemertes Neesii*, *Cephalothrix bioculata* and the other Nemertea. *Acanthodoris pilosa* and *aspera*, *Jorunna Johnstoni*, *Favorinus albus* and *Pleurobranchus plumula* again occur, with many of their congeners. The Annelids *Polymnia nebulosa*, *Lanice conchilega* and *Siphonostoma diplochætos* are fairly abundant. Lastly, there exists here a rich Echinoderm fauna which we did not thoroughly examine. *Holothuria nigra*, *Cucumaria cucumis*, *Ocnus brunneus* and *O. lacteus* were some of the more obvious forms.

Very different from this fauna is that inhabiting the muddy shore of Lough Mark, which is largely a submerged peat-bog. In the wood a species of *Pholas* burrows, and the Gephyrea *Thalassema Neptuni* and *Phascolosoma tenuicinctum*, McCoy (= *Ph. elongatum*, Keferstein) are present in the peat; the last, which was found originally by McCoy on this coast (*Ann. Mag. Nat. Hist.*, vol. xv., 1845) being very plentiful. *Lamellidoris bilamellata* was found here accompanied by very large specimens of *Facelina coronata* (spawning) and one or two other Eolids, including a stranded specimen of *Lomanotus Genei*, two inches long. *Nymphon gallicum*, Hoek (male with eggs), was the most interesting Pantopod. It is a southern form and was first described by Hoek from the coast of Brittany.[1] In a patch of gravel off Reenglass Point, the purple urchin (*Str. lividus*) occurs. On the shore of the Caher river at Ballycarbery Castle, *Myxicola infundibulum* is plentiful. It may be mentioned that this is a locality for *Bufo calamita*, the Natterjack Toad.

Turning now to the fauna obtained by dredging, it must be premised that as we only had the use of a rowing boat and were not able to dredge effectually outside the harbour, the results were in many hauls not unlike those of shore-collecting at low-springs. We discovered, however, two banks of shells

---

[1] Hoek, *Arch. Zool. Expt. et Gen.* ix: 1881, p. 445. See also Carpenter, "Pycnogonida of Irish Coasts." *Proc. Roy. Dub. Soc.*, vol. vii. (n.s.) pt. ii. 1893.

(*Pecten maximus*, *P. opercularis*, *Mya truncata*, &c.) which yielded excellent results. The rest of the bottom is covered with vast numbers of *Ascidiella aspersa*, and elsewhere with meadows of *Zostera* rooted in mud, except off Glanleam, where there is a bottom of sand and gravel, containing a limited but well-differentiated fauna.

The Hydroids were not well represented. The abundance and small size of the Medusa of *Corymorpha nutans* in the water of the harbour, argued the presence of the Hydroid in the immediate neighbourhood, but in spite of arduous labours we did not find it. In fact, notwithstanding the presence of several medusæ with known hydroid stocks, none of the latter were obtained. *Halecium Beanii* was dredged once (with gonophores) in the harbour. The two species of *Antennularia* were common, and upon these were young specimens of *Lomanotus Genei*, *Doto coronata* and *D. fragilis*. *Doto pinnatifida* occurred a couple of times on the shelly ground in company with the following:—*Epizoanthus Couchii*; TURBELLARIA:—*Prostheceræus vittatus, Oligocladus sanguinolentus, Eurylepta cornuta* and the other Polyclads taken in the littoral zone. NEMERTEA: —*Amphiporus dissimulans*, Riches, *Tetrastemma flavidum* (var. *longissimum*), *Carinella aragoi, Lineus bilineatus, Micrura fusca, M. fasciolata, M. purpurea*. ANNELIDA:—*Pontobdella muricata, Phascolion strombi, Phascolosoma papillosum*. OPISTHOBRANCHIA:—*Polycera ocellata, Eolis angulata, Coryphella Landsburghii, Cratena amœna, C. olivacea, Amphorina cærulea, Embletonia pulchra, Galvina picta*.[1] PYCNOGONIDA:—*Phoxichilus lævis, A. petiolatus,*[2] *Pallene brevirostris*, and great numbers of *Ammothea echinata*.

On the muddy ground of the harbour *Ascidiella aspersa* itself contains a small fauna. Its test was covered with *Antedon europæa* and riddled by *Crenella marmorata*, whilst amongst the mud of its attachment, the three species of *Micrura*, *Siphonostoma diplochætos* and *Phascolosoma tenuicinctum* were found. The Turbellaria and Nemertea were identical with those of the shelly ground. *Amphiporus lactifloreus* however

---

[1] Prof. Haddon in a list of forms from Valencia, July, 1887, which he has kindly communicated to me, notes *G. Farrani*, now, according to some authors, a variety of *G. tricolor* Forbes.

[2] Along with *Anopl. petiolatus*, Kr., we obtained specimens of *A. pygmæus*, Hodge. Canon Norman (*Ann. Mag. Nat. Hist.* (6) xiii., 1894, pp. 153-4) considers the latter to be immature examples of *A. petiolatus*.

occurred here, but not *A. dissimulans*. Among the Annelids *Ammotrypane aulogastra*, Rathke, was common, and a species of *Chætopterus* occurred a few times. *Philine aperta*, *Ph. punctata*, *Ph. catena* were very characteristic Opisthobranchia.

A word or two remains to be said concerning the occurrence of a species of *Polygordius* in fair numbers on patches of gravel off Glanleam. It is difficult to state which of the known species this approaches most closely, and we hope to investigate the matter further. Comparison with M'Intosh's specimens of *P. apogon* from Bressay Sound in the Shetlands, seems to indicate that our specimens resembled this species more than the others, although the eyes, which are a diagnostic feature of the northern form, were absent. Since the discovery of *Polygordius* at Valencia, we have found it off Port Erin (Isle of Man), and also at Plymouth, associated usually with *Glycera capitata*, *Embletonia pulchra*, and a few other forms which affect a gravelly bottom.

In conclusion I may draw attention to some of the more interesting forms which fell to our lot while shore-collecting and dredging. In reference to these, previous Irish records have been consulted so far as the time at my disposal has permitted. But the publication of faunistic notes relating to the Irish marine Invertebrate fauna, in many often inaccessible journals and papers, renders this a matter of the greatest difficulty.

Messrs. T. and A. Scott[1] have published descriptions of a new genus (*Lomanticola insolens* n.g. n.sp.) and two new species (*Aplostoma Beaumonti* and *A. hibernica* n.spp.) of parasitic Copepoda which were found respectively in *Lomanotus Genei*, Ver., and in Compound Ascidians, at Valencia. A species of a genus of Hydroidea (*Rhizogeton* sp.) new to the British seas is in Mr. Browne's hands for description. The Pycnogonid *Anoplodactylus virescens*, Hodge, is apparently new to the coast of Ireland. Of the Nudibranchiate Mollusca, *Amphorina cœrulea* (Mont.), *Antiopa hyalina*, A. & H., *Lomanotus Genei*, Ver., and *Embletonia pulchra*, A. & H., are noteworthy forms, if not new to the coast. The abundance of species of *Micrura*, and the occurrence of *Amphiporus dissumulans*, Riches, are perhaps the more interesting results of Mr. Beaumont's work at the Nemertea. Among the

---

[1] *Annals and Mag. Nat. Hist.*, Ser. 6, vol. xvi., 1895, p. 353.

Turbellaria, the list of which I fully expect to increase very considerably, *Prostheceræus vittatus*, Mont., *Oligocladus sanguinolentus*, Lang, and, *Stylochoplana maculata*, Quatref., are worthy of mention. Finally the occurrence of a species of *Polygordius* has, I believe, not before been signalised from the coast of Ireland.

PROCEEDINGS OF IRISH SOCIETIES.

ROYAL ZOOLOGICAL SOCIETY.

Recent donations include a Badger from the Earl of Granard, a pair of Peacocks from A. Bell, Esq., a Macaw from V. W. Brown, Esq., and a pair of Herons from E. Blake Knox, Esq. Two St. Kilda lambs, a hybrid calf, and a pigmy calf, have been born in the Gardens.

8,070 persons visited the Gardens during March.

DUBLIN MICROSCOPICAL CLUB.

MARCH 19th.—The Club met at Mr. W. N. ALLEN'S.

Mr. MOORE exhibited *Nectria aurantium*, Kick. At a previous meeting Mr. Moore had exhibited a pseudo-bulb of an unnamed species of *Anguloa* from South America, which was infested with a fungus. The fungus was the species now exhibited. It is remarkable that several distinct species of *Nectria* have been found growing on Orchids in the houses at Glasnevin. The species in question is uncommon. It had previously been recorded as growing on the Laburnum and Aspen Poplar in Thuringia, and on the Ash tree in Belgium.

Mr. G. PIM showed the æcidiospores of *Puccinia Lapsanæ*, Schultze, sent by Mr. Burbidge, from the Trinity College Gardens. The fungus produces crimson spots on the leaves on which nestle the clusters of pale yellow peridia, forming a very pretty low-power object.

Mr. MCARDLE exhibited fertile specimens of *Cephalozia Turneri*, Hook., which were sent to him by Mr. M. B. Slater, F.L.S., of Malton, Yorkshire. They were collected in Maine Co., California, in May, 1894, by Professor Marshall A. Howe, of the University at Berkely.

In Ireland it is one of the rarest liverworts; it was first found by Miss Hutchins near Bantry, Co. Cork, who sent it to Sir William Hooker, and he named it to perpetuate the memory of his friend Dawson Turner; an excellent description and figure of the plant is given in his grand work on the "British Hepaticæ." From the date 1811, ? when it was collected by Miss Hutchins, we have no record that it was found again until 1873, when it was collected in small quantity at Cromaglown,

Killarney, by Professor Lindberg. In England it is known to grow in one station in Sussex, rare and local in France, found also in the Canary Islands (Webb) near Tangier, Africa (Salzman.) This curious and pretty plant is remarkable in having pectinato-dentate leaves, and in its close affinity to several genera, especially *Anthelia*

MARCH 16th.—The Club met at the house of Prof. GRENVILLE COLE, who exhibited a large section, prepared for the Royal College of Science, from an opal-bearing rhyolite occurring on Sandy Braes, Co. Antrim. Radial chalcedonic groupings occur in clear amorphous opal, the structure being, as usual, well brought out by crossed nicols.

Mr. PIM showed, on behalf of CANON RUSSELL of Geashill, a minute *Nectria*, probably *N. sanguinea*. The perithecia are scattered, somewhat pyriform, papillate, and of a deep red colour; the sporidia are uniseptate and uno-bi-seriate.

Mr. M'ARDLE exhibited a fertile specimen of the rare liverwort *Scapania compacta*, Dumort., which he found last year amongst rocks on the bank of the River Barrow near Borris, Co. Carlow, when collecting for the Flora and Fauna Committee of the Royal Irish Academy. Dr. D. Moore, in his work on the Irish Hepaticæ, states that the only specimens he collected of the true plant are from the neighbourhood of Brandon, Co. Kerry, which were sterile in both places where it was observed growing.

Mr. A. VAUGHAN JENNINGS exhibited a leaf of *Arisarum vulgare* from Bordighera, North Italy, containing the endophytic alga *Phyllosiphon arisari*, Kühn, which is only known on that plant, and only from the Riviera and West Italian coast. A preparation under a low power showed the unicellular (cœnocytic) branching filament spreading through the leaf-tissues, and its contents breaking up in parts into very minute spores. Another slide showed these spores under a high power, when they were seen to be oval bodies with a central nucleus and a bright spot toward each pole. The plant resembles closely a green siphonaceous alga such as *Vaucheria*, but it seems to live to a great extent parasitically on the leaf-tissues, which it destroys. No sexual organs are known; and the method of asexual reproduction differs entirely from that of *Vaucheria*, the immense number of minute spores having almost a fungoid aspect.

Mr. G. H. CARPENTER showed specimens of the minute crane-fly *Molophilus ater*, Mg., recently collected by Mr. J. N. Halbert, near Roundstone. This species, probably common in hilly and northern districts, is of interest on account of the great reduction of the wings in both sexes.

Mr. HENRY J. SEYMOUR showed sections of a hornblende schist from Killiney. The rock occurs just north of the garden wall of Killiney Park, near the junction of the granite and slate. In the slides a schistose structure is clearly seen, and hornblende, a pyroxene, some quartz and numerous plagioclase crystals can be identified. The rock may have been originally a diorite or a pyroxene aphanite. A photo-micrograph of the section taken by Mr. Mitchell was also shown.

BELFAST NATURALISTS' FIELD CLUB.

MARCH 17th.—The PRESIDENT in the chair. Prof. COLE, F.G.S., read a short paper on the Rhyolites of Co. Antrim. Subsequently the Fifth Annual Meeting of the Microscopical Section was held, the evening being devoted to a display of microscopical objects, and to demonstrations of mounting, &c. The following exhibited—Rev. John Andrew (Chairman of the Section); J. J. Andrew, Miss M. K. Andrews, Miss S. M. Thompson, Mrs. Blair, J. O. Campbell, W. B. Drummond, P. F. Gulbrausen, W. A. Firth, L. Roscorla, James Murdoch, William Gray, A. M'J. Cleland, James Stelfox, W. S. M'Kee, J. Lorrain Smith, Cecil Shaw, H. M'Cleery, Joseph Wright, W. F. de V. Kane, and W. D. Donnan (Sec. of the Section).

BOTANICAL SECTION.—MARCH 28th.—Mr. J. H. DAVIES read an interesting paper on Casuals. It was illustrated by a fine set of mounted plants, kindly lent for the occasion by an old friend of the writer, a Yorkshire botanist, Mr. William Foggitt, who has given considerable attention to this class of plants. Mention was made of the spread within recent years of *Veronica Buxbaumii*, *Silene noctiflora* and *Trifolium agrarium*. *Silene dichotoma*, first noticed in our district two years ago by Mr. David Redmond, has been known to produce 330 capsules on one plant. Many of these plants are brought in with foreign seed, and one cannot but speculate as to the future possibilities of their spreading. Mr. Richard Hanna, who contributed a remarkable list of these alien plants to the recent "Supplement to the Flora of N.E. Ireland," exhibited some which he had collected in the neighbourhood of Belfast distilleries and flour mills.

GEOLOGICAL SECTION.—A week of geological studies, conducted by Professor G. A. J. Cole, terminated on Tuesday, March 24. A paper on the structural details of the Antrim rhyolites, read at the Club's microscopical meeting, fitly commenced the course, lantern slides showing the microscopic characters of these lavas, varied by others of rhyolitic areas in other parts of Great Britain. The first field excursion was to Squire's Hill, where the series of Cretaceous quarries were visited, Professor Cole pointing out and explaining the methods in which the many dykes had intruded through the sedimentary rocks, also drawing the attention of his students to the difference between our Cretaceous series and that of England. A visit to the basaltic quarry led the party across Carr's Glen to the Cavehill quarry, with its great dyke, showing horizontal columns, which traverses the Chalk and the overlying basalt. The second excursion made an early start for Stewartstown, involving a walk of ten miles through fine, rolling country, to Tullyconnell for the Permian strata that are so rare in Ireland, a block *in situ*, nine or ten feet long, with stray fragments in an adjacent cottage garden, being all that here remains. The Castle Farm quarries at Stewartstown furnished fossils from the Carboniferous limestone, some pits in the lower Coal-measures being passed on the return drive to Dungannon. Friday saw the party walking from Dundonald through the interesting esker of partially-cemented gravels full of travelled pebbles, by the old road to Scrabo. The intrusive sheets and dykes of Scrabo have acted as a protective skeleton, and preserved the hill and its capping of dolerite when the surrounding unprotected area was denuded away. Saturday was devoted to the rhyolitic area, which has been specially studied by Professor Cole for some years, and magnificent weather favoured the party as they drove from Doagh to Sandy Braes.

After the welcome rest of Sunday, the geologists made a fresh start on Monday, the place selected being Barney's Point, near Magheramorne, where an abundant store of lower Lias fossils was obtained, including *Ceromya gibbosa*. Fragments of Rhætic rocks led Professor Cole to point out that these Liassic beds had probably overridden the lower strata. Walking across the backbone of Islandmagee, the party inspected the fine cliffs at the Gobbins. Yet more splendid weather favoured the final excursion on Tuesday, and the 7.30 train saw ten members on their way to Newcastle. The dykes that traverse the uplifted Ordovician strata (in some cases themselves traversed by later dykes) were inspected under Professor Cole's guidance. Professor Cole subsequently led the party up by Bloody Bridge and Glen Fofanny valley to the ridge above, which led to an explanation of the origin of the great detrital fans, which have hitherto been regarded as moraines. Mr. La Touche, of the Geological Survey of India, also mentioned the making of such fans in the Himalayas in a few hours by a flood. An ascent of Thomas Mountain to inspect the Ordovician rock that overlies the granite—a reminder of the great sedimentary arch under which the latter molten rock accumulated —was the prelude of the final descent through the grounds of Donard Lodge.

APRIL 1st.—The Secretary's annual report of the section's work was read by Mr. F. W. LOCKWOOD, and, being passed, was sent on to the Committee of the Club. Miss M. K. ANDREWS subsequently gave a brief account of some of the investigations of the Swiss "Gletscher-Kommission" into the results and cause of the remarkable glacier-avalanche that occurred at the Altels on the 11th September, 1895.

APRIL 6th.—An excursion to Murlough Bay on Easter Monday was carried out. A party of 15 started by the 6.30 train from Belfast, and drove from Ballycastle to Murlough Bay, probably the most picturesque bit of coast in County Antrim. The geology is also of great interest, the most ancient rocks in the county (metamorphic), occurring near sea level, followed by the basal conglomerates of the Carboniferous period. Ascending in altitude and in geological line, the spectator admires the fine slopes of ruddy Trias, upon which rest the interesting pebble beds that indicate the western shores of the great Cretaceous ocean that once rolled between this and the Crimea. A considerable time was spent in searching for the fossils that occur somewhat sparingly in this conglomerate, which is not developed in England. The homeward walk along the noble cliffs of Fair Head fitly introduced the period of volcanic activity, whose results have made Antrim what it is, preserving many rocks from denudation that have vanished in other parts of our island. The weather was splendid, and a glorious sunset gratified the travellers on the homeward journey.

APRIL 21.—The annual meeting of the Club was held, the outgoing president (Mr. F. W. LOCKWOOD) in the chair. Before the regular business was proceeded with, Mr. WILLIAM GRAY, M.R.I.A., delivered the report of his visit to Dublin, Cork, and Limerick as the delegate of the Club under the auspices of the Irish Field Club Union. A few slight additions to the Club's rules were then agreed to, after which the president called upon the honorary treasurer (Mr. W. H. PHILLIPS) to read the statement of accounts, which were satisfactory, a small balance being to the credit of the Society. The honorary secretary then read the annual report, of which the following is an abstract. The Committee of the Belfast Naturalists' Field Club now lay before the members the 33rd Annual Report. The work of the Club has been steadily carried on during the past year, some good results having been obtained especially by the different sections of the Club, whilst an interesting co-operation with the different other scientific Societies of Ireland has been maintained. The Conference of all the Irish Field Clubs held in Galway during July under the auspices of I. F. C. Union, was a hearty stimulus in this direction. The creation of an entrance fee has acted as desired in keeping the membership of the Club within working bounds without materially affecting the finances of the Club. The membership now stands at 480—32 new members having been elected during the year, and 68 having been struck off. During July the London Geologists' Association visited Belfast, and were officially received and entertained by the Club. During their stay different members of the Club acted as their guides during their excursions, and their programme and arrangements were attended to by the Honorary Secretaries. The Home Reading Union was treated in a similar manner. During March a week's good geological work was done in a systematic way under the instruction of Professor Cole, there being an excursion to different places of interest each day and a class each evening. The Geological Section with Miss S. M. Thompson as Secretary has been most active during the Session. The Microscopical Section has also been fairly active. The Celtic Class having been nurtured to maturity under the sheltering care of the Club has now formed a separate organization, "The Belfast Gaelic League," which is both active and prosperous. The Botanical Section formed during the year under the guidance of the Rev. C. H. Waddell, B.D., has made satisfactory progress, and will doubtless continue to keep this important study in the forefront of the Club's work. This section is the practical outcome of Professor Johnson's course of botanical lectures last session. Your Committee trust that during the coming session more individual research will be done by the members. In conclusion, your Committee express their satisfaction with the lengthened notices of the Club's proceedings given from month to month in the *Irish Naturalist*. The officers were then elected, as follow:—Lavens M. Ewart, M.R.I.A., President; Rev. C. H.

Waddell, B.D., Vice-President; William H. Phillips, Treasurer; William Swanston, F.G.S., Librarian; F. J. Bigger and Alex. G. Wilson, Honorary Secretaries; with the following Committee:—Miss S. M. Thompson, F. W. Lockwood, W. Gray, John Hamilton, W. J. Fennell, S. A. Stewart, R. J. Welch, Joseph Wright, John Vinycomb, and J. St. J. Phillips, Various suggestions in regard to the summer excursions were then taken up and considered. The following new members were then elected ;— Charles MacLorinan, LL.D., and Robert Ardill.

Dublin Naturalists' Field Club.

APRIL 21.—The evening was spent in hearing reports on the scientific results of an Easter trip to Connemara, in which a number of members took part. The chair was occupied by the PRESIDENT (Prof. GRENVILLE COLE). Mr. R. LLOYD PRAEGER gave a general account of the week's work, describing the beautiful district of which Roundstone is the centre, and its scientific attractions. Specimens were shown illustrative of the botany of the district, and of the rich shell-sand of Port-na-fedog. Lantern illustrations of the district were also shown, taken from photographs by Mr. R. Welch, Belfast. Dr. HERBERT HURST followed by exhibiting some frog's bones from Inis Mac Dara, a remote islet off the Connemara coast. The opinion was expressed that the frog was not a native of the island, the bones having probably been brought by a bird. Mr. LYSTER JAMESON spoke on the marine zoology of the district, and exhibited the results of dredgings carried out by the party. Mr. J. N. HALBERT described the insect life of the district, and showed a number of rare beetles and moths. Prof. T. JOHNSON spoke on a large collection of sea-weeds which were on exhibition, gathered during the week by a lady member of the party. The various reports mentioned above will appear in our pages when completed.

Subsequently Mr. PRAEGER showed, on behalf of Mr. A. Roycroft, bones, shells, &c., from a kitchen-midden at Lough Shinny, Co. Dublin. The PRESIDENT exhibited in the lantern slides illustrating the esker of Greenhills, Co. Dublin. Rev. MAXWELL CLOSE discussed the origin of these remarkable gravel ridges. The following were elected members of the Club :—Miss L. Allen, Miss M. Allen, J. C. Burlington, Mrs. Coffey, J. de W. Hinch.

APRIL 25.—The first excursion took place. A party of 36, which swelled to 57 *en route*, took the 1.45 train to Bray, and passing the new harbour, examined the old forest-bed underlying marine clay on the shore at low water, recently described before the Club by Mr. Praeger, who now pointed out on the ground the relations of this deposit to the neighbouring beds. After an hour's work examining the peat and clay, and shore-hunting, the party proceeded by the 4.0 o'clock train to Killiney, while a few remained to collect seaweeds at Bray. At Killiney, under guidance of the President (Prof. Cole) the famous junctions of the Ordovician and granite were visited, and Prof. Cole explained the geological phenomena displayed. Numerous specimens of the schist full of andalusite crystals were brought away for examination. The party returned to town by the 6.11 train from Dalkey.

FIELD CLUB NEWS.

The Easter excursion to Roundstone, in which a number of members of the Belfast and Dublin Field Clubs, and others, took part, was an unqualified success. No rain marred the enjoyment of the party, and investigations into the fauna, flora, and archæology of Connemara proceeded steadily. The scientific results, which were laid before the Dublin Club on April 21st, will appear duly in our pages.

A better centre than Roundstone for those desiring a holiday in a beautiful district abounding in interest for the naturalist could not be found. Situated on a sheltered arm of the Atlantic, in the midst of lovely scenery, all sorts of ground are within easy distance for the explorer—bays with a rich marine fauna, high mountains, sandy beaches, rock-pools, extensive bogs, innumerable lakes, and an excellent little hotel.

The Belfast Naturalists' Field Club has received the valuable gift of a large box of geological specimens from Mrs. Smythe, of Tobarcooran, Carnmoney. The collection belonged to the late General W. J. Smythe, R.A., C.B., formerly President of the Club.

NOTES.

BOTANY.

PHANEROGAMS.

Lathræa squamaria in Co. Down.—It may be of interest to some botanical readers to know that *Lathræa squamaria* is to be found growing in the woods in Lord Annesley's demesne at Castlewellan. It is most likely indigenous, as I have found it growing in several of the plantations nearly a mile apart, mostly under Portugal Laurels (*Cerasus lusitanicus*) of great age, also I have found it growing near the Bird-cherry (*Prunus padus*) and under some Elms (*Ulmus campestris*).

It would be interesting to know if *Lathræa squamaria* has been found growing in other districts in Ireland, and where?

T. RYAN, Castlewellan, Co. Down.

Early Hawthorn.—On 19th April, near Cabinteely, Co. Dublin, I saw a large Hawthorn tree in almost full bloom; there was nearly as much on the shady side as on that exposed to the sun. From the condition of the flowers, it was obvious that some must have been out at least on the 15th inst., if not sooner. Since then I have seen Hawthorn "May" (*sic*!) in various other places, including Rutland-square. Is this not almost a record for earliness?

GREENWOOD PIM, Dublin.

ZOOLOGY.

INSECTS.

Formica rufa, L., in Co. Wexford.—Though I am not a "formicologist" I have been for many years familiar with the large Wood Ant (*Formica rufa*) as a denizen of old Killoughrim Forest, in the County Wexford; and I forward this note on seeing that the Rev. W. F. Johnson in the April number of the *Irish Naturalist* asks for information concerning its Irish localities, and expresses some doubt as to its indigenousness in this country.

The great size of this ant, its wood-haunting habit, and the remarkable nest, resembling a hay-cock in shape, which it builds of sticks, grass, leaf-stalks, &c. (or pine-needles where these happen to be accessible to it) are sufficiently distinctive, I hope, to guarantee one who has not scientifically studied the order against risk of erroneous identification.

As to the question of its indigenousness, the character of the habitat is to my mind practically conclusive. Killoughrim Forest—the main remnant of the old natural wood of Oak, Birch, Hazel, Holly, Guelder-rose, and Broom, which in bygone years covered a great part of the county—is, so far as I have been able to observe, almost completely free from introduced vegetation, while several of our very local but undoubtedly native insects (as *Thecla betulae* and *Nisoniades tages*) are apparently confined to this wood, or occur outside its limits only in a few isolated spots, once part of the forest, that still retain the original sylvan character. It seems most unlikely that the ants would be so thoroughly at home as they are, in such a place as this if the species were an imported one. In fact it has grown into an axiom with me that whatever is in Killoughrim is indigenous. Even the Squirrel, now for six years established and common in all the woods of the adjacent parts, declines to be tempted by the only hazel-nuts the district offers to ground whereon he instinctively knows there is neither Beech nor Pine.

I regret to add that the dense scrub which has sprung up in Killoughrim since the last felling of the oaks ten years ago has so obliterated many of the old pathways and open spaces that it is no longer the easy matter it once was to visit *Formica rufa* in her haunts. Spots where I have found, I should say, a dozen Wood Ant's hillocks in village-like juxtaposition are now difficult to identify, and besides the ants themselves shift their ground from time to time.

Despite their defensive capabilities, not ineffective against Man, and stated to be infallible security against the Pheasant and Partridge (see remarks by "A Son of the Marshes" on "Our British Game Birds"), they have at least one formidable enemy in the Hedgehog, and probably, though I have no certain evidence of this, another in the Badger; at any rate, even the former animal now and then gives them such a mauling as to compel the abandonment of a site.

I have found a few nests of *Formica rufa* outside Killoughrim Forest, under plantation timber at Ballyhyland, and in other woods not far off; and in these instances I took note of the fact that pine-needles, for obvious reasons lacking in Killoughrim, were largely used in the construction of the tumuli. These outside colonies, probably formed by emigrants from the Forest, in every case have proved curiously short-lived, and last summer I searched all the localities (exclusive of the Killoughrim settlements) without finding a single nest of the Wood Ant.

I will see to securing a few "neuters" of this Ant for authoritative inspection during the coming summer, but meanwhile I have very little doubt that other Irish localities for it will be readily forthcoming—enough, perhaps, to dispense with any special need for corroboration by specimen of my County Wexford record. So interesting and striking an insect is in all probability familiar by sight to many observers ignorant of its scientific name, who, when once attention is drawn to the subject, will be able to add largely to what is known of its distribution.

C. B. MOFFAT, Dublin.

MOLLUSCA.

Some Slugs from North-West Ireland.—I have recently received from Miss Amy Warren a small collection of slugs from Ballina, Co. Mayo, and as records from this district are very few, a note concerning the same may be of interest. There are eight specimens referable to the following species:

Arion empiricorum, Fér. (immature) (3).
    var. allied to *Bocagei*, Simr. (2).
A. subfuscus, Drap. (1).
A. hortensis, Fer. (1).
A. fasciatus, Nils. (1).

The occurrence of forms of *A. empiricorum* allied to Simroth's variety *Bocagei* is most interesting.

WALTER E. COLLINGE,
Mason College, Birmingham.

BIRDS.

Spring Migrants.—I saw two Sand Martins on the 20th March and a solitary Wheat-ear on the 1st April. The latter are our first spring migrants here, and seem later in coming than usual.

W. A. HAMILTON, Ballyshannon.

THE TERNS OF KILLALA BAY.
BY ROBERT WARREN.

Of the tern family, four species are regular summer visitors to Killala Bay, and breed within the district—the Sandwich, Common, Arctic, and Little Terns; while one, the rare Black Tern, has only once been known to visit the bay.

Up to the summer of 1851, very little was known of the SANDWICH TERN (*Sterna cantiaca*) in Ireland, and was first mentioned as an Irish visitor by the late Wm. Thompson in the *Proceedings* of the Zoological Society of London for 1833 from a specimen shot on the 14th of September, 1832, in Belfast Bay: again, on the 28th of July, 1838, an adult bird was shot opposite "The Grove" and several others were seen there in September, 1839, and during the same month in 1844: while another specimen shot in Strangford Lough on the 16th of August that year was sent to Belfast for preservation; the above being all that was known to Wm. Thompson of this bird on the northern coast. This writer, proceeding to speak of its occurrence on the Dublin coast, mentions a specimen having been shot near Clontarf in October, 1831; and in July, 1834, two more were obtained near the same locality. In September, 1837, several were seen near Howth; and one was seen at Dollymount strand on 11th May, 1842; while from that date up to 1850, individuals were seen every summer, in June and July, between Portmarnock and Malahide, and one was shot on 15th June that year on Ireland's Eye.

The late Mr. J. J. Watters was the first to discover that it bred on the coast, for on 17th June, 1850, when visiting that great breeding-haunt of Terns on the Dublin coast, the Rockabill (now long since deserted), he saw three birds flying about, and found a broken egg on the rocks, and although he saw 70 or 80 Roseate Terns, and at least twice that number of Common and Arctic Terns on the wing, he was unable to identify more of the Sandwich Terns than the three individuals already mentioned, thus showing that these three birds were mere chance stragglers from some larger breeding-haunt of the species, at that time unknown.

The preceding information being all that was known of this tern in Ireland up to the date of the publication of Wm. Thompson's work in 1851, I had the great pleasure of adding

A

something to it; for on 7th April the same year I met this beautiful Tern near the island of Bartragh, Killala Bay. Having previously resided in the South of Ireland, it was quite unknown to me, and when the attention of my brother and myself was first attracted by its very peculiar cry (which if once heard can never be mistaken or forgotten), we were much puzzled, as for a long time we could not make out what had uttered it, or from what direction it proceeded. However, chancing after some time to look upwards, we were just able to perceive some birds, wheeling about, and soaring at an immense height, all the time screaming loudly. This wild flight and strange cry, so unlike that of any bird we knew, induced us to watch them closely, and after some time they gradually lowered their flight to the water. Seeing that they were some species of tern, we got into our boat, and having succeeded in shooting a couple, found that they were this lovely tern, and in such a perfect state of plumage that their breasts and bellies had quite a rosy tinge almost as deep as that of Roseate Terns. This peculiar habit of soaring to such a height as to be almost invisible, and wheeling in wide circles, occasionally chasing each other and screaming loudly, is most frequently seen early in the season before they begin to hatch, although occasionally in August and September, a pair may be seen acting in a similar manner, but almost invariably on fine bright days. As these terns remained all the season feeding about the bay and estuary, we were most anxious to find their breeding-station, but although we made many inquiries and searches we quite failed, and what made the failure the more annoying was, that at the time the birds were hatching the male birds were seen daily flying inland in the direction of Lough Conn, with Sand-eels in their bills to feed their sitting mates. Lough Conn, however, was visited twice without our seeing any trace of the Sandwich Terns either on or about the lake, the only birds met with being Blackheaded Gulls and Common Terns. Our search for the breeding-haunt having thus failed, I gave it up for a time, but in May, 1857, I was told of a small lough where a number of small gulls bred, and which was situated close to the residence of the late Mr. Gardiner of Cloona, two miles from the town of Ballina, and about four from the estuary. On visiting the lough I found it to be surrounded on two sides by a turf bog and on other two by the fields of Mr. Gardiner. It was about 20 or 30 acres in extent and had a wooded island in the centre, having a large quantity of reeds and bullrushes on one end, extending out some distance into the water. A large colony of Blackheaded Gulls were breeding amongst the reeds, and on the tussocks of coarse grass along the margin, while a small colony of Sandwich Terns were located on a low flat mudbank, scarcely above the level of the water. Some of the terns had scarcely any nests, but laid their eggs in slight depressions of the soil thinly lined with a few dried blades of grass, and three, I think (as well as I can remember), was the average number of eggs in each nest. When returning I took half a dozen eggs, and when attempting to blow them found that the greater number were so near being hatched that it was impossible to prepare them for my collection, thus showing that this species breeds much earlier than the smaller species of terns, and in further proof of their early breeding I have seen young birds accompanying their parents about the river and estuary as early as the 24th of June.

The following winter and spring being unusually wet, the level of the lake was raised so high, as to cover the mudbank upon which the terns had their nests, and as the bank continued under water during the summer of 1858, the terns deserted the lake altogether, and removed to the little moorland lough of Rathrouyeen, situated midway between Ballina and Killala, and within 300 yards of, and in sight of the high road between these towns.

This lough is considerably larger than Cloona, and is nearly surrounded by bog, with very swampy shores, except on the east side, and has a considerable quantity of reeds growing on the margin, in some places extending to a small island in the middle of the lake. This island is nearly circular in form, and is about 25 or 30 yards in diameter, and has some tall bushes growing round the outer edge, while the middle of the island is bare, except where some long grass grows.

A very large colony of Blackheaded Gulls have nests all over this island, and amongst the reeds, and on the tussocks along the boggy margin, while a smaller colony of Sandwich Terns breed together on a bare part of the island, as well as amongst the Gulls' nests. This lake and the adjoining land were the property of the late Sir Charles Knox-Gore, who, with the spirit of a true naturalist, strictly preserved it, and did not allow either Gulls or Terns to be disturbed or molested, and had the long grass and weeds, and some bushes cleared off it to give more space to the birds for their nests, so that now from being so well protected, this beautiful tern has increased in numbers, so largely, that Miss Knox-Gore told me that when visiting the island in 1886, she counted 150 nests of Sandwich Terns, and as the present owner preserves the lake as strictly as the former, there is every probability of this breeding-haunt continuing for many years.

This tern is the earliest of our spring visitors, sometimes appearing in the estuary as early as 20th March; and appears to be little affected by cold, for during the unusually cold weather of March, 1892, they arrived in the estuary on the 27th, when there were four inches of snow on the ground, and the thermometer indicated six degrees of frost. Up to the present date, Rathrouyeen is the only breeding haunt of this tern in Ireland, of which we have any record, except the deserted ones of Rockabill and Cloona, though of course there may be others unnoticed on some remote and unfrequented parts of the coasts or lakes. There is very probably one on the North Sligo coast, somewhere between Raughly and Mullaghmore, for when I visited Horse Island (that great haunt of the Arctic Tern) in July, 1894, I saw several Sandwich Terns flying about, but saw no trace of their breeding on the island with the Arctic Terns.

When the pairing season commences it is very amusing watching the absurd antics of the males trying to attract the attention of the females. When the tide is out, at low-water, the terns generally assemble on a sandbank to rest after fishing, and there the males strut about amongst the females, with their heads thrown back and wings drooping (almost touching the sand), but after a time if there is no response from the females, who generally look on the performance with the greatest unconcern, one goes off for a little and returns with a Sand-eel in his bill, and commences again strutting about with wings and head in same position and moves about amongst the females, offering the Sand-eel from one to another as he passes along unnoticed, until at last he meets a hen who accepts his offering, and then sits down alongside of her to settle their future arrangements.

COMMON TERN (*Sterna fluviatilis*).—A summer visitor, generally appearing in the bay and estuary about the first week in May, and sometimes delaying its visit if the weather is cold and stormy. It is an abundant species and widely distributed during the breeding season amongst the freshwater lakes and sea-shores. Large numbers breed on a low gravelly island near Errew Abbey in Lough Conn, and on another island at the Pontoon end of the lake, while lesser numbers are scattered about the lake, solitary pairs breeding on the stony points of many of the smaller islands. They also breed on islands in Loughs Mask and Carra, also in Mayo, while I have seen a small colony on an island in Lough Gill, near Sligo. Of their marine breeding-haunts the principal one on the North Mayo coast is that of the Inch, a low gravelly island in Killala Pool, where they breed in company of the Lesser and Arctic Terns; a few pairs also breed on Horse Island, near Raughly, Sligo Bay, amongst the crowd of Arctic Terns.

ARCTIC TERN (*Sterna macrura*) is not so numerous in the bay and estuary as the Common Tern, and although I had occasionally shot specimens in company of the Common Tern it was not until the past summer that I ascertained that they bred in this locality, when I found them breeding on the Inch with the Common and Lesser Terns. I had in previous years shot birds at the Inch, that from the darkness of their under plumage when seen in flight I took to be Arctic Terns, but in every instance they proved to be the Common; so that I find it impossible to identify an Arctic Tern on the wing by the colours of its plumage. Indeed my experience is, that unless seen close enough to discern the lake-coloured bill, the colours of plumage will not distinguish this bird from the Common Tern. Other means of distinguishing between the two species when flying are the much sharper cry, when alarmed, than that of the Common Tern, and the greater length of the tail feathers, but these are not always perceptible to the observer.

When visiting the Inch on 14th June, 1895, I remarked that several of the Terns emitted the same sharp cries that I had heard previously at breeding-haunts of the Arctic Terns, at other places, but still I could not perceive any difference in appearance between any of the large numbers of birds flying about, until walking over to some nests of the Lesser Terns, one of the larger species rose off eggs at my feet, and uttering the sharp cry, kept soaring round out of shot. While doing so, the unusual length of its pointed tail feathers, and its excessive wildness (so unlike the habits of the Arctic) caused me to think that it might be the rare Roseate Tern, and being very anxious to identify the bird, or shoot it, I lay down behind a little hillock, about 50 yards from where the eggs were laid on the bare sand, and though after a time the bird returned to her eggs, yet, whenever I attempted to move, or stand up, she always got up quite out of shot, soaring about in wide circles; several times for over half an hour all my attempts failed in obtaining a shot, and her great wildness made me feel so confident that she was a Roseate, that I was more anxious than ever to shoot her. So trying another plan, I put her off the eggs, and then lay down behind the hillock on the chance of obtaining a shot as she circled round ; remaining quite still, she lowered her flight, and in one of her circles, coming within range, I brought her down, and to my great disappointment she proved to be an Arctic Tern.

When at the summer assizes of Sligo in July, 1894, a friend told me of a large breeding-haunt of terns on Horse Island, near Raughly, off Brown's Bay, about 12 miles from Sligo, and I gladly accepted his offer to drive me there. Reaching Raughly, we stopped on our way at Artarmon to call on Mr. C. Jones Henry, who very kindly took us in his boat to the island. It is seven or eight acres in extent, and all in pasture. The terns lay their eggs all about the island on the grass, and on the rocks and stones above high-water-mark, all round the island. On landing we were soon surrounded and mobbed by the largest flock of terns that I ever saw. At the least estimation fully 500 to 700 pairs were flying about us, and from their sharp cries all were evidently Arctic Terns. I did not recognise the note of a single Common Tern, and all the specimens we shot were of the first-named species, and the only evidence we had of the presence of Common Terns, was two or three young birds we found running about the rocks. This great flock of Arctic Terns was to me one of the most interesting sights I had witnessed for a long time, and Mr. Henry told us that when he visited the island some three or four years before, the number of birds was far larger, and that when walking on the island, he found it almost impossible to avoid treading on the eggs, so thickly were they scattered about. We found that only about fifty or sixty pairs had eggs on the short pasture, and on the rocks; not more than half a dozen young birds were seen, although it was so late as the 7th July, but the birds had been much harassed and disturbed by previous visitors taking the eggs out of mere wanton mischief, and leaving them in heaps on the grass. We found one heap of 50 or 60 eggs left near the landing-place, all nearly incubated, and this wanton destruction of the eggs easily accounted for the few nests found by us, and the small number of young birds seen.

William Thompson was not aware of this tern having any inland breeding-haunts, but considered it strictly marine in all its habits, and both Mr. Yarrell and Mr. H. Saunders appear to have been of the same opinion, for neither in the last edition of "British Birds," nor in Saunders' "Handbook," is there any mention of this bird breeding on fresh water within the British Isles.

The first intimation I had of this tern breeding on fresh water, was from my old and valued friend, the late Mr. A. G. More, who, when botanising along the shores and islands of the Mayo lakes, met this bird breeding in company with Common Terns on an island on Lough Carra; and I was also informed in 1891 by Mr. W. H. Good, of Westport, that he met with it breeding on islands, both on Loughs Mask and Carra: which statements I verified, when visiting these lakes in the company of my friend Mr. W. Williams, of Dublin, in June, 1893, for we obtained specimens on both lakes, and brought young and eggs from an island off Cushlough on Lough Mask.

This tern is remarkable for the great extent of its breeding range, which extends from the inland lakes of Ireland, to Smith's Sound in the Arctic regions, as far north as the foot of civilized man has trod; Colonel Fielden of the late Arctic discovery expedition under Captain Nares, having met with this bird near the Alert's winter-quarters on the 16th June, 1876. In August of the previous year, he found eight pairs breeding on a small islet at the mouth of Discovery Bay, and a newly-hatched young bird in a nest surrounded by snow.

The LITTLE TERN (*Sterna minuta*) is a regular summer visitor, generally arriving in the estuary during the first or second week of May, and although I have long observed them about the locality, it was only of late years that I have ascertained their breeding-haunt on the Inch, between Killala and Bartragh (their only breeding-haunt on the North Mayo coast). Here a small colony of ten or twelve pairs, used to breed in company with Common and Arctic Terns, until the past summer of 1895, when their numbers suddenly, and most unaccountably increased, and as they had not sufficient scope on the gravelly Inch, they spread over the adjacent sandy peninsula of Ross. When I visited the Inch on the 14th of last June, I was surprised at the large numbers of these terns, and estimated that at least 60 to 70 pairs were seen all about—both on the wing, resting on the sands, and sitting on their eggs, The birds had spread along the Ross shore for nearly half a mile laying their eggs on the sandy flat, and round the gravelly base of some hillocks, from which the sand had been blown away; no nests had been made; the two or three eggs of each pair lay on the bare sand or gravel. Just across the narrow channel, on the extreme end of Bartra Island, I found four pairs hatching a little above high water mark, and below the line of Bent-grass, the eggs also on the bare sand, and where no birds had ever before been known to breed.

The sudden increase of this tern is very interesting and mysterious, for it cannot be accounted for by any larger number than usual having been reared on the Inch the previous summer. Unless by the desertion of some distant breeding-haunt it is difficult to account for this influx of breeding birds to the Inch and neighbourhood. Besides this North Mayo breeding-haunt, there are several along the Sligo coast; one at Rosses Point, Sligo Bay, where a small colony of eight or ten pairs frequent a little sandy bay off the Rabbit-burrows, another on the northern side of the point in Drumcliffe Bay, where thirty to forty pairs breed on the wide expanse of sand-flat, which extends nearly across the upper end of the bay. This wide expanse of sand is generally bare all the summer, and apparently is only covered by the high spring-tides of spring and autumn; so the terns can hatch and rear their young in safety, for as they lay near the centre of the flat nearly a mile from the land, they are seldom molested, being quite out of the way of either cockle-pickers or bait-diggers. A third breeding-haunt is situated three or four miles further north, near Raughly, in Brown's Bay, where a dozen pairs frequent a flat at the base of the sandhills, and lay on the bare pasture between the tufts of bent grass.

The BLACK TERN (*Sterna nigra*).—So rare a species in Ireland has only once come under my notice as a visitor to Killala Bay, and it was by the merest chance I came across it as I was fishing for Sea-trout near Bartragh on the 12th of October, 1859.

My boat was anchored in the channel between Baunross and a wide stretch of sand-banks left bare by the ebb-tide, and while fishing I remarked a group of four or five small terns resting on the sand-bank close to the channel, but at first, thinking they were young Common Terns, I paid no attention to them. However, after a while they rose from the sand, and began hawking after some flies, and the very sudden and adroit twists and turns they made in the pursuit of their diminutive prey showed they were birds strange to me. I at once got up my anchor and rowed after them, and as they were not at all shy I easily succeeded in shooting a pair of Black Terns in the first season's plumage. This little party, a family of terns, were evidently on their way south from their breeding-haunt, but whether they were bred in this country on some remote bog or mountain lough, is difficult to say, for there is no record of the Black Tern having ever bred in Ireland.

NOTES ON THE ROCK POOLS OF BUNDORAN.
BY J. E. DUERDEN, A.R.C.SC. (LOND.),
Curator of the Museum, Kingston, Jamaica.

In addition to the notes in the *Irish Naturalist* for January, 1895, upon the "Rock-pools of Bundoran," I find I have a few other observations which removal from Ireland has prevented from further amplification. This latter occurrence may perhaps be considered sufficient apology for their disconnected nature; while the fact that some of the specimens were collected and handed to me by Prof. Johnson renders it obligatory upon me to present them.

In examining the Hydroids the greenish, somewhat flask-shaped tests of the Protozoan *Folliculina ampulla*, Mull., were met with on the stems in considerable numbers.

The sponge *Hymeniacidon celata*, Bowk. (*Cliona celata*, Grant), occurred perforating the hard Carboniferous limestone near the Fairy Bridge at the eastern end of Donegal Bay.

The patches at the surface exhibited a very characteristic appearance, and upon splitting the rock it was found to be closely perforated by the sponge for a depth of two or three inches. A well-known boring sponge, *Cliona* is commonly found inhabiting oyster and other shells all round the coast, but only occasionally is it met with in limestone. Bowerbank records it thus only from the limestone rocks around Tenby.

Among the Crustacea, a single specimen of the small Isopod, *Dynamene Montagui*, Leach, was obtained by Prof. Johnson from amongst the sea-weeds. It has previously been recorded from Bantry Bay.

Many specimens of the Sea-Hare, *Aplysia punctata*, Cuvier, were met with in the shallow rock-pools west of Bundoran, and also near Aughrus Point. Most were in the act of laying their strings of brown-pink spawn. The majority were of a uniformly dark olive green colour, while others were sprinkled with small opaque white patches over various parts of the body. Mr. Garstang has shown (*Journ. Mar. Biol. Assoc.* (n.s.) vol. i., No. 4, 1890, p. 403) that this species changes with growth from a violet, purplish, or rose-red colour, through brownish-red and brown to olive-brown or olive-green. The rock-surface of the pools in which the present specimens were found was coated with the pink *Lithothamnion polymorphum* to which the dark *Aplysiæ* offered a great contrast.

Prof. Johnson found the rare Nudibranch, *Hermæa bifida*, Montagu, while examining the weeds collected at low-water. It was living upon *Halurus* (*Griffithsia*) *equisetefolius*, to which the lake-red colour in its dorsal papillæ presented a remarkable resemblance. This protective or warning resemblance to the objects upon which Nudibranchs live has lately been the subject of various papers by Prof. Herdman, Mr. Garstang, and others. *Hermæa bifida* has been the object of some of Mr. Garstang's experiments at Plymouth (*Journ. Mar. Biol. Assoc.* (n.s.), vol. i., No. 2, Oct., 1889, p. 173) where it is interesting to find that the creature, which there was also collected by Prof. Johnson, lives upon the same Alga as at Bundoran. It is shown that its colour is purely adventitious, being determined mainly by that of the food within it undergoing digestion.

I obtained one specimen of the small greenish Nudibranch, *Hermœa dendritica*, Ald. and Hane., living amongst the green Algæ *Bryopsis* and *Codium*. Kept in captivity it laid a characteristic round mass of spawn. It refused to live upon the *Codium*, and in a few days lost most of its green colour, becoming yellowish brown. Garstang's experiments show that this species entirely avoids the red sea-weeds, upon which its colour would render it conspicuous.

Many examples of the Nudibranch, *Eolis coronata*, Forbes, were found living amongst colonies of *Tubularia larynx* collected from the Fairy Caves, their colours harmonising with the light red of the polypites.

A SUBMERGED PINE-FOREST.

BY R. LLOYD PRAEGER, B.E.

(Read before the Dublin Naturalists' Field Club, March 9th, 1896.)

ONE day in February last, Mr. R. Welch and I strolled along the beach northward of the new harbour at Bray, and just within the confines of the County of Dublin. At the verge of low water, where the slope of coarse shingle gives way to a more level stretch of fine sand and boulders, which is only left dry at spring tides, we noticed some stumps and boughs of trees, and on examining them, found that they were embedded in a compact layer of peat, which dipped southward at a low angle. The peat was full of branches and roots, and of cones of the Scotch Fir. On the southern side it disappeared under a bed of fine blue clay containing sea-shells; to the north, its broken edges overlay a stratum of coarse grey sand, with rounded fragments of granite. We had but cursorily examined the spot when the tide crept up again and soon hid it from view.

Here evidently was a geological story to be unravelled; a long history lay buried with this old peat-bed under the mud and shingle which the sea had heaped upon it; and it was for us to read that history, if we could. Thus it came about that in two days' time we again visited the place, and Mr. Welch secured several excellent photographs of the deposit; and a little later, selecting a spring-tide, Mr. Lyster Jameson and I went down and thoroughly examined the spot, and determined the extent of the different beds and their relative position and thickness. What we found may be shown in the form of a section north and south along the beach (fig. 1). The newest

FIG. 1.

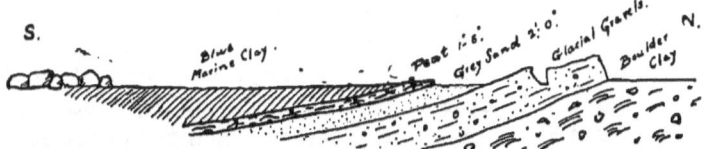

bed is the blue marine clay, which may be well seen in the space lying inside of the crescent-shaped heap of large boulders which forms a conspicuous object on the shore at low water about a quarter of a mile north of Bray Harbour. The clay is extremely fine and tough, and is full of the shell *Scrobicularia piperata*, a species whose habitat is between tide-marks on mud-flats and in estuaries. In most cases the pairs of valves are still in juxtaposition, and upright, showing that the shells are lying undisturbed in the place where they lived and died. With this shell was the well-known *Tellina balthica*, which lives in similar situations ; and a specimen of *Littorina litorea*, the Common Periwinkle, was also found. We had not brought excavating implements with us, but with the aid of a broken coal-shovel, kindly lent to us by the nearest resident, we found that towards the southern extremity of its area the bed of clay is at least six feet thick. Especially in its lower portion, the clay contains fir-cones and fragments of wood, washed out of the underlying peat. The peat-bed was next examined. Careful excavation round a selected stump, a large one standing almost upright, revealed the fact that it was firmly rooted in the peat ; the spreading branching roots so characteristic of the Scotch Fir could be clearly traced from their junction with the trunk to their interlaced extremities. Although it was evident that various plants had contributed to the formation of this old forest-bed, no other species could be identified in the short time at our disposal. The peat rested abruptly on a couple of feet of coarse grey sand, in which no organic remains were detected. A little further on, the glacial sands and gravels that form the upper part of the fine coast section between Bray and Killiney rose out of the shingle, cemented into a hard conglomerate, as they are at other places in the neighbourhood. Beyond this the strand was occupied by a denuded surface of boulder-clay, burrowed by that pretty shell *Pholas candida*.

Two facts in the above description deserve our special attention. Firstly, the trees were *rooted* in the peat, showing that they *grew* there, and were not drifted by currents or carried down by streams. Secondly, the marine shells in the overlying clay *lived* where we now find them. And thus we obtain the key to this little earth-story. Fir-trees do not grow in the sea, nor do marine shells flourish on dry land. These beds of peat and clay tell us clearly of changes in the relative level of land and sea. To appreciate these changes, and to confirm our interpretation of the phenomena before us, we turn to a locality where beds of this kind attain a more extensive development, and can be better studied than on the storm-swept shore at Bray. The greater part of the City of Belfast is built on thick deposits of post-glacia lage, and the deep and wide excavations made from time to time in the construction of new docks, have afforded golden opportunities for their investigation—opportunities which have not been altogether neglected. We will take a typical section from the Alexandra Dock Works[1] (fig. 2).

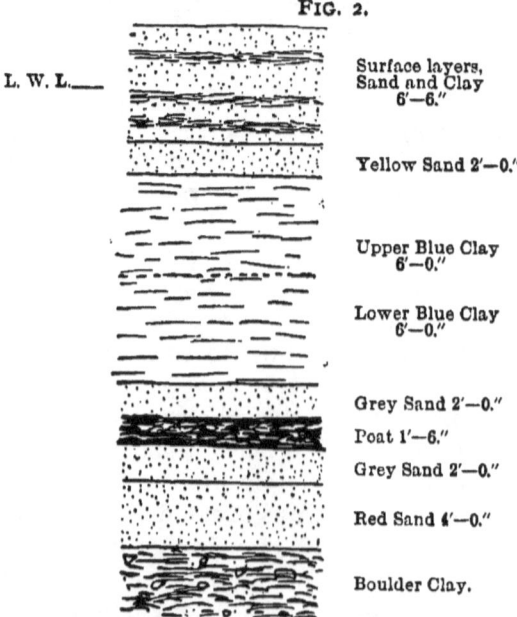

FIG. 2.

L. W. L.

Surface layers, Sand and Clay 6'—6."

Yellow Sand 2'—0."

Upper Blue Clay 6'—0."

Lower Blue Clay 6'—0."

Grey Sand 2'—0."
Peat 1'—6."
Grey Sand 2'—0."

Red Sand 4'—0."

Boulder Clay.

---

[1] See Praeger, "The Estuarine Clays at the new Alexandra Dock, Belfast." *Proc. B.N.F.C.* for 1886-87, *Appendix*.

Here, below some feet of sandy and muddy beds, the recent creation of the River Lagan, we find a bed 12 feet thick of blue clay, which examination shows to be clearly divisible into two zones—an upper clay, exceedingly fine and pure, full of a rich and luxuriant fauna characterized by species which live in from 5 to 10 fathoms of water; and a lower zone, more sandy, which yields in abundance remains of the Grass-wrack, *Zostera marina*, and shells, such as *Scrobicularia piperata*, *Tapes decussatus*, and *Tellina balthica*, that are usually found living with the Grass-wrack on muddy shores between tide-marks. Under these clays we see, intercalated between thin beds of grey sand, a layer of peat, which contains remains of Scotch Fir, Hazel, Alder, &c., as well as bones of the Red Deer, Wild Boar, and Irish Elk.[1] The next bed in order of descent is a fine red sand, a deposit that in many places in the neighbourhood of Belfast attains an extensive development, and which, though its stratigraphical relations have not yet been worked out, there is good reason for supposing to correspond with the sands and gravels which form so important a feature in the glacial series about Dublin. And lastly, this bed of sand reposes on Boulder-clay.

Comparing now this section with the beds on the foreshore at Bray, we will be immediately struck with the exact parallelism. The deep-water clay which forms the uppermost bed of the series at Belfast is indeed unrepresented at Bray, but the others correspond zone for zone, and the clay and peat are even characterized by the same fossils. And we may with advantage carry our comparison a little further. The peat-bed is to be found in many spots in the north-east; and in other places at Belfast, and at Downpatrick, it is to be found underlying thirty feet or more of the blue clay. Again, at Larne, the *Scrobicularia* clay (as we may call the lower zone), which is also very persistent along the north-eastern shores, has, superimposed on it, 19 feet of stratified marine gravels, which contain flint implements of Neolithic age from top to base, though none are found in the clay. At Kilroot, midway between Belfast and Larne, the beds present an appearance exactly like that seen at Bray, for here, near low water-mark,

---

[1] Praeger, *op. cit.*, and *Proc. B.N.F.C.* for 1891-92, p. 416.

we have a patch of *Scrobicularia* clay which rests on peat, both lying in a shallow basin in the Boulder-clay, which crops out close at hand. At Ballyholme, again, on the opposite or southern shore of Belfast Lough, the peat may be seen on the shore between tides, with 15 feet of stratified marine gravels overlying it, and Boulder-clay below. Similar instances might be multiplied.[1]

The sections just described throw much light on the beds at Bray, and will assist us to form an idea of their age, and of the conditions under which they were laid down. The peat evidently represents a period when the land stood slightly higher than at present. The cold that characterized the glacial epoch appears to have quite passed away, for the plants and animals of the peat, so far as they are known, point to a climate resembling that which this country at present enjoys. Then came subsidence, and the accumulation of marine clays on the former land-surface. This may have been the period of Palæolithic man; we know at least that it is the zone underlying the lowest which contains Neolithic implements at Larne. It may be noted that the characteristic shell of these clays—*Scrobicularia piperata*, which is present in countless thousands both at Bray and in the many places where this deposit is found in Antrim and Down—while it still lives about Dublin, has become completely extinct in the north-east of Ireland, and many other shells of the clays have disappeared along with it. The Bray series carries us no further, but the deep-water clay and extensive raised beaches that overlie the *Scrobicularia* clay in the North-east are evidence of a further period of depression before the land rose to its present level.

And thus, as we stand on the sea-shore at Bray and gaze along the storm-swept edges of these old beds, we are, as it were, looking down the corridors of time—glancing at a tale, which, though long, occupies but the last page, nay, but the last sentence, of the great book of geological history. The peat tells us of a forest of dark fir-trees, under whose shadow wandered herds of stately Red Deer, and packs of Wild Boars and Wolves, and perhaps the great Irish Elk, while year by

---

[1] See Praeger; Report on the Estuarine Clays of the north-east of Ireland. *Proc. R.I.A.* (3) ii., No. 2, 1892.

year the trees shed their cones and needles to form the firm brown mass at our feet. A different chapter of the story is revealed by the fine blue clay, which points to a shallow muddy shore-line, like that which we still find on the Murrough of Wicklow. Immediately above the bed of clay, the broad shingle of the present beach catches our eye, recalling the never-ceasing wear and tear of the ocean, ever carving and levelling, and still making new land out of old; while beyond all, and over all, we catch a glimpse of the villas and spires of Bray, and hear the rattle of vehicles and rumble of trains, to remind us that from the dim twilight of the past, we have emerged into the broad daylight of the present.

THE SONG OF BIRDS.

The Evolution of Bird-Song, with observations on the Influence of heredity and Imitation. By CHARLES A. WITCHELL. London: A & C. Black, 1896. 5s.

Mr. Witchell's ten years "scientific investigation of the various features of bird-song" has borne fruit in a volume comprising less than 250 pages— a fact proving that the author possesses in full the faculty of judicious compression. Besides making it his object to acquaint himself as far as possible with the notes of all his feathered neighbours, and to ascertain for each variety of bird-note the kind of occasion on which it is uttered, Mr. Witchell has addressed himself to the task of resolving the songs of birds into their component parts; and his account, given in these pages, of the probable course of development of the phenomena of bird-song, is in the main, well calculated to command general acceptance. Mr. Witchell's theory is not a very elaborate one. The most primitive bird-sounds he believes to have been combat-cries, which passed with more or less of modification into defiance-cries and alarm-cries, while the latter, as employed between members of a family, would form the origin of the call-note. The earliest and of course simplest songs were mere repetitions of the call-note, or sometimes "possibly" (p. 58) of the defiance-cry. (Mr. Witchell might surely, on his own showing, have laid more stress on this latter element; and did he never hear a hen-whitethroat, frenzied with rage at some peril to her new-fledged brood burst into hysterical snatches of her lord's song?) Simple songs would be varied by being more rapidly and "forcefully" uttered, rivalry between male birds occasionally instigating other modifications which, if agreeable to the females, would tend to become hereditary. Finally, male birds excelling in range of voice would learn new notes from their environment, and develop into more or less accomplished mimics. Mr. Witchell's chapter on the influence of imitation is the part of his book which is likely to be read with most suspense of judgment. It contains some excellent remarks (pp. 192-3) on the difficulty of detecting mimicry—especially when imperfect—and on the general impossibility of subjecting to proof the statements of an observer who claims to have heard particular imitations. No one with the least susceptibility to Mr. Witchell's evident love of nature would question for a moment the strict fidelity of his record—so far, that is, as his observations can be severed from his inferences. But are *casual* resemblances so rare among natural sounds that mimicry may fairly be inferred or conjectured when a heron (p. 182) croaks like a frog (N.B.—the *dead* heron does this automatically); or a landrail (p. 189) salutes his bride in measured tones attuned like munches of a grazing cow? The suggestion by the way of the proximity of the latter kind of animal would be a bit disquieting to the sitting female, and a display of doubtful tact on her mate's part. The following rendering of a thrush's song, in which " a phrase without recognizable mimicry is indicated by an 'O'" will serve as a sample of Mr. Witchell's readiness in detecting what he deems imitative resemblances:—"Frocester, Glos., near the church, 17th May, 1892. Thrush singing :—Golden plover —golden plover—O—crow—corncrake—be quick—O—O—wood warbler's sibilous notes—cuckoo (in rough tones)—O—young starling's cry after leaving nest—O—butcher-bird—be quick—O—O—whitethroat's alarm— great tit (cry)—O—O—end" (pp. 203-4.)

That a few strains are here somewhat too willingly classed as imitations cannot, indeed, be proved but it can be fairly surmised. Sometimes, certainly, Mr. Witchell does make too much of mere similarities between sounds. For instance, the resemblance of the wren's to the hedge-sparrow's song is quite superficial, and requires no such hypothesis as Mr. Witchell offers in explanation,—viz., that both were "derived from some persistent source" (p. 191)—as an alternative to the utterly absurd idea that one of these birds copied the other. The remark, too, that robins, even in winter, often " reproduce *exactly* " the unique and beautiful song of the willow-warbler (p. 207) is startlingly questionable, though here again a slight similarity in cadence is frequently noticed. And surely it was riding a hobby to death to hint (p. 187) that the yellow-hammer's song is a mimicry of the grasshopper's, when on a previous page (p. 48) the same well-known melody had been grouped among those inferior efforts which are obviously " more or less repetitions of the call-note "

C. B. M.

SOME RECENT NATURAL HISTORY PAPERS.

The last-issued part of the *Proceedings of the Royal Irish Academy*, (3) vol. iii., No. 4, December, 1895, contains several natural history papers of considerable interest. Prof. Sollas writes "On the Crystalline form of Riebeckite," the blue hornblende characteristic of the "micro-granite" of Ailsa Craig, pebbles of which have been found in Irish glacial drifts from Greenore to Greystones. A pebble from Portrane contained cavities large enough for well-formed crystals of riebeckite, whose angles Prof. Sollas was able to measure. The results were slightly but obviously abnormal, and the author suggests in explanation, that "the crystals are far from simple, and may best be regarded as crystal complexes, simulating and making a close approximation to a simple crystal form."

Mr. G. H. Kinahan contributes a paper on "Quartz, Quartz-rock, and Quartzite." His views on the origin of these rocks have been laid before the readers of the *Irish Naturalist* (vol. I., pp. 162, 184.) At the end of the paper is the reference to Mr. W. W. Watts' examination of sinter from Iceland which led to some correspondence from that gentleman published in our last volume (p. 340.)

The third of the local surveys undertaken by the Dublin Anthropometric Committee is described by Dr. C. R. Browne in his important paper on "The Ethnography of the Mullet, Inishkea Islands, and Portacloy, Co. Mayo." After describing the physiography of the districts which are most isolated, Dr. Browne deals with the anthropography, sociology, folk-lore, archæology, and history of the inhabitants. It is needless to say that the information on these subjects is of the greatest interest, the people preserving many curious primitive customs. The original inhabitants seem never to have been driven out, though often conquered, but one or two recent immigrations are known to have taken place. The people of Inishkea differ in many respects from their neighbours of the mainland, and are probably the most unmixed representatives of the original population.

Mr. W. J. Knowles' "Third Report of the Pre-historic Remains from the Sandhills of the Coast of Ireland" is of interest to naturalists for its reference to the abundance of bones of the Great Auk, referred to by Mr. Barrett-Hamilton in his paper in our last month's issue.

Mr. John Hood, of Dundee, has communicated through the Flora and Fauna Committee an important paper "On the Rotifera of Co. Mayo," enumerating 220 species of those highly interesting microscopic animals. There are excellent figures of some of the rarer forms. Two species, *Pterodina bidentata*, Ternitz, and *Eosphora elongata*, Ehrb., are recorded as new to the British Isles. On account of the number of lakes and vast tracts of unreclaimed land, Mr. Hood considers that Ireland should furnish a rich harvest to the rotifer-collector. He gives a list of all the species found in Ireland by Miss Glascott and himself, amounting together to about 275, and suggests, in some cases, the identity of species described as new by Miss Glascott with forms described by previous authors.

Mr. H. H. Dixon contributes two papers on the histology of the vegetable cell. The first, "On the Chromosomes of *Lilium longiflorum*," deals with the number of those bodies formed by the nuclear thread in mitosis. Investigations into the division of the pollen mother- and daughter-cells and of the cells of the embryo-sac are described. Variations in the number of the chromosomes were noticed, a phenomenon which the author believes not to have been hitherto described as occurring in the gametophyte of flowering-plants, prior to the differentiation of the sexual cells. Mr. Dixon's second paper is a "Note on the Nuclei of the Endosperm of *Fritillaria imperialis*." Nuclear division, as observed here, was found to be extremely variable, and forms intermediate between normal karyokinesis and direct division are referred to as of special interest.

In the *Transactions of the Manchester Geological Society*, vol. xxiv., pt. 7, appears a paper by Mr. G. H. Kinahan, "On possible Land-Connections in Recent Geological Times between Ireland and Great Britain." This communication seems to have been suggested by Dr. Scharff's preliminary report "On the Origin of the Irish Land and Freshwater Fauna" (*Proc. R.I.A.* (3), vol. iii., p. 479, *Irish Nat.*, vol. iii., p. 260). Mr. Kinahan maintains that all the Irish plants and animals passed into the country in late Pleistocene times. Apparently he has not taken the trouble to read Dr. Scharff's paper, as in each of the first two paragraphs he attributes to that naturalist the use of the term "Pliocene" in connections where "Pleistocene" was really used, while, a little further on, Dr. Scharff is credited with the statement never made by him that all the lakes inhabited by varieties of the "pollen" (*sic*) communicate directly with the Irish Sea. Mr. Kinahan asks why Dr. Scharff should found his argument on ten mammals only, and "eliminate specially the rat, rabbit, bat, roebuck, and wild cat." Dr. Scharff in his paper plainly said why, because the ten only are undoubtedly indigenous. What naturalist ever included the Roebuck among native Irish mammals? Mr. Kinahan suggests that the land-connections across which the Irish animals and plants came consisted of shoals formed by tide-action, one at the north-east and the other at the south-east corner of Ireland, and adds that such frail bridges would be rapidly washed away. He brings forward, in evidence of the southern drift, the startling statement that the Killiney gravels are largely composed of fragments of Wexford rocks. There is no attempt to answer Dr. Scharff's argument for the Pliocene age of the Irish Fauna, from the existence in Great Britain in Pleistocene times of those animals which are British but not Irish, but which should have found their way to Ireland had Pleistocene land-connections existed.

PROCEEDINGS OF IRISH SOCIETIES.

ROYAL ZOOLOGICAL SOCIETY.

Recent donations comprise a Hare from Master Ball, and a Hedgehog from Mr. W. M'Donnell. A very fine pair of Burchell's Zebras, three Mona Monkeys, a Wanderoo Monkey, a Siamese Ape, a Nigger Monkey, a Siamese Civet Cat, a Binturong, three Virginian Opossums, a Wombat, a Golden Eagle, and two dozen small birds have been purchased.

18,000 persons visited the Gardens in April.

CORK NATURALISTS' FIELD CLUB.

The Annual Meeting was held April 21st, when about 25 members attended. Mr. J. H. BENNETT, V.P., occupied the chair. The Secretary read the fourth Annual Report, of which the following is an abstract:—We are glad to report an increase of membership—46 paid-up members, as against 33 of the previous year. We believe this to be the result of increasing interest owing to the union of the Field Clubs, and their growing importance.

The following places were visited during the summer of 1895:—
May 11.—The Lee Valley, with the object of noting the physical geography of the district, under the able guidance of Prof. Hartog, D.Sc., V.P. May 25.—Fota. June 15.—Ballyednmund, Midleton. July 10.—Upton and Innishannon. August 5.—Doneraile Court and Buttevant Abbey. August 24.—Warren's Court, by permission of Sir Augustus Warren, who entertained the party. September 7.—Castlemartyr, Lord Shannon's demesne.

Owing to the Gilchrist Lectures, which our Club, jointly with the Literary and Scientific Society, were instrumental in securing, being held, and also the Extension Lectures, it was deemed advisable not to multiply meetings, and accordingly only three Club meetings were held during the Winter Session:—

November 27, 1895.—Lecture: "The Galway Field Club Conference, 1895," by R. Lloyd Praeger, Hon. Sec. D.N.F.C. and F. C. Union. December 12.—Lecture: "The Scenery of Co. Antrim," by W. Gray, B.N.F.C. February 11, 1896.—Paper by William Miller: "The Climate of Cork," which gave rise to an animated discussion, and is to appear in the *Cork Historical and Archæological Journal*, followed by "Notes on Rousslet's method of mounting Rotifers," by Prof. Hartog, D.Sc. (which has already appeared in the *Irish Naturalist*).

On November 5th, 1895, your Secretary attended the Conversazione of the Dublin Naturalists' Field Club, and on March 10th, 1896, a Conversazione was held jointly with the Cork Historical and Archæological Society in the Imperial Hotel, attended by members of the Dublin and Limerick Clubs, and which was most successful. The finances, including a few subscriptions since paid, just about balance for the year.

The following Officers and Committee were elected:—
W. H. Shaw, President; Prof. M. Hartog, T. Farrington, Miss Martin, J. H. Bennett, J. Gilbert, Vice-Presidents; J. L. Copeman, Hon. Sec. and Treasurer; R. A. Phillips, Curator; D. Franklin, H. Lund, Mrs. Peyton, E. B. Hughes, F. R. Rohu, Committee.

MAY 2nd.—The first excursion took place to Fota, Mr. A. Smith-Barry's demesne, and proved a record one, about 50 members and friends attending. Under the guidance of Mr. W. Osborne Stewart, the grounds were viewed, and the various rare pines and palms with which they abound examined. Some specimens of larvæ, &c., were taken in the ponds, including a "singing" *Corixa*, which seems to have been the first noticed from near Cork, those noted by Mrs. Thompson all coming from the Fermoy district.

FIELD CLUB NEWS.

Lavens M. Ewart, the new President of the Belfast Field Club, is interested chiefly in the archæological side of the Club's work. He is a well-known collector of local prints, &c., and his collection of old maps of the Belfast district is the finest in existence. Rev. C. H. Waddell, the new Vice-President, has for many years devoted himself to botany, particularly mosses and hepatics, and more recently to phanerogams also. The formation of the new Botanical Section of the Club was largely due to his influence.

On the invitation of the Hon. R. E. Dillon, a party of naturalists will spend a week in June at Clonbrock, Co. Galway, exploring eastern Galway and Roscommon. This district is almost virgin ground to the naturalist, and Mr. Dillon's startling discoveries among the Lepidoptera there augur well for the success of the expedition. The publication of the results will be looked forward to with interest.

The Secretaries of the Belfast Club desire us to make it known that a dredging excursion has been arranged for Saturday, July 4, of which they invite members of the various Field Clubs to take advantage. A paddle steamer from the Clyde has been engaged for the occasion. The marine fauna of the waters adjoining Belfast Lough is rich and interesting, and it is intended to plunder the treasures of the Turbot Bank, made famous by the explorations of Hyndman and Waller.

Cheering news comes from Cork, where Mr. Copeman, at the annual meeting of the Field Club on April 21, was able to report a substantial rise of membership, and increased interest in the work of the Club, which he believed to be largely due to the formation of the Field Club Union, and to its influence. The Cork Club has now passed the somewhat trying period of infancy, and naturalists in Ireland will watch with satisfaction its continued progress.

NOTES.

Seasonable Notes from Cushendun.—Swallows appeared here on April 2nd; Wild Anemone in flower, 5th; Hawthorn in flower, 19th; *Cardamine pratense* in flower, 22nd; *Orchis mascula* in flower, 22nd; Cuckoo calling, 22nd; small white Butterfly, 19th; Corncrake calling, May 2nd; *Vicia sepium* in flower, 3rd; St. Mark's Fly, 3rd; Swift, May 9th.

SL. ARTHUR BRENAN, Cushendun.

BOTANY.

PHANEROGAMS.

Ranunculus tripartitus, DC., an Addition to the Irish Flora.—While botanizing on the 3rd of April last among the rocky hills which lie to the south of Baltimore, Co. Cork, I discovered in a small lake not far from the sea a distinct and pretty little Batrachian *Ranunculus*, which Messrs. H. and J. Groves have kindly identified for me as *R. tripartitus*, DC., type. This is certainly an addition to the flora of Ireland and possibly to that of the British Isles also, as, according to the *London Catalogue*, 9th ed., it is represented in Great Britain only by the variety (or species) *intermedius*, Knaf., which occurs in a few of the southern English counties. It is also an addition to the characteristic group of South-west European plants native in Ireland, its foreign distribution being limited to Portugal, Spain, France, South Italy, Belgium, and Germany.

R. A. PHILLIPS, Cork.

Lathræa squamaria in Co. Down.—I have within the last thirty years frequently found *Lathræa squamaria* growing in the Tollymore Park woods of the Earl of Roden, a locality which is mentioned in Dickie's *Flora of Ulster*, and Stewart and Corry's *Flora of the North-East of Ireland*. Mr. Ryan will find many Irish localities for this plant given in the above-named books, and also in Moore and More's *Cybele Hibernica*. I may mention two Co. Armagh localities that are known to me, Ardmore Glebe, on the shores of Lough Neagh, and the Lower Demesne, Tanderagee, where my daughter found it 7th May, 1896.

H. W. LETT, Loughbrickland.

Lathræa squamaria.—In reply to T. Ryan's note (*I. N.*, p. 142). Stewart and Corry's *Flora of N. E. Ireland* says the Toothwort is frequent in Antrim, Derry, and Down, and gives many localities. I have seen it in Tollymore Park. On account of its early flowering in April and May it is sometimes overlooked. In Kerner's *Natural History of Plants*, p. 137, an account is given with illustrations of the structure of this plant, from which it appears not only to be parasitic but also carnivorous in its habits. This interesting and splendidly illustrated work ought to do much to promote a more general knowledge of the life of plants.

C. H. WADDELL.

Lathræa squamaria in King's Co.—*Lathræa squamaria* is found growing freely in this county. It is well developed on the lawn of Geashill Rectory under Beech-trees, and quite lately I found it about nine miles from here on a ditch along the road through Clonad Wood. The plant fastens itself to the roots of the Beech by small attachments or discs; but it also grows round the roots, forming a sort of envelope or outer sheath; a section which I have prepared shows well the way in which the cellular tissue of the plant passes into that of the wood.

C. D. RUSSELL, Geashill.

Lathræa squamaria.—I see an inquiry in your May number as to the occurrence of *Lathræa squamaria*. It is found at Heywood, near Clonmel; my impression is that it is parasitic upon Elm there. It also grows in Strabane Glen, Co. Tyrone, on the roots of Hazel.

A. H. DELAP, Strabane.

Allium triquetrum, L., in Co. Cork.—This interesting South European plant occurs in at least two stations in this county. In 1890 I found it (about 20 or 25 plants) in a grassy hollow near Dunkettle on the northern side of Cork Harbour, where it has since continued to hold its own, and this year Surgeon W. G. Axford, R.N., has discovered it at Monkstown, some eight miles south and on the opposite side of the harbour. Though not a native, the occurrence of this species here in a wild state is remarkable, as its British distribution, like that of many other Cork plants, is limited to Cornwall, where it is thoroughly naturalized, and the Channel Islands, while on the continent it is found only in S. France, Spain, and Italy.

R. A. PHILLIPS, Cork.

ZOOLOGY.

SPIDERS.

Discovery of the genus Atypus in King's Co.—A very interesting addition to our Irish list of spiders has been made by the discovery of the tubular nest of a female *Atypus* by Rev. Canon Russell of Geashill, near Tullamore. The specimen was kindly sent by him to the Dublin Museum and has been authenticated by Rev. O. P. Cambridge. Pending the discovery of the maker of the nest the species must remain doubtful, though it will probably be the less rare British form, *Atypus piceus*, Sulz. *Atypus* is the only British genus of the *Aviculariidæ*, the family which contains the great "bird-eating" spiders of the tropics and the trap-door spiders of southern Europe. This spider constructs a long silken tube in the earth, but there is no trap-door; the end of the tube protrudes for a few inches above the surface. The nest sent by Canon Russell contained a caterpillar of *Hepialus humuli*, which may have been dragged in by the spider as prey.

GEO. H. CARPENTER.

INSECTS.

Formica rufa.—This ant occurs sparingly in a wooded glen in the Co. Waterford, near Clonmel, about two miles south of the town.

A. H. DELAP, Strabane.

REPTILES.

A Stray Snake near Coleraine.—On the evening of April 22nd, a lady friend called to tell me that she had killed a snake in her garden, which is in the immediate vicinity of Coleraine. It is upon the right bank of the river Bann, and about a quarter of a mile south of the town. She described the reptile's hiss and her own alarm in such a graphic way, that in spite of the legend about our Patron Saint and his expatriation of all Ophidians, the incredulity with which I at first regarded her story gave way, and I accompanied her to the spot and found upon a grass plot in front of her house the newly-killed snake. It is a Ringed Snake (*Tropidontus natrix*) measuring twenty-five and three-quarter inches in length. In depriving it of its supposed power to do harm she had not used it gently. Nevertheless, though somewhat mutilated, the specimen was well worth preserving, and so I committed it to a bottle of spirits. It is not necessary to say that Ringed Snakes are not native here, but where this one came from, or how it came here, I have been as yet unable to make out.

JAMES BELLAS, Cronbannagh, Coleraine.

BIRDS.

Scarcity of Land Rail.—For some reason the Corncrake is either very late to come or very scarce this year in this district. While the Cuckoo has been here since 15th April, and is plentiful, I have only heard one Corncrake on 14th May, where they usually abound.

C. H. WADDELL, Saintfield.

Arrival of Spring Migrants in Londonderry District.—The Chiff-chaff was as usual our earlier visitant; it reached us on 31st March. The Sandmartin and Swallow were much behind their usual time; the former arrived on 12th April, and the latter on 13th April. The Willow Wren was also very late of coming; I did not hear its song until 23rd April. The Cuckoo was first heard on 21st April, and the Corncrake on 22nd April.

D. C. CAMPBELL, Londonderry.

The Magpie in the Isle of Man.—Referring to Mr. C. B. Moffat's note in your April number (p. 116), I may mention that the Magpie *is* an introduced species in the Isle of Man. In the history of the Island by Bishop Wilson[1] (cp. 1698-1755) it is stated—" It is not long since a person, more fanciful than prudent or kind to his country, brought in a brood of Magpies, which have increased incredibly, so as to become a nuisance."

P. RALFE, Laxey, Isle of Man.

---

[1] In Manx Society's Publications, vol. xviii. The exact date of the work does not seem to be given.

THE GULLS OF KILLALA BAY.
BY ROBERT WARREN.

OF the eight species of gulls met with in this locality, five are resident and breed—namely, the Great Blackbacked, Lesser Blackbacked, Herring, Common, and Blackheaded Gulls; one, the Kittiwake, is only a summer visitor, departing after the breeding season is over; while two, the Glaucous and Iceland Gulls, are irregular winter visitors, only occasionally seen.

The GREAT BLACKBACKED GULL (*Larus marinus*), the largest of our native gulls, is common, but not numerous, a few pairs frequenting the estuary and sands of the bay in winter, while two or three pairs of non-breeding birds remain about the sands during summer.

The nearest breeding-haunt to Killala Bay is Doonbrista, the pillar-like rock off Downpatrick Head, near Ballycastle (six miles from Killala), where twelve or fifteen pairs have their nests on the flat, grassy summit, and rear their young in perfect safety, for the rock is quite inaccessible; and strange to say, though perfectly safe from disturbance of any kind, their numbers do not seem to increase, for about the same number of breeding birds are now to be seen frequenting the rock as were observed thirty years ago when I first visited Downpatrick Head. The next breeding-station of this gull on the North Mayo coast is that on the Stags of Broadhaven, fifteen or twenty miles west of Downpatrick Head, where a few pairs breed on the largest of the rocks.

The Stags of Broadhaven are situated about three miles from Portacloy, and are four huge isolated rocks, the largest about 300 feet in height, and give one the idea of four miniature Ailsa Craigs with sharply triangular outline. A peculiarity of the rocks along that coast, especially at the base of the cliffs, is their broken shattered appearance and their sharp and rugged points and edges, seen appearing along the surface of the water when the tide is low, in some places extending for many yards beyond the cliff's base.

Some years ago the Great Blackbacked Gulls of this locality were nearly exterminated by poison, laid by the tenant

A

of Bartragh Island for the destruction of rats. A plague of rats destroying the young rabbits in the burrows, thinned them out considerably, and he, wishing to protect them, laid poisoned meat and fish amongst the burrows on the sand-hills, which the gulls (always on the look-out for dead or dying Rabbits) greedily devoured, and the result was that numbers of both Blackbacked and Herring Gulls were afterwards seen lying dead in all directions about the island; and for three or four years after very few were seen about the sands.

These great gulls always hovering over the sands and shores, are like vultures, on the look-out for carrion, dead fish, or weakly, or wounded birds. They become a perfect nuisance to the wild-fowl shooter, alarming the birds he is setting up to for a shot; for the instant he lies down to his gun, the gull, seeing him in such an unusual position, begins to suspect danger, and flies over, and round the punt (out of shot), looking down on the shooter, and giving out his harsh alarm note, which immediately causes the ducks, or Widgeon to be so much on the alert, that the fowler is unable to approach within shooting distance. However, if he does succeed in coming within range, and obtain a shot, any of the dead or wounded birds that escape him are sure to become the prey of the gulls. I well remember on one occasion I knocked down fifteen Widgeon at a shot, while a "dropper" fell dead some distance off, and while I was picking up the dead, and chasing the cripples, a Blackback, that had been watching, and trying to alarm the flock of Widgeon, on seeing the dropper fall, at once made for it, and settling down on the water alongside began tearing the breast, and by the time I had secured my dead and wounded birds, I reached the dropper only in time to find a well-picked skeleton. A dead, or wounded bird is seldom (in winter) found lying on the shore for any time without being clean picked, and many a rare specimen cast up by the sea is destroyed long before the naturalist finds it. I was one day so fortunate as to rescue two fine specimens of the Fulmar from being destroyed by these gulls; they had been thrown up by the surf on the Enniscrone sands, in so weak and exhausted a condition as to be unable to stand, when I came on the gulls just attacking them.

The HERRING GULL (*Larus argentatus*) is the most numerous of the large gulls on this part of the coast. They have many breeding-stations on the cliffs along the North Mayo coast, from Lacken Bay to Bunwee Head. Small colonies of a few pairs are to be seen scattered for miles along the cliffs, while the large colonies are located on the ledges and shelves of Doonbrista, and Downpatrick Head, at Keadue beyond Ballycastle, between Glenglosera and Belderig, Moistha Island, between the last-named place and Porturlin, on Pig's Island, west of the latter place, and also between it and Portacloy, while a few pairs also breed on the Stags of Broadhaven. In fact, there is scarcely a high cliff anywhere between Downpatrick Head and Portacloy, without some Herring Gulls breeding there, being almost as widely distributed as the Kittiwakes. On the North Sligo coast there is a very large colony—one of the largest I have seen—on Aughris Head, about midway between Sligo and Killala Bays.

The LESSER BLACKBACKED GULL (*Larus fuscus*) is not so numerous as the Herring Gull, and is seldom seen in the bay or estuary, for its chief breeding station in Mayo is at present on Lough Mask; though at one time it bred on Lough Conn, as mentioned to the late Wm. Thompson by Mr. B. Ball, which statement was corroborated to me by my late friend, Mr. Henry Knox, of Palmerstown, Killala, who told me that when he was a young man and fishing on Lough Conn he found large numbers of these gulls breeding on islands in the lake. A pair have of late years been seen every summer about the lake, but the nest was not found; and until last summer no good evidence of its breeding was had, when Mr. H. Scroope, of Ballina, saw a pair of young birds in the nestling plumage, following the old ones, showing that they had been bred somewhere about that lake or the adjacent Lough Cullen.

Mr. W. H. Good, of Westport, told me that this gull bred on Lough Mask in large numbers, on one of the islands, and that odd pairs were scattered about through the lake breeding on some of the smaller islands also, which statement I found correct when visiting Lough Mask with my friend, Mr. W. Williams, on the 19th of June, 1893. The gulls' island is situated on the western side of the lake, opposite the Partry Monastery, and is about 200 yards in length, quite low, and thickly covered with rocks and large loose stones, amongst which a few bushes and patches of long grass are growing. The gulls make large nests of the dried grass thrown up by the winter's floods, under the bushes and between the stones. Most of the nests (about twenty) had been robbed a short time previous to our visit, and we found only three or four in which the birds had begun to lay, with one or two eggs in each. We also found on the terns' island two gulls' nests, in one of which there were three eggs, and our boatman informed us that throughout the lake many solitary pairs had nests on many of the small islands. In June, 1895, my friend, Mr. R. J. Ussher, visiting Lough Corrib, found this gull breeding in small numbers on the islands about the lake between Cong and Oughterard, and also found a few pairs breeding on Lough Erne, Co. Fermanagh. I have not myself found this bird breeding on the sea-cliffs of Mayo, although when visiting the north coast in May, 1893, I saw a solitary bird flying along the cliffs between Porturlin and Portacloy, but saw no trace of a nesting-place.

The COMMON GULL (*Larus canus*) is not so numerous as the smaller gulls, though it is extending its breeding-range to places where a few years ago none were to be seen. I first met this gull breeding on a small island in Lough Talt, about twelve miles from the sea, in the heart of the Ox Mountains, Co. Sligo, in 1855; only two or three pairs bred on the lough. I saw the nests (one with an addled egg) on a little rocky islet, and some young birds just able to fly, following their parents about the lake. Since that date the gulls have deserted Lough Talt as a breeding-haunt in consequence of boats having been placed on the lake for the convenience of trout fishers, who frequent the water during the breeding-time in May. They disturbed the gulls so much as to cause them to leave altogether.

This was all I knew of the gulls breeding in this locality, until some years later, when I was told of their breeding on Lough-na-Crumpawn (the lake of the stumps) about ten miles from Ballina, between Glenmore and Crossmolina, but thinking the gulls mentioned must be the Blackheaded, I did not visit the lough until the 17th of May, 1882, when in the company of my friends, Dr. S. Darling and his brother James, we drove to Glenmore, and taking a boy as our guide walked to the bog, which was a wide expanse of low peat moor, with many little loughs and pools scattered all over it. Many of these loughs had little islets, or rather clumps of turf covered with heath and coarse grass. On reaching the first of the loughs, we observed a gull resting on a clump in the middle, but seeing only a solitary bird that flew off at our approach, we had no idea of a nest being there.

Dr. Darling and I went on ahead; James Darling remaining to take another look round, and wading out to the clump of turf, found a nest of dried grass on it containing three eggs. This "find" was most encouraging, for not seeing any gulls about except the solitary one on the clump, we were beginning to fear that our journey would have proved in vain. We then walked on to a group of loughs a quarter of a mile further on, and there we saw two gulls resting on clumps, and in a few minutes we had three pairs of the Common Gull circling round us and screaming, plainly indicating by their anxiety, that at least three nests must be somewhere about the islets on the loughs; but unfortunately for us, owing to the great depth of the soft black mud on the bottom of these loughs, it was quite impossible to wade out to the islands and search for the nests. While walking round the lough, vainly seeking for a passage to the islet, we disturbed a pair of Dunlins, but were unable to find their nest.

Although so far fortunate in finding a breeding-haunt of the Common Gull, yet we had not found the particular lough reported to me, and of which we had come in search. We again questioned the boy, but he knew of no other loughs, nor of one where the gulls built their nests on the tree stumps of an old submerged forest, as had been described to me. So finding the boy of no further use as a guide, we decided on going in different directions over the bog, and, while time allowed, persevering in our search for the missing Lough-na-Crumpawn, "the lake of the stumps." Dr. Darling and I then proceeded to examine some pools about a quarter of a mile away, while James Darling and the boy went off in the opposite direction to a little ridge, from which they could have a better view over the surrounding bog, and perhaps discover the particular lough of which we were in search. Soon after we heard the boy whistle, and saw James Darling run to meet him; we afterwards learned that he had just then come on a Dunlin's nest with four eggs.

We then saw them walk to the top of the ridge, when James Darling whistled, and waving his hat to us, disappeared over the ridge. Not seeing him return we concluded that he had found the lough, so we hastened after him, and on reaching the top, we saw to our great delight, in a hollow about half a mile off, the long-sought for lough easily identified by the tree stumps studding its surface; a number of gulls were flying over our friend, who was wading out through the muddy water to where the nests were. On reaching the lough we soon had eight pairs of *Larus canus* flying over us, and saw eight nests composed of dried grass on the tree stumps; James Darling visited seven of these, six contained eggs; the eighth he was unable to reach, in consequence of the great depth of the black mud on the bottom of the lough.

The foregoing was all the information I had of the breeding of this gull in Sligo and Mayo, until June, 1890, when my friend, Mr. R. J. Ussher, on his way from Belmullet to Ballina, found a large colony of at least fifty pairs breeding on an island in Lough Dohybaun, near Corick, in the last named county. Since then I have met them breeding on Loughs Conn and Cullen, where they had not been seen until a few years ago. On Lough Conn some odd pairs breed on the stony points of the small islands at the upper end of the lake, near Enniscoe and Errew abbey, and are probably scattered all about the lake, for I met them also on the lower end, near Pontoon Bridge; and in Lough Cullen they are scattered about also, while there is a colony of twelve to fifteen pairs on the shores of a small island close to the land, between Garrison Island and the bridge. I have also found the Common Gull breeding on the shores of islands in Lough Mask, but not so numerous as in Lough Cullen.

There is no doubt that these Gulls are extending their breeding-range in this district, more especially to Lough Conn, where fifteen or twenty years ago none were to be seen, when I used to visit the lake in search of breeding birds, and particularly during my close search for the Sandwich Terns, at which time only Blackheaded Gulls, and Common Terns bred about the lake. This gull, during the breeding season, appears to have been more widely distributed throughout the north-west counties than was expected, previous to the visits of my friend Mr. R. J. Ussher, who found them in pairs and small colonies on the loughs in Connemara, as well as in N.W. Donegal, and Mayo; and probably when Clare is explored, they may be found breeding in that county also.

The KITTIWAKE GULL (*Larus rissa*) is very abundant round this coast in summer, but very few are to be seen in winter, and then only a bird in miserable condition is occasionally seen. I have sometimes found birds lying dead on the shore in winter evidently starved to death; any I have shot at that time of year were always in the same miserable state, mere bundles of bones and feathers. This gull breeds in many small colonies along the cliffs extending from Lacken Bay to Downpatrick Head, where there is a very large colony breeding on the shelves and ledges of the head, as well as on those of Doonbrista, the rock on which the Great Blackbacked Gulls breed. The next breeding-haunt is about ten miles further west near Belderig, where many thousands breed on the cliffs between that and Porturlin, and also on the range of cliffs between the latter place and Portacloy; while one of their largest colonies is on Pig's Island, near Porturlin.

The numbers of Kittiwakes, and their numerous breeding-haunts along that line of coast, are really astonishing, and must be actually seen to be realized.

There is also a great breeding-haunt of Kittiwakes on the Sligo coast, Aughris Head (about twenty-four miles from Ballina), where the gulls are in two large colonies, one on a range of cliff about 300 yards long, and the other on one about 50 or 60 yards shorter, and as the shelves and ledges are very regular in their formation, the gulls sitting on their nests can be seen to great advantage, as they appear in long rows, tier above tier, on the face of the cliff. This is the largest colony of Kittiwakes I have yet seen, for although there are greater numbers on the Mayo coast they are more scattered, and not so many are seen at one colony as at Aughris.

The BLACKHEADED GULL (*Larus ridibundus*) is the most numerous of our residents, and a few years ago had two large breeding-haunts within two and three miles of Ballina, Cloona, and Rathrouyeen, but the former has been deserted for some years, for after the death of Mr. Wm. Gardiner, who strictly preserved the lough, the new tenant neglected doing so, and in consequence the gulls were so disturbed and harassed by the country boys robbing their nests year after year, that they left the lake altogether and shifted their quarters to Rathrouyeen, where they now may be seen in thousands. When I first visited Rathrouyeen, over thirty years ago, there were probably not more than between two and three hundred pairs of gulls breeding, chiefly on the small island, where I counted close on 200 nests, while perhaps there were 30 to 50 nests amongst the reeds and rushes about the lake. But now they have overflowed so much that the nests are built everywhere amongst the reed-beds and Bullrushes, and all round the margin of the lake on the tussocks of coarse grass and bunches of rushes; and when any one approaches the shore of the lake the noise of the screaming thousands is deafening. There is also a small colony breeding on a low gravelly island in Lough Conn near Errew Abbey and Enniscoe.

These gulls are the first to suffer from a hard winter and a long-continued frost. In 1894 they suffered more than in any winter that I can remember, and they were so reduced that only a mere tithe of their numbers assembled at their breeding-haunt the following spring. During the severe frost of that winter the unfortunate birds were so hard-pressed for food that they came into the farmyards to feed with the pigs and the poultry; large numbers came into my poultry-yard and piggery feeding on the potatoes and turnips. I fed them every day while the frost lasted, but each morning their numbers lessened by death; one day over a dozen came into the kitchen, and were so tamed by hunger as to feed close round the fire and almost to snatch the food out of the hands of the girl who was feeding them. They even came into the town of Ballina, feeding in the streets and yards of the houses.

The GLAUCOUS and ICELAND GULLS (*Larus glaucus* and *L. leucopterus*), being irregular winter visitors, are only occasionally seen, and as I have given an account of those coming under my notice in the *Irish Naturalist* for October, 1892, there is no need of my now repeating the information given in that number.

THE PLANTS OF INISMURRAY, CO. SLIGO.
BY R. LLOYD PRAEGER, B.E.

On June 8th, on the return of the Rockall expedition, the party landed for an hour on Inismurray, famous among antiquarians for its wealth of primitive edifices. Mr. R. M. Barrington and I spent the time in botanizing, and as no botanist has apparently examined this island previously, a short note on its flora may be interesting, even though that flora is poor and devoid of any special interest. The island is composed of Carboniferous sandstone, and is low and flat. Only a portion is cultivated. The rest consists of stunted heath, marshy in places. In the hour spent on the island, I listed 145 species, almost all of which are plants of universal distribution in Ireland.

In the meadows and marshy spots, the Purple Loosestrife (*Lythrum Salicaria*) grew in enormous profusion. It was not yet in flower, but one could imagine the sheets of purple with which these green spots would soon be covered. Among the grass, and on the heaths, three Orchids brightened the ground by their abundance—*O. maculata, O. latifolia (?)*, and *Habenaria bifolia*. The quantity of the last-named plant, coupled with the almost complete absence of its ally *H. chloroleuca*, was a remarkable feature in the flora of Inismurray; for almost everywhere in Ireland these proportions are reversed. Along the edges of the meadows, and on banks, great masses of Royal Fern grew; it was a surprise to us to find it in such luxuriance in a locality so bleak and wind-swept. The other ferns observed on the island were *Polypodium vulgare, Lastrea Filix-mas, L. dilatata, Athyrium Filix-fœmina, Pteris aquilina,* and *Asplenium marinum;* the last-named grew among boulders on the exposed western shore. A leaf of Sea-Kale, lying in a boggy meadow, made me watch for this plant on the stony shores, but it was not seen. The Golden Rod (*Solidago virgaurea*) grew on dry banks, and in wet places were tufts of *Œnanthe crocata*. The only plants that grew in the few pools and drains were *Apium inundatum, Pot. polygonifolius,* and *Scirpus fluitans; Peplis portula* was straggling over muddy ground close at hand. The commonest weed in the corn-fields was *Sinapis alba; Veronica Buxbaumii* grew with it

The only roadside plant worthy of mention was *Sagina maritima*. Perhaps the most curious plant of the island was a diffuse form of *Juncus conglomeratus*, the stems of which, instead of growing erect in a compact clump as usual, spread out at every angle, from horizontal to vertical, giving the plant a very strange appearance, and recalling the habit of *Schœnus nigricans;* this curious rush was abundant in damp places with the typical form. Mr. Barrington found *Radiola linoides* and *Carduus pratensis*, two species which did not occur to me.

CANIS VULPES MELANOGASTER, BONAP., IN IRELAND.

BY R. F. SCHARFF, PH.D.

This variety of the Fox is characterised by having the underparts of the body and tail black or dark brown instead of white. A specimen recently acquired by the Dublin Museum has all the underparts of the body and tail greyish black. It is a full-grown rather undersized female, and came from the County Kildare. I had never seen an Irish specimen before, but Mr. Ed. Williams, informs me that he has stuffed several for people in the country.

The chief interest of the occurrence of this variety of the Fox in Ireland lies in its geographical distribution. As far as I know, there is only one previous record of this variety having been observed in the British Islands, viz., in Warwickshire (Bell's "Brit. Quadrupeds," 2nd Ed., p. 231).

Nilsson described it as existing in Scandinavia, and there is also a record from France. But it is distinctly a southern form, and has been observed in Greece, Southern Italy, Spain, Portugal, and in the Mediterranean Islands. We may suppose it to have originated in Southern Europe and then to have spread along the Atlantic shores in times long gone by, when the British Islands were still connected with the continent, for the Fox must be looked upon as probably the most ancient of the British Mammals.

I should be glad if any readers of the *Irish Naturalist* would inform me if they have met with this variety of the Fox.

THE MEDUSÆ OF VALENCIA HARBOUR, COUNTY KERRY.

BY EDWARD T. BROWNE.
Zoological Research Laboratory, University College, London.

My friend and colleague, Mr. F. W. Gamble, published in the May number of this Journal a preliminary account of the results obtained by dredging and shore-collecting in Valencia Harbour. It falls to my share to give a list of the Medusæ collected during April and May, 1895.

In selecting the locality on the West Coast of Ireland it was necessary to find a place not only suitable for dredging and shore-collecting, but also for tow-netting, a place well-protected from the swell and storms of the Atlantic. For tow-netting I found Valencia Harbour an exceedingly good place, naturally well-sheltered, and with an excellent pelagic fauna. When the tide was flowing in from the ocean it was only necessary to anchor the boat and to cast the net overboard. By this method the lovely siphonophore *Agalmopsis* could be taken in perfect condition, without the loss of even a swimming-bell. Everyone who has worked on delicate pelagic animals, knows that it is not only important to catch them in perfect condition, but also to be able to examine them very soon after the net has been taken on board. A tow-netting not examined within an hour is usually of little use, as most of the delicate animals are either in a dying condition or dead. The examination of the specimens was greatly facilitated by the short distance of the laboratory from the place for tow-netting.

Only a very few species of Medusæ had been recorded from the West Coast of Ireland, and they conveyed only a vague idea of what might be expected to be found there. As many rare and interesting animals had been taken along the West Coast I naturally expected to meet with a few rare and interesting Medusæ. The species which I collected were not very rare, and most of them I had already seen either at Port Erin, in the Isle of Man, or at Plymouth; but some, even the commonest, were of great importance from a systematic point of view. I was able to collect many early stages and a few complete series showing the development of some of the commonest Medusæ, and to extend the area of distribution of many species in a westward direction.

I have described in detail many of the specimens collected at Valencia in a paper on "British Hydroids and Medusæ" which was read at a meeting of the Zoological Society of London on March 17th, and will be published in the *Proceedings* of the Society in August.

I intend here to give only a list of species taken, omitting a few doubtful ones which require the collection of more specimens to establish for a certainty their identity.

HYDROMEDUSÆ.

ANTHOMEDUSÆ.

Margelis britannica (Forbes) [=*Bougainvillea britannica*, Forbes].— Some very large adult forms taken in May.

Podocoryne carnea, Sars. —Only a single specimen taken.

† **Corymorpha nutans,** Sars.—Very abundant during April and May. The hydroid was not found.

† **Hybocodon prolifer,** Agassiz [=*Amphicodon fritillaria* (Steenstrup)].—A few specimens found at the beginning of April. Some carried young hydræ in the umbrella-cavity.

* **Lar sabellarum,** Gosse [=*Willsia stellata*, Forbes].—Fairly common during April and May.

* **Dipurena halterata,** (Forbes) [=*Slabberia halterata*, Forbes.]— Only a single specimen taken in April. Miss Delap sent me a specimen taken in the harbour on July 8th, and another on September 6th.

* **Euphysa aurata,** Forbes.—Scarce during April, but increased in number during May.

* **Tiara pileata** (Forskal) [=*Oceania episcopalis*, Forbes].—A few early stages seen and some splendid adult specimens taken at the end of May.

* **Lizzia blondina,** Forbes.—A few taken at the end of May.

* **Margelllum octopunctatum** (Sars.) [=*Lizzia octopunctata* (Forbes)].—Fairly common during April and May.

LEPTOMEDUSÆ.

* **Laodice calcarata,** Agassiz.—Three specimens taken in April.

† **Dipleurosoma hemisphæricum** (Allman) [=*Ametrangia hemisphærica*, Allman].—A few taken in May.

* **Tiaropsis multicirrata** (Sars.) [*Thaumantias melanops*, Forbes].— Two early stages taken at the beginning of April.

* **Euchilota pilosella** (Forbes) [=*Thaumantias pilosella*, Forbes].— Three specimens taken in April and one in May.

---

* New to the Irish Fauna.
† Not previously recorded for the West Coast of Ireland

- * **Phialidium cymbaloideum** (Van Beneden) [=*Thaumantias cymbaloides*, Van Beneden].—One of the commonest Medusæ in the harbour during April and May.
- * **Phialidium temporarium,** Browne.—Fairly abundant throughout April and May, specially the early stages.
- * **Saphenia mirabilis** (Wright).—Two specimens taken at the end of May.

Specimens were also taken of Medusæ belonging to the following genera—*Sarsia, Cytæandra, Obelia* and *Aglantha*.

SCYPHOMEDUSÆ.

The complete absence of the Scyphomedusæ during April and May at Valencia is an interesting case in the distribution of pelagic animals at different periods of the year. I did not see a single specimen, not even an early stage. The Misses Delap continued the tow-nettings during the summer. The Scyphomedusæ began to appear about June 11th; some belonging to the genus *Chrysaora* measured a foot in diameter. *Aurelia aurita* appeared about a week later, and *Cyanæa* at the beginning of August; the latter was very abundant. A specimen of *Rhizostoma pulmo* was seen on October 10th.

FIELD CLUB NEWS.

We have received from the Secretaries of the Belfast Club particulars of their Dredging Expedition fixed for the 4th July. The steamer will leave the jetty, Queen's Bridge, at 9.45 a.m., and return at about 7 p.m. All facilities will be given for studying the marine forms of life which may be collected, and tea will be provided on the steamer, which contains a comfortable ladies' cabin. As announced in our last month's issue, the Belfast Club generously invite members of other Field Clubs to take advantage of the opportunity. Those who wish to join should send immediate notice to the Secretaries, Rea's Buildings, Belfast. Tickets are 5s. each.

The arrangements for the Field Club Union excursion to Cavan in July are completed, and have been announced to members. The party will reach Cavan at midday on July 10th, and spend the afternoon in examining the Farnham district. July 11th will be devoted to Lough Oughter, and Monday, 13th, to Slieve Glah. It is to be hoped that a large party will take the opportunity of visiting a beautiful and little-known locality.

SCROPHULARIA UMBROSA (DUM.) IN IRELAND.

BY NATHANIEL COLGAN, M.R.I.A.

As this somewhat critical species has not hitherto been ascertained to occur in Ireland, the *Flora of Ulster* records for Antrim having been rejected by the authors both of the *Cybele Hibernica* and of the *Flora of North-east Ireland*, its discovery in the county Dublin will be of interest to Irish botanists. In August, 1894, I met with a few plants growing by the side of the Liffey in Lucan demesne, and on making further search in the September of last year, lower down the river, between Knockmaroon and Woodlands, it was found again, and in considerable quantity, on both the right and left banks, associated with its congeners, *S. aquatica* and *S. nodosa*. My suspicions as to the identity of the Liffey plant with *S. umbrosa* (Dum.)=*S. Ehrharti* (Stev.) have been confirmed by Mr. Arthur Bennett, the Rev. E. S. Marshall, and the Rev. W. Moyle Rogers, who have kindly examined specimens. The occurrence of the three species in association on the Liffey banks makes it easy to observe in the field the marked differences which separate them. Intermediate in many points between *S. aquatica* and *S. nodosa*, *S. umbrosa* is yet separable at a glance from either by the peculiar form of its inflorescence. The rigid branches of the lax and widely-spreading cyme are almost filiform in their slenderness. By an error, which has no doubt caused much confusion amongst British botanists, the terms descriptive of the cymes of *S. umbrosa* and *S. aquatica* have been transposed in the 3rd Edition of Hooker's *Student's Flora*, those of the first being set down as *contracted* and of the second as *lax*. Further search along the Irish rivers may be expected to extend to other districts, the range of this interesting plant, which seems fully entitled to take specific rank.

PROCEEDINGS OF IRISH SOCIETIES.

ROYAL ZOOLOGICAL SOCIETY.

Recent donations comprise a Rhesus Monkey from Mrs. Tisdall, a Herring Gull from Captain Boxer, a Hedgehog from J. Keegan, Esq., a Grey Parrot and an Angolan Vulture from A. H. Hanley, Esq., and a Jackdaw from W. Williams, Esq.

DUBLIN MICROSCOPICAL CLUB.

May 21st.—The Club met at the house of Mr. GREENWOOD PIM, who showed in the lantern photo-micrographs of various objects, including an ant, sections of basalt, sucker of *Rhingia*, portion of frond of *Hymenophyllum* showing chlorophyll grains and nuclei, group of conceptacles from *Æcidium ranunculacearum, Coscinosdiscus, Jungermannia*, &c. The negatives were taken with a Leitz microscope, objectives from No. 3 to No. 7 (and in one case a Beck 3-inch). The ocular was used in every case, and the ordinary achromatic single lens of the camera left in situ, according to Mr. Mitchell's plan. No adjustment for difference between visual and actinic foci was made, and the definition left nothing to be desired. The *Æcidium* was taken as an opaque object with light condensed from above.

Mr. MCARDLE exhibited male plants of *Scapania umbrosa*, Schrader, one of the minutest of that group of liverworts, which he collected in some quantity at Anniscaul, Co. Kerry, in 1894. It is generally found in very small quantities amongst the larger Hepaticæ. The Anniscaul plants were found growing in compact tufts on decayed wood. The upper portion of the shoots bear from one to three antheridia in the saccate base of each leaf; the stems and the lower portion of the leaves which cover the antheridia are of a brilliant scarlet colour, which gives the plant a peculiarly handsome appearance; in this way, and by its smaller size, truly serrated leaves which are recurved at the apex, and by the truncate and entire mouth of the perianth, it is easily known from all other *Scapaniæ*.

DR. MCWEENEY showed a cultivation of the mould-fungus *Eurotium herbariorum*, showing the sexually produced reproductive bodies or perithecia. These are small yellow globular bodies containing a number of nearly globose asci, each of which has eight spores. The point of interest is that this mode of reproduction is seldom resorted to by the fungus, save under special circumstances, the usual mode being by asexual conidia produced in a globose head.

BELFAST NATURALISTS' FIELD CLUB.

May 23rd.—Excursion to Armoy and Ballycastle. The party left the train at Armoy, and at once made for the Church, where the remains of the fine old round tower still stand in the graveyard. Leaving the church a short halt was made at the chapel to see a couple of rude crosses in the yard.

The district is full of botanical interest, especially as regards the cryptogamic flora, but the find of the day was the rare Whitlow grass, *Draba muralis*. This is rare as a British plant, and as regards Ireland still more rare. It is stated that one plant was found long since growing on the walls of Blarney Castle, in the south, and Dr. Dickie said it was naturalised on old walls near Belfast, but it does not seem to have been seen by any living botanist in either place. On the walls of an old bridge near Armoy, however, it is plentiful and luxuriant. *Draba muralis* has also been found on walls of Glasnevin, where it was supposed to have escaped from the Botanic Garden. The occurrences in Ireland of this plant have all been attributed to accidental escapes from gardens, but, if not indigenous, it is more probable that they are still lingering relics of a more extensive cultivation at a remote period.[1]

The ruin of the old church locally known as *Goban saers* was visited; perched on an overhanging ridge, its rude, strong masonry afford evidence of its early building. The ruined fort of Dun Rainey, having been passed and the Mairge crossed, a halt was made at the ruins of the Old Franciscan Abbey of Bun-na-Mairge. In the old abbey the Rev. J. A. S. Woodward, A.M., read a short paper descriptive of the ruins and their history. At five o'clock all assembled in the Antrim Arms, Ballycastle, where an excellent tea was provided by Mr. Hunter.

JUNE 6th.—The Club held their second summer excursion, and a fine afternoon brought the large number of over 100 members together in time to catch the 2.15 train to Carrickfergus, from which station the whole party proceeded to the salt mines at Duncrue, some two miles distant. Here they were met by Mr. Pennall, the courteous representative of the owners, who placed his services at the Club's disposal during the afternoon. The tedious business of lowering the large party into the pit was then begun by the two shafts, down each of which the buckets carried four persons at a time, one of the buckets being raised at the same time that the other was lowered and by the same engine. The depth of the shaft is about 750 feet, so that the mines are considerably below the sea-level. On arriving at the bottom each member was supplied with a candle, and when enough were collected a party was formed, under the guidance of some one of the miners and of one of the geological members, to explore the galleries. A number of Bengal and coloured lights were brought down, which gave an extremely good effect among the vast piers that have been left to support the roof—often forty or fifty feet above the floors—while the crowd of little twinkling lights seen at the far end of one of the numerous drives was most picturesque. So, numerous was the party that the first section was up again before the

---

[1] We have seen specimens of this plant recently collected at Newry by Rev. H. W. Lett, on a wall near Messrs. Roger and M'Clelland's nursery—no doubt imported.—EDS.

last was down. At appropriate times Mr. William Gray and Mr. Alexander G. Wilson (Hon. Secretary) briefly described the geological features of the Triassic period and the salt-beds in particular, Mr. Gray explaining the lithological characters and Mr. Wilson giving a *resumé* of some of the recent discoveries of the fauna and flora of the period.

The salt is here worked by being quarried from the matrix, often in an almost pure state, and when raised to the surface in buckets is tipped into a reservoir, from which the brine flows down to the evaporating pans near the town. The best thanks of the Club are due to Mr. Alexander Miscampbell, the Irish Manager of the Salt Union, for his courtesy in allowing the members to visit the mine. On reaching the surface the members walked back to Carrickfergus, some of them loitering in the neighbouring fields, the result of which was the discovery of the "Water Soldier" (*Stratiotes aloides*), and the Wood Vetch (*Vicia sylvatica*). The former plant was a most interesting find, as in Stewart and Corry's flora it is marked as "now extinct" in the three recorded localities, and this is a new station for it, and therefore the only known one in Ulster. The vetch is also rare, but the station has been previously recorded. Those who were not able to go by the earlier train left Carrickfergus by the 8.5 train, thus giving them all time to visit the fine old Church of St. Nicholas, where Mr. W. J. Fennell read a short paper on the architectural features of the building, which was illustrated by a most excellent series of photos and drawings.

The GEOLOGICAL SECTION held an Excursion on 16th May to Squire's Hill, for Cretaceous strata, and basaltic dykes and flows. A considerable number of the usual Chalk and Greensand fossils were obtained, from various horizons, and several photos were taken of the remarkable dykes, from one of which was taken the beautiful junction of chalk and basalt recently exhibited at the Club's meetings by Mr. R. Bell.

Another excursion of the section was held on the 13th June, to Woodburn, for the lower beds of the Cretaceous series. A number of the usual Chalk and Greensand fossils, such as *Janira*, *Pecten*, *Terebratula*, *Exogyra*, *Rhynchonella*, *Catopygus*, &c., were taken, though none were new to the local list. Those who were also botanists were pleased to see the glen abundant in the Wood Vetch and Guelder-rose in full flower. The beautiful *Equisetum sylvaticum* was also in quantity.

DUBLIN NATURALISTS' FIELD CLUB.

MAY 30th.—Excursion to Lambay Island. This excursion was of exceptional interest. A party of 46 left Dublin at 10.0 a.m. on board the s.s. "Erin's King," and, steaming round the cliffs of Howth, were soon close to the island of Lambay. The water was quite smooth, and the sky, which was cloudy at starting, speedily cleared, and a day of glorious sunlight ensued. The steamer passed close inshore right round the island, and the great colonies of sea-birds, the sheets of wild flowers on the slopes and cliffs, coupled with the brilliancy of sea and sky, formed a scene not readily to be forgotten. The party were soon ashore in the little harbour, and, under the leadership of Mr. J. E. Palmer, the steep slopes and cliffs of the eastern side of the island were visited. Here the Herring Gulls were breeding in great numbers among the herbage and stones, and care had to be taken not to tread on the dark-spotted brown eggs, or the young birds, equally inconspicuous in their coats of dark mottled down. On the steeper portions, Guillemots and Razorbills were perched in rows beside their large blue and brown eggs, which lay on the ledges of bare rock, and hundreds of Kittiwakes occupied every cranny with their nests of grass. Many of the grassy slopes were riddled with holes made by the Puffins, which, in their beautiful black and white plumage and brilliant red beaks and legs, stood like sentinels at the mouths of their burrows, guarding their solitary large, whitish egg in the nest within. In a deep crevice a Cormorant's nest was visited, in which were three young birds, already nearly fledged. The botany of the island was interesting, and the masses of colour presented by certain species, such as *Lychnis diurna, Sedum acre,* and *Silene maritima* were very striking. Enormous groves of the Henbane, *Hyoscyamus niger,* were observed, four feet in height, and covering considerable areas. Close to the coastguard station a rare clover, *Trifolium striatum,* was obtained. The beetles, of which Mr. H. K. G. Cuthbert kindly supplies a full list, included *Badister bipustulatus, Bradycellas harpalinus, Pterostichus striola, Amara aulica, Trechus minutus, Philonthus varius, Stenus guttula, Helodes marginatus, Corymbites cupreus* (type and var. *aeruginosus*), *Grammoptera ruficornis, Crypticus quisquilius.* As to Hymenoptera, in the *Chrysis* group, Mr. Cuthbert met with *Chrysis ignita,* L., and *Hedychrum lucidulum,* Latr., and in the Aculeate group, *Megachile maritima,* Kirb. (an addition to the Irish list), *M. centuncularis, Andrena fulvicrus, A. minutula, Sphecodes dimidiatus, Odynerus pictus, O. parietinus, O. trimarginatus,* and *Vespa sylvestris.* The last-named species was nesting in a bank, an unusual circumstance in the case of an arboreal wasp, an instance having been once before recorded by the late Mr. Frederick Smith. A very interesting find of another kind was the occurrence of flint-flakes and cores in low mounds of clay and pebbles near the southern extremity of the island; quite a large series was obtained. Messrs. Greenwood Pim and R. Welch obtained a number of photographs of the birds and their nests and eggs, which will no doubt duly appear on the lantern screen at some winter meeting of the Club. All assembled at the harbour at 6.0, where Miss Gardiner had tea ready. Embarkation being safely effected, the "Erin's King" left at 7.45. The evening was dead calm, and lovely effects of light were enjoyed on the homeward run. The party reached Dublin at 9.45, delighted with all they had seen, and very grateful to Count Considine, by whose kindness they were permitted to explore the island.

CORK NATURALISTS' FIELD CLUB.

MAY 30th.—The third excursion took place, the destination being Ballyphehane Bog and Vernon Mount. Owing to the prolonged drought the bog was practically dry and but few of the moisture-loving plants for which it is esteemed, were observed. The Yellow Sedge (*Carex flava*) was seen well in fruit, *Sparganium ramosum* was in flower, and some luxuriant specimens of the smooth horsetail (*Equisetum limosum*) 3-4 feet high were collected. In a neighbouring hedge the Guelder Rose (*Viburnum opulus*) was found flowering handsomely. The excursion was well attended and much interest was shown in the collection of plants. Opportunity may be taken to record the presence of *Brassica tenuifolia*, Boiss. (*Diplotaxis tenuifolia* of older botanists), at Haulbowline Island, where it has been found growing plentifully in waste ground by a member of the Club. This plant with a scanty distribution in the south of England has hitherto been only doubtfully recorded from Co. Cork. In the present case its identity has been verified by Mr. R. A. Phillips of Cork.

ROYAL IRISH ACADEMY.

JUNE 22nd.—The Earl of ROSSE, President, in the Chair. Rev. W. S. GREEN read a paper on a visit to the islet of Rockall, which lies in the Atlantic 220 miles from Tory Island, and 178 west of St. Kilda. On the night of the 6th inst., he and his companions reached the rock in the S. S. "Granuaile," which had been placed at their disposal by the Congested Districts Board. The sea was then breaking heavily all around, and attempts made to dredge resulted in the loss of the gear. On the 7th, the sea still running high, the "Granuaile" steamed away eastward, and a trawling was made in 130 fathoms. The gear was badly torn, but some specimens were obtained. The weather showing no sign of improvement, the vessel steered for Killybegs, which was reached on the evening of the 8th. A fresh start was made on the night of the 13th, and on the 15th Rockall was again sighted. Dredgings were made in from 50 to 100 fathoms. The ship remained close to the rock all night, and on the following morning the rock was approached to within twenty yards, but landing was impossible. Every bird on the rock was recognised, and some were shot and picked up. The weather giving no promise of improvement, a course was steered for St. Kilda, a dredging being made on the Rockall Bank. The result of the dredging was very varied, and some valuable specimens were obtained. Over a dozen species of sea-birds were noted on the rock and in its vicinity.

NOTES.

BOTANY.

PHANEROGAMS.

Recent Notices of Irish Plants.—In the *Journal of Botany* for June, Messrs. E. S. Marshall and W. A. Shoolbred publish an important list of plants observed by them during a fortnight's stay in July, 1895, at Clonbur, near the S.W. corner of Lough Mask, and on the borders of Mayo and Galway; a few notes from Kilkenny and Clare are also included. Of the more interesting plants recorded, the following may be mentioned:—*Ranunculus Drouetii, Subularia aquatica, Polygala oxyptera, Agrimonia odorata, Filago minima* "not recorded from the West of Ireland" *(Cyb. Hib.)*; *Utricularia ? neglecta, Polygonum maculatum, Epipactis atrorubens, Potamogeton filiformis, Carex aquatilis,* var. *elatior,* Bab., *C. Pseudocyperus, Festuca Myuros, Lycopodium inundatum, Pilularia globulifera.* Some of the above furnish very important extensions of the known range of the several plants. In a long list of *Rubi,* the following are new records for Ireland—*R. erythrinus, R. dumnoniensis, R. argentatus, R. Sprengelii, R. Babingtonii.*

The Twelfth Annual Report of the Watson Botanical Exchange Club, just issued, contains references to a number of Irish plants, sent to the Club by the late Mr. H. C. Levinge, and the Revs. C. H. Waddell and H. W. Lett. Few of these call for special remark, but we are glad to see definite confirmation of the occurrence of *Ranunculus floribundus* in the North-east (see *Flor. N.E. I. Suppl.*). Mr. Lett adds *Anthriscus vulgaris* to the Armagh Flora, and some interesting *Rubi* are recorded.

Flora of North-East Ireland.—On the 25th May I noticed on Slemish Mountain, County Antrim, the following plants:—*Vaccinium Vitis Idæa* sparingly on the north face; and *Hieracium iricum,* with the *Vaccinium;* and *Habenaria albida* plentiful at the S.W. base. None of these are abundant plants, and the first is very rare in the north-east of Ireland.

H. C. HART, Portsalon, Letterkenny.

Draba verna at Poyntzpass.—I noticed this spring on one of the walks in my flower garden a plant very like *D. verna.* In order to make sure I sent it to Mr. Praeger who confirms my determination.. It occurs also on the road between this and Poyntzpass and at the railway station. The only other locality in County Armagh is I believe the Sheep-walk at Armagh, but Mr. Praeger thinks it has escaped notice elsewhere from its small size and early habit of flowering.

W. F. JOHNSON, Poyntzpass.

The Globe Flower in Co. Fermanagh.—It may interest botanical readers to know that the Globe Flower (*Trollius europæus*) grows in an unquestionably wild state on the shores of one of the larger Fermanagh lakes. Mr. Pike of Sydenham Hill, London, first brought the circumstance under my notice.

W. MACMILLAN, Enniskillen.

Measurement of a Scotch Fir Stump in Fanet, Co. Donegal.
—In July, 1892, in company with the Rev. A. Delap, I took measurement of a trunk of a Scotch Fir, bared by recent drainage on the shore of Ballyhork Lake, in the "Between Waters," Fanet. The trunk was 3 feet 6 inches in diameter. The root at base of trunk were *in situ*. Obviously the tree had been felled, and the stem was gone. The bark was still on, the peat having been but recently removed. Hazel nuts and oak-wood were in company with the fir. We counted the rings from the centre; he made out 264, and I made them 234.

H. CHICHESTER HART, Portsalon, Letterkenny.

ZOOLOGY.

Our Introduced Species.—I am glad to see Mr. P. Ralfe's note on the introduction of the Magpie into the Isle of Man. I had not previously heard of the fact, though Bishop Wilson is also the principal authority for the introduction (in his time), and rapid increase of the Frog. The marked parallelism between the recorded introductions in these two islands (Ireland and Man) is an interesting piece of circumstantial evidence in favour of the correctness of both records, and therefore strengthens the case for the opinion generally held, but to some extent disputed by Dr. Scharff, that the Frog was really unknown in Ireland till 1696.

C. B. MOFFAT, Dublin.

WORMS.

Freshwater Annelids: An appeal.—During a visit which I recently paid to the north of Ireland, I was fortunate enough to find some very interesting forms of freshwater worms. What I saw convinces me that the ponds, canals, and loughs of Ireland will yield many valuable forms, if only they can be carefully worked. In order that I may make my forthcoming reports as full as possible, I want to appeal to all who are interested in the progress of science in Ireland to help me. The work I want my fellow-collectors to undertake is simple, easy, and not unpleasant. I ask all those who are living near, or visit places where there are ponds, lakes, canals, or other sheets of water, to send me wide-mouthed bottles filled with algæ, pond weed, and decaying debris floating about, with just a little water, in the hope that some new forms of *Nais* and other microscopic annelids may be discovered. I found at least one new species among such material in a small branch of Loch Erne, and have no doubt but that others will be forthcoming. Those who do not mind dredging, or putting their hands into the silt by the side of streams, ponds, and ditches or gutters, might also render good service by sending the material thus collected, either in tins or wide mouthed bottles, labelled Natural History Specimens.

HILDERIC FRIEND, Cockermouth, Cumberland.

INSECTS.

Entomological Notes from Poyntzpass.—My earliest captures of lepidoptera were *Phigalia pedaria* and *Hybernia marginaria*, which I took on February 13th in the glebe grounds. A nice specimen of *Selenia illunaria* was brought to me on March 13th. *Bombus terrestris* put in an appearance on March 20th, and *Vanessa urticæ* on the 22nd, and on the evening of the same day there was a remarkable swarm of Dor Beetles (*Geotrupes stercorarius*, L.) at the railway station in Poyntzpass. They must have been in great numbers, for two boys brought me about seventy, and the next morning I saw numbers lying on the pathway where they had been trodden on by passers by. I can only suggest as the cause of their assemblage the quantity of cowdung left in that vicinity after the cattle fair. I have noticed these beetles particularly numerous this Spring, I think more so than I ever observed before. Of other early butterflies I noticed *Pieris napi* on April 17th, and *Euchloë cardamines* and *Satyrus egeria* on the 22nd. I saw the first wasp on the wing on April 23rd. Sallows are rather scarce here, and I only obtained the commoner species of *Tæniocampa*, viz., *gothica*, *stabilis* and *incerta*.

Among coleoptera I have not met with anything very remarkable in this immediate locality. On February 26, I gathered a bag of moss from one of my fields, the best species in which were—*Bembidium Mannerheimi, Encephalus complicans, Megarthrus depressus, Silpha opaca, Hister neglectus, Euplectus ambiguus,* and *Miccotrogus picirostris*. In March I took *Lithocharis ochracea* in a hot-bed at Acton House, and *Olophrum piceum* when digging in the side of a drain in one of my fields. On the shore of the lake at Loughbrickland on April 9th I took a single specimen of *Enochrus bicolor*; the only previous record for Ireland is Mr. Halbert's who took it in quarries near Raheny (*I. N.*, 1894, p. 203). My specimen is lighter in colour than those I have from English localities, but not otherwise distinguishable.

On May 6th I received from Rev. J. Hamilton of Coolmore, Co. Donegal, a box of larvæ, which, on examination, I found to be those of *Melitæa aurinia*. He kindly sent me a further supply, and mentioned that they had appeared in the greatest profusion in that neighbourhood much to the alarm of the country folk. It will be remembered that I reported (*I. N.*, 1895, p. 161), a number of this butterfly being washed up on the beach at Coolmore, and I then supposed that they had been blown across from the opposite side of the bay, but the present capture of larvæ shows that my supposition was incorrect, and that they were in the immediate neighbourhood, probably somewhat further south towards the mouth of River Erne. The larvæ have fed upon Honeysuckle, and pupated, and I hope soon to have a number of nice specimens. On May 7th, in the Lower Demesne at Tanderagee, I captured *Leistotrophus nebulosus*, and Mrs. Johnson picked up *Geotrupes sylvaticus*, in both cases only a single specimen was met with. Lepidoptera are now (June) plentiful; and I have captured in my garden here *Chærocampa elpenor, Plusia festucæ, P. pulchrina, Cucullia umbratica*, &c. I hope as I become better acquainted with this locality to be able to report more interesting captures.

W. F. JOHNSON, Acton Glebe, Poyntzpass.

Acherontia atropos at Bessbrook.—On September 26th, 1895, I received a specimen of the Death's Head Moth which had been captured at Bessbrook, and was kindly forwarded to me by Mr. E. M'Clelland. It is a very fine example, measuring five inches across the expanded wings.

W. F. JOHNSON, Poyntzpass.

Carabus clathratus, L. in Co. Wicklow.—In Mr. Carpenter's paper, lately published in the *Irish Naturalist*, on the "Mingling of the North and the South," I find the non-occurrence of *Carabus clathratus* in the East of Ireland is specially commented on. I may state that I captured some of these beetles on the Great Sugar-loaf in Co. Wicklow, in September, 1891, and October, 1892

H. G. CUTHBERT, Dublin.

FISHES.

The Allis Shad in Irish waters.—A specimen of this rare fish (*Alosia communis*) was caught at Donaghadee early this year, and has been presented to the Museum of the Belfast Natural History and Philosophical Society. Londonderry is the only locality given for the species in Thompson's "Natural History of Ireland."

BIRDS.

Irish Birds.—In the *Zoologist* for May, Mr. R. J. Ussher writes concerning the reported occurrence of the Gold-vented Thrush and Spotted Eagle Owl in Ireland. The writer gives full particulars, as far as known, of the history of the specimen of each of these birds alleged to have been shot in Ireland, and the evidence which he adduces is strongly in favour of the view that the records are perfectly *bona fide*, and that these two African species were actually shot in this country. Mr. H. A. Macpherson gives an extract from a letter from Major-General Vallancey to J. C. Walker, dated from Cove, January 25th, 1794, and published in Thirteenth Report, Historical Commission, concerning a bird shot in Co. Cork, which from the description Mr. Macpherson suggests may have been the Buff-backed Heron. Mr. H. Chichester Hart in the same number records the occurrence of three Wood Wrens at Carrablagh, Portsalon, Co. Donegal.

Spring Migrants at Poyntzpass.—In spite of the remarkable mildness of the season the arrival of these birds was not earlier than usual. The Chiffchaff came on March 24th, the Willow Wren April 8th, the Swallow April 18th, the Sand-Martin April 23rd, the Corncrake April 27th, the Cuckoo April 30th, the Swift May 9th, and the House Martin May 11th.

W. F. JOHNSON, Poyntzpass

The Grasshopper Warbler in Co. Dublin.—On the 4th May I saw and heard a Grasshopper Warbler (*Acrocephalus nævius*) near Templeogue; it was not at all shy, and allowed me to come within a few yards of it without stopping its song. It remained in the same spot for three days.

G. P. FARRAN, Templeogue.

Stock-Dove in Co. Galway.—During the week ending April 18th, my steward, who is well acquainted with all local birds, told me several times that he had heard or seen what appeared to be a Wood Pigeon, which uttered an (to him) entirely strange note. It frequented a chain of fir plantations near the house, and in one of these I heard it myself on Monday, April 20th, and at once recognized the note as being that of a Stock-Dove (*Columba œnas*). One morning early that week my steward had a good view of it as it sat "cooing" on an oak tree, and when it flew he could see no white bar on the wing. We heard it frequently until May 1st, on which day I first caught sight of it as it flew out of a tree in a wood. The bird was evidently alone. I see in Seebohm that it is "unknown in Ireland except in the N.E., where, however, it is very rare."

R. F. HIBBERT, Scariff, Co. Clare.

[The Stock-Dove has extended its range in Ireland during the last few years. It has been noticed in Co. Wicklow (*Irish Naturalist*, vol. ii., p. 202), and in Co. Carlow (vol. iv., p. 296). Its occurrence in the far west now noted is of great interest.—EDS.]

Quail in Co. Cork.—I heard the Quail near Bandon this evening (31st May). There were two of them crying to each other from opposite sides of a country road, and I have no doubt that they are nesting there. It is said that Quail were once common in the south of Ireland, but I never heard one here before. The unusually warm dry weather probably accounts for their settling.

ALLAN P. SWAN, Bandon.

Iceland Gull on the Sligo Coast.—I picked up dead on the strand at Mullaghmore, Co. Sligo, on the 5th June, an adult Iceland Gull (*Larus leucopterus*, Fab.). It had evidently been shot at, as both legs were broken, and there were wounds in its neck and stomach. It was identified by Messrs. Williams of Dublin.

CHARLES LANGHAM, Tempo Manor, Co. Fermanagh.

GEOLOGY.

Submerged Peat-bogs in Co. Donegal.—Among submerged peat-bogs it may be worth while to note those of Inver Bay, County Donegal. The most conspicuous is on its N.W. shore, a little beyond the old house and wood of Kilmacreddan (?) It is visible enough at low water of springs, and I have found in it fragments of *Pinus sylvestris* and entire Hazel-nuts.

It may here be noted that a considerable depression of the opposite coast of North America seems to have been, geologically speaking, not far from contemporary. Farther away in Bombay Harbour, a forest of trees, of an existing species (*Acacia catechu*) of the Peninsula, was found some years ago, in digging the Prince's Dock, many feet below low water level. The stumps stood upright on their roots, just as they do in many Irish bogs; and the wood was good enough to make beautiful walking sticks.

W. F. SINCLAIR, London.

THE FIELD CLUBS IN CAVAN.
BY R. LLOYD PRAEGER,
Sec. I. F. C. Union.

CAVAN, according to the programme issued to all members of Irish Field Clubs, was selected for this year's joint excursion, on account of its being a promising county, which was almost unknown to the naturalist. And, indeed, of all the counties of Ulster, Cavan, the most southern, was the one concerning the flora and fauna of which our knowledge was most incomplete. The party which assembled there on July 10th, therefore, had before them the pleasure which ever pertains to the examination of comparatively virgin soil, although, on account of the highly cultivated character of the greater part of the district, and the extensive draining that has been carried out, no discoveries of a startling nature were anticipated.

It was a bright morning when we left Dublin and rapidly crossed the level limestone plain to the lake district of Westmeath, and thence northwards through undulating ground, and then over the great bog which fills the valley of the Inny, to the rolling Ordovician hillocks of Cavan town. The Belfast party had meanwhile been travelling south-west to join us, and welcomed us on the railway platform, where were also congregated several country members and local friends who had converged towards our rendezvous. Thanks to the joint meetings of the last few years, and the almost constant intercourse between the different Clubs that the Field Club Union has fostered and brought about, the meeting of the Belfast and Dublin parties was no longer a meeting of strangers, as it was on the occasion of the first joint excursion to the Boyne some few years ago, but was more like a meeting of old acquaintances, pleased with the prospect of renewing their friendships. The whole party, in number thirty-six, met without delay at early dinner at the Farnham Arms Hotel, which was headquarters during our stay, and by 2 o'clock we were mounted in brakes *en route* for the woods of Lord Farnham's demesne. The vehicles took us through the deerpark, where under trees the Broad-leaved Helleborine (*Epipactis latifolia*) grew in luxuriance, and I had the good fortune to spot the Bird's-nest Orchid (*Neottia Nidus-avis*) below a great Beech; the former

A

plant proved to be common in the Cavan district. A brief halt was made at Farnham House, where, by the kindness of the steward, Mr. Hamilton, we visited a mineralogical museum brought together by a former owner, in which there was a remarkably fine collection of ambers. Pushing on, we dismounted in Derrygid wood, with several pretty lakes flanking us on the right and left. The party soon scattered in pursuit of their different hobbies. The continued rains of the past week, which concluded with the torrential downpour of July 8 and 9, had almost drowned the country, and we found all the lakes and streams risen several feet above their normal limit, rendering the search for aquatic and paludose species often difficult and sometimes impossible. The woods did not prove productive, but the stony and often-flooded margin of Farnham Lough, fringed with a scrub of native Birch and Aspen, furnished excellent hunting-ground. There at many points the Buckthorn (*Rhamnus catharticus*) grew, loaded down with green berries. In wet ground the Purple and Yellow Loosestrife (*Lythrum salicaria* and *Lysimachia vulgaris*) brightened the thick growth of grass and sedges, among which the beautiful and local plant, *Carex Pseudo-cyperus* was conspicuous by its abundance. The Great Water-dock (*Rumex Hydrolapathum*) and Great Spearwort (*Ranunculus Lingua*) were also among the species noted.

The conchologists were well pleased by finding abundance of the land shell, *Clausilia laminata*, which in Ireland is confined to a very limited area in the central portion of the country. Lepidoptera also came in for a good deal of attention. The best species noted were *Uropteryx sambucaria*, *Lasiocampa quercus* var. *callunæ*, and larvæ of *Chærocampa elpenor*. Others took advantage of the picturesqueness of the scene and brilliant light for sketching, and got some pretty "bits," where the tall oaks and dark pines rose above the birchen thickets that fringed the calm waters of the lake. All spent a profitable afternoon, and met at 9 o'clock supper, well pleased with their first experience of Co. Cavan.

Next morning the well-known whistle summoned the party to breakfast at 8 o'clock, and before 9.0 we were out in the brilliant sunshine and off for a long day's exploring. Driving south-westward, the first halt was made at Kilmore Cathedral. There the archæologists came to the front, and discussed the wonderfully-preserved ornament of the beautiful old doorway, taken from Trinity Abbey on Lough Oughter, and now built into the wall of the recently-erected church, which was carefully examined and its graceful proportions admired. The tomb of the famous Bishop Bedell, in the old graveyard, was duly visited, and also a very fine earthen fort, with a deep fosse, in a meadow adjoining. There I noted the Rough Chervil (*Chærophyllum temulum*), a rare plant in Ireland. When the party were once again brought together, and Mr. Welch had finished photographing the doorway and tomb, we proceeded towards Crossdoney. Near Lisnamandra the geologists, under Prof. Cole, found in a field by the roadside an interesting section, showing a dark andesitic intrusion, baking the overlying Carboniferous sandstones, which are here almost horizontal. Close at hand, a grey eurite appears, probably an offshoot from the pre-Carboniferous granite of Crossdoney. A larger rock-exposure occurs by the roadside close to Crossdoney, where excellent hand-specimens of the biotite-granite were obtained. Thence a short drive brought us to Bellahillan bridge and the Erne, where a brief halt was made. We turned northward now, and having surmounted a couple of steep hills on foot, a rapid drive, with lovely and ever-changing peeps of Lough Oughter, brought us to Killykeen cottage, and lunch, within three minutes of the appointed time, 2 o'clock. Killykeen cottage is situated on a long promontory among the mazy windings of Lough Oughter. Straight opposite a similar promontory, occupied by the woods of Gartnanoul, projects till the lake between is narrowed to the width of a stone-throw. To left and right, the water extends, branching on each side among a series of wooded points and grassy islands. Lunch was speedily disposed of on the grassy sward by the water's edge, and then a movement was made towards the boats, which had been most kindly placed at the disposal of the party by Messrs. H. H. Moore, W. H. Halpin, and Samuel Jones. In these the majority of the party started southward to visit the ruins of Trinity Abbey. A second detachment crossed to the Gartnanoul side to collect in the woods and on the shores, while others elected to explore the woods of Killykeen. On the young Aspens that fringed the water on the Gartnanoul shore Mr. Kane discovered the larvæ of the rare moth, *Cymatophora or*, and a band of willing helpers assisted him to collect the pairs of leaves between whose fastened-together edges the larvæ were to be found. Almost the whole party eventually met at Clogh Oughter Castle, or Bedell's Tower, a mile to the northward—a massive circular keep, one-half of it now fallen down, standing on an islet in the centre of one of the reaches of the lake. The return to Killykeen was made in time to allow a half-hour's hunt over the bog at Derrywinny, where, on a preliminary visit to Cavan in May, I had noted several uncommon plants. These were all found, and some additional species of interest. The flora of the bog includes the Great Sundew (*Drosera anglica*), Marsh Andromeda (*A. polifolia*), three species of Bladderwort (*U. vulgaris, U. intermedia, U. minor*), the Frog-bit (*Hydrocharis Morsus-ranæ*), White Beak-rush (*Rhynchospora alba*), Cyperus Sedge (*Carex Pseudo-cyperus*), and Spinulose Bucklerfern (*Lastrea spinulosa*). A drive along beautifully wooded roads brought us back to Cavan. In the evening the tables were cleared, and bottles, jars, collecting boxes, and drying paper took the place of knives and plates, and we had an exhibition and examination of the specimens collected on our first two days. Prof. Cole, Miss Thompson, and A. G. Wilson showed the rock-specimens obtained in the Crossdoney district. W. F. de V. Kane, Hon. R. E. Dillon, and Endymion Porter produced their entomological finds. H. Lyster Jameson had two species of bats, and the rare shell *Clausilia laminata*. W. D. Donnan and I had some flowering plants; and others contributed according to their means. By request, the Dublin President (Prof. Cole) gave a brief general sketch of the geological construction and history of the district. He said that the geology of the vicinity afforded some contrasts, beneath the uniform scenery of rounded hills and intervening little lakes, which are such a feature of Co. Cavan. The floor of the country is formed of Ordovician shales and sandstones, finely seen upon Slieve Glah, and uptilted, as usual, by earth movements prior to the Carboniferous period. At Crossdoney, a biotite-granite, with associated veins of compact grey eurite, penetrates the Ordovician beds, probably as an accompaniment of these same movements. The alteration of the Ordovician shales along the junction had been well seen in several sections. To visitors from Dublin, the comparison with the muscovite-granite of the Leinster chain, which occurs similarly, made Crossdoney of especial interest. Unconformably on the Ordovicians, the Lower Carboniferous sandstone was laid down, and was succeeded by the great Carboniferous Limestone, which forms the country west of Cavan, and which includes the basin of Lough Oughter. The sandstone, which is only of local occurrence, had been seen below Lisnamandra. The relations of a small exposure of eurite to the adjacent rocks had not been determined in the short time available; but there is little doubt that the eurite belongs to the Crossdoney series, and was cold and denuded before the grey quartzite, now seen close against it, was deposited as a sand-bed in the Carboniferous sea. The true position of this eurite is, however, a matter of much interest, as it may, after all, represent a post-Carboniferous intrusion, like the adjacent andesite. The glacial deposits consist of thick boulder-clay, with very little sand and gravel. The boulder-clay capping so many of the hills gives them and their slopes the typical dome-like contour, whether the underlying rock is Ordovician or Carboniferous; but the limestone of the latter period has larger lakes upon its surface, solution doubtless aiding their formation; and the broad hollow of the Erne lies in it, stretching away from Cavan to Enniskillen.

Afterwards, I was called on to give a short account of the Bladderworts and their allies, as these interesting plants had been particularly in evidence that day. Then a pleasant function was performed as Prof. Cole presented to Henry Hanna a prize recently awarded to him by the Committee of the Belfast Club for the best set of twenty-four microscopical slides showing general excellence. Afterwards we returned to our specimens, and until a late hour the crowd of town's-people round the hotel windows showed the interest that the inhabitants of Cavan took in our mysterious researches.

Cavan is notoriously a wet county, and the statement made with some positiveness by local members, that there *could* not be more than two such fine days in succession, proved correct. Sunday morning was gloomy, and after breakfast heavy rain began to fall. But, indeed, if it *had* to rain, the weather was most considerate, for a less inconvenient time for rain during our stay could not have been found. The church-goers were in no way deterred, and a large party started off for Killykeen in excellent spirits in the very heaviest downpour. We had a six-mile drive in the rain, and a swim in the lake, and as we sat at lunch in the little tea-house, the clouds lifted, and soon the sun came out, and a brilliant and delightful afternoon succeeded. In three boats we rowed northward, and again visited Bedell's Tower, and explored the adjoining lake-shores; and then, leaving a contingent sketching on the margin, we rowed back by a narrow and tortuous channel, only navigable in flood-time, with splendid woods rising on either hand. On one small islet we found, submerged below about six inches of water, half a dozen terns' nests with eggs, showing how great was the flood. We re-assembled at Killykeen for tea, and on the way home had another hour on the bog at Derrywinny, and got further specimens of its interesting plants—including a large quantity of delicious wild Raspberries. Even the approach of darkness did not put an end to scientific enquiry, for long after our late dinner a bat-hunting party set out in the dusk, to scour the district for these little-known mammals.

Our last day (Monday) was finer than ever, and in brilliant sunshine we left the "Farnham Arms" at 9.0 a.m. and drove south-east to the base of Slieve Glah, and by 10.30 our advance guard had taken possession of the summit. Though only 1,057 feet high, this hill looks imposing from any point of view, on account of its isolated position; and for the same reason a remarkably extensive view is obtained from its summit. This day was not exceptionally clear, and yet we could clearly identify no less than fourteen counties. To the east, beyond the fertile fields of Cavan, stretched the plains of Meath and Louth, with the ridge on which Tara stands, and the high ground about Collon clearly distinguishable. To the north-east, a haze or shower hid the mountains of Mourne; but beyond the undulations of Monaghan, Slieve Gullion in Armagh rose faint and blue. Tyrone was probably in view, but we could not identify any particular point. To the north-west stretched the valley of the Erne, and on its southern side the limestone mountains of Fermanagh and Leitrim rose clear and high, with Cuilcagh in the centre. Westward stretched the plains of Roscommon and Longford, with the moat and chapel spire of Granard to the south-west. Southward lay the valley of the Inny, with

Lough Sheelin spread in the foreground, and the limestone hills that overlook Lough Kinale and Lough Derevaragh in Westmeath standing up conspicuously, and far beyond these lay the long blue outline of the Slieve Bloom Mountains, on the borders of King's and Queen's Counties. To the southeast we probably saw Kildare, though it could not be identified, but beyond it the high granite range of Dublin and Wicklow rose wonderfully clearly, its southern end fading into blue dimness, its northern end boldly standing out in the Two-rock and Three-rock Mountains. In the foreground the rolling hills and fertile fields of Cavan spread in every direction, with lakes and woods giving variety to the scene.

The appearance of so large a party on the mountain had thrown the district quite into a commotion, and by this time most of the neighbours had joined us, one old fellow being particularly obliging in retailing information respecting the locality, giving due prominence to the giants, witches, and fairies of both past and present days. Descending the hill to the northward, our party scattered, and several finds were made. The Stag's-horn Club-moss, *Lycopodium clavatum*, was found in considerable abundance, and already in fruit; and Miss Kelsall obtained a single specimen of the Moonwort (*Botrychium Lunaria*). The entomologists took *Acronycta myricæ* var. *montivaga*, and larvæ of *Saturnia carpini* and *Eupithecia nanata*. After lunch it was time to return to Cavan, and the bustle of packing was succeeded by a final cup of tea, when many plans for future excursions were discussed, and many invitations exchanged between the members of the different Clubs. The northern party were the first to leave, amid friendly farewells, and they were accompanied to the train by several of the Dubliners, and by Messrs. H. H. Moore and S. Jones, who had been indefatigable in their efforts to assist the visitors, and whose local knowledge proved of the greatest service. An hour later the Dublin members departed, and all reached home delighted with their visit to Cavan, improved in health and spirits by their long days in the open air, and many of them bearing with them material for scientific papers, which will, no doubt, in due course find their way into these pages.

HEPATICÆ COLLECTED IN CO. CARLOW.
(For the R.I.A. Flora and Fauna Committee.)
BY DAVID M'ARDLE.

On the 30th of March last year I joined Dr. R. F. Scharff and Mr. J. N. Halbert,[1] of the Science and Art Museum, at Borris, where they were investigating the fauna; and we were soon on our way to the banks of the River Barrow. In a small plantation amongst granite rocks near the bridge at Graigue, I was fortunate in gathering *Scapania compacta* in a fertile state. The late Dr. D. Moore considered it a very rare liverwort, and the only specimens he collected of it were found in two localities in the County Kerry, in both places sterile. *Scapania æquiloba* and *S. aspera* also grew plentifully amongst the moist crumbling rocks. We returned through the demesne to Borris. The following day was spent collecting on both sides of the river between Ballyluglea Bridge at Borris, and Goresbridge, distant about five miles. Amongst other liverworts I collected *Lejunea flava*, var., and *L. patens*, and on damp rocks in a wood the rare *Lophocolea spicata*. Part of a day spent in Oakwood Park near Carlow concluded this interesting excursion.

In the following list of Hepaticæ I enumerate 33 species and 3 varieties, many of them rare and of botanical interest, such as fertile specimens of *Metzgeria conjugata*, *Jungermania alpestris*, &c. It may be of interest to note that we have no previous list or even a locality quoted for liverworts in the County Carlow that I am aware of. Had our visit been of longer duration I could have pushed on to the Blackstairs Mountains, and possibly I would have been enabled to further extend this list. Hepaticæ are very scarce in the granite districts, but a few genera, such as *Scapania*, *Nardia*, &c., abound. On the limestone formation they are more abundant both in genera and species.

Frullania dilatata, Linn.—Wood by the roadside at Graiguenamanagh, Goresbridge, Oak Park demesne, on trees, common.

F. tamarisci (Mich. L.)—Spreading in large patches on rocks and trees about Graigue, Goresbridge, Oak Park demesne, very common.

Lejeunea serpyllifolia (Dicks.) Libert.—On a damp bank, Graigue. On trees in the wood near Goresbridge.

---

[1] Mr. Halbert has published a list of the Coleoptera which he captured, in the *Irish Naturalist* for December, 1895, p. 330.

L. patens, Lindberg.—Wood by the roadside, Graigue, and Goresbridge, rare. There is an excellent figure of this plant in Moore's "Irish Hepaticæ."[1]

L. flava, Swartz, var.—Damp places amongst rocks about Graigue, and on trees near Goresbridge, rare.

Radula complanata, Linn.—Common on the trunks of trees about Graigue, Oak Park demesne, and Goresbridge.

Lepidozia reptans, Linn.—Damp places near the River Barrow, Graigue. On decayed wood at Goresbridge, *fertile*.

Bazzania trilobata, Linn. (Hook. Brit. Jung., tab. 76; *Mastigobryum trilobatum*, G. L. et N. Syn. Hep., p. 230).—Amongst rocks near the bridge at Graigue, rare.

Cephalozia bicuspidata, Linn.—Damp places about Graigue and Goresbridge, very common.

C. catenulata, Huben. (Hepaticol. German., 169; Carrington in *Trans. Bot. Soc. Edin.*, vii., p. 449, t. 11., fig. 2).—Amongst damp rocks near the bridge, Graigue, rare.

Lophocolea bidentata, Linn.—Common.

L. spicata, Taylor.—Amongst damp rocks in the wood near Goresbridge, very rare.

Kantia trichomanes, Dicks.—Common.

K. arguta (N.M.) Lindb. (Eng. Bot. tab. 1875).—Damp bank in wood by the roadside, Graigue, rare.

Saccogyna viticulosa, Mich.—On a damp boggy place in wood by the roadside, Graigue.

Scapania compacta, Dumort. (*Jungermania compacta*, Roth, Germ. 3, p. 375; Lindenb. Synop. Hep., p. 58; *Jungermania resupinata*, Hook. Brit. Jung., tab. 23, excellent fig.; Sm. Eng. Bot., tab. 2498.)—Amongst granite rocks, bank of the River Barrow near Graigue (fertile), rare. Dr. D. Moore in his work on the Irish Hepaticæ states this is a rare plant in Ireland; the only specimens he collected were from the neighbourhood of Brandon, Co. Kerry, sterile in both places where it was found growing.

S. æquiloba, Dumort. (Carrington, Brit. Jung., p. 81, no. 3, pl. 8, fig. 26).—On rocks near the River Barrow at the bridge at Graigue, plentiful.

S. æquiloba, var. near *S. aspera*.—On rocks near the bridge at Graigue.

S. aspera, Müller and Bernet. (Pearson in *Journal of Bot.*, Vol. xxx. p. 353. plate 329, 1893).—Amongst damp rocks, side of the River Barrow near the bridge at Graigue, plentiful.

S. nemorosa, Dumort.—Amongst damp rocks, side of the River Barrow at Graigue.

S. undulata, Linn.—Margin of a stream near the bridge at Graigue.

Diplophyllum albicans, Linn.—Damp banks in the plantations about Graigue, very common.

Plagiochila asplenioides, Linn.—Damp banks in Borris demesne and plantations about Graigue, common.

P. asplenioides, Linn., var. **minor** (=*P. Dillenii*, Taylor). On rocks, in damp wood, Graigue.

P. punctata, Taylor.—Damp banks in a wood at Graigue, rare.

---

[1] *Proc. R.I.A.* Ser. 2, vol. ii.

Jungermania (Lophozia) alpestris, Schl. (*Jung. alpestris*, Schleich, Exs., cent. 2, n. 59; Nees Europ. Leberm; II., p. 104; G. L. et N. Syn. Hepat., p. 113.)—Dioecious. Stem strong, creeping or erect from the upper half, simple or divaricately branched near the apex, clothed on the under side with white rootlets proceeding from the often violet-coloured stem. Leaves in two rows, vertical, increasing in size from the base upwards, sub-quadrate, two-lobed, rarely three-lobed, segments of various depths, acute or obtuse, often widely and shallowly notched at the apex, in some leaves sinus scarcely perceptible. Perichætial leaves three or four times acutely divided, stipules none. Perianth obovate or obovate oblong, terminal or lateral. Antheredia remarkably large, placed singly at the base of each leaf, which are closely imbricated and saccate at the base, patent at the apex, recurved, of a pale violet colour. Amongst damp rocks near the side of the River Barrow at Graigue. Very rare.

J. (Gymnocolea) affinis, Wilson (in Hook. Brit. Fl., II., p. 128; *Jung. turbinata*, Wils., in Eng. Bot. Suppl., t. 2744, nec Raddi).—Quarry bank near Goresbridge.

Nardia emarginata, Ehrh.—Amongst damp rocks, side of the River Barrow near the bridge at Graigue. Plentiful.

N. scalaris, Schrader.—Amongst damp rocks, side of the River Barrow at Graigue.

N. hyalina, Lyell.—Moist bank in a plantation, Graigue. Rare.

Pellia epiphylla, Dill. (L.)—Damp places. Common.

Conocephalus conicus, Neck.—Banks of the River Barrow. Common.

Metzgeria furcata, Linn.—On the trunks of trees about Graigue; Oak Park near Carlow. Common.

M. furcata, Linn. var. **fruticulosa,** Dicks. (Lindberg's Monogr. *Metzgeria*; *Jungermania fruticulosa*, Eng. Bot., Vol. 35, tab. 2514. *J. furcata* var. *æruginosa*, Hook., Brit. Jung., 55 et 56). On the trunks of trees in the wood at Goresbridge. A very distinct form growing in compact crisped tufts not unlike some large alga. Fronds tapered near the apex, sharply forked, with the margins shallow and closely recurved, giving the ramuli the appearance of being reduced to the nerve. Colour near the apex a brilliant verdigris green, or blue green apex erect, bearing copious gemmæ.

M. conjugata, !Dill. (Lindberg's Monogr. *Metzgeria*), Autœcious. Fronds robust, not much elongated, more or less dichotomous, irregularly pinnated or decomposite, linear, narrower in some parts than in others, in transverse section semilunar, hairs longish, stout, often in pairs on margin and divergent. The paucity of hairs and more solid substance of the frond with copious innovations, and above all the autœcious inflorescence abundantly distinguishes this species from *Metzgeria furcata*, which is dioecious, and all other known species of this singular genus. On granite rocks, banks of the Barrow at Graigue (*fertile*), on the trunks of trees in the wood near Goresbridge (*fertile*).

Riccardia pinguis, Linn.—Crevices of rocks in a quarry at Goresbridge.

THE QUAIL IN IRELAND:
ITS PRESENT AND RECENT VISITS.
BY C. B. MOFFAT.

THE re-appearance in 1896 of the Quail has already been reported from the counties of Cork,[1] Tipperary,[2] and Wicklow,[3] and doubtless observers in many other localities have, like myself in Co. Wexford, heard and seen the bird.

The general conditions prevailing this year so strongly resemble those of 1893, when Quails excited attention in a number of localities throughout Ireland, that the return of the birds in 1896 will scarcely cause surprise; but it would be a mistake to make too little of our erratic visitant, for whose next re-appearance on our shores we may have many years to wait.

At the time when the *Irish Naturalist* was founded in 1892 the Quail was looked upon as practically lost to our fauna. There were still a few counties in which it could not be said to have ceased to breed, at least occasionally—(Donegal, Louth, Dublin, Roscommon, and Wexford were those from which Mr. Ussher had recent notes of its nesting); but the localities were very few, and the records therefrom I believe rather meagre. At Ballyhyland (in the last-named county) it had been unknown for many years. In the first number of this periodical Mr. Ussher referred to the rapid decrease in Ireland of the Quail, Golden and Sea Eagles, and Marsh Harrier—all four species being then apparently on the verge of extinction.

Rather curiously, it was in the summer of the same year that the Quail began to put in his appearance again, though the incursion of 1892 was little noticed at the time by ornithologists in this country. I happened, that summer, to spend several whole nights in the fields in the neighbourhood of Ballyhyland, partly for the purpose of improving my acquaintance with a family of Nightjars; and it was on one of these occasions that I first heard the cry of "wet-my-lip" (or "quick-whip-it" as it rather sounds to my ear) with which the Quail is wont to enliven the cool hours. The moon being

---

[1] See p. 192.   [2] *Field*, July 11th.   [3] *Land and Water*, June 13th.

full, the Quail called incessantly from midnight till twenty minutes before sunrise, at which time, following the Fern-owl's example, he ceased; though the Grasshopper-warbler, who had been similarly vociferous through the night, still reeled on unwearied. This was in July, and it seems to me more than probable that there was then a nest in the vicinity.

A few months later a number of letters in the *Field* drew attention to the fact that 1892 had been decidedly a Quail-year in England; but it was not till the next year, when a considerably larger incursion took place, that the return of the birds was at all generally noticed in Ireland. However, in reading the communications on this subject forwarded by different observers to the *Irish Naturalist* in 1893, I was struck by the fact that several of them incidentally mentioned reports of the Quail's having also been heard the year before: so that the Quail-wave of 1892, if not a heavy one, would still appear to have been widely distributed over the British Islands.

At Ballyhyland I found, as might have been expected, plenty of Quails in the summer of 1893; but as far as I could ascertain, they were strictly confined to the immediate vicinity of the ground on which I had heard them in 1892. The Quails were sometimes in grass-fields, sometimes in barley, and sometimes in potatoes; one night a pasture-field in which I stood seemed thick with Quails, emulously whistling all around me in the faint light; in the day-time also a few were sometimes audible at the same spot; but no other ground than that occupied in 1892 appeared to contain a Quail. This I think tends to show that our '93 visitation was merely a return in increased force of the wave of '92.

It is to the same ground, again, after a two-summers' absence, that the Quail has returned in June, 1896. In fact it was in crossing the very field (half pasture and half furze-knock) where I first heard its note four years ago, that, as if again in response to the song of my old friend the Nightjar, who was strumming in the heath on one side, I heard in the grass on the other a gentle "quick-whip-it." It was an hour past sundown, and the bird was of course quite invisible on the ground. I walked up to it, however, when it rose and skimmed for a short distance, to drop again in the dry, dewless grass. This attachment to a particular spot seems singular in the case of a bird which comes to us only at irregular intervals.

The general similarity which subsists between 1896 and 1893 does not extend to 1892, but the three Quail-years resemble one another in the unusual dryness of their spring months—March, April, and May. I extract from the Ballyhyland register the following figures, showing the rainfall here for each of the spring months for the past twenty years:—

	1877.	1878.	1879.	1880.	1881.	1882.	1883.	1884.	1885.	1886.
March,	3·59	1·22	2·49	4·17	3·68	2·40	1·92	4·56	3·85	3·99
April,	5·52	3·76	2·68	3·91	2·13	5·87	3·23	1·01	4·12	2·53
May,	3·97	5·01	1·68	1·09	2·98	3·02	2·52	2·61	2·89	4·08
Total,	13·08	9·99	6·85	9·17	8·79	11·29	7·67	8·18	10·86	10·60

	1887.	1888.	1889.	1890.	1891.	*1892.	*1893.	1894.	1895.	*1896.
March,	1·76	4·04	1·32	4·26	1·31	1·16	0·56	1·94	3·81	3·04
April,	1·82	2·51	2·46	1·67	2·87	1·02	0·78	4·67	2·33	0·72
May,	1·36	3·19	3·85	3·60	3·99	3·75	2·17	4·51	0·45	0·07
Total,	4·94	9·74	7·63	9·53	8·17	5·93	3·51	11·12	6·59	3·83

* Indicates the Quail-years.

The above figures as they stand show that the springs of '93 and '96 were the driest of the series, and that, with the sole exception of the Jubilee year (1887), the remaining Quail-year, '92, ranks next. On the whole, they favour the view that unusual drought in spring directs the flight of *Coturnix communis* towards this island; but it may be objected that on this hypothesis we ought to have had Quails in the year of Her Majesty's Jubilee, when, if they came to us, they certainly attracted no special notice.

The similarity in the rain-gauge results for my three Quail-years is, however, far from being fully brought out by the above table; for, on looking closer, I find that in each of those years the greater part of what rainfall we had was enjoyed either early in March or late in May. Now, supposing that the Quail, which crosses the Mediterranean in April, has to select its breeding ground in our latitude by about the middle of

May, the fact of a continuous drought having characterized the preceding 8 weeks might in several ways do much towards influencing its choice. It appears, then, that

In 1892 the rainfall for 8 weeks ending May 11th was 1·63;
„ 1893 „ „ „ May 15th „ 1·65;
„ 1896 „ „ „ May 17th „ 1·22;

and in nearly every other year of the series, including '87, the heaviest of these rainfalls was surpassed in April alone. The only exceptions were 1884, when, however, the 6 weeks ending May 4th were sufficient to produce 2·45 inches, and 1890, when the same 6 weeks produced 4·20. The three years in which I have found the Quail (apparently breeding) at Ballyhyland therefore easily distance all other recent years in the severity of their droughts for the period precedent to the middle of May.

I do not for a moment suggest that extraordinary drought attracts the Quails; it appears to me far more probable that the consequent sparseness of vegetation in their Continental resorts may at such times drive the birds further afield in search of localities where cover and food are more obtainable. If Mr. Howard Saunders is right in including slugs[1] among the principal ingredients of the Quail's diet, an additional reason for its spreading further in dry seasons is at once apparent.

One can scarcely suppose that any of the ordinary requisites of Quail-life are lacking in Ireland in a normal summer, considering how common the bird formerly was here, many as a rule even staying the winter: during which season, as we learn from Thompson, seven-eighths of its food consisted of seeds of such invariably plentiful plants as Chickweed (*Stellaria media*) and different species of Dock, Plantain, and Knot-grass. True, reclamation of waste land may have reduced its facilities for enjoying this island as a winter home; but the discontinuance of its summer visits remains an apparently insoluble puzzle. The diminished cultivation of wheat is sometimes assigned as the cause; to this view, however, there are several objections, besides the fact that in my

---

[1] Thompson found slugs in only one of thirty Quails whose crops he examined; these birds, however, had all been shot in winter or early spring. The one Quail had eaten 11 specimens of that highly mischievous slug, *Agriolimax agrestis*.

(of course local) experience Quails show no partiality whatever for wheat-lands, but, if their distribution indicates a choice, prefer barley. In England, certainly, the Quail's decrease set in long before it did here; and though wheat has never ceased to be extensively grown in that country, Quails, according to Mr. More (*Ibis*, 1865) had more than thirty years ago almost ceased to breed regularly in Britain. Moreover, Quails abounded in Elizabethan Ireland, scarcely a paradise of wheat-growers. The enormous numbers yearly netted on the Mediterranean passage have suggested another explanation, but apparently this cause had not, till quite recently, affected their abundance on the Continent; in 1892 Mr. More (*Irish Sportsman*, May 21) cited evidence to the negative. Still it is refreshing to learn that the French Government now strenuously combats this traffic; giving us additional grounds for hope, that, should caprice of climate again fetch it to nest with us for a few successive seasons, the Quail's lost habit of annually visiting our shores may be re-acquired.

A NEW BIRD-BOOK.

A Concise Handbook of British Birds. By H. Kirke Swann. London: J. Wheldon and Co., 1896. 3s. 6d.

The portableness and cheapness of this little volume fairly justify its claim to serve as a "handy text-book for reference that has had as yet no rivals." It purports to give some account of every species occurring in the British Islands, defining the habitat, or range in the breeding season, of each, with brief descriptions (except where these are held to be unnecessary) of plumage, nidification, and general habits. To fulfil this task within the limits of 208 fcap. 8vo. pages was somewhat of a *tour de force*, and it must be added that the type of the book is good and not overcrowded. The principal shortcomings are such as might, under the circumstances, have been expected. Conciseness frequently degenerates into vagueness, as where a species is merely stated to nest in the "Northern Palæarctic region." The uselessness of this phrase becomes apparent when we find it applied without further detail to the breeding areas of such a heterogeneous assortment of birds as the Merlin, Black Grouse, Lesser Spotted Woodpecker, Tengmalm's Owl, and Jack Snipe! We should certainly be surprised to hear of the last named species nesting either with *Tetrao tetrix*, in the Apennines, or, with *Dendrocopus minor*, in the Azores. Again, the curiously intercrossed Continental ranges of the Hooded and Carrion Crows deserved some delineation. It is disappointing to find "Europe, excepting extreme north"—at once too little and too much—the sole definition of habitat accorded *Corvus corone*. To come nearer home, it is an encouraging fact that upon the subject of the Irish fauna our author has been at pains to compile his information from the best sources; but here, too, it is to be feared that he has sacrificed too much to compression; *e.g.*, we read that the Blackcap "in Ireland breeds locally in nearly every county." Mr. Ussher in 1894 recorded it as known to breed regularly in four counties and occasionally in five others; there was therefore a wide margin remaining to be filled. Mr. Swann's boiling-down process occasionally also mars his descriptions. The male Crossbill's plumage is described as "suffused with light crimson"; the fine clear yellow, which several ornithologists believe to indicate his full maturity, despite Mr. Seebohm's conjecture that it belongs, perhaps, to "old and barren birds," is not mentioned. The Pheasant is likewise assumed to need no description; although, as the author rightly observes that most of our Pheasants are of hybrid descent, it might have struck him that some mention of the distinguishing marks of a pure-bred *Phasianus colchicus* could not be absolutely uncalled for. Nor would descriptions of the *young* Pied Wagtail and Blue Titmouse, which differ much from the adult females, have been superfluous. The Black-headed Gull is said to breed "all round our coasts." This is misleading, for its breeding places are generally inland. Among the Jackdaw's nesting sites, rookeries and rabbit-burrows should have been mentioned (by an odd slip this bird's habitat is stated to be the "*Eastern* Palæarctic region"); and the description of the Willow-wren's nest as "rarely on ground" will surprise many, and possibly puzzle not a few. The author's list of birds does not include *Turdus migratorius* or *Chionis alba*, both obtained in Ireland of late years under circumstances that seemed to indicate actual migration; they might at least have received a place in the Appendix, in which thirty such doubtful "Britishers" as the Golden-winged Woodpecker (*Colaptes auratus*) are decorously shelved. Our author adopts "trinominals" for each of his seventeen sub-species Thus our indigenous Dipper is *Cinclus cinclus aquaticus* (Bechst.), and "*Loxia curvirostra pityopsittacus* (Bechst.)," is the Brobdingnagian title of the Parrot Crossbill, of which handsome bird it is fervently to be hoped that, no new variety needing a quadrinominal appellative will be discovered.

C. B. M.

THE BELFAST CLUB AND ITS WORK.

Annual Report and Proceedings of the Belfast Naturalists' Field Club for the Year ending 31st March, 1896. Belfast: Printed for the Club, 1896.

This, the narrative of the thirty-third year's work of the Belfast Field Club, has just been issued. It occupies sixty-six octavo pages, and furnishes interesting reading. From the annual report, we learn that " the creation of an entrance fee has acted as desired in keeping the membership of the Club within working bounds." As a matter of fact, it has had the effect of reducing the membership (which had been steadily rising for many years) from 516 to 480—a result certainly not to be deplored, for, as we took occasion to remark last year, one of the weaknesses of this Society was the strength of its membership. The report contains several items which give evidence of the activity and width of scope of the Club's work. Thus, the Geologists' Association, London, and the Home Reading Union, had, during their visits to the North of Ireland, the hearty co-operation of the local Society, and this means a great deal where long excursions, often to somewhat inaccessible regions, are the order of the day. A hard week's work in geology was carried out under Professor Cole, each day being devoted to field work, each evening to practical petrography. The Celtic Class has now forsaken the sheltering wing of the Club, and has started an independent existence as the Belfast Gaelic League. Nineteen pages are devoted to an account of the excursions of the year. These appear to have been uniformly successful, and we are glad to note at least a slight improvement on last year in the way of scientific results. The next fourteen pages go to the winter meetings, and brief, very brief, abstracts of the papers brought forward. Then follow reports from the Secretaries of the Microscopical, Geological, and Botanical Sections. The Geological Section has again a good deal to show for its year's work, and here, indeed, the energy of the Club appears to be centred. Glacial geology occupies the chief place, and if the listing of erratics, examination of boulder-clays, and general examination of the district is continued systematically, the results cannot fail to throw much light on the Glacial Period in the North-east of Ireland. The " Proceedings " are neatly printed on good paper, but we regret to notice not unfrequent misprints—surely the Committee might avoid such a disfigurement of their publications. The volume is swelled by an 80-page appendix —" A Bibliography of Irish Glacial and Post-Glacial Geology "—which will be noticed in our next number.

R. LL. P.

INSECTS COLLECTED ON LUGNAQUILLA AND IN GLENMALUR VALLEY, CO. WICKLOW.

(For the R.I.A. Fauna and Flora Committee.)

BY J. N. HALBERT.

OWING no doubt to the difficulty of access, many of the most interesting parts of the highlands of Co. Wicklow are practically unknown as regards their insect fauna. Probably none of the old collectors possessed a greater knowledge of the county, exclusive of Lepidoptera, than the late A. H. Haliday, to whom, from certain evidence afforded by his collection, it seems to have been a favourite hunting ground. Yet unfortunately he left few systematic notes of his own experiences for the assistance of future workers, resting contented with the recording of a comparatively small number of his captures, as for example, his discovery of the most interesting ground-beetle *Calathus nubigina*, Hal., from the summit of Lugnaquilla. Accompanied by my friend Mr. M'Ardle, I paid a brief visit to this district at the end of last month. The day selected for the attempt seemed at first unfavourable, threatening clouds had gathered and mists hung about the hills, but as we approached Drumgoff the weather fortunately cleared and we succeeded in reaching the summit of the mountain, after a toilsome climb under a scorching sun. We made the ascent by the Clohernagh Brook, which seemed to be the readiest way from the Drumgoff side, although a safer route might be found in a wet season. On the following day we explored the fine old birch and oak wood clothing the eastern side of the valley for over a mile of its extent. This wood seemed to teem with larvæ, and I have no doubt a collector of Lepidoptera would reap a rich harvest by a little hard work, as the possibilities of finding rare species are undoubtedly great. The following list contains the most notable of the Coleoptera and Hemiptera, excluding many common species.

COLEOPTERA.

Carabus catenulatus, Scop.—Slopes of Lugnaquilla. It was decidedly disappointing not to find either *C. glabratus* or *C. clathratus*; no doubt both occur; the latter has been taken by Mr. H. G. Cuthbert on the Great Sugar-loaf.

Notiophilus palustris, Duft.—Abundant. Also on summit.

Nebria Gyllenhall, Sch.—Abundant, both the red and black-legged forms occurred on the summit.

Calathus melanocephalus, L., var. **nubigena,** Hal.—Specimens of the variety occurred both on the summit and lower slopes, having the thorax entirely suffused with black, and having the legs and antennæ pitchy. The type seems to be extremely rare, or absent from the district.

Taphria nivalis, Panz.—Common in Glenmalur valley.

Trechus minutus, F., var. **obtusus,** Er.—Abundant on summit, where I found one example of the type; all had the wings rudimentary, not exceeding one and a half mm. in length. Type specimens from the lowlands are said to be always winged.

Patrobus assimilis, Chaud.—A fine series obtained on summit.

Philonthus addendus, Sharp. } Glenmalur Wood.
Halyzia xvi-guttata, L.

Byrrhus pilula, L.—Common under stones on the slopes and summit of Lugnaquilla.

B. fasciatus, F.—One specimen.

Phyllopertha horticola, L.—This insect, the well-known 'June-bug,' simply swarmed in the valley and over the hill-sides. It will probably be very abundant this season in Ireland. A few examples of the dark form were noted.

Corymbites quercus, Gyll.—Common with variety **ochropterus,** Steph.

Dascillus cervinus, L.—Frequent on Bracken.

Podabrus alpinus, Payk.—Common in Glenmalur Valley by sweeping, also beaten off Larch, Broom, etc. All having the elytra black. A local species, has occurred near Dublin, in Tollymore Park, Co. Down, and at Rostrevor (Furlong).

Telephorus pellucidus, F.—With preceding, but rarer.

T. figuratus, Mann.—Taken by sweeping rushes at the edge of the Clohernagh Brook. Although never definitely recorded, this insect occurs in other localities, but has hitherto passed under the name of *T. hæmorrhoidalis,* F. These Glenmalur specimens seem to be quite dark enough to pass for *T. scoticus,* Sharp; but as they do not agree *in toto* with the description of that variety, it is more satisfactory to refer them to the type. (I am indebted to Mr. G. C. Champion for verifying this identification.)

T. paludosus, Mann.—In same locality as the foregoing. Not previously recorded from Ireland. Mr. Haliday's collection contains a single example marked as Irish, but bearing no locality label. This is, in all probability, from the same place. The species is found in northern and mountainous districts in Britain.

Rhagonycha pallida, F.—Abundant in Glenmalur Wood.

Donacia discolor, Panz.—Common in swampy places on the lower slopes of Lugnaquilla.

Deporaus betulæ, L.   } Both abundant on Birch in Glen-
Polydrusus cervinus, L.   malurWood.

HEMIPTERA.

The following species were taken in Glenmalur Wood:—*Acanthosoma hæmorrhoidale, Calocoris striatellus* off Oaks, *Cyllocoris histrionicus, Harpocera thoracica, Phylus melanocephalus, Psallus varians*. In the valley and on the lower slopes of Lugnaquilla occurred:—*Velia currens, Miris holsatus*, and *Heterocordylus tibialis*, the last abundantly off Broom. The sub-alpine species *Gerris costæ*, H. S., occurred on small bog-pools at a considerable altitude on Lugnaquilla in company with the common *G. lacustris*.

NOTES.

BOTANY.

Teesdalia nudicaulis in Ireland.—On June 28th I had the pleasure of receiving from Mrs. Leebody fine specimens of this plant, which she had gathered on 26th inst. on the sandy shore of Washing Bay, on Lough Neagh, in Co. Tyrone. This locality is at the south-west corner of the lake, in a remote and unfrequented place, and Mrs. Leebody reports that the plant grows in abundance there. Although *Teesdalia* is distributed all over England, and in Scotland as far north as Elgin, it has not hitherto been known in Ireland, and furnishes an interesting addition to our flora.

R. LLOYD PRAEGER.

Lepidium Draba, L.—In the Journal of Botany for July, Mr. Britten notes the receipt of a specimen of this alien from roadside near Enniscorthy, Co. Wexford. The finder's name is not stated.

Pinguicula grandiflora, Lam., introduced in Co. Wexford.—I think it may be of interest to record the successful establishment of a colony of *Pinguicula grandiflora* in Co. Wexford. About half-a-dozen roots were brought from Co. Cork in 1879, and planted in a bog at the foot of Blackstairs Mountain; these have now increased to twenty-seven plants, and they bloom beautifully every year in May. The only butterwort which is indigenous to these parts is *Pinguicula lusitanica*.

E. V. COOPER, Killanne, Co. Wexford.

Mercurialis perennis in Co. Monaghan.—Mr. W. F. de V. Kane has sent me specimens of this plant from Bellanode near Monaghan, where it grows in a hedge-bank. It has long been known to grow in the adjoining county of Armagh, but is local and rare in Ireland.

R. LLOYD PRAEGER.

ZOOLOGY.

CRUSTACEANS.

Trichoniscus roseus, Koch.—This very rare wood-louse I find fairly plentiful among damp cinders and old bricks in a corner of my own yard. Dr. Scharff, who verified the specimens for me, found it under similar conditions in Dublin in autumn (*I.N.*, 1894, p. 26).

R. WELCH, Belfast.

INSECTS.

Vespa norvegica, F., at Omeath, Co. Louth.—I spent June 25th at Omeath, and while searching for beetles on some young fir trees, I nearly ran against a wasp's nest hanging from the branch of a Larch. Having retreated to a safe distance, I watched my opportunity and succeeded in capturing several specimens of the workers, and obtained a male from another nest which had been taken close by. The yellow base of the antennæ showed me that I had got something different from *V. vulgaris*, and on my return home I found that the specimens I had captured belonged to the above species. The wasps were too busy to be vicious, for I stood only about eight feet from the nest while catching them, and none attempted to attack me.

W. F. JOHNSON, Poyntzpass.

SPIDERS.

Atypus in King's Co.—Rev. Canon Russell writes that the *Atypus* tube from King's Co., recorded in the *Irish Naturalist* for June, was found by Mrs. Reamsbotham.

MOLLUSCS.

Helix arbustorum.—During a short visit to Ballycastle, North Antrim, in May, I spent a day collecting at Murlough Bay, and was fortunate enough to find some fine specimens of this beautiful shell among Nettles in the plantation, which I had often searched before without success. Thompson recorded it from Larne, and specimens collected by Waller about thirty years ago, are labelled Drumnasole (near Carnlough). Dr. Scharff tells me that he does not know of any other finds later than those for this district. The three other localities in which this shell was lately found, are in Donegal, Armagh, and Sligo, as recorded in the *Irish Naturalist*.

R. WELCH, Belfast.

West of Ireland Mollusca.—Messrs. Edward Collier and Robert Standen contribute to the April number of the *Journal of Conchology* a good paper on the mollusca collected on the Galway excursion of the Field Club Union last year. Mr. Standen contributed to this Journal a full list of the species found, which was published in the special "Galway Conference" number (September, 1895). The present paper is more detailed, and deals particularly with the species and varieties of land and fresh-water shells collected on that excursion.

BIRDS.

American Robin in Connaught.—During a recent visit to Carrick-on-Shannon, I was informed by Mr. C. C. Beresford Whyte that his keeper at Newtown Manor, near Lough Gill, had shot there and preserved a strange thrush with a red breast. On visiting the place, I was shown the bird by Mr. Robert West, whom I found to be a most observant and careful man. I placed him in communication with Dr. Scharff, and the result is that the bird is now in the Science and Art Museum, Dublin, the second example obtained in Ireland; the previous one, also in the Museum, having been shot in Co. Dublin on 4th May, 1891. Mr. West writes about his bird—"The thrush was shot on or about 7th December, 1892, in a large water-meadow very near the shore of Lough Gill, Newtown Manor side, feeding with a similar bird, also with Snipe, Lapwing, Fieldfares, and Redwings. By my diary I find the heavy snow began to thaw on the 5th." Unlike the previous occurrence in May, this specimen was obtained at the end of a very severe period of frost and snow in December.

R. J. USSHER, Cappagh, Co. Waterford.

Occurrence of the Crane (Grus communis) at Inch, Lough Swilly.—On 24th June, Mr. John M'Connell, of Burtslob House, brought me for identification a fine male specimen of the above species, which he had shot the previous evening on Inch Slobs. The following are particulars taken by me. Total length, 42½ inches; wing, 22½ inches; expanse from tip to tip, 6 feet 5 inches; bill, 4 inches; weight, 8 lbs. 12 ozs. The plumes were very slightly developed, the red brown warty patch on the top of head was very prominent. The plumage was light gray, tinged very faintly with brown, primaries and secondaries black, latter tinged with gray. This is another rarity added by Mr. M'Connell to the list of Inch birds.

D. C. CAMPBELL, Londonderry.

The Quail in Co. Monaghan.—On 26th May I heard the Quail in the neighbourhood of Newtownbutler.

W. MACMILLAN, Enniskillen.

Cormorants in Co. Donegal.—Mr. H. C. Hart contributes to the *Zoologist* for June, a note on the nesting habits of the Great and Green Cormorants, as observed by him near Portsalon.

Razorbill on Lough Neagh.—Whilst sailing on Lough Neagh yesterday a Razorbill passed flying close to the boat and alighted on the water some 200 yards further.

H. D. M. BARTON, Antrim.

Stock Doves in Co. Down.—Some years since I addressed a note to your paper on the subject of these birds being seen and nesting in Co. Antrim. Since that time I have frequently seen them in this locality, but have only now learned that they breed in considerable numbers in the Mourne Mountains, Co. Down. This year I have had reliable information of no less than five nests being found, all of them placed in rabbit holes on the face of a rather steep mountain and within a radius of less than half a mile.

H. D. M. BARTON, Antrim.

PROCEEDINGS OF IRISH SOCIETIES.

ROYAL ZOOLOGICAL SOCIETY.

Recent donations comprise a seal from L. Powell, Esq.; a monkey from C. S. Donnelly, Esq.; a pair of Axolotls, and six Japanese Fantail Goldfish from J. B. O'Callaghan, Esq., and a Squirrel from Sergt. Talbot. 12,200 persons visited the Gardens in June.

DUBLIN MICROSCOPICAL CLUB.

JUNE 18th.—The Club met at the house of Mr. F. W. MOORE, who showed *Sphærostilbe flavo-viridis*. This species belongs to the same group of Fungi as *Volutella* and *Myrothecium*, species of which had been exhibited by Mr. Moore on former occasions. The present species was found growing on the condensed sap which had exuded from a cut shoot of *Beaumontia grandiflora* in a stove house at Glasnevin. The peculiar stem-like structure, made up of a number of hyphæ joined together, was well shown. The conidia-bearing ends formed a roundish structure of small dimensions, of a yellowish green colour. The species is scarce.

Mr. G. H. CARPENTER showed *Chernes phaleratus*, Simon, a false-scorpion new to the Irish fauna, taken at Woodenbridge, Co. Wicklow, by Mr. J. N. Halbert. The species occurs in the New Forest, England, and at Fontainebleau, France.

Mr. HENRY J. SEYMOUR showed a thin section of the phonolite from Blackball Head, discovered by Mr. W. W. Watts, and mentioned in his Guide to the Geological Survey's Collection of Rocks (p. 91). This rock, which is very compact, and of a dark green colour, is the only recorded occurrence of a phonolite in Ireland.

IRISH FIELD CLUB UNION.

A general account of the joint excursion made to Cavan and Lough Oughter on July 10th to 13th, appears on a previous page of the present number.

BELFAST NATURALISTS' FIELD CLUB.

JUNE 20th.—GLENARM. On account of the inclement weather, only a very small number went to Glenarm, and little work was done. A couple of souterrains were visited at the Sallagh Braes and the old fort, and a few ordinary plants collected. The return was made by the coast road past Carncastle.

GEOLOGICAL SECTION, 24th JUNE.—F. W. LOCKWOOD in the chair. Miss S. M. THOMPSON exhibited specimens and sections of the riebeckite-bearing rocks of Skye and Ailsa Craig, obtained from the collection in Jermyn St., through the kind assistance of W. W. Watts, F.G.S., etc. Other rock specimens were shown, and twenty-four microscopic sections presented by the Rev. J. ANDREW; pamphlets by Prof. COLE; erratics by R. BELL, and a collection of Red Crag fossils by the Chairman.

An Excursion to Glenavy on the 18th July proved fruitless, owing to the flooded condition of Lough Neagh, which prevented access to the leaf-beds which formed the object of the expedition.

DUBLIN NATURALISTS' FIELD CLUB.

JUNE 27.—BECTIVE AND THE BOYNE.—A party of about twenty-five members proceeded to Kilmessan by the 9.30 train, and walked thence to Bective, to explore the portion of the valley of the Boyne. The well-known and picturesque ruin of Bective Abbey was first visited, and then the members scattered, a botanical party making for the marshy margins of the rivers, while others proceeded to Trim, to examine the antiquities of that historic town. The botanists found the reedy margins of the Boyne highly interesting, and many rare plants were gathered, including the Meadow Rue (*Thalictrum flavum*), Spearwort (*Ranunculus Lingua*), Marsh Stitchwort (*Stellaria glauca*), Narrow-leaved Water Parsnip (*Sium angustifolium*), Great Water-Dock (*Rumex Hydrolapathum*), Frog-bit (*Hydrocharis Morsus-ranae*), Sweet Flag (*Acorus Calamus*), Lesser Bank Sedge (*Carex paludosa*), and Reed Meadow Grass (*Glyceria aquatica*), while the great groves of reeds and bull-rushes, 9 or 10 feet in height, added picturesqueness to the scene. On the dry banks overlooking the marshes were the Gromwell (*Lithospermum officinale*), Vervain (*Verbena officinalis*), Teazel (*Dipsacus sylvestris*), and Goat's-beard (*Tragopogon pratensis*). Entomology was not represented in the party, but the botanists discovered in the stems of the Reed-mace the larvæ of *Nonagria typhæ*. Subsequently the party returned to Kilmessan, where tea was served by Miss Gardiner. Time was still left for a stroll, and in a gravel pit in the village the botanists again scored, finding among other plants the Henbane (*Hyoscyamus niger*), three of the four British species of poppy (*P. Rhœas, dubium, Argemone*), the purple Hempnettle (*Galeopsis Ladanum*), the Swine's Cress (*Senebiera Coronopus*), and other uncommon plants. By roadsides and in fields during the walk there were noted the Field Chamomile (*Matricaria Chamomilla*), Wild Mignonette (*Reseda lutea*), Toothed Corn-Salad (*Valerianella dentata*), Good King Henry (*Chenopodium Bonus-Henricus*), and Rough Chervil (*Chærophyllum temulum*). The party returned to town at 8.45.

CORK NATURALISTS' FIELD CLUB.

JUNE 10.—A small party visited the grounds of Ballincollig Powder Mills and the Lee Valley.

JULY 1.—Carrigaline and Revine's Point were visited. Thirteen members went and had a most enjoyable drive of about twenty miles each way. Several stoppages were made to enable botanists and others to collect, and a good number of specimens were obtained, though no records were made.

JULY 11.—The glen between Waterfall Station and Ballincollig was explored by a good number, and yielded a good supply of flowers and insects to collectors.

NOTES ON THE FAUNA AND FLORA OF CLONBROCK, CO. GALWAY.

PREFATORY NOTE.

BY E. J. McWEENEY, M.D., AND R. LLOYD PRAEGER, B.E.

AMONG the many results which have followed, directly or indirectly, the Galway Conference of the Irish Field Clubs in 1895, and the gathering and intercourse of naturalists on that occasion, few will be looked back to with greater pleasure and interest by those who were so fortunate as to participate in it, than the week spent in June last by a representative party of the Dublin Naturalists' Field Club at Clonbrock, Co. Galway, on the invitation of our fellow-member, the Hon. R. E. Dillon. A very deep debt of gratitude is due to our host and hostess, the Right Hon. Lord Clonbrock and Lady Clonbrock, whose unfailing kindness was only exceeded by the interest they displayed in our researches, and the assistance they rendered us in numberless ways. When to this is added the fact that every corner of the large estate was thrown open to us, and all the resources of the estate placed at our disposal, it will be seen that we pursued our field work under circumstances of unusual advantage and pleasure.

It may be well to preface the scientific notes of the different members of the party with a general narrative of our doings.

On Tuesday, June 16th, the party, consisting of R. F. Scharff, PH.D., E. J. McWeeney, M.D., David M'Ardle, and J. N. Halbert, left Dublin by the 9.15 train for Ballinasloe, which was reached at 12.30. The party was met at the station by one of Lord Clonbrock's carriages, into which M'Ardle and Halbert lost no time in transferring themselves, whilst Scharff and McWeeney mounted their machines, and the $8\frac{1}{2}$ miles to Clonbrock were quickly negotiated. The party was received by Lord and Lady Clonbrock and the Hon. R. E. Dillon, and after lunch were accompanied round the ground and gardens, and through the more nearly adjoining woods. They visited the "Old Orchard," a veritable jungle of densely packed plant-life, and passing into the open wood were shown the bank on which grows that most remarkable fungus *Morchella elata.* This bank in Clonbrock Wood and its immediate neighbourhood are the only British localities for the "Tall-growing Morel."

Ocular demonstration of its existence here was afforded by the numerous shrivelled and dried-up specimens with which the slope was studded.

After dinner Mr. Dillon conducted a party to examine the contents of an apparatus devised by himself for trapping moths, whilst the non-entomologists sat in the large drawing-room—converted, by the way, into an admirably commodious laboratory—and discussed plans for the morrow.

Wednesday opened windy and wet. The enthusiasm of the party scorned such slight drawbacks, and it was not long after ten when they started, under the leadership of Mr. Dillon, for the western pine-wood and neighbouring boggy land. The chief botanical feature which was observed in the pine-wood was the enormous abundance of the Tway-blade (*Listera ovata*), which was here quite the commonest herb. McWeeney observed a cluster-cup fungus growing abundantly on the back of its leaves, and betraying its presence by yellow spots on the upper surface. It proved to be a stage in the life history of a "rust," *Puccinia moliniæ*. A rare ladybird beetle, *Chilocoris bipustulatus*, was taken by Halbert, who also secured on Sheep-pool Bog a crab-spider, *Xysticus sabulosus*, new to Ireland, and a rare and interesting wolf-spider, *Pardosa herbigrada*, also new to Ireland, figured in the current number (Plate 3).

At two o'clock all were back at the house for lunch, and afterwards most of the party started off to explore the south side of the river as far as the avenue; others, having a considerable number of specimens to work through, remained at home. Mr. Dillon had occasion to go across the lawn to the pheasantry, which he uses as a breeding-place for moths and butterflies, and returned in a few minutes with two fungi that he had found in the pheasantry. One of them, a red club-shaped specimen, about two inches long, was growing out of a huge chrysalis, and was none other than the famous *Cordyceps militaris*, which mysteriously originates from Lepidopterous larvæ. This carnivorous fungus, though not absolutely uncommon in England, has been detected hitherto in Ireland only at Powerscourt (*Irish Naturalist*, Oct., 1893). The other specimen was a beautiful little agaric, *Lepiota felina*, Fr., which has not previously been recorded from Ireland.

The day concluded with a demonstration of specimens after dinner—and the usual moth-hunt, from which the enthusiastic lepidopterists were in nowise deterred by the heavy rain.

On Thursday the whole party went to the woods and separated, each collector going whithersoever his instinct led him to hope for booty. *Lachnea hemisphærica*—a fungus new to Ireland—was found on the damp soil in the pine-wood; while Halbert secured the rare ground-beetle, *Calathus piceus*, in the oak-wood, and *Orectochilus villosus* in Clonbrock River. After lunch most of the party returned to the wood. The evening was spent arranging specimens and looking at microscopic preparations, M'Ardle's demonstration of the rotatory movements of the protoplasm in an internodal cell of *Chara* being much appreciated.

On Friday morning the party separated, Mr. Dillon proceeding on foot with M'Ardle and Halbert to Doon Wood, whilst Scharff and McWeeney cycled to near Mount Bellew, and did some collecting along the road. Doon Wood proved a good entomological locality, yielding a beetle, *Phalacrus substriatus*, and two spiders, *Cornicularia vigilax* and *Tetragnatha obtusa*, all new to Ireland. Returning to Clonbrock at 1.0, they picked up a well-stocked luncheon basket at the house, and rejoined their colleagues at Doon Wood. Some good work was done by M'Ardle in the domain of flowering plants. He had taken the Bee Orchis (*Ophrys apifera*), and Marsh Helleborine (*Epipactis palustris*) to preserve. A striking feature of Doon Wood is the enormous abundance of *Listera ovata*, and the luxuriant development of the plant. One specimen, which measured 27 inches in height, was brought home, but Praeger, on being shown the specimen later on in the evening, recollected having found this plant four feet high, which caused the Doon specimen to hide its diminished head. Starting on the homeward journey, the party passed through the deer-park. Here Mr. Dillon pointed out *Iris fœtidissima*. In turning over a large trunk, McWeeney came across a fluffy fungal mass which proved to be *Botryosporium diffusum*, Ca., one of the most exquisite of British moulds. At dinner the party was joined by Praeger, who had come through from Londonderry, *via* Belfast and Dublin, since the previous evening.

On Saturday afternoon Scharff and McWeeney had to leave for Dublin, much to their regret, so they did not join the party which started at 10.0 in a wagonette for some extensive bogs to the northward. We first examined a wood near Tycooly House, and then spread out over the adjoining bog. Here Praeger made an interesting find, the Brown Beak-rush (*Rhynchospora fusca*), a very rare plant in the British Isles, and in Ireland known previously only from stations much nearer the western ocean. It was subsequently found again growing in profusion on bogs at Killasolan, with its congener *R. alba*. Tramping over an extensive bog, we visited the banks of the Shiven River, which were ornamented with tufts of Royal Fern, and came back by the Killasolan bogs. A rapid drive brought us back in time for dinner, and a long evening among our specimens.

Sunday dawned fine. At breakfast specimens of the Birds-nest Orchis (*Neottia Nidus-avis*) were produced by Praeger, gathered under beech-trees not far from the house. His morning ramble had a more important result, for a pondweed collected in the Clonbrock River, and at the time unknown, is believed by Mr. Arthur Bennett to be a new form of the rare *Potamogeton lanceolatus*; study of the growing plant will, it is hoped, settle its identity. M'Ardle, Halbert, and Praeger were early afoot, and investigated the bog beyond the "Lurgan Plantation" and the Clonbrock River adjoining. In the afternoon, accompanied by Lord and Lady Clonbrock, we explored the Deer-park, and pushed on to Doon, where the abundant Orchid-flora of that place—including the Bee Orchis, Marsh Helleborine, Sweet-scented Orchis, Butterfly Orchis, Frog Orchis, Tway-blade, and others—was again studied with admiration and interest. Specimen of *Choleva fumata*, a beetle new to Ireland, occurred in dead birds in the woods.

On Monday morning we drove eastward to the River Suck, which here bounds the counties of Galway and Roscommon, and spent some highly profitable hours collecting along its banks in the neighbourhood of Bellagill bridge. This place yielded a rich haul of flowering plants to the botanists, though poor in cryptogams; while the entomologists secured in *Trechus discus* a ground-beetle new to Ireland, and in *Erirrhinus æthiops* a very rare weevil. But our work was doomed to interruption in the afternoon. The rain, which had threatened all morning, at last came down in earnest, and it was a drenched and bedraggled party that reached Clonbrock at about four o'clock. The rain continued, so we spent a very busy afternoon putting away specimens, and sorting and arranging the spoil of the last few days.

The pleasantest time must have an end, and on Tuesday morning we bade a grateful adieu to our host and hostess, and drove to Ballinasloe, stopping for an hour at some gravel-pits by the roadside, which yielded a number of plants which we had not seen at any other place in the district—plants, such as the poppies, which love light soils. Ballinasloe was reached in good time, and in due course we once again glided under the familiar roof of Broadstone terminus.

LAND PLANARIANS AND LEECHES.

BY R. F. SCHARFF, PH.D.

Several specimens of the only British land planarian, *Rhynchodemus terrestris* (almost all planarians being either marine or freshwater species), was secured under dead tree-trunks in Clonbrock forest. This little worm, as I pointed out in *Nature* (vol. 50, p. 617), is exceedingly rare, and is only known from about a dozen European localities. This is the second Irish record, having been first discovered in Ireland at Blackrock, near Dublin, by Miss Kelsall. It is a very inconspicuous black slug-like worm, about half an inch in length, and it seems to love damp shady places.

Halbert and I took several hauls in the Clonbrock river on the second day, and among other interesting objects, secured two species of freshwater leeches, viz., *Glossiphonia complanata*, L., and *G. heteroclita*, L. They are both about half an inch long when at rest, and are parasitic on water-snails. The former, which is the commoner of the two, is of a reddish-grey colour and semitransparent, so that its internal organs are plainly visible. Another curious feature about this leech is that it carries its young about with it, and one of the specimens taken had about a dozen very minute leeches fixed to the underside of the mother by their posterior sucker. The other leech is yellowish, and its six eyes are arranged in a triangle, so that with an ordinary lens only three are visible, though each of these is really composed of two.

EARTHWORMS.

BY REV. HILDERIC FRIEND, F.L.S.

Through the kindness of Dr. Scharff I have been able to examine a typical set of Earthworms from Clonbrock, Co. Galway, which contained several species already recorded for other parts of the country. I submit a full list of species received.

Lumbricus herculeus, Savigny (Common Earthworm). Usually known as *Lumbricus terrestris*. A fine typical specimen, well developed, with girdle extending over segments 32-37. On one side of segments 25, 26, there were ventral papillæ such as often occur in adult forms. The specimen was placed in spirits and returned to Dublin.

Lumbricus rubellus, Hoffmeister (Red Worm). This worm has the good fortune to be without synonyms. It is known by the girdle extending across segments 27-32. Sometimes it begins abnormally on segment 26. The colour is purple and iridescent. It is much smaller than the last, and often twice as large as the next, which in other respects it very closely resembles. It has no papillæ on segment 15 in connection with the male apertures.

Lumbricus castaneus, Savigny (Purple Worm). Long known as *L. purpureus*. A small, clean, lively worm, with girdle on segments 28-33. There is here also an absence of glandular swellings on the fifteenth segment.

Lumbricus rubescens, Friend (Ruddy Worm). Beddard regards this as synonymous with the *Enterion festivum* of Savigny, and the *Lumbricus festivus* of Dugès. Though the accounts of the worm given by these two authors are brief and imperfect, I am prepared to accept the identification, in which case the worm will be known as *Lumbricus festivus* (Savigny). I first described it in *Nature*, 1891, p. 273.

Allolobophora fœtida, Savigny (Brandling). A well-marked species, abundant in old manure, and much sought after by the angler. It exudes a yellow fluid when irritated, and is known by its alternate yellow and ruddy-brown coloured bands.

Allolobophora subrubicunda, Eisen (Gilt-tail). A worm with a large list of names, first differentiated by Dr. Gustav Eisen, in 1873. It is often no more than an inch in length, though it sometimes reaches three inches. The girdle covers segments 26-31, and it is a great favourite with certain kinds of fish.

Allolobophora chlorotica, Savigny (Green Worm). There is usually little difficulty in identifying this species, first on account of its well-marked colour and habits, and next because of the three pairs of pores (*tubercula*) on alternate segments 31, 33, 35. It usually coils itself up when disturbed, and is very sluggish.

LAND AND FRESHWATER MOLLUSCA.
BY R. F. SCHARFF, PH.D.

As one would expect from the abundance of wood, most of the species of *Hyalinia* are abundant in the Clonbrock demesne, especially the otherwise rare Garlic Snail (*Hyalinia alliaria*). When writing my paper on the Irish Land and Freshwater Mollusca (*Irish Naturalist*, vol. i., 1892), I was under the impression that the European range of this species was much more restricted than it really is, having since taken it on the Brünig Pass in Switzerland (see *Nachrichtsblatt d. d. Malakol. Gesellsch.* 1895). Another uncommon species which is known only from three or four Irish localities is *Hyalinia Draparnaudi*. The commonest species were *H. nitidula*, *H. cellaria*, and *H. crystallina*. Both *H. pura* and *H. radiatula* were noticed under decaying leaves and twigs, and also *H. fulva*.

As regards slugs, they were not so abundant, not even the ubiquitous *Agriolimax agrestis*, whilst *A. lævis* was not to be seen anywhere. The only really common slug was *Limax marginatus (arborum)* which gracefully glided up and down the dripping tree-trunks after the heavy showers we had. Under leaves and dead wood were secured *Arion ater* (the brown and black forms), *A. subfuscus*, *A. hortensis* (the bluish variety), *A. circumscriptus (Bourguignati)*, and *A. intermedius (minimus)*, also *Limax maximus*, but I was much surprised not to meet with a single specimen of the keeled slugs— belonging to the genus *Amalia*.

I was delighted to meet with such a number of the rarer *Helices* at Clonbrock. The stems of the stately Beech-trees are tenanted by numerous *H. fusca*, one of the rarest species of British *Helices*, and which in other localities I had only observed among the leaves of *Luzula sylvatica*. Other rare species found among leaves on the ground were *Helix lamellata*, *H. aculeata*, and *H. pygmæa*, whilst *H. rupestris* occurred among the crevices of old limestone walls. McWeeney was fortunate in discovering a scalariform monstrosity of *Helix rotundata* among the small fungi he was examining. I had never seen such a form before, and quickly transferred it to my collection. *H. rufescens*, our commonest

Dublin garden snail, is exceedingly rare at Clonbrock. Other species of *Helix* observed were *H. hispida*, *H. ericetorum*, and *H. nemoralis*. Not a trace anywhere of the common *Helix aspersa*. *Cochlicopa lubrica* and *Clausilia bidentata* abounded; indeed, as Mr. Dillon observed, the denomination *bidentata* seems somehow or other to have always been applied to very common species.

The rare *Pupa anglica* — a species confined to southern Europe and a few British localities—was abundant; at any rate it was more common than *P. cylindracea* (*umbilicata*). *Vertigo* was represented by the sylvan *V. edentula*, whilst *V. pygmæa* was noticed under stones at the roadside on the way to Mount Bellew.

Near the river I found among the thickly-growing reeds *Succinea Pfeifferi*, which I think should be looked upon as a distinct species, and not as a variety of the South European *S. elegans*, as I formerly thought.

In the Clonbrock river itself were taken *Limnæa stagnalis*, *Physa fontinalis*, *Bythinia tentaculata*, *Valvata piscinalis*, and *Neritina fluviatilis*. In a cold spring near the house, I found numerous very fine examples of a form somewhat intermediate between the typical *Limnæa peregra* and *L. ovata*, and on Doon Bog I secured specimens of *L. truncatula*.

The more remarkable absentees, besides those already referred to, include the following: *Helix acuta*, *H. virgata*, and *H. intersecta*, *Balea perversa*, *Clausilia laminata*, and the genera *Planorbis*, *Ancylus*, and *Sphærium*.

Altogether the demesne and the surrounding country of Clonbrock are thoroughly good hunting-grounds for the conchologist, and I am convinced that further search, especially along the river Suck, whence Halbert brought me *Limnæa palustris*, would yield an additional number of species.

ISOPODS.

BY R. F. SCHARFF, PH.D.

THE large grey *Oniscus asellus* is exceedingly abundant under logs of wood, under stones, and under all kinds of refuse. The very minute red woodlouse (*Trichoniscus pusillus*) is common in Clonbrock wood under moss, and indeed everywhere where there is sufficient dampness to suit its comfort. *Philoscia muscorum*, which swiftly darts about among the twigs and moss, and *Porcellio scaber* frequent much drier localities. All these are species which occur in almost all parts of Ireland, and, except *Metoponorthus pruinosus*, no rare woodlice were observed. The latter occurs at Clonbrock only among garden refuse, and even there it is very scarce.

The most striking feature is the absence of the 'Pill Woodlouse' (*Armadillidium vulgare*), a species which is so abundantly met with around Dublin.

SPIDERS.

BY GEORGE H. CARPENTER, B.SC.

UNABLE to join the Clonbrock collecting-party myself, I looked forward eagerly to the examination of the spiders and harvestmen which Scharff and Halbert were so good as to secure for me from that now famous locality. The result proves most gratifying, as the thirty-three species of spiders collected comprise five which I had not before identified from any part of Ireland. Several of the other species are now recorded as Irish for the first time. This collection must represent but a small fraction of the spider-fauna of the district, and many other novelties and rarities doubtless await discovery there.

I had some hopes that traces of *Atypus*—our only British genus of the *Aviculariidæ*, whose nest has recently been discovered in King's Co.[1]—might have been found at Clonbrock. These expectations, however, were disappointed; nor was a species of the *Dysderidæ* to be found in the collection, though several probably occur in the district. The large family of the *Drassidæ* was represented only by the ubiquitous *Clubiona reclusa*, Cb., and the more interesting *Anyphæna accentuata*, Wlck., a species not included in Workman's list[2], but collected

---

[1] See p. 167 of this volume. [2] *Entomologist*, vol. xiii., 1880, p. 125.

and received by me from many Irish localities, and apparently generally distributed. There were two species of *Dictynidæ*—*Dictyna uncinata*, Thor., and *D. latens*, Bl.; I do not think that the latter has ever been recorded from Ireland, though Mr. Freeman first took it near Dublin several years ago. No representative of the *Agelenidæ* was secured.

The small *Theridiidæ*, which comprise the majority of our spiders, are not numerous in June. *Theridion sisyphium*, Cl., was common, as might have been expected. *Linyphia montana*, Cl.,—a species that with us seems to be found in parks and gardens—was taken in the demesne, together with *L. pusilla*, Sund., *L. hortensis*, Sund., *Labulla thoracica*, Wid., *Leptyphantes tenuis*, Bl., and *L. Blackwallii*, Kulcz. The common species *Erigone atra*, Bl., and *Gonatium bituberculatum*, Wid., were also secured, as well as the tiny *Maso Sundevallii*, Westr. The only other theridiid taken was one of the prizes of the expedition—*Cornicularia vigilax*, Bl., a very rare species in the British Isles, found only in Dorsetshire and North Wales[1], with a wide but discontinuous continental range from France to Galicia[2], and occurring also in the United States. Both sexes of this species were secured by Halbert, a male at Doon and a female in the demesne.

Six species of the *Epeiridæ* or orb-weavers were collected. Besides the common *Tetragnatha extensa*, L., Halbert secured, by sweeping heather on Sheep-pool Bog, a female of *T. obtusa*, C. Koch, a species with less elongate abdomen, hitherto unknown as Irish. Since determining this spider, I have found another female in a collection sent me last year from Skibbereen, Co. Cork, by Mr. J. J. Wolfe. As might be expected, *Meta segmentata*, Cl., *Epeira diademata*, Cl., and *E. cornuta*, Cl., were common. The other epeirid taken, *Singa sanguinea*, C. Koch, is a valuable addition to the Irish list, being rare in Great Britain, and apparently confined to the southern counties[3].

There were three *Thomisidæ* or crab-spiders:—*Philodromus aureolus*, Cl., and *Xysticus cristatus*, Cl.—both common species everywhere—together with another addition to the Irish fauna, also found by Halbert on Sheep-pool Bog—*X. sabulosus*,

---

[1] O. P. Cambridge, "Spiders of Dorset," Sherborne, 1879 (p. 113).
[2] E. Simon, "Arachnides de France." Tome v., Paris, 1881 (p. 848).
[3] O. P. Cambridge, *op. cit.*, p. 248.

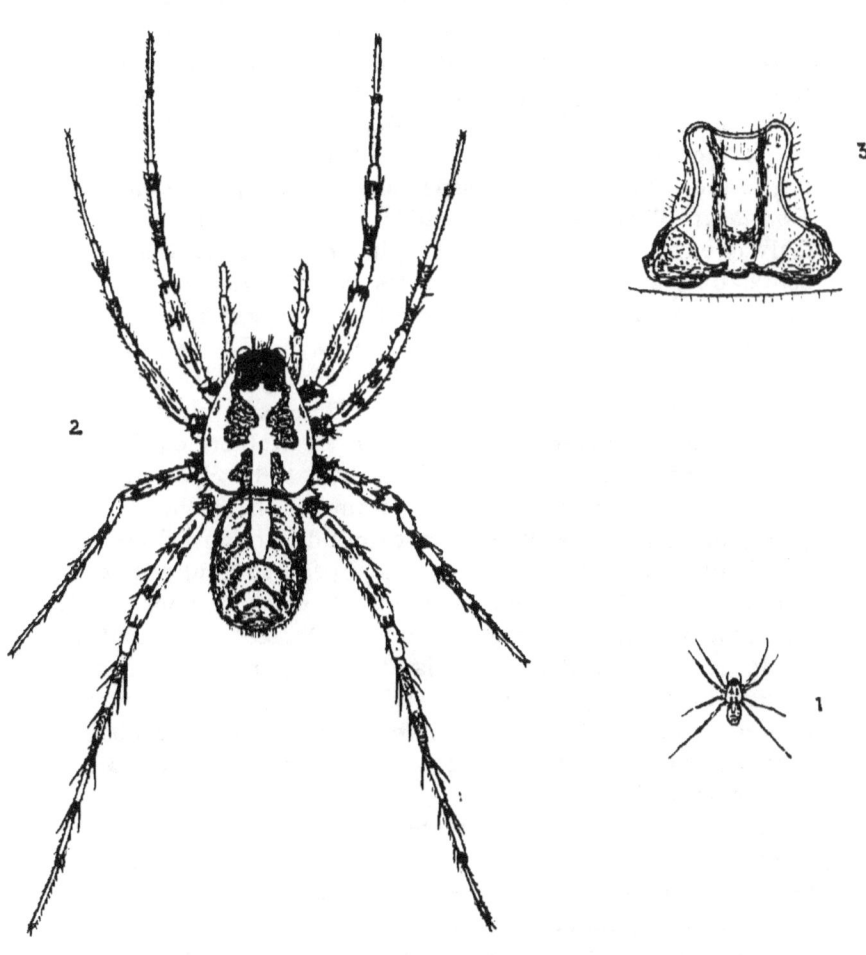

Fig. 1. *Pardosa herbigrada*, Bl., female, natural size.
Fig. 2.   „   „   „   magnified.
Fig. 3. Epigyne, highly magnified.

Hahn. This handsome species was known as a British spider only from the south of England[1] until its recent discovery in Inverness-shire[2]. It is of interest to be able now to record it for one of the western counties of Ireland, its known range in the British Isles being thus strangely discontinuous, though it doubtless awaits discovery in intermediate localities.

Coming lastly to the *Lycosidæ* or wolf-spiders, it was interesting to find several immature specimens of the great *Dolomedes fimbriatus*, Wlck., which attracted so much attention on the Galway expedition of last year[3]. The genus *Lycosa* was represented only by two common species—*L. pulverulenta*, Cl., and *L. ruricola*, DG.; while there were five species of *Pardosa*. *P. amentata*, Cl., *P. pullata*, Cl., and *P. palustris*, L., are probably common species everywhere, while *P. nigriceps*, Thor., is generally distributed and not scarce. The remaining species represented by a single female taken by Halbert on Sheeppool Bog running close to a drain, proves to be *P. herbigrada*, Bl., a very handsome addition to the Irish fauna. Since determining this specimen I have found another female in a collection made by Prof. D'Arcy Thompson at Roundstone, in August, 1894. This spider has a peculiar discontinuous range. In Great Britain it has been found in Dorset[4], Northumberland[5], and the Scottish Highlands[6]. On the continent it occurs in Norway, Sweden, and Galicia[7]. According to Simon[8], it has not been found in France; but it probably inhabits at least the north-west of that country, as it has lately been discovered in Guernsey[9].

This beautiful spider (see Plate 3) is remarkable among the species of *Pardosa* on account of the extensive area of the yellow markings on the cephalothorax, the dark lateral bands being generally, as in the present specimen (fig. 2), interrupted. Most species of the genus are predominantly

---

[1] Carpenter and Evans, *Ann. Scott. Nat. Hist.*, 1894, p. 233.

[2] O. P. Cambridge, *op. cit.*, p. 301.

[3] *Irish Nat.* vol. iv., 1895, p. 255.

[4] O. P. Cambridge, *op. cit.* (p. 385.)

[5] O. P. Cambridge. *Proc. Berw. Nat. Club*, 1875.

[6] Carpenter and Evans, *l. c.* (p. 235).

[7] T. Thorell, "Remarks on Synonyms of European Spiders," Upsala, 1870-3, (p. 282).

[8] "Arachnides de France," Tome iii. (p. 323).

[9] F. O. P. Cambridge " *Trans. Guerns. Soc. Nat. Sci.*, 1894.

dark in colour, the yellow bands tending to become narrow and broken up. The nearest ally of *P. herbigrada* is *P. palustris*, L., an abundant spider in which the cephalothorax is mostly of a black-brown colour, showing three narrow yellow bands, the central drawn out to a fine point in front. But in the specimen of *P. palustris* taken at Clonbrock the central band is somewhat widened behind the eyes. This form I have received from several Irish localities and the series goes far to bridge the gap between typical *P. palustris* and *P. herbigrada*. In the females of both these species the epigyne is very large and of a truncated triangular form. This structure in these and allied species has recently been carefully described and figured by Rev. F. Pickard-Cambridge[1]. In *P. herbigrada* it is relatively larger and more prominent than in *P. palustris*, but it varies somewhat in different individuals of the same species, and in the present specimen the hind corners are extremely prominent and rugose (fig. 3).

It is of interest to note that in some of the dusky species such as *P. amentata*, Cl., and *P. agricola*, Thor., the yellow colour is predominant in the cephalothorax of very young specimens; as the spider grows older, the amount of dark colour in the pattern increases. This suggests that *P. herbigrada*, with its broad expanse of yellow when adult, represents an old stage in the evolution of the genus, a suggestion supported by the rarity and discontinuous range of the species. While its dark-hued relation *P. palustris* is spread abundantly over our islands, and is found on the Continent from Lapland to Italy, *P. herbigrada* is apparently absent from the greater part of Central Europe, and almost restricted to northern and western regions in Scandinavia, Britain and Ireland. It would seem, therefore, that *P. palustris* is the younger and more vigorous species, and has largely superseded *P. herbigrada* in the struggle for existence. The problem remains whether the darkening of the cephalothoracic pattern has been itself an advantageous factor in the conflict, or whether it is but the necessary accompaniment of other and deeper causes.

---

[1] *Ann. Mag. Nat. Hist.* (6), vol. xv., 1895 (p. 34, pl. iv.)

HEMIPTERA

BY J. N. HALBERT.

THE Hemiptera or Plant-bugs are summer insects, though a comparatively few hibernate through the winter. A great number were in the immature state when we were at Clonbrock, yet the early season had caused some species to appear, in the adult condition before the usual time. There is little doubt that specimens of a large shield-bug, in the larval state, occurring on the heaths about Clonbrock, are referable to *Podisus luridus*, Fab., but as the species has not been recorded, from the country it must be given with reserve until fully developed specimens are found. I swept several examples of *Cymus grandicolor*, Hahn. off Flags in marshy places. *Microphysa elegantula*, Baer., was a rather satisfactory capture. It occurred freely by beating old lichen-covered Sloes near the Deer-park. I had not met with this species previously, the only Irish specimens that I know of being in Mr. Haliday's collection. *Myrmedobia tenella*, Zett., also occurred by general sweeping; it is said to be rare, though from its small size it is probably overlooked by collectors. I found *Tetratocoris Saundersi*, D. and S., in a marshy field beside Doon wood, very similar to localities in which it had occurred on the east coast. *Allodapus rufescens*, H. S., has not been previously recorded from any Irish locality. A single macropterous specimen occurred by sweeping heather, at dusk, and it is apparently a rare species in England. Several species of *Psallus* were more or less common in the woods, the rarest being *P. diminutus*, Kb. now recorded as Irish for the first time.

Amongst other captures were the following:—

Nabis flavomarginatus, Scholtz., common; *N. ericetorum*, Scholtz., on heath; *Salda scotica*, Curt., river banks; *Acompocoris pygmaeus*, Fall., *Dicyphus stachydis*, Reut., and *Plesiocoris rugicollis*, Fall., the last in some numbers off Willows at Sheeppool Bog. I managed to secure a good many Homoptera, including several species I had not previously met with, but it is necessary to reserve these as they include many critical forms still in the hands of Mr. J. Edwards, F.E.S., awaiting further investigation.

COLEOPTERA.

BY J. N. HALBERT.

THE great success attending Mr. R. E. Dillon's researches amongst the lepidoptera of East Galway are now well known to all students of the order. This success is mainly due to the varied nature of the district, comprising some fine remnants of natural forest and extensive moorlands, and to no small extent also, to steady collecting in the same localities for the greater part of the year. In an order so numerous in species as the Coleoptera, we could only hope during our visit to obtain a general idea of the species occurring in the district, and as three-fourths of the collecting was done on boggy heaths, a general sameness in results to those obtained in many places in west and central Ireland, was to be expected. We managed, however, to secure a fair number of local forms. Mr. Dillon had preserved a small collection of beetles from the immediate neighbourhood; amongst these were two or three rarities taken during the previous month, that all our efforts failed to refind, showing that on account of the abnormal earliness of the spring, many species were practically over at the time of our visit. The following notes refer only to the less common species.

The *Carabidæ* or ground-beetles are rather poorly represented at Clonbrock, as in such inland localities they are chiefly to be found on the stony margins of lakes and rivers; and it is to the scarcity of these conditions that the absence of such species as *Carabus clathratus* and *Pelophila borealis* may perhaps be attributed.

The first species to be noticed in our list is *Carabus arvensis*, F., here of the usual shining bronze colour. Mr. Dillon found two specimens running on a pathway earlier in the year; it is widely distributed, though local, occurring chiefly on heaths. *Calathus piceus*, Marsh., was fairly common in damp mossy places in the Oak-wood, where also *Dromius quadrimaculatus*, L., abounded under bark. Perhaps the best place for ground-beetles was along the banks of the Suck; here I was fortunate enough to meet with *Trechus discus*, F., a very local species, not previously recorded from Ireland. Other notable captures in this locality were *Chlænius nigricornis*, F., *Bembidium guttula*, F., *B. assimile*, Gyll, and *B. bipunctatum*,

L., the last occurring abundantly amongst shingle at the edge of the river.

We were much too late to do any good with the water-beetles, the rivers seemed to produce very few species; the best results were obtained in the pools and drains half choked by vegetation. There were amongst others *Haliplus fulvus*, F., *Hydroporus erythrocephalus*, L., and *Agabus Sturmii*, Gyll. I took a single *Hydroporus memnonius*, L., by sweeping at dusk, at some distance from water. *Orectochilus villosus*, Mull., a nocturnal beetle, occurred freely in the Clonbrock river, lurking amongst a thick growth of weed.

The *Staphylinidæ* or rove-beetles were not numerous in species. *Alcochara brevipennis*, Grav., is noteworthy, as it is one of those species, restricted, so far as we can at present judge, to a southern and western range in Ireland, though of wide distribution in Britain. I found *Gyrophæna affinis*, Mann., in *Boleti*, an addition to the Irish list, and *Philonthus quisquiliarius*, Gyll, a local southern species, occurred under stones on the banks of the Suck.

We kept a careful look out for all dead animals for the *Necrophaga* or carrion-feeders. One of the less common black and orange burying-beetles, *Necrophorus mortuorum*, F., swarmed in a dead squirrel, while Dr. Scharff got *Necordes littoralis*, L., in a rat. This species is of local occurrence inland, but it is much commoner in maritime localities.

Numbers of a species of *Choleva* occurred in dead birds in the woods, proving to be *C. fumata*, Spence, as far as I can ascertain not previously recorded from Ireland. Mr. A. H. Haliday possessed Irish examples, bearing, however, no definite locality. I was very pleased to meet with *Silpha dispar*, Herbst., when collecting on the banks of the Suck. This is one of the rarities so far monopolized by the Rev. W. F. Johnson, in the north of Ireland, where he has taken it on the south shore of Lough Neagh, and also near Armagh; this extension of range is therefore of interest. Several common species of *Coccinellidæ* abounded in the woods, the only one of interest being *Chilocoris bipustulatus*, Ill., found on willows in boggy places. This also seems to be a south-western species, at least it does not seem to have been recorded from any eastern locality. Near Doon Wood I found by sweeping in a marshy meadow two uncommon beetles, *i.e.*, *Phalacrus substriatus*, Gyll., and *Antherophagus pallens*, Gyll., the former indeed being unrecorded from Ireland; a single example only, which is considerably larger than certain types in the museum collection, but agrees with them in every other respect; and I may add that Mr. G. C. Champion, F.L.S., has kindly verified this identification. *Epuræa deleta*, Er., was not uncommon in fungi on trees, and *Elmis Volkmari*, Panz., under stones on river-banks.

Passing over many common insects, the next species of note is *Elater pomorum*, Herbst., a handsome shining black click-beetle with deep red wing-cases; Mr. Dillon found it commonly enough on birch in the beginning of May. Although said to be very local in England, it would seem to be not uncommon with us, as it has now been recorded from Co. Armagh[1], the Bog of Allen near Tullamore[2], and I have just seen a specimen taken by Mr. F. Neale in south Clare, close to a lake-shore, where he discovered the beautiful ground-beetle, *Panagæus crux-major*, L., that formed such an unexpected addition to our Irish list. *Corymbites tessellatus*, F., another large species, occurred occasionally on the heaths. The Longicorns were singularly scarce at the time of our visit; we really expected to meet with some novelties, seeing that the district is so suited to their habits, but unfortunately no new species rewarded our search. Mr. Dillon found *Leiopus nebulosus*, L., earlier in the year. The large and handsome *Rhagium bifasciatum*, F., is evidently not uncommon in the fir-woods, and a small black *Grammoptera ruficornis*, F., found on flowers, were all that were observed.

In water-plants in the Clonbrock river several species of *Donacia* occurred, but all were common with the exception perhaps of *D. impressa*, Payk., a species that has now been recorded from at least three localities in the south and west. Other captures were *D. discolor*, Panz., frequent on the heaths, *Chrysomela hyperici*, Forst., and *Haltica oleracea*, L.

The *Heteromera*, a section of the Coleoptera containing such well known insects as the "cellar-beetles" and "meal-worms," are very poorly represented in Ireland. One small species, *Salpingus castaneus*, Panz., occurred by sweeping at edge of a fir-wood; all the previous records for this species are from the east. The Oil-beetles (*Meloe*) also belong to this section, but search should be made for these very early in spring.

---

[1] W. W. Fowler. "Coleoptera of British Islands," vol. iv. (p. 91).
[2] *I. Nat.*, vol. iv., 1895, p. 173.

The *Rhynchophora* or weevils usually come last in beetle lists; they are without exception vegetable-feeders, the greater number being extremely conservative in keeping to their respective food-plants. The first weevil deserving of notice in the Clonbrock list is *Rhynchites minutus*, Herbst., found on two occasions by sweeping near willows. This species was added to the Irish list last year by Mr. J. J. Walker, who found it at Queenstown.[1] *Apion Gyllenhali*, Kirby, and *A. marchicum*, Herbst., were the best species of that extensive genus; although I had previously collected the latter, generally in marshy places, I have never succeeded in taking more than one or two specimens on any occasion. Sweeping large patches of *Equisetum* in drains produced *Grypidius equiseti*, F., a queer beetle looking not unlike a seed-head of that plant, to which it is exclusively attached. One of the most satisfactory discoveries made on this excursion was the occurrence of *Erirrhinus æthiops*, F. I found a single specimen of this rare weevil under a stone, on the banks of the Suck. Up to the present it had been found only by the Rev. W. F. Johnson in Co. Armagh[2]. According to Canon Fowler, the species is of extreme rarity in England, but it occurs in several Scotch localities; it will probably be found commonly enough when the midlands are better worked.[3] Amongst other captures I may mention the following:—*Polydrusus cervinus*, L., *Orchestes rusci*, Herbst., and *O. ilicis*, F., *Dorytomus maculatus*, Marsh., abundant; *D. pectoralis*, Gyll., *Cœliodes rubicundus*, Herbst., and *Poophagus sisymbrii*, F.

The beetles occurring on the banks of the Suck afforded a rather typical example of the gathering of northern and southern forms, that adds such interest to collecting in Ireland. In company with *Erirhinus æthiops*, which has a decidedly northern range, I found a ground-beetle (*Trechus discus*) having for its habitat the river-valleys of the midland English counties, while with both might be found a rove-beetle (*Philonthus quisquiliarius*), a species that has apparently Cambridgeshire for its northern limit in Britain. Examples of this mingling may be found in almost any part of Ireland, but they are undoubtedly most characteristic of the west.

---

[1] *I. Nat.*, vol. iv., 1895, p. 209.   [2] W. W. Fowler, *op. cit.*, vol. v. (p. 270.)

[3] I have just seen a fine series of this beetle in a collection made at Tempo, Enniskillen, by Mr. C. Langham.

FUNGI.

BY E. J. MCWEENEY, M.A., M.D.

HYMENOMYCETES.

Lepiota felina, Pers. Pheasantry. New to Ireland.
Mycena juncicola, Fr. Fir-wood.
M. tenerrima, Bk.
Omphalia fibula, Bull.
Pleurotus acerosus, Fr. New to Ireland.
Claudopus depluens, Batsch.
Hypholoma sp.
Irpex sp. immature.
Exidia glandulosa, Fr.
Tremella indecorata, Somm.
Dacryomyces stillatus, Nees.

MUCEDINES and DEMATIEI.

Monilia aurea, Genel. New to Ireland.
Botryosporium diffusum, Ca.
Rhinotrichum repens, Preuss.
Peronospora parasitica, Pers.
Stachylidium cyclosporum, Grove. New to Ireland.

UREDINEI.

Puccinia primulæ, D.C. Teleutospores much commoner than œcidia.
P. lychnidearum, Link.
P. moliniæ, Tub. Œcidia abundant on *Listera ovata*.
P. saniculæ, Grev.
P. violæ, Schum.
P. caricis, Schum. Œcidia on *Urtica dioica*.

UREDINEI.—*continued*.

Uromyces valerianæ, Schum. Spermogonia only, in fir-wood. New to Ireland.
? *Œcidium sonchi*, Johnst. New to Ireland.
Œ. sp. On *Carduus palustris*.

DISCOMYCETES and PYRENOMYCETES.

Morchella elata, Fr. On a mossy bank in Clonbrock wood—the only British locality for this species.
Peziza atrobrunnea, Phil. New to Ireland.
Lachnea hemisphærica, Wigg. New to Ireland.
Dasyscypha virginea, Fckl.
Lachnella corticalis, Pers. Not hitherto recorded from Ireland.
Propolis faginea, Karst. Not hitherto recorded from Ireland.
Phyllachora ægopodii, Fckl.
Cordyceps militaris, Fr. On buried lepidopterous larvæ and pupæ in pheasantry.
Hypoxylon multiforme, Fr.
Rosellinia mastoidea, Fr.
Sphæria. Two sp. undetermined.

MYXOMYCETES.

Œthalium septicum, Fr.
Lycogala epidendrum, Fr.
Trichia sp.

MOSSES AND HEPATICS.
BY DAVID M'ARDLE.

THE number of species of Mosses found at Clonbrock is low, and there was a striking similarity of collections made on different parts of the estate. A peculiar feature on the Sheeppool bog was the patches of *Funaria hygrometrica*, yards in extent; the brilliant red colour of the countless numbers of setæ and sporangia of the matured plants at once attracted attention, and was visible for a considerable distance. Most of the trees had their stems clothed with many forms of *Hypnum cupressiforme*, notably the var. *filiforme*, which hangs in long festoons. *Orthotrichum crispum* selected the tips of branches and luxuriated in neat compact tufts. *O. affine* was common on the trunks near the base. The ground in the woods was carpeted with *Hypnum triquetrum* and *H. proliferum*, with large patches of *Dicranum palustre*. On the bogs *Leucobryum glaucum* grew in large hassocks; *Campylopus fragilis* and *C. setifolius* were very common; and in wetter places *Aulacomnion palustre*. On the drain-banks *Dicranella varia* and *Fissidens adiantoides* were plentiful, in the streams the water-moss *Fontinalis antipyretica* was abundant. The Sphagnums were plentiful, and large patches of *S. cymbifolium*, *S. papillosum*, and *S. rubellum*, with many forms of *S. acutifolium* were collected, in the bog-pools *S. cuspidatum* var. *plumosum* was plentiful; it is by no means a common plant. On Doon bog I found *S. papillosum* var. *confertum*, a rare plant, only found by Professor Lindberg and myself on Connor Hill, Co. Kerry; it is very close to the rarer *S. Austini*, which I took it for at Clonbrock as I did in Kerry, but the microscopical difference is very marked. In the cell-walls the papillæ are regular and conical. On Tycooley bog, near the banks of the Shiven River, I was fortunate in finding the rare *S. Austini*, which differs in its peculiar branching, and in having the cell-walls of the leaves furnished with pectinate ridges. It was first found in Ireland by the Rev. H. W. Lett, in a bog at Glenariff, Co. Antrim, in 1889, and he afterwards collected it in a bog near Geashill, King's Co. (*I.N.*, vol. ii., p. 22), as did Rev. Canon. Russell and myself. These are the only known localities for this rare *Sphagnum*. There is an excellent figure and description of the plant in the *Monthly Microscopical Journal*, June

17th, 1871, p. 215, by Dr. Braithwaite, and the following account of its distribution "Hab. swamps Farrago, Ocean county, New Jersey, United States (*Austin*). In Europe only found in Sweden, Hunneberg Mountain, Westrogothia, 1859, (*Lindberg*). Viby, Nerike, 1860 (*Zetterstedt*), both sterile." He writes me that the Clonbrock specimen is referable to the var. *imbricatum*, and identical with specimens taken in Lewis by Dr. Moore.

The investigation of the Hepaticæ was the principal object of my visit. I endeavoured by every means to make as complete a collection as possible. In the Oak-wood alone I made thirty-three gatherings, and on Doon bog and adjacent woods thirty distinct gatherings. These and many others collected on other parts of the Clonbrock estate were subjected to a careful microscopical examination, with, I regret to say, very poor results, on account of the similarity between the specimens collected on different bogs and in different woods and plantations, although remote enough from each other. Out of all the material collected I enumerate only thirty species of Hepaticæ. Of these the following eleven species only are local on the estate; the remainder are widely distributed there, and I may truly say through Ireland.

Lejeunea hamatifolia, Hook.—On trees, Tycooley wood.

Lejeunea serpyllifolia, Libert.—In the oak-wood.

Lepidozia reptans, Linn.—Bog at Killasolan.

Jungermania exsecta, Schmidel—Sheep-pool bog, oak-wood, Doon bog. A rare species.

Jungermania affinis, Wilson.—Damp bank in oak-wood, Doon bog.

Cephalozia divaricata, Smith.—Doon bog.

Cephalozia catenulata, Huben.—Doon bog.

Cephalozia Lammersiana, Huben.—Doon bog.

Astrella hemisphærica, Beauv.—Doon bog.

Riccardia latifrons, Lindberg.—Doon bog, rare.

Scapania undulata, Linn. -Doon bog.

The small number of species of *Lejeunea* which were met with is remarkable. Out of the three which were collected *L. hamatifolia* only is rare in Co. Galway; it was collected in the woods at Kylemore Castle demesne, by the late Dr. D. Moore, in 1874, and, in July, 1895, I found it sparingly on Carn Seefin in the same county. The commonest liverwort in the district is *Lejeunea minutissima*. I collected it on all parts of the estate; it luxuriates on the trunks of the huge Beech-trees which dot the verdant lawn, and in the woods adjacent to the bogs, on almost every tree.

Out of fourteen species of *Lejeunea* known to grow in Ireland the number of species collected at Clonbrock is very small. They are curious little plants in their structure and habits, and love the moist warm glens, and tell of climatal conditions in as marked a manner as the rare flowering plants do. Amongst some of the liverworts that were remarkable by their absence I may mention *Lophocolea heterophylla*. *L. bidentata* was very common, but the former is a distinct plant, and I searched for it in vain on the decayed logs. It differs from the latter in having some of the leaves bidentate, others with the apex plane or slightly obtuse, and above all in having parœcious inflorescence, *i.e.*, the antheridia are in the axils of the leaves just beneath the perianth. By this character it is well separated from *L. bidentata*, which has the antheridia in spikes or amentæ.

Cephalozia sphagni was abundant on all the bogs, but no specimen of the rare *C. denudata* was found, which grows so abundantly on the Hill of Howth, and Corslieve Mountain, Co. Mayo, also sparingly on Bear Island; these are the only localities known in Ireland. The range of *C. sphagni* is probably wider than that of any other species belonging to this singular family of plants. It abounds in the north temperate zone, and luxuriates in the hot forest plains of the equator; it is always found on living plants of *Sphagnum*, *Leucobryum*, &c. *C. denudata*, on the contrary, is found mostly on decaying vegetable matter, such as rotting logs, peat, &c.; and is a plant of the hills. *C. sphagni* is found on the plains, and rarely at high elevations. *Cephalozia curvifolia*, one of the prettiest of the genus, reported from Kylemore, was not to be found. I searched the drains and moist banks for any species of the curious genus *Riccia*, but without success. One of the commonest plants amongst the frondose section was *Metzgeria conjugata*, which was first collected at O'Sullivan's Cascade, Killarney, in 1873, by Professor Lindberg, who pointed out its remarkable autœcious character, *i.e.*, its having the antheridia on one branch of the thallus, and the calyptra which contains the capsule and spores on a separate branch of the thallus, of the same plant; by this character it is separated from all the other species of *Metzgeria*, which are dioecious, having the antheridia or male inflorescence on one plant, and the calyptra which contains the female inflorescence on another plant. Recent researches of myself and others, show that the plant is to be found in almost every county; it is as widely distributed in Ireland as *M. furcata*. In specimens of both species collected at Clonbrock, I have been struck by the remarkable examples they exhibit of adventitious budding or branching, and it is obvious that they reproduce themselves more by this method than they do by spores. I shall quote one instance where this means must be adopted to reproduce the species. *Metzgeria pubescens* is a rare plant, confined to a few stations in Co. Antrim. We have only the male plant in Ireland; the female has not been found, so far as I am aware. In the *Irish Naturalist* for April last year, from copious specimens I have been enabled to demonstrate the subject of adventitious branching or budding with a figure of *Metzgeria conjugata* bearing young plantlets, which I trust will serve to explain this singular mode of reproduction.

Amongst the rarer species which I collected *Jungermania exsecta*, Schmidil, must not be forgotten. I found it once before, in Co. Wicklow. It is a curious plant, not like any other liverwort that I know. The leaves are in two rows, ovate in outline, the apex bluntly bi- or tridentate, and having about the middle on the upper margin a strong tooth, pointing obliquely upwards across each leaf. The specimens from Sheep-pool bog are luxuriant; they were growing amongst *Jungermania incisa* and bore gemmæ, but no fertile specimen was found. The plant is beautifully figured by Sir J. W. Hooker, in his grand work on the British Hepaticæ, at tab. 19, and supplement, p. 1. In his description of the plant, he writes—
" This singular species of *Jungermania* seems to be confined to the two most eastern counties in the Kingdom (Norfolk and Suffolk), at least I never heard of its being found in any other places, excepting indeed, very lately, near Bantry, by Miss Hutchins, of whom it may almost with truth be said, that she finds everything." It has since that time been found by Dr. Carrington at Killarney; and at Gleniff, Co. Leitrim, and at Sallagh Braes, Co. Antrim, by the late Dr. D. Moore. We have no previous record for Co. Galway.

FLOWERING PLANTS AND VASCULAR CRYPTOGAMS.
BY R. LLOYD PRAEGER, B.E.

WHEN the time arrived for our visit to Clonbrock, I was far out at sea, exploring that inhospitable islet of Rockall, in the N.E. Atlantic; and a heavy gale off the Hebrides further delayed junction with my colleagues, so that I did not reach Clonbrock till the pleasant week was half spent. My notes on the phanerogamic flora are, therefore, not so complete as might be desired; but they will convey, nevertheless, a fair general idea of the botanical character of the district.

The area in which Clonbrock is situated is composed entirely of the Carboniferous limestone formation, and is, in every particular, a characteristic piece of the great Central Plain. The streams flow sluggishly in broad shallow basins, through pasture and marshy meadows. The only hills are gently-swelling and inconspicuous ridges. The rock is seldom seen. Eskers are wanting, though one or two mounds of gravel occur. The pasture and tillage is broken by great bogs, which stretch for miles; their edges are often wooded, chiefly with Scotch Fir. Large areas are under timber, chiefly Oak, Beech, and conifers. Lakes there are none. From this description, it will be seen that the flora to be expected was that which characterizes the Central Plain, and that neither the lake or mountain rarities of Connemara, nor the limestone pavement flora of Burren, was likely to be represented, although both of these interesting districts lie within fifty miles. As a matter of fact, just one characteristic West Coast species turned up—*Rhynchospora fusca*, furnishing an important extension of range of this rare plant, fifty miles east of its most easterly recorded station. In mentioning briefly the more interesting plants found, they will be dealt with in the natural order, for convenience of reference.

Of *Ranunculaceæ*, the most conspicuous species was the Great Spearwort (*Ranunculus Lingua*), which grew abundantly on the marshy edges of the Shiven River, and on both the Galway and Roscommon banks of the Suck. The Marsh Meadow-Rue (*Thalictrum flavum*) was seen on the Roscommon bank of the River Suck.

Fumaria Borœi grew on both sides of the River Suck in cultivated land; with it was *F. officinalis*. *F. muralis* was gathered on the Roscommon bank. *Viola canina* was noted on old worked-out bog at Killasolan.

The Poppies were well represented for a district so far to the westward. The Long Prickly-headed (*P. Argemone*) grew on roadsides and in gravel-pits a couple of miles on the Ballinasloe side of Ahascragh—the only gravel-pits in the neighbourhood; with it were the two smooth-headed species (*P. Rhœas* and *P. dubium*) in abundance, and these two occurred in many places south and east of that spot.

Among crucifers, the Marsh Cress (*Nasturtium palustre*) and Water Radish (*N. amphibium*) grew by the River Suck, and in fields it was noticed that the White Mustard (*Sinapis alba*) in this district quite took the place of the usually all too common Charlock (*S. arvensis*), which was hardly seen at all, while its ally was most abundant.

Caryophyllaceæ had no representatives of much rarity, but the Three-nerved Sandwort (*Arenaria trinervia*) grew in many places, and was much more abundant than the commoner Thyme-leaved Sandwort (*A. serpyllifolia*).

Five species of St. John's-wort were noted—*Hypericum Androsæmum, perforatum, dubium, quadrangulum, pulchrum.* The third is the only one which is not generally distributed in Ireland.

The only Rosaceous plant of interest was the Bird-cherry (*Prunus Padus*), which grows in great profusion in one old wood at Clonbrock. A few brambles were collected, but have not yet been submitted to a specialist.

The beautiful Grass of Parnassus (*Parnassia palustris*) was everywhere abundant in marshy land. On the bogs all three species of Sundew (*Drosera anglica, intermedia, rotundifolia*) grew in charming profusion, often brightening the wetter portions by the large patches of red-haired leaves, glistening as the sunlight caught the heads of viscous fluid with which all the hairs are copiously tipped. Two species of Millfoil were found—*Myriophyllum verticillatum* on the Galway side of the Suck, and the commoner *M. alterniflorum* in various places.

Umbelliferous plants were not largely represented, the only uncommon species being the Broad-leaved Water-Parsnep

(*Sium latifolium*) which grew on the Galway bank of the Suck. Of the Valerian tribe, the Toothed Corn-salad (*Valerianella dentata*) was one of several plants found only in the neighbourhood of the gravel-pits already mentioned.

To come now to the large order of Composite plants, the Mountain Cudweed (*Antennaria dioica*) was quite conspicuous by its abundance everywhere. The Bur-Marygold (*Bidens cernua*) grew by the Shiven River. A much rarer plant, the Field Chamomile (*Matricaria Chamomilla*) occurred in many places on roadsides; though possibly originally introduced with seed, as it certainly is sometimes, it appears in this district to have settled down as a resident. Among the Thistles, *Carlina vulgaris* occurred but sparingly. The Slender-flowered Thistle (*Carduus tenuiflorus*), a species usually found near the coast, grew in the gravel-pits; the Bog Thistle (*C. pratensis*) was one of the most abundant plants in the district. Among the *Liguliflorœ*, or Dandelion-like plants, the Yellow Goats-beard (*Tragopogon pratensis*) was found in one field half way between Ballinasloe and Ahascragh. The Hairy Hawkbit (*Leontodon hirtus*) was common; its ally, the Rough Hawkbit (*L. hispidus*) was not seen; it appears to be a much rarer plant in Ireland, and I doubt if it has a wider range, as stated in *Cybele Hibernica*.

Of that beautiful order of which the Heaths are the type, two interesting plants abounded on the bogs—the Cranberry (*Vaccinium Oxycoccos*) whose delicate pink flowers had in many places already given way to the large berries; and the Marsh Andromeda (*A. polifolia*), its lovely pink bells still lingering on a few belated shoots. One gentian, *G. Amarella*, was found, though not yet in flower, still sufficiently advanced for determination. Its ally, the Yellow-wort (*Blackstonia perfoliata*) occurred sparingly. The Primrose order was represented by eight species—the Yellow Loosestrife (*Lysimachia vulgaris*), which grew by the Suck, and with it the Brook-weed (*Samolus Valerandi*), and the tiny Bog Pimpernel (*Anagallis tenella*); in the woods the Moneywort (*L. nemorum*) was remarkably abundant; while the Scarlet Pimpernel, Cowslip, and Primrose made up the balance.

Of *Boraginaceæ*, the only uncommon species was the Field Gromwell (*Lithospermum arvense*) gathered in a potato-patch on the Roscommon side of the Suck. Of *Scrophulariaceæ*, the Mullein (*Verbascum Thapsus*) flourished at the gravel pits, and the Cow-wheat (*Melampyrum pratense*) on Tycooly bog ; of ten species of *Veronica* noted, the only one worth mentioning is *V. polita*, gathered on the Galway side of the Suck.

Two of these interesting carnivorous plants, the Bladderworts, grew in the bog-holes, both in blossom—the Common (*Utricularia vulgaris*) and Lesser (*U. minor*) ; that characteristic west coast species, *U. intermedia*, was not found. Of their equally interesting allies, the Butterworts, two species were noted—*Pinguicula vulgaris*, the common species, and the rarer Pale Butterwort (*P. lusitanica*) usually a mountain plant, but here growing on an old worked-out bog at an elevation of only about 150 feet. The great Water Dock (*Rumex Hydrolapathum*) grew with other marsh-loving species on the Galway bank of the Suck.

The native trees included both species (or varieties) of the Birch (*Betula pubescens* and *B. verrucosa*) which everywhere fringed the bogs, along with Willows, of which seven species were noted, all common except *Salix pentandra* and *S. purpurea*. The remaining indigenous *Amentiferæ* were the Oak, Alder, and Hazel.

Orchids were well represented, and one of the prettiest and most interesting sights we saw was at Doon, where, on a rough piece of boggy land, sparsely dotted over with low stunted fir-trees, a remarkable variety of Orchids grew together. The large white or pinkish flowers of the Marsh Helleborine (*Epipactis palustris*) were perhaps the most conspicuous. M'Ardle found some plants in which the whole flower was suffused with a rich rose-red. With it grew the beautiful Bee Orchis (*Ophrys apifera*), and great abundance of the Sweet-scented (*Gymnadenia conopsea*), and Tway-blade (*Listera ovata*), and in less quantity the Smaller Butterfly Orchis (*Habenaria bifolia*), Frog Orchis (*H. viridis*), Broad-leaved (*Orchis incarnata*), and Pyramidal (*O. pyramidalis*). The only species found in the district which were not at Doon were the Early Purple (*O. mascula*), gathered in fruit ; the Greater Butterfly (*H. chlorantha*) which was very rare, while *H. bifolia* was common ; and lastly, the rare Bird's-nest (*Neottia Nidus-avis*), which grew under trees at Clonbrock.

Of Pondweeds, three species grew abundantly in the River Suck—*Potamogeton lucens, P. Zizii,* and *P. heterophyllus* var. *graminifolius*. In the Clonbrock River, not far from the house, were gathered *P. plantagineus,* and another form of much interest, on which Mr. A. Bennett supplies the following note:—

"This plant is doubtless, in a wide sense, to be placed under *P. lanceolatus,* Smith, but differs from the Anglesea, Cambridge, or French specimens, as such supposed hybrids would do. It seems that these specimens may have been produced by *P. heterophyllus,* Schreb., v. *graminifolius,* as the one parent, and *P. pusillus,* L., as the other. The difficulty of reference to any known form, causes one to wish that it could be cultivated; the hybrid theory is an easy way out of a difficult problem, and yet it is not easy to suggest in this case any other. 'Make a new species of it,' would be another way, and easy enough from some views, but if eventually *proved* an error, is only adding to synonymy unnecessarily. As a supposed hybrid, it is an uncertain quantity, and leaves it open for experiment. I consider all supposed hybrids that have not been actually produced by cultivation, as doubtful plants, although naturally the amount of faith or credence that may be placed in them is very variable.

The present specimens, by their longer and broader (relatively) upper leaves, with a much smaller part of the leaf occupied by the chain-like areolation, so conspicuous in the Anglesea and Cambridgeshire specimens[1], bear the same proportion, as to shape and size, that the others do to *their* supposed parents. On these specimens the glands of the *graminifolius* section are very conspicuous.

If a name is required for it, it might be called var. *hibernicus* (or f. *hibernicus*). characterized by its longer, and broader upper leaves, longer lower leaves, slightly longer flower-spikes, and the structure of the leaves."

Among the Sedges and their allies, the most interesting find was the Brown Beak-rush (*Rhynchospora fusca*), which has been already referred to in the general account of our trip (p. 220). Of sixteen sedges collected, the best was *Carex teretiuscula,* which was found in marshes by bog-holes in many places. Mr. A. Bennett remarks of specimens submitted to him, "very near, if not identical with β. *Ehrhartiana.*" The twenty-five grasses found offer nothing of special interest; *Bromus racemosus, B. commutatus,* and *Festuca loliacea,* Huds., were gathered within the Galway area.

---

[1] In *P. pusillus,* L., when having spathulate upper leaves (as in *P. panormitanus,* Bivona), the tendency is to produce this chain-like areolation.—A.B.

Ferns were tolerably well represented. The abundance of *Lastrea spinulosa* was remarked. The Scale Fern (*Ceterach officinarum*) grew at Clonbrock, and the great rarity of the Black Spleenwort (*Asplenium Adiantum-nigrum*) was noticed; it is equally rare in King's and Queen's Counties, and perhaps it shuns the Limestone Plain. The Royal Fern (*Osmunda regalis*) grew in several places; the Moonwort (*Botrychium Lunaria*) was gathered sparingly at Killasolan; and the Adder's Tongue (*Ophioglossum vulgatum*) grew in pastures at Clonbrock. The only Club-moss found was the little *Selaginella spinosa*, which grew on worked-out bog at Killasolan, and abundantly on the gravel-ridge near Ahascragh.

The total number of plants noted in the three days I had at Clonbrock was 360, but a number of critical plants were also collected, which have not yet been determined; these will bring up the list to close on 400 species.

PROCEEDINGS OF IRISH SOCIETIES.

ROYAL ZOOLOGICAL SOCIETY.

Recent donations comprise a Peregrine Falcon from L. Powell, Esq.; a Moose Deer from the Earl of Aberdeen; a Sparrow Hawk from Master Stubbs; a pair of Cockatoos from V. W. Brown, Esq.; a pair of Doves from Miss Perry; freshwater fish from F. Godden, Esq.; a pair of Horsefield's Tortoise from A. Jamrach, Esq.; and some Rabbits from Mrs. Lennan. A pair of Siberian Cranes, a Brazilian Cariama, twenty Budgerigars, a pair of Ibex, a pair of Toggenburg Goats, and a Tibet Goat have been purchased; while four Puma cubs have been born in the Gardens.

13,360 persons visited the Gardens during July.

DUBLIN MICROSCOPICAL CLUB.

AUGUST 6th.—The Club met at the house of PROF. T. JOHNSON, who exhibited a section of *Asperococcus compressus*, a brown alga, recently obtained by Miss Hensman and himself by dredging off Go Island (Co. Donegal). *A. compressus* was dredged by the exhibitor three years ago in Bantry Bay. It is now recorded for the first time as a member of the Irish marine flora; a southern type of weed, its occurrence so far north is of interest.

Mr. GREENWOOD PIM showed sections of the petioles of *Nymphæa alba* and *N. marliacea*, and drew attention to the curious internal hairs which occur in the air-canals in these and in other aquatic plants. They seemed especially numerous in *N. marliacea*, a hybrid raised by M. Marliac, and now common in gardens where water-plants are grown.

Prof. Cole showed a section of andesitic volcanic tuff, as an example of the series known as "pyroxenic rocks" near the summit of Slieve Gallion, west of Lough Neagh. These rocks had hitherto been regarded as metamorphic, but Prof. Cole hoped to show that a considerable volcanic series occurred as a capping above the granite of that area, which had intruded into it at a later date.

Mr. M'Ardle exhibited specimens of *Jungermania exsecta*, Schmidel, a rare liverwort which he collected last June on Sheep-pool Bog, Clonbrock. The leaves are arranged in two rows, ovate in outline, with their apex bluntly bi- or tridentate, and having about the middle of the upper margins a strong tooth which points obliquely upwards. The plant is very local. Dr. Carrington found it at Killarney, and Dr. D. Moore recorded it from Gleniff, Co. Leitrim, and Sallagh Braes, Co. Antrim. It has not been previously found in the Co. Galway.

Mr. W. Haughton showed specimens of *Tribolium ferrugineum*, Fab., which had been found on empty flour-sacks. These small beetles often occur in large numbers in mills and warehouses among flour, and multiplying at a high rate, are very injurious and hard to exterminate.

Belfast Naturalists' Field Club.
Dredging Cruise.

On Saturday, 4th July, the Belfast Club held a somewhat unusual excursion: a dredging cruise having been arranged to Belfast Lough and adjacent bays. There has not been a dredging trip in this neighbourhood for some time, so that it was of some interest. Unfortunately for the enjoyment of the party, the morning proved very wet and drizzling, but no way deterred a party of nearly fifty from assembling on board the Steam Tug "Storm Light" before ten o'clock; at which time the whistle blew for the last time, and the vessel started for the day's work. The guiding genii of the day held a conference almost immediately, to settle the plans of action, following which the boat was headed for Carrickfergus: on arrival at the desired locality, all the appliances having been previously made ready, the vessel was slowed down, and the first dredge lowered over the side. Ten minutes or so was allowed for the filling of the net, and on the signal being given, a number of willing helpers lent a hand, and soon had the first haul on board: a cast of the lead showing $3\frac{1}{2}$ fathoms. The take proved to contain a large quantity of corallines of various species, with much other material, all of which was emptied out into large flat trays and distributed about the after end of the vessel, for purposes of examination. Hitherto the weather had been getting steadily worse, until at this point the collecting of specimens was eagerly being carried on amid a downpour of rain. Meanwhile the "Storm Light" proceeded at full speed to the second station, three quarters of a mile from Whitehead, where a scrape in $9\frac{3}{4}$ fathoms brought up a most miscellaneous haul, which kept the collectors of ascidians, crustaceans, seaweeds, worms, &c., occupied until the vessel was well under the great cliffs of the Gobbins. Here, sailing close under the precipitous face, the steam whistle's blast raised from their ledges a cloud of seagulls, whose screaming cries and wheeling flight distracted the scientists' attention from the spoils of the deep, in order to gaze at the beautiful picture, with the blue sky, now fast clearing of clouds, as a background.

No time was lost, however, but another haul was made in fourteen fathoms, at about a quarter of a mile from the cliffs, bringing up a great mass of small pebbles, among which, however, two *Terebratulæ* were found, to the delight of many (or indeed most) of the party, who had never previously seen a living one. The hopes of getting more rarities in the deeper waters of this locality induced the party to try a fisherman's mussel-dredge of large mesh, in twenty-five fathoms, close by the last station. This appliance brought up very little in bulk, but among its contents was a very large and perfect sponge, measuring nearly four inches across; there were also two sea-urchins in splendid condition, whose movements in one of the large belljars on deck provided much interest to many of the members. Several crabs of different quaint-looking species (*Hyas, Portunus*) also disported themselves in an adjoining jar to the detriment of a fine worm, which rapidly disappeared, and to the amusement of the watchers. Meanwhile, the gallant little tug was making all possible speed outwards towards the "Maidens," but owing to the roughness of the water where unprotected by the land, the project of taking a netful from the deep water of mid-channel had to be abandoned for fear of losing the tackle; fate however was adverse, and on trying to make a haul off Larne, one of the dredges was carried away altogether, and the other, a brand new one of novel make, came up with its frame bent, and quite empty. This so disgusted members, that full speed was at once made for Whitehead, under whose sheltering cliffs tea was quickly prepared and most thoroughly enjoyed.

Clearance of tea-things having been made, it was suggested that the next trial should be made off the centre of the mouth of the lough; which proposal being acted on, resulted in another empty net. The increasingly rough water, on the southern side of the lough, made it advisable not to risk the remaining dredges, so orders were given to return in Kilroot direction, where a haul resulted in an enormous number of dead *Venus* shells being brought up.

Time now began to run short, and no time was lost in making for Belfast again. On nearing the jetty at Queen's Bridge, Mr. Alec. G. Wilson (Hon. Sec.) proposed briefly that a hearty vote of thanks be given to Mr. Waterson, the owner of the "Storm Light," for his invaluable assistance in making the trip the success it proved to be. This was passed without further ceremony by a hearty round of applause. Three new members were then elected. During the trip, the Club was pleased to entertain four members of the Dublin Club, who availed themselves of the invitation to the other Club, and whose services during the day proved of great value, Prof. Johnson and Dr. C. H. Hurst being specialists in their respective lines of marine botany and zoology. Prof. Johnson's notes on the Algæ collected and Dr. Hurst's list of the animals observed will be published next month.

NOTES.
BOTANY.
PHANEROGAMS.

Veronica peregrina L. in Ireland.—This plant was recorded from Belfast in 1857 by Rev. W. M. Hind, who found it "fully established as a weed of the soil at The Lodge" (*Phytologist*, n.s. ii. p. 47). It does not appear to have made headway in this district, as it has not been found near Belfast by any subsequent botanist, and Mr. Stewart remarks (*Flor. N.E.I.*) "perhaps extinct about Belfast." In Co. Tyrone it was observed so far back as 1836, according to *Cybele Hibernica*, "growing abundantly within the demesne of Barnescourt" [Baron's Court], and subsequently "in several localities between that place and Londonderry," and in More's "Recent Additions," (*Journ. Bot.*, 1872), three Donegal localities are added, two on the authority of Mr. Hart, the other on that of Mr. Hind; also the more distant stations of Rockingham in Roscommon, and Hazelwood in Sligo, on the authority of Dr. Moore. In Donegal it would appear to have become quite naturalized, for Mr. Hart says of it in 1883 "in many places from east to west of Donegal this has become the commonest garden weed. Except in gardens I have not met with it" (*Journ. Bot.*, xxi., p. 208.) In its head-quarters in the valley of the Foyle, it appears to have thoroughly established itself, as Mrs. Leebody has this season sent me fine specimens which she collected in abundance in gardens at Duncreggan near Londonderry, while she has also found it abundant in a nursery garden near the same town, and at Culmore (all these stations are on the Donegal side of the Foyle); also at Favor Royal and Donaghmore, both in Co. Tyrone. This plant, therefore, would appear to be thoroughly established in cultivated ground in the north-west of Ireland, and the fact is of interest, as, so far as I can find, it is unknown in England, and in Scotland is recorded from Perth alone. In the "London Catalogue" it does not find a place, being apparently treated as merely a casual, and unworthy of insertion, but the above records show that it merits recognition as a British plant quite as much as, say, *Camelina sativa* or *Cotula coronopifolia*. *Veronica peregrina* is an American species, now found, according to Nyman's *Conspectus*, in Spain, France, Belgium, Holland, Germany, Italy, &c., and it appears to be one of the several American immigrants that has settled down as a colonist on European soil.

R. Lloyd Praeger.

Scirpus parvulus, R. & S. (= S. nanus, Spreng.)—Mr. R. M. Barrington sends fresh specimens of this very rare little plant, collected on July 14th at Arklow. It is interesting to know that, despite recent changes, the plant still survives in its only Irish station.

R. Lloyd Praeger.

ZOOLOGY.

MOLLUSCS.

Littorina obtusata at Bunowen, Connamara.—On the occasion of the Easter trip to Roundstone and district by a number of members of the Belfast and Dublin Field Clubs, many of those who were at Bunowen Bay, near Slyne Head, noticed the great numbers of this common little shell, at one end of the strand. There is a small cove at the westward end, cut off from the main beach; in this cove the surface of the sand above highwater mark was covered with shells.

From the surface I collected at random as many shells as covered about two to three square yards, taking care not to select special patches. The following is the list of species thus gathered:—*Littorina obtusata*, 509 individuals; *Trochus cinerarius*, 57; *T. umbilicatus*, 55; *Littorina littorea* 16; *Helix ericetorum*, 15; *Purpura lapillus*, 10; *Trochus zizyphinus*, 2; *Patella vulgata*, 1; *Helix acuta*, 1. In addition to these, which were all practically unbroken shells, were the following:—Small pebbles, 5; fragments of *Cardium edule*, 1; fragment of *Ostrea*, 1. This list seems so remarkable that I am sending it up for publication, in order to find out any parallel instances of great preponderance of one species.

A. G. WILSON, Belfast.

Spirialis retroversus in Killala Bay.—During the recent neap tides and in fine calm weather I visited the Island of Bartra, lying across Killala Bay, and having a long range of sandy beach exposed to the Atlantic. I thought it would be a favourable day for shell drift, but the most interesting occurrence was the immense deposit of *Spirialis retroversus*. It lay along the water-mark in a broad band varying in width from three feet to a few inches, and heaped up in some places to a depth of two inches. This deposit extended along the beach for about a mile, where it lay like froth. Though in colour a pale milky chocolate, the mass had evidently been wafted in alive, as the odour was most unpleasant, and remained on those I brought away for some days. Besides this froth-like deposit, which extended for quite a mile, there was a smaller quantity mixed with the usual drift all along the beach.

Once before I met with this shell in the froth-like masses, though not to such an extent. The shells were, for the most part, very small.

AMY WARREN, Ballina.

FISHES.

The Allis Shad in Irish Waters.—The July number of the *Irish Naturalist* mentions that a specimen of the Allis Shad had been lately taken near Donaghadee, and quotes Thompson as an authority for saying that Londonderry is the only Irish locality where it has been found.

Dr. Day on the other hand quotes this same Thompson as reporting that it is often abundant in some parts of Ireland, and specially mentions two or three instances from Donegal, and I have myself seen two specimens taken in Inver Bay on the west coast of that county.

W. SINCLAIR, Strabane.

[Thompson (*Nat. Hist. of Ireland*, vol. iv., p. 178) gives Londonderry as the only Irish locality on the authority of the Ordnance Survey.—EDS.]

MEDICAGO SYLVESTRIS IN IRELAND.

BY R. LLOYD PRAEGER, B.E.

IN June, 1894, on a dry sandy bank at the southern extremity of the Portmarnock dunes, opposite the village of Baldoyle, I noticed among the close-cropped herbage the leaves of a plant, apparently a *Medicago* or *Trifolium*, with which I was not familiar. A search revealed the fact that it grew on several other dry banks in the vicinity, but no trace of flower or fruit could be found. On looking up "Cybele Hibernica" and the "British Association Guide," I could find no plant recorded from Portmarnock with which the short leafy shoots of my plant appeared to correspond, so I went back at the end of July, in hopes that it would then be in flower, but no appearance of blossom could be detected. Walking into Malahide, I found a large patch of the same plant on the sand-dunes near the Baths. Roots from Portmarnock were brought away and cultivated; they grew vigorously, and in August of the next year (1895) they came into blossom; and at first sight, judging by its large size and clusters of purple flowers, I took the plant to be a form of *Medicago sativa*. But before the plant had ripened its fruit, which in the Medicks furnishes the most satisfactory specific criterion, it was accidentally cut down to the ground, and the opportunity of critically examining it was lost. I visited Portmarnock and Malahide again, but although there was an abundance of leafy shoots, no flower or fruit had been produced, or if it had, had been eaten down by the rabbits. This year, however, the cultivated specimens shot up, and flowered sparingly at the end of July, and when the fruit ripened in August I found it to consist of a pod twisted in the shape of a single flat or slightly spiral ring, thus corresponding exactly with *Medicago sylvestris*, Fries, a very rare plant, known in Great Britain to grow only in sandy or gravelly places on one limited area, which extends into the counties of Suffolk, Norfolk, and Cambridge. A fortnight later, Prof. G. F. Fitzgerald, F.R.S., sent me specimens of the plant in flower and fruit from Malahide for determination, suggesting the name *Medicago sylvestris*. I again visited

Portmarnock and Malahide, and found the plant flowering and fruiting at both places. At Portmarnock it could be traced along the dry banks over a considerable area, but flowering very sparingly. At Malahide it appeared to be confined to the limited area in which I had first noticed it; here most of the flowers assumed the peculiar greenish-yellow colour that is characteristic of the plant, others being purple, while at Portmarnock almost all the flowers were bright purple, a few only being greenish-purple. Though there could be no doubt as to the identity of the plant, specimens were sent to Mr. Arthur Bennett, who promptly confirmed my determination, adding the remark, "closely approaching in habit the wild Suffolk plant as I have gathered it."

Two points in connection with this plant and its occurrence in Co. Dublin invite comment—its standing (1) as a good species, and (2) as a native. As regards its specific distinctness, and its relationships, botanists appear to be much at variance. Fries[1] first described it as a species. Hooker and Arnott[2] treated it as a variety of *M. falcata*; Reichenbach[3], and Grenier and Godron[4], considered it a hybrid between *M. falcata* and *M. sativa*; Wallroth[5] and Koch[6] called it *M. falcata β. versicolor*. Syme[7] states that he never saw the plant alive, and therefore "adopts the middle course" of giving it sub-specific rank under *M. falcata*. Babington treated it as a good species in the last edition of his "Manual," and the same course is followed in the latest edition of "London Catalogue."

Discussing the question of its hybridity, and Fries' emphatic denial of the possibility of this, Syme states that in England it frequently occurs where *M. sativa* is absent. A similar argument against its hybrid origin might now be advanced as regards its Irish stations, for *M. falcata* is unknown in Ireland except as a rare casual, and the other supposed parent, *M. sativa*, only occurs occasionally where sown. Indeed, the occurrence in some quantity of a hybrid where one parent is absent, and the other is a fleeting plant of cultivation, strikes one as very improbable.

---

[1] *Mant.* III. [2] *Brit. Flora*, ed. 8. [3] *Fl. Germ. Excurs.* [4] *Flore de France*, I.
[5] *Sched. Crit.* [6] *Synopsis Fl. Germ. et Helv.*, ed. 2. [7] *Engl. Bot.*, ed. 3.

Again, there does not appear to be any reason for supposing the plant to have been introduced in its Irish stations. True, there are scattered cottages near its Portmarnock home; but there is very little cultivation around or near these cottages. The close-cropped mossy grass extends on every hand, and no other introduced plants accompany the Medick. The Malahide station is nearer the influences of agriculture and civilization, but the occurrence of the plant here, in a habitat exactly similar to the Portmarnock one, and at a distance of three and a half miles, is itself an argument against the theory of introduction. Portmarnock has long been known as productive of alien plants, it is true, but these appear to have their home among the cultivated fields around the head of the Portmarnock inlet, and not among the natural sward at the extremity of the promontory, where several rare native plants, such as *Viola hirta*, *Vicia lathyroides*, and *Epipactis palustris*, have long been known to flourish. Another plea might be put forward in favour of its introduction—that so large a plant is not likely to have so long escaped notice in localities which have been thoroughly known to botanists for a century past. But as a matter of fact, *M. sylvestris*, growing stunted among short herbage along with *Ononis*, *Trifolium*, and other similar-leaved plants, is in reality quite inconspicuous, the more so on account of its sparse and late blossoming; when it took me three seasons to discover its identity, it appears possible that botanists have overlooked it, or, even if gathered, that it was passed by as an indeterminable fragment of probably a common species.

When once studied, *M. sylvestris* may be easily recognised, even in the absence of flower or fruit. The leaflets are smaller and narrower, and the stems thinner, more branched, and much more spreading than in *M. sativa*, and the whole plant, even when fully developed (as it appears to never be in its Irish stations, thanks to rabbits and sheep) is smaller than that species. In blossom, the smaller flowers, in shorter racemes, furnish an additional feature, not to mention their peculiar colour when typical. In fruit, the pod, coiled in a single plane or slightly spiral circle, supplies a character that cannot be mistaken. I have not had an opportunity of comparing it with *M. falcata* in a living state.

ALGÆ FROM THE NORTH SIDE OF BELFAST LOUGH[1].

(Dredged by the B. N. F. C. Expedition, 4th July, 1896.)

BY PROF. T. JOHNSON, D.SC., AND MISS R. HENSMAN.

To the request of the B.N.F.C. Secretaries, that we of the Dublin Field Club who happened to possess any special knowledge of marine fauna and flora investigation, should go over and help them, there could be, having regard to the kindly welcome for which Belfast is noted, but one answer. Accordingly Dr. C. H. Hurst, H. Lyster Jameson, Miss Hensman, and I, joined the dredging excursion, of which some of the results are here recorded.

Remembering that the weather was so rough the day the excursion took place that the Belfast Regatta was postponed, the results of the excursion, as recorded below, must be considered satisfactory. A little organization of the enthusiasts who faced the lough on the 4th of July should produce some good algologists.

The Belfast Field Club would do a splendid piece of natural history work, if it would make such arrangements as would enable some of its members to examine thoroughly, by shore-hunting and dredging, the coast of Co. Antrim, in the neighbourhood of Cushendall and Cushendun. Practically nothing has been added to the knowledge of the marine flora of the N. E. of Ireland since the time of Harvey, when, mainly through the work of W. Thompson and Dr. D. Moore, the district was as well known as any other.

During the past few years a committee has been investigating the marine flora of the Clyde sea area, and, thanks more especially to E. A. L. Batters (whose lists have been published), a better knowledge of this district is now possessed. Several competent members of the Club (whose names need not be mentioned) should be encouraged to do a similar piece of work for the N. E. of Ireland.

So far as time has allowed the examination of the material collected to proceed, some sixty species have been identified, of which the more interesting are here given.

---

[1] For a general account of the Dredging Excursion on which these algæ were obtained, see pp. 245-6.

Names preceded by † are now recorded for the North-east of Ireland for the first time. Names preceded by * are first records[1] for Ireland. Perhaps the most interesting of all is *Halicystis ovalis*, a green stalked alga, the size of a small pin-head. This alga, though known to occur on the French and Scandinavian coasts, has been only once before recorded for Britain—from the Clyde district by the late Prof. Schmitz and G. R. Murray, F.L.S.

CYANOPHYCEÆ.

†*Hyella cæspitosa.*
†*Plectonema terebrans.*
†*Mastigocoleus testarum.*

CHLOROPHYCEÆ.

***Halicystis ovalis.*
***Pringsheimia scutata.*
†*Epicladia Flustræ.*
†*Gomontia polyrhiza.*

PHÆOPHYCEÆ.

Arthrocladia villosa.
Stilophora rhizodes.
Sporochnus pedunculatus.
†*Aglaozonia reptans.*

RHODOPHYCEÆ.

†*Conchocelis rosea.*
†*Erythrotrichia carnea.*
†*Scinaia furcellata.*
Phyllophora Brodiæi.
***Actinococcus subcutaneus.*
Rhodophyllis bifida.
†*Gonimophyllum Buffhami.*
Odonthalia dentata.
†*Rhodochorton membranaceum.*
***R. mesocarpum.*
Ceramium diaphanum.
†*Melobesia Lejolisii.*
†*M. Corallinæ.*
***Lithophyllum Lenormandi.*
†*Lithothamnion calcareum.*[2]
†*L. corallioides.*

---

[1] It should be stated that though the records are new, many of the species have been already found by the writers at other points on the Irish coast.

[2] It was interesting to find a coralline off Carrickfergus, identical with the much discussed *Melobesia compressa*, which M'Calla found in Dalkey Sound.

OLDHAMIA IN AMERICA.

BY PROF. GRENVILLE A. J. COLE, M.R.I.A., F.G.S.

Oldhamia, the obscure ridge-like and radiating marking that occurs in the shales of the Bray series, has made the county of Wicklow famous among geologists throughout the world. Continental text-books have figured these problematic objects, adding, perhaps, even greater firmness to their outlines, and greater symmetry to the disposition of their rays. The handsome specimens in the Survey collection in the Dublin Museum are, indeed, enough to stimulate curiosity, even if they are disappointing to those who look for distinct organic structure. The supporters of the organic view of *Oldhamia* will, however, receive much encouragement from the discovery of similar objects in America *in strata of Cambrian or Lower Ordovician age*. Mr. C. D. Walcott, Director of the U. S. Geological Survey, has published (*Proc. U. S. National Museum*, vol. xvii., p. 313) a valuable description of *Oldhamia occidens* Walcott, from shales near Troy, New York State. I am indebted to the author for kindly sending me a copy of a paper not easily accessible.

Mr. Walcott throws doubt on Hall's *Oldhamia fruticosa*, from the Trenton Limestone (Upper Ordovician) of Wisconsin, but accepts Lapworth's determination of an *Oldhamia*, species uncertain, from the Cambrian slates of Farnham, in the province of Quebec.

The specimens on which the new record are based were sent, with various indeterminable tracks and impressions, by Mr. T. N. Dale to his chief in 1893. *Oldhamia occidens* is placed under the sub-genus *Murchisonites*, proposed by Brady for *O. antiqua* in 1865; but it differs from that species by the fact that each fan-like tuft springs serially from the summit of that preceding it—or, as appears from the figure, from some point slightly behind the summit, so that the "fans" are grouped along a straight line, the broad edge of one just overlapping on the point of origin of that following it.

The description of the beds, which are "post Lower Cambrian and pre-Trenton," reminds one very strikingly of those of Bray.

The literature relating to the Irish examples was quoted in the first number of the *Irish Naturalist* (vol. i., p. 13). Although the American specimens do nothing, as Mr. Walcott points out, to advance "the position of *Oldhamia* in the classification of organic forms," yet the whole question is evidently still an open one; while the absence of the structure from post-Ordovician shales has still to be explained by those who regard it as inorganic.

CONTRIBUTIONS TO GLACIAL GEOLOGY.

A Map to show the distribution of Eskers in Ireland. By Prof. W. J. Sollas, LL.D., F.R.S. (*Sci. Trans. Royal Dublin Society*, vol. v., part xiii. Price 2s.)

In this paper we have another example of that excellent system of publication, by which single memoirs, read before a learned society, are made accessible to the outer world. As a review of the literature of eskers alone, this part of the Transactions of the Royal Dublin Society should be in the hands of most geologists and of all "glacialists." Its title is misleading, for it is far more than a map; and the map given, by-the-bye, illustrates only a certain part of Ireland. In the north especially, numerous fine eskers exist, which are not set down upon the maps of the Geological Survey, these sheets having been already hachured; but in the region between Galway and Dublin, Longford and Roscrea, Prof. Sollas has been able to extract the eskers from the unshaded 1-inch maps, and from the documents of the Geological Survey, and has brought together a striking picture of their distribution and of their confluence. He sums up his own observations as telling strongly in favour of the subglacial origin of eskers; the materials of the esker have been accumulated in the lower part of the ice-sheet, and have been left behind when the mass melted away. Hummel, in 1874, suggested that streams running beneath an ice-sheet, or beneath a local glacier, hollow out tunnels, which become choked with sand and gravel; the eskers are to be regarded as casts of these tunnels. Holst, two or three years later, held that eskers originated in the gravel washed into the ravines and beds of rivers which were cut in the surface of the ice; the glacier, on melting, yielded up the drift which it contained at various levels within it, as well as that which lay upon its surface, and this material became arranged along the beds of the streams; finally, the complete melting of the ice left these river-accumulations in the form of ridges, their sides having been, until then, banked up by the ice. Dr James Geikie adopted the englacial or subglacial view of eskers in 1877, and it is to him that geologists in the British Isles are indebted for an introduction to Hummel's and Holst's most suggestive papers. Prof. Sollas does justice to other independent workers, such as Winchell and

Upham in America; but should not Mr. J. G. Goodchild also appear prominently in this connexion? Mr. Goodchild (¹) put forward in 1874 the somewhat curious view that drumlins and eskers accumulated on rock-bosses and rock-ridges *between* the channels of subglacial streams, *i.e.*, between the channels of greatest flow; but, if he did not independently proceed precisely on Hummel's lines of argument, his papers contain much that is strikingly original, and much that appears to anticipate the work of Holst. Had he been more familiar with Irish eskers, his theory would doubtless have widened, and he would have no longer demanded a rocky boss as a base for every accumulation. His papers contain consistent and valuable explanations of the form and inner structures of drift-mounds, as well as the suggestion that the occasional contortions are due to the settling down of ice-blocks in the glacier-mass (²). Prof. Sollas, after his review of the literature, gives a topographical account of the principal esker-systems in the area selected by him, showing how each "presents a remarkable resemblance to a map of a river-system. The narrow linear outlines, the meandering course, the branches converging like tributaries, or diverging like the channels of a delta, the loops and knots are singularly alike in each" (p. 817). He ranges himself as an adherent of Hummel's view rather than that of Holst, the materials of the esker having "been deposited on the place where they are now found by the action of running water," and not "precipitated in mass from the bottom of sinking ice-canons" (p. 819). The striking observations of Russell on the Malaspina glacier certainly afford the strongest support to the subglacial rather than the englacial theory. Where eskers run across the general direction of glacial striæ in the district, their origin is somewhat boldly attributed to crevasses, at the base of which the gravel is held to accumulate.

Certainly, when we see an esker, like those in the romantic district west of Cookstown, running up and down across a valley, with the air of the Great Wall of China, and breached at right angles by the stream, we feel that we have still a good deal to learn. But Prof. Sollas has done for Ireland what has been done for parts of eastern America and Scandinavia, and has given us a comprehensive view which raises probability a long way towards proof. The map is beautifully printed, in four colours and a groundwork, and two portions are given in the text on a larger scale. There is also a "fig. 3," apparently showing the relation of eskers to lines of bog; but to this we have been unable to find a reference. As we have already hinted, the treatment of the subject in the text is even more important than the map; and the paper becomes a permanent work of reference upon eskers.

G. A. J. C.

(¹) "On Drift." *Geol. Mag.*, 1874, pp. 509 and 510. Also "The glacial phenomena of the Eden Valley, &c." [Read June 24, 1874]. *Quart. Journ. Geol. Soc. London*, vol. xxxi. (1875), p. 95.

(²) *Geol. Mag.* 1874, p. 508, and *Q. J. Geol. Soc.*, vol. xxxi., p. 96.

A Bibliography of Irish Glacial and Post-Glacial Geology. By R. Lloyd Praeger, B.E. (*Proc. Belfast Nat. Field Club*, vol. ii., Appendix 6; 1896).

This work appears as one of the now well known series of appendices published by the northern Field Club; but it is also issued in a separate form, so as to be accessible to all geologists. And, indeed, it is difficult to name the geologist to whom it might not prove useful; even the continental student of post-Pliocene faunas will find such a bibliography of constant service.

Mr. Praeger brings to his task, involving the selection and cataloguing of 767 works and pamphlets, the knowledge and method of a librarian. But, unlike some bookmen who have essayed such duties, he has also the judgment of a naturalist, and is able to give us a note on every paper, briefly indicating its scope. The arrangement is alphabetical, according to authors, and two indexes follow, one grouping the papers under their geological aspects, while the other classes them under counties.

No such list can ever be complete, for there must be passing references to Irish soils, or to discoveries of shells or bones, in works dealing with subjects far other than glacial geology. But Mr. Praeger has gone as far as he could, short of reading every work in which Ireland is accorded prominence, and he has thus given us Young's reference to Mitchelstown Cave in "A Tour in Ireland," and Parkinson's account of the great Irish deer in "Organic Remains of a former World." Even human bodies found in bogs, if sufficiently far down, come within his scope; and he has found it very hard to draw the line between flint gravels and chipped flints, between post-glacial geology and human archæology. Mr. Praeger's tendency to give even trifling references is surely very much on the safe side, and he seems to have kept well clear of vain repetitions and purely second-hand sources of information. The handsome printing of the list will enable us to insert any later references as foot-notes, or in the margin; but we shall hope for an appendix from Mr. Praeger himself every ten years or so, and a complete new edition about A.D. 1926. Were the present bibliography never touched or reproduced, its value to geologists would remain; it is a pleasant gift from a busy worker to his fellows, and will vastly lighten the labours of all who deal with recent deposits in the British Isles. As to those who call themselves "glacialists," they will do well to keep the list constantly at their elbow; and its comprehensive character may make us indeed hesitate, before we add one sheet of foolscap to the controversial side of glacial geology. May we look in time for a digest of the whole matter from Mr. Praeger, a history of Ireland in post-Pliocene times, which shall bring together the scientific results of his own observations, together with those of the authors whose works he has so carefully kept before us?

G. A. J. C.

THE SKUAS OF KILLALA BAY.

BY ROBERT WARREN.

ONLY three species of the skua family have as yet been known as visitors to this bay and estuary—the Pomatorhine, Richardson's, and the Longtailed or Buffon's Skua.

The POMATORHINE SKUA (*Lestris pomatorhinus*) up to the date of Wm. Thompson's "Birds of Ireland," was very little known as an Irish visitor, only nine specimens being recorded by him, of which two were obtained in Belfast Bay; one in the autumn of 1834, and the second on the 16th of October, 1848, both immature birds.

My first acquaintance with this skua began in 1862, when large numbers visited the bay on their way to the south. For several days previous to the 22nd of October the weather had been very stormy, the wind blowing in wild squalls from the south-west, accompanied by heavy showers of rain. On that morning I was standing at the parlour window of Moyview, looking down the estuary towards Bartragh, when suddenly a flock of ten or twelve dark-coloured birds appeared in view, flying slowly up the river from the sea. I immediately took my gun and ran down to the shore, but only reached it in time to see the skuas pass out of shot. My disappointment, however, did not last long, for a few moments after a flock of five birds passed, out of which I was so fortunate as to secure a fine specimen of the Pomatorhine Skua in almost perfect adult plumage. Several other flocks passed on afterwards, and I was able to obtain a second bird in a similar stage of plumage. But soon after I had shot the last bird I was called away to attend to some business matters, which delayed me for some time, and when I returned to the shore found that the flight of skuas had ceased for that day.

On the morning of the 23rd the gale still continued, but had changed round to the west-north-west, and consequently the skuas in their flight up the river kept close to the eastern (or Mayo) side, and none came within shot of the Sligo side, upon which Moyview is situated. On both days the skuas after keeping along the tidal course of the river for about two miles directed their flight across the country to the south-west.

I had an excellent opportunity for observing those that passed on the 22nd, and have little or no hesitation in considering the greater part, if not all, to have been Pomatorhines; the first flock that passed were undoubtedly of that species, their great size and clumsy-looking tails clearly pointing them out as such, and all exhibiting white underneath, and long tails which proved them to have been adults.

When seen during flight the Pomatorhine Skua's tail presents a very clumsy, awkward appearance, in contrast to the elegantly pointed tails of the smaller skuas; this is caused by the two elongated tail-feathers being bluntly rounded at the ends and twisted for nearly half their length at almost right angles to the plane of the short tail-feathers, so that when a side view of the bird is taken the full breadth of the long tail-feathers is shown, giving the tail that thick, clumsy appearance which so easily identifies this species of skua on the wing.

Very few dark-coloured birds were seen on either day—probably not one to ten of the white-breasted ones.

I could not be quite certain as to which species the birds seen on the second day belonged, for they passed at too great a distance for me to judge of their size and appearance; but as the first day's flight was undoubtedly made up of Pomatorhines, it may be safely inferred that the second day's was a continuance of the first, and therefore was of the same species.

A very interesting letter from J. C. Neligan, of Tralee, was read at a meeting of the late Dublin Natural History Society, in March, 1863, describing his meeting with a large flight of skuas (many of them Pomatorhines) in Tralee Harbour on the 25th of October, 1862, just two days after the last of the skuas left this on the 23rd, and, I think, almost satisfactorily proving that the skuas after leaving this bay, and crossing the island, continued their flight along the coast to Tralee Harbour, where they took shelter and remained while the stormy weather lasted.

Since the above date, this skua, so far as I am aware of, has only occasionally occurred in this and the adjoining County of Mayo; four specimens only having come under my notice. An adult bird of the black variety was shot on Lough Conn by my friend, Mr. John Garvey, of Ballina, on the 24th of

October, 1890; and on the 8th of November same year, the late Dr. Burkitt sent my friend, Mr. R. J. Ussher, of Cappagh House, Co. Waterford, an adult bird that he had found dead in a field close to his house, near Belmullet, County Mayo. Then, during the last week of November, 1890, Dr. Scott of Enniscrone gave me an immature specimen of the black variety, that was shot by his nephew, as, in company of two or three others, it was flying over a bog near Kilasser, twelve or fourteen miles from the sea. And a fourth specimen, a very fine adult, with long tail and white under-parts, was found lying dead (but quite fresh) on the Enniscrone sands by Miss Amy Warren on the 2nd October, 1892.

RICHARDSON'S SKUA (*Lestris crepidatus*) visits the bay and estuary much oftener than either of the other two species, some being observed nearly every autumn, during the migratory months of September and October.

This skua first came under my notice in October, 1851, when residing with my brother, Mr. E. H. Warren, on the island of Bartragh. We observed the first of the skuas on the 8th, when, as we were returning from Killala to Bartragh, two flocks of six and eight birds were seen at a great height coming from the open bay, and passing across the country to the south-west; but these were only the precursors of the large numbers that followed on the 15th and 16th. . The wind had been blowing in wild squalls, with heavy showers of rain on the morning of the 15th, when my brother observed four skuas flying from the bay; about half-past nine o'clock, nineteen birds passed, one of which I shot (an immature Richardson's). At eleven, I saw twenty-two pass; about twelve, I saw ten, and at one o'clock, seventeen birds passed over; all flying in the same direction, up the river to the south-west. These flocks, together with the stragglers that passed singly while we were watching, altogether made up the number to seventy-two birds, counted without mistake. On the morning of the 16th the flight still continued, the birds passing in small flocks, and up to eleven o'clock (we were unable to remain longer) upwards of one hundred birds were seen.

They appeared to be all Richardson's (I did not notice the large Pomatorhine amongst them), and the greater part were dark-coloured birds, and mostly immature, for very few longtailed, or white-breasted ones were seen; some of the skuas appeared tired with their long flight against the wind, and would occasionally light on the water, resting for a few minutes, and then rise and follow their companions. Strange to say, though there were plenty of gulls about the sands on both days while the skuas were passing, yet we never saw any attempt to chase the gulls, though quite close to them.

The next occasion on which I had the pleasure of seeing skuas on migration was on the 18th September, 1869—a fine bright calm day, as I was in one of my fields looking on at some reapers at work, and chancing to look upwards, my attention was drawn to a flock of fifteen birds passing at an immense height on their usual course to the south-west, and if the day had not been so clear I could not have recognised them as skuas, for I was only just able to make out their dark long tails against the clear blue sky. Again on the 3rd of October, 1874, I was fortunate in witnessing a small flight of skuas migrating in the usual direction. The weather had been very stormy, with heavy showers for some days before: wind north-west on this day, when about ten o'clock I observed a flock of twenty birds flying up the river from the sea; a short time afterwards four more passed; then a little flock of three, which were followed by four, and in about a quarter of an hour, a solitary bird (which I think was a Pomatorhine) brought up the rear, and as far as I saw ended the flight for the day.

I have frequently observed, and shot solitary birds of this species during the migratory months of September and October, but their spring visits are very rare.

In May, 1877, a party of six birds accompanied a large flight of Common and Arctic Terns visiting the bay and estuary: three of the skuas were in light-coloured plumage, and three in the very dark, or black stage, and I imagined at the time, from seeing a light and a dark-coloured bird keeping company, that these colours marked the male and female, and in order to ascertain if my surmise was correct, I shot three birds, a light-coloured one, a bird in an intermediate stage of plumage, and a dark, or nearly black one, all three having long tails, showing that they were adults. However, much to my surprise, on skinning and dissecting them, they all three turned out to be females, the ovaries of each containing eggs varying in size from No. 8 to B shot.

The LONGTAILED or BUFFON'S SKUA (*Lestris parasiticus*) is of very rare occurrence on this part of the coast, and has only on two occasions come under my notice—first, on the 24th of October, 1862, I was on the shore near Scurmore, looking out for any rare birds that might have been driven in by the gale of the two previous days, when a small skua flew past, which I fired at and wounded, but it escaped over the sandhills. On the following day when walking along the Enniscrone sands, on the bay side of the sandhills, and nearly in the same place where on the previous day I had found two fine specimens of the Fulmar Petrel, I picked up a dead skua, and fancied it was the bird I had fired at the day before. After I got home I skinned the bird and found that it was wounded by No. 6 shot, the same that I had used, so felt pretty certain that it was the bird I had wounded. It proved to be an immature specimen of Buffon's Skua.

The second specimen was given to me by the late Mr. N. Handy of Ballintubber, near Killala, on the 18th of October, 1867, who told me he met it when out grouse-shooting, and shot it as it rose from the carcase of a hare, upon which it had been feeding. This was also an immature bird, but as it had been kept too long, I was unable to preserve it.

The only instance that I am aware of this skua being seen on its spring migration in Ireland, is that mentioned by Lieutenant Crane, of the 67th Regiment, in a letter read at a meeting of the late Dublin Natural History Society on the 7th February, 1862, in which he says:—

"The specimens of Buffon's Skua were shot by me on the 16th of May, 1860, on the Shannon, about five miles south of Athlone.

"I was out with two brother officers shooting Land-rails, which are very plentiful on that part of the river. The day was very stormy, and cold for the season, the wind from north-west. I was sitting in a boat at a place called Longisland, when a flock of about twenty skuas passed over. I saw at once that they were not common birds: the long tail feathers marked them at once; but as I was sitting in the bow, the flock had nearly passed over before I saw them, but I succeeded in killing one. Sometime after another flock of about the same number passed, but I could not get a shot; but a third flock came over, out of which I killed one with each barrel, making three in all. I gave two of them to the late Mr. Glennon, and he then showed me another, which he told me had been killed from a flock in the Co. Donegal on the 17th, the day after I got mine. The birds were following the course of the Shannon, flying north. I gave the third specimen to Major Newton, R.A., who sent it to his brother, Alfred Newton, Esq., so well known for his work on eggs. I saw between sixty and seventy in all."

From the foregoing notes on skuas seen on their southern migration, and from the fact that my brother, when residing on Bartragh island from February, 1851, to December, 1855, observed skuas every October passing over Bartragh, and crossing the country to the south-west, I think it may be safely inferred that the line of flight of a part of the southern migration is along our north-west coast until Killala Bay is reached, and then, to avoid the longer course round the rugged coast-line of Mayo and Galway, they enter Killala Bay, and taking the shorter and more direct course over Bartragh, continue their south-west route across the country, and striking on the coast again, probably at Galway Bay, continue their flight to the south.

It may also be noted that the skuas were never seen in any large numbers, unless during very stormy weather occurring in October: and that if the weather was calm and fine during that month, only a few straggling birds were seen, probably birds not strong enough to keep up with the main flight.

PROCEEDINGS OF IRISH SOCIETIES.

ROYAL ZOOLOGICAL SOCIETY.

Recent donations comprise a magnificent pair of Crown Cranes from L. O. Hutton, Esq.; a pair of Bibron's Frogs from A. E. Jamrach, Esq.; a pair of Wild Cats from Miss Cunningham; a Merlin from Sir Douglas Brooke; a snake from the Editor of the *Irish Field*; two parrots from J. H. Davidson-Houston, Esq.; an eagle from F. H. Young, Esq.; a Merlin from C. J. Wisdom, Esq.: a Cape Canary from Mrs. Cannon; and some Loach from Miss Phillipson. Two Lion cubs and two Capybaras have been born in the Gardens, and a Somali Lioness has been purchased.

19,928 persons visited the Gardens in August.

BELFAST NATURALISTS' FIELD CLUB.

AUGUST 15.—The Club held an excursion to Slieve Gallion, in County Derry. The party, numbering over twenty, left the Northern Counties Station at eight o'clock, arriving at Moneymore at ten. Cars were at once taken, and the long drive will be a pleasant recollection to all the party, the hedgerows being bright with blackberries and the brilliant scarlet of the honeysuckle-berries. Arriving at Lough Fea, a boat was kindly provided on the lake by Mr. Russell to explore the crannog showing so conspicuously in the centre. A short notice of the geology of the district was read, written by Professor Cole, who had been working out the local rocks, the main features being the intrusion of granite in pre-Carboniferous times into the much older pyroxenic and hornblendic rocks, formerly supposed to have been altered shales and sandstones, but now recognised as being volcanic in origin, ashes and tuffs having been found in considerable quantity, and vesicular structure being often seen. The melting up of the older rock by the intrusive granite seems to have produced a curiously mixed rock on a regional scale. This is described by the Geological Survey and elsewhere as diorite, and was supposed to have been of separate origin. It is also of considerable interest to see the small capping of our familiar basalt and Chalk, showing what a gigantic amount of denudation has gone on in geologically recent times in order to clear all the basalt and most of the Chalk from the great valleys on either side of the mountain. The members were then free to ascend the mountain or explore the lake; but the party decided to climb, so a start was at once made over the fields and by cart lanes until the open heath was reached. Investigating each crag and exposure of the rock, the party gradually reached the summit (1,623 feet), from which the view proved somewhat disappointing owing to the heavy clouds covering the sky. After a short rest the descent was undertaken, passing exposures of the mingled rock above referred to. Another long and lovely drive brought the members to the top of Carndaisy Glen. The little stream has cut down through gravels and sands until it now has got some way into the rock, the sides of the gorge rise steeply, beautifully timbered on either hand, while the carriage road runs down close by the stream. Leaving the vehicles, the members scattered in pursuit of their various avocations, the fungi being (though still early) especially noticeable. The Hedgehog Mushroom (*Hydnum repandum*) was in considerable quantity, as were several species of *Russula*, *Boletus* (including the locally rare *B. satanas*), *Amanita* and *Peziza*. Halfway down the glen the surprising sight was seen of the stream apparently rushing against the steep bank, and having cut through it, flowing at right angles to its old course, now quite dry. This has been caused by a second stream cutting its way from outside, till its bed was lower than the main one, thus, when cut far enough back, tapping the larger stream and producing the above effect. On arriving at the end of the glen cars were again mounted, and the few miles separating Carndaisy from Moneymore were soon covered, bringing the party quickly to the

Drapers' Arms, where tea was in readiness. It should be mentioned that some members of the Gaelic League accompanied the Field Club, and succeeded in finding quite a number of Irish-speaking people, though even the magic key of silver failed to extract Gaelic from the younger members of the community.

SEPTEMBER 5.—The last long excursion of the season was held to Ballynahinch and Slieve Croob, where a pleasant and enjoyable day was spent amongst the rocks and mountains of what is, with the exception of the Mournes, the wildest portion of County Down. The party drove through Ballynahinch, past the historic height of Ednavaddy, to where the Belfast Water Commissioners are having a section made of their new Mourne scheme. Here a short halt was called to allow the members to inspect a deep cutting through which a concrete tunnel has been made. Shortly after this, the little village of Dromara was reached, and then the mountain road was taken skirting the Lagan. A good climb up the beds of different streams, each party intent on discovering the real source of the Lagan, soon brought all the members to different little wells of limpid water, where lunch was taken. The sloping sides of Monahoor were then passed, and the heights of Cratlieve left behind, making it but an easy pull up to the topmost cairn, 1,755 feet high, of Slieve Croob itself. Here a halt was called, and some photos taken around the great cairn, which has been pulled down and erected into small modern piles. A little work would restore this cairn to its original conical condition—the covering and monument of some long-forgotten hero. From the cairn the descent was easy and rapid to the vehicles, which were soon mounted, and the road taken to the little chapel of Dunmore, high perched upon a rocky knoll. Here Father Quail, who had been the Club's local guide throughout the day, showed the members some geological specimens and other things of interest. Time did not permit of a long delay, so the road was once more taken to the Spa, where an excellent tea was provided by Miss Brelsford, after which the following new members were elected:—The Rev. G. Foster, Mrs. Stevens, and the Rev. Richard Cole. The President, Mr. Lavens M. Ewart, M.R.I.A., in a few well-chosen words, then thanked Father Quail, on behalf of the members, for his great kindness and hospitality throughout the day.

GEOLOGICAL SECTION.—This section met in the Museum on the 29th July, when Mr. A. G. Wilson, Honorary Secretary, described a recent visit with Professor Cole to the Slieve Gallion district, illustrating his remarks by a collection of rock specimens, which he subsequently presented to the Club. Mr. R. Bell mentioned that the well-known Rhætic beds in Colin Glen, which had been inaccessible for many years, are exposed by recent floods, exhibiting specimens of the bone bed. He also presented a series of rhyolites from Cloughwater, Kirkinriola, Ballyloughan, and Eslerstown. After some discussion, the Pomeroy excursion was relinquished, as the section to be visited occurs in the bed of a stream. The recent excursion to Glenavy was also spoiled by the severe rain, which had made Lough Neagh unusually high.

DUBLIN NATURALISTS' FIELD CLUB.

AUGUST 15.—KELLY'S GLEN. A party numbering close on thirty proceeded by car and cycle to Whitechurch, and thence on foot up Kelly's Glen. Some elected to search along the stream, where rough banks strewn with rocks invited the naturalist; others struck up the heather-clad side of Tibradden Mountain, and along its high ridge to the summit, where, from the ruined sepulchral carn, a fine view of the Dublin and Wicklow hills was to be had. The party re-assembled at a whitewashed cottage at the head of the glen, where tea was spread on the grass. Close at hand rose the green slopes that covered a deposit of much geological interest—the highest of the celebrated series of Dublin high-level glacial gravels. The descent was made across the ridge to Ticnock, and thence to Dundrum. The season was rather advanced for flowering plants, but *Trifolium medium* was observed in one of its few Co. Dublin stations; with it grew the Golden Rod (*Solidago virgaurea*). The Sweet-Scented Orchis (*Gymnadenia conopsea*) and Grass of Parnassus (*Parnassia palustris*) were still in flower in damp spots, and the mountain variety of the Cow-wheat (*Melampyrum pratense* var. *montanum*) was gathered both on Tibradden and Kilmashoge. Among the Liverworts collected by Mr. M'Ardle were *Scapania nemorosa, S. umbrosa, Nardia gracillima,* and *Riccardia multifida* var. *pinnatifida.*

SEPTEMBER 5.—BRITTAS BAY. A rainy morning kept a few members away, but a party of close on twenty disembarked at Wicklow from the train leaving Dublin at 10.0. The day brightened as the party drove southward, through pretty undulating country and hedges laden with sloes, hips, haws, and blackberries. The sands of Brittas Bay were reached shortly after mid-day, and as the sun burst forth the party scattered among the dunes. Here that fine and rare rush, *Juncus acutus,* grew plentifully. Specimens were measured seven feet in height. Other plants of the sand-hills were *Carlina, Cynoglossum, Euphorbia paralias,* and *E. portlandica.* On the sand-hills the entomologists noted a fair number of species. Amongst the beetles the following are noteworthy:—*Demetrius atricapillus, Dromius nigriventris, Otiorrhynchus ovatus,* and a very white form of the common *Philopedon geminatus.* In the marshy ground behind the sand-hills *Aphodius foetens* occurred, a very local species in Ireland. Two uncommon plant-bugs were found on the sand-hills, *Metacanthus punctipes* and *Nabis lativentris.* The former occurred in abundance under *Lotus corniculatus*; it had previously occurred only on Portmarnock sands. The Spiders collected included *Lycosa leopardus, L. picta, Pardosa monticola,* and an immature *Drassus* (probably *D. delinquens*) new to the Irish Fauna. Along the rocks of Mizen Head were found *Statice occidentalis* and *Carex extensa. Foeniculum* and *Artemisia Absinthium* grew on roadsides adjoining. A note on the fungi taken will be found on p. 268. At 3.30 a sumptuous tea was provided by Mrs. Johnson, and subsequently the party drove back to Wicklow, and caught the mail train to town. Hon. R. E. Dillon and Brigade-Surgeon Wellington Gray were elected members of the Club.

CORK NATURALISTS' FIELD CLUB.

AUGUST 12.—ROSTELLAN AND CASTLE MARY. Fifteen members left by 12.10 train, and proceeded by steamer to Aghada from Passage. Driving to Rostellan the grounds were explored, and along the boggy margins of the lake were found the Common Skullcap (*Scutellaria galericulata*) in abundance, the Gipsywort (*Lycopus europæus*), the Marestail (*Hippuris vulgaris*), and the Marsh Willow-herb (*Epilobium palustre*). Crossing the fields to Castle Mary, the Dwarf Spurge (*Euphorbia exigua*) was noted, a species local in Ireland. Two fungi were collected, *Boletus edulis*, frequent in the moist woods at Rostellan, and *Coprinus comatus* under the beeches at Castle Mary. The margins of the lake at Rostellan were evidently rich in insect life, but time prevented many captures. Numerous fine specimens of *Argynnis aglaia* were seen. After tea at Cloyne the fine old cathedral was visited, and the round tower inspected. A drive of four miles back to Aghada, then steamer and train, and Cork was reached at 9.45, after a most delightful day's outing.

FIELD CLUB NEWS.

The Dublin Club has recently been elected a Corresponding Society of the British Association, and was for the first time represented at the Corresponding Societies' Conference at the recent meeting at Liverpool. Prof. Johnson, Treasurer of the Club, was the delegate on this occasion.

Several English conchologists—Dr. Chaster, Mr. R. Standen, and Mr. Hardy—have recently been collecting in North Antrim, under the able guidance of Mr. R. Welch. We trust some account of their results will shortly appear in these pages.

We note with pleasure that the Hon. R. E. Dillon, who initiated and organized the recent week's field-work at Clonbrock, the results of which filled our last issue, has been elected a member of the Dublin Club. Mr. Dillon's name is already well-known on account of his remarkable entomological discoveries in Co. Galway.

Mr. Charles Elcock, long a member of the Belfast Field Club, and a microscopical manipulator of great skill, has been appointed Curator of the Art Gallery and Museum at the Free Public Library in Belfast, in place of Mr. J. F. Johnson, whose recent mysterious disappearance caused some sensation locally.

The Cork Club are losing a valued member by the removal of Surgeon W. G. Axford, R.N., F.L.S., from H.M.S. Black Prince, Queenstown, to Devonport, where he has been appointed Surgeon to the Dockyard at Keyham. His presence on the various excursions this year have been most helpful to the members, and while congratulating him on promotion, they much regret his removal.

NOTES.

BOTANY.

FUNGI.

New Irish Fungi.—Mr. Praeger has lately sent me the following specimens:—*Glyceria aquatica* affected with the long linear sori of *Ustilago longissima*, Sow., which ultimately cause the leaves to split up and die, and the stem to wither away without flowering. The spores are very small; it would take sixty-four millions to cover a square inch! The affected grass was gathered at Bective, and near Enfield, Co. Meath. *Ustilago caricis*, Pers. (= *U. urceolorum*, Tul.), is a smut-fungus which converts the fruit of sedges into a little mass like a grain of charcoal. Its spores are four times as large as those of *U. longissima*. It was found on *Carex panicea* near Enfield by Mr. Praeger. From the same locality comes an inflorescence of *Holcus* sp., with a large-spored smut, *Tilletia Rauwenhofii*, Fischer v. Waldheim, a species allied to the well-known "bunt" of wheat, and like it smelling of herring-brine when rubbed. All three fungi are new to Ireland, and the last-mentioned species has not to my knowledge been hitherto published as British, but Dr. Plowright, the British authority on the subject, informs me that he found it on *Holcus mollis* near Doncaster, in 1891.

ED. J. McWEENEY, Dublin.

Fungi from Brittas Bay Excursion, D.N.F.C.—The following were the rarest of the few agarics collected:—*Clitopilus carncoalbus*, Wither; *Entoloma jubatum*, Fr.; *Stropharia inunctus*, Fr.; *Inocybe rimosa*, Bull. (This common agaric is mentioned on account of the peculiar locality where it was found, viz., amongst the sand-hills on the seashore; the pileus was in many cases quite coated with sand). Of *Uredinei* and *Ustilaginei* one species was found (by Mr. Halbert) which I have not hitherto met with, though I have often sought for it, *Puccinia hydrocotyles*, Lk., forming pustules chiefly on the upper side of leaves of the Marsh Pennywort. Mr. M'Ardle found *Puccinia calthæ*, Lk., a decidedly rare species, within a few yards of Mr. Halbert's capture, on the marshy land west of the coast-road to Arklow and north of the cross-road at Brittas Bay. The other Fungi taken comprised *Erinella apala*, Mass., an exceedingly beautiful tiny *Peziza* growing on dead culms of rush. It is covered with long hairs, whitish round the margin, fawn-coloured elsewhere, and its spores, resembling compact bundles of slender rods ($40\mu \times 2\mu$), form an interesting high-power object. *Cyphella villosa*, Karst., a minute woolly species, closely resembling a *Peziza*, was also found. It covered a considerable area of a dead herbaceous stem. This is the first occasion on which I have found this species. My measurements of the spores come out a little smaller (9×7) than those given in Massee, but the agreement is otherwise perfect.

E. J. McWEENEY, Dublin.

PHANEROGAMS.

Flora of Lough Derg.—The following notes as to some of the rarer species which I observed in the neighbourhood of Lough Derg in June and July, 1895, may perhaps be of interest:—

Thalictrum collinum.—A few plants among rocks near mouth of Rossmore river (Co. Galway). *Thalictrum flavum.*—Abundant on banks of Borrisokane river (Co. Tipperary). *Aquilegia vulgaris.*—Frequent in stony places throughout the district. *Erysimum cheiranthoides.*—One plant at Brocka (Co. Tipperary). *Geranium sanguineum.*—Plentiful among rocks at Drominagh (Co. Tipperary.) *Galium boreale.*—Abundant at Brocka. *Inula salicina.*—A fine clump of this striking plant found on rocky shore of Lough Derg at Curraghmore, seen also on Brynas Island, both on Tipperary shore of Lough. *Carduus pratensis.*—Abundant in bogs. *Teucrium scordium.*—In profusion among rocks on shore of Rossmore river, and also at Drominagh. *Ophrys apifera.*—Frequent in limestone pastures at Borrisokane. *Epipactis palustris.*—Moderately abundant in a rocky meadow at Bellevue, on the Tipperary side of Lough. *Habenaria conopsea.*—Frequent at Brocka. *Sisyrinchium angustifolium.*—Growing freely on rocky shore at the mouth of Rossmore river. The district is a most interesting one to a botanist, as it yields some species not found elsewhere in the United Kingdom, and appears to be the only European habitat of the beautiful *Sisyrinchium angustifolium*.

C. J. LILLY, Larne.

Sisyrinchium californicum, Dryander, in Ireland.—To the *Journal of Botany* for August, Rev. E. S. Marshall contributes a note on the occurrence of this plant in marshy meadow-land north of Rosslare station, Co. Wexford, where he states it grows in abundance, among plants all of which are undoubtedly indigenous. *S. californicum* is a native of California and Oregon, and Mr. Marshall says he is " quite convinced that this plant has not been accidentally introduced" in its Co. Wexford station.

Dryas octopetala in Co. Antrim.—Among some plants which I gathered in 1884 at the Sallagh Braes, in Co. Antrim, and which had got astray among my papers, I have recently found a specimen of *Dryas octopetala*. This discovery is interesting, as the only record of this plant from Co. Antrim is in Mackay's *Flora Hibernica* (1836), without any locality being mentioned, viz.:—" County Antrim, *Mr. Templeton*"; on which the editors of the *Flora of the North-east of Ireland* (1888), p. 48, remark : " In *Flora Hibernica* Mr. Templeton is erroneously credited with finding this plant in Antrim." I have since heard from my friend Mr. Stewart, the surviving editor, that neither he nor his coadjutor, the late Mr. Corry. found in Templeton's MSS. any note of *D. octopetala* in Antrim, hence their reason for doubting the correctness of the statement in the *Flora Hibernica*. Mr. Stewart has seen my plant, which has come as a surprise to him. He has often searched the Sallagh Braes, but as my plant is an old barren one, it was probably overlooked from its habit of creeping close to the ground, and resembling *Salix repens*. To me it is very satisfactory to be able to verify Mr Templeton's record.

H. W. LETT (in *Journ. Bot.* for August).

[We are not sanguine that the foregoing note will convince Irish botanists as to the occurrence of *Dryas octopetala* in County Antrim. The fact that a plant so striking and distinct was not recognised at the time, but should turn up long afterwards amongst papers admittedly mislaid, does not tend to inspire confidence or conviction. The remark that "as my plant was an old barren one, it was probably overlooked from its habit of creeping close to the ground, and resembling *Salix repens*" strikes one as strange. The resemblance to *Salix repens* is surely fanciful, and our experience is that old plants do not creep closer to the ground, or flower less than younger ones. It must be noted also that several records credited to Templeton by various writers, but not mentioned in his own notes, have already proved erroneous, *Euphorbia hiberna* and *Chrysosplenium alternifolium* for instance, and that the Sallagh Braes have been well searched by botanists ever since Templeton's time, notably so by the late Dr. Moore. From these considerations the desirability of Mr. Lett's verifying his specimen by the discovery of the plant *in situ* is manifest, and while we do not for a moment cast doubt on the *bona fide* nature of his communication, it appears to us that there are now two records which invite verification—Mr. Templeton's, and Mr. Lett's.—EDS.]

Carex teretiuscula, Good., in County Down.—This sedge has just now been re-found, July, 1896, in a wet sphagnous bog near the Giant's Ring at Ballylesson, Co. Down, which was in all likelihood Orr's original locality, and it is thus a restoration to the county of a plant which was excluded by the authors of *Flora N. E. Ireland* as not now being found. Indeed, until it was lately discovered at Killelagh Lough in County Derry, by Mrs. Leebody and Mr. Praeger, as recorded in the Supplement to the Flora, it was considered as probably extinct in the north of Ireland. The history of the occurrence of this species in the district, particularly as relating to County Antrim, is amusingly curious. It was believed that there was neither bog nor marsh at or near the Giant's Ring. The habitat in the case of Templeton's locality in County Antrim, given by him as "old moss holes" at Cranmore (which place was for a long time the residence of that careful and indefatigable naturalist) was, in transcription, changed to marl hole, and then from marl hole it was altered, in *Flora Hibernica*, to the marble hole, Cranmore, and again transformed in *Cybele Hibernica* to Marble Hall, Carnmoney; but nobody seems to be aware of the existence of any Marble Hall at that place or elsewhere in the county, nor is the plant to be found in the neighbourhood of Carnmoney. Possibly it may still exist at Cranmore, but since Templeton's time it does not seem to have been seen there. In conversation with my friend, Mr. Stewart, concerning this species, he told me that, as mentioned in the *Flora*, he did not know of any bog near the Giant's Ring, but stated that he had sought for it between that singular relic of antiquity and the River Lagan, where, as a matter of fact, there is no bog. Recollecting that some years ago I had examined, bryologically, a bog at the foot of the eastern slope of the Giant's Ring, close by the roadside, the approach to which is by a lane directly opposite the Ballylesson National School, we concluded it to be highly probable that this might prove to be the spot, where, on the authority of David Orr, *C. teretiuscula* had been detected by him more than half a century ago; and I determined, though too late in the season to find the plant in perfection, to adventure in quest of it, if haply it might still be found there. The result showed our supposition to be correct. A very few specimens of a starved form of the plant were obtained in different parts of the bog, but for the most part it is confined to a cutting running at right angles with the road, where it occurs, growing in the water, in considerable profusion and luxuriance. At the time of my visit, the latter end of July, the fruit was thoroughly ripened, and indeed most of it had disappeared, but sufficient was secured to facilitate the accurate identification of the plant, in the examination of which I had the friendly assistance of Mr. Stewart. The height of this sedge is given in Babington as one to two feet, which may be generally correct, but the Ballylesson plant is fully three feet high, and many specimens were found measuring very little under four feet. The rediscovery of the species in the county may not be without some interest to North of Ireland botanists. When *Cybele Hibernica* was published the plant could be recorded for only two counties, Down and Antrim, but it is more widely distributed than it was then known to be, and there are specimens to vouch for its occurrence in Tyrone, Derry, and Donegal.

J. H. DAVIES, Lisburn.

ZOOLOGY.

Fauna of Belfast Lough.—The following is a record of species taken on a dredging expedition, on July 4th, 1896, organised by the Belfast Naturalists' Field Club. Names in parentheses ( ) are given on the authority of Dr. Hurst alone; those in brackets [ ] on Mr. H. Hanna's authority alone. Those without brackets on the authority of both :—

PROTOZOA.—(*Ceratium*, sp.)

PORIFERA.—[*Leucoselinia botryoïdes.*] [*Sycon coronatum.*] [*Euspongia*, sp.]

HYDROZOA.—*Plumularia*, sp. *Tubularia indivisa*. [*Obelia geniculata*.] *Sertularia abietina*. [*Sertularia pumila*.] [*Filellum serpens*.] (*Clytia Johnstoni*.) (*Calycella syringa*.) (*Diphasia rosacea ?*.) (*Garveia nutans*.) (*Antennularia ramosa*.) (*Coryne*, sp.) (*Hydrallmania falcata*.)

POLYZOA.—*Pedicellina* (*cernua*). *Flustra* (*foliacea*). *Flustra* (*securifrons*). *Crisia* (*eburnea*). (*Vesicularia spinosa*.) (*Amathia lendigera*.) (*Mucronella Peachii*.) (*Gemmellaria loricata*.) (*Cellaria sinuosa*.) (*Scrupocellaria scruposa*.) *Valkeria uva*.) (*Eucratea chelata*.) (*Bugula plumosa*.) (*Bugula flabellata*.)

BRACHIOPODA.—(*Terebratula*, sp.)
CHÆTOPODA.—[*Serpula pectinata.*] [*Sabella vesiculosa.*] Hermione, sp. *Nereis*, sp.] [*Polynoe propinqua.*]
CRUSTACEA.—(*Hyas coarctatus.*) (*Portunus depurator.*) (*Ebalia Pennantii.*) (*Pandalus annulicornis.*) (*Eurynome aspera.*) (*Balanus*, sp.)
PYCNOGONIDEA.—(*Ammothea lævis*.)
ECHINODERMATA.—(*Echinocyamus pusillus*—dead.) (*Ophiacantha*, sp.) (*Ophioglypha albida.*) (*Echinus sphæra.*) (*Spatangus purpureus.*)
MOLLUSCA.—(*Venus casina.*) (*Astarte sulcata.*) (*Aporrhais pes-pelicani.*) (*Dentalium*, sp.—dead.)
TUNICATA.— [*Ascidia*, sp.] [*Ciona intestinalis.*] [*Aplidium elegans.*] [*Lepidium*, sp.] [*Perophora Listeri.*] *Clavellina lepadiformis.*

This list is of course very far from being complete.

Some species I have been unable to identify with certainty, and in such cases I have given Mr. Hanna's names, or no specific name at all, or indicated my doubt by a note of interrogation.

No special comment is called for in the case of any of the above species: all are well known as occurring in British waters, and most, if not all, of them have been previously recorded from the same district.

C. HERBERT HURST, Dublin.

INSECTS.

Wasps catching Flies on Cattle.—On August 28th, about 1 P.M., I noticed a number of wasps buzzing about my cows, which were lying down quietly chewing the cud, and whisking their tails now and then in a lazy fashion to remove the flies. It was a field between two woods, and the cows were lying far away from any bank or hole likely to contain a wasp's nest. I could not therefore imagine what the wasps were doing—four to eight about each cow—and as the cows did not mind them in the least, it was evident that the wasps were not stinging them. Closer inspection revealed a most interesting sight. The wasps were all busy catching flies—darting quickly hither and thither along the cows' flanks—and pouncing with the rapidity of hawks after birds on the flies as they tried to settle or rest on some favorite part of the cow. One white cow drew more wasps than any of the others, because the moment a fly alighted it was seen at once against the skin. I do not think, however, that wasps can see very well—because one little black speck which looked like a fly (but was not) was pounced on by a disappointed wasp more than once. When a wasp catches a fly it immediately bites off both wings (this is the work of an instant)—sometimes a leg or two, and I believe occasionally the head. I saw some of the wasps when laden with one fly catch another—without letting go the first, and then fly away with both. They were coming and going as long as I watched—there was a constant stream of wasps carrying away flies—I suppose to feed the larvæ in their nests, and returning again to the cows to catch more. In about 20 minutes I estimate between 300 and 400 flies were caught, on two cows lying close to where I stood.

RICHD. M. BARRINGTON, Bray.

Entomological Notes from N. E. Ireland.—In a collection of insects made by the Rev. H. W. Lett, when a boy, in the neighbourhood of Clough, Co. Antrim, I found a specimen of *Carabus clathratus*. This appears to be the furthest N. E. record for this beetle. Mr. C. B. Moffat, who is preparing for publication the journals of the late Mr. A. G. More, found a note of the capture of *C. clathratus* by Rev. G. Robinson on Deer's Island, in Lough Neagh. Mr. Robinson frequently told me that he had taken *C. clathratus* at Tartaraghan, among turf. In fact the beetle seems particularly attached to turf, for all the captures that I am acquainted with have been made where there was turf, or bog suitable for turf.

The records given above are interesting, as showing the junction in the line of its distribution with its Scottish habitats. In Rev. H. W. Lett's collection were also *Blethisa multipunctata*, *Pelophila borealis*, *Chlaenius nigricornis*, *Stomis pumicatus*, *Amara spinipes*, *Silpha opaca*, a very narrow brown form of *Silpha subrotundata*, and *Barynotus obscurus*.

Both *Blethisa* and *Pelophila* thus like *C. clathratus* complete the line of connection with Scotland, though the former is by no means so northern a species as the latter. Mr. Lett had also some lepidoptera in his collection, of which I may mention the following:—*Chrysophanus phlaeas* var. *Schmidtii*, this is the only specimen of this form that I have seen in Ireland, and I do not know of any record of it from this country; *Chaerocampa elpenor*, *Smerinthus populi*, *Saturnia pavonia*, *Apamea didyma* (a very black form), *A. basalis*, *Xylocampa lithorrhiza*, and *Hybernia progemmaria*.

I have two fresh localities for *Sirex gigas*—on July 22nd, a specimen was forwarded me from Caledon, Co. Tyrone, where it was found on a Larch, and two days later a specimen was found close to the glebe here, also on Larch. These captures would seem to indicate a spread of this Saw-fly in the country, a thing by no means to be desired, as it is very injurious to timber.

On June 6, I paid a short visit to Greencastle, on the Co. Down shore, opposite Greenore. I had only about half an hour to search for insects, and confined my attention to the beach, where I met with *Calathus fuscus*, *Amara fulva*, *Heterothops leinotata*, *Lathrobium tricolor*, and *Mecinus pyraster*, also numbers of *Otiorrhynchus atroapterus*. *Lathrobium tricolor* also occurred at Omeath when I was there on June 25th. I have captured a few Hymenoptera here, among them being *Halictus rubicundus*, *Andrena cineraria*, *Bombus agrorum*, *B. lapidarius*, and *B. smithianus*; of this last I found a couple of very strong nests in my lawn when the hay was being cut. They were very fierce, and chased me a considerable distance when disturbed. This appears to be the first record of their occurrence in Ireland. *Megachile centuncularis* I captured in my garden on July 21st, in the act of cutting a piece out of a rose leaf. *Vespa norvegica* occurred on July 27th. *V. vulgaris* is not as plentiful as I had expected after the mild winter and spring, but there is quite a sufficient supply. Among the butterflies I have noticed a great abundance of *Pararge egeria* here; it quite swarms in my garden, and abounds along the roads and lanes. I have seen a couple of *Vanessa atalanta*, but *V. urticae* has not been at all as plentiful as usual; possibly the torrential rains of last month had something to do with its scarcity. I may mention that the larvæ of *Melitæa aurinia*, which I mentioned in a former note (*I.N.*, vol. v., 190) duly pupated and emerged, giving me a very handsome series of this pretty butterfly, some being very dark.

W. F. JOHNSON, Acton Glebe, Poyntzpass.

MOLLUSCS.

Marine Mollusca of Co. Galway.—In April last, the following species were collected on the extensive strand between Bunowen and Slyne Head, Connemara, in addition to the many commoner ones that characterize the shell-sand of Roundstone (see *I.N.*, 1895, pp. 264-5). The shells have been kindly determined by Dr. Chaster.

Aclis minima, Jeff.; *A. supranitida*; *A. unica*; *Scalaria communis*; *S. clathratula*; *Homalogyra atomus*; *H. rota*; *Odostomia rissoides*; *O. nivosa*; *O. insculpta*; *O. diaphana*; *O. Warreni*; *O. nitidissima*; *Eulima incurva*; *Cerithiopsis concatenata* (=*pulchella*, Jeff.); *Rissoa fulgida*; *R. obtusa* (=*soluta*, Jeff.); *Cyclostrema serpuloides*; *C. nitens*.

R. WELCH, Belfast.

Mollusca of Cavan Excursion.—Land and Freshwater Shells collected near Cavan, 10th to 13th July, 1896:—*Vitrina pellucida*, Kilmore graveyard; *Hyalinia cellaria*, Kilmore graveyard; *H. Draparnaudi*, Kilmore graveyard; *H. alliaria*, Kilmore and Farnham woods; *H. fulva*, old quarry at Crossdoney; *H. crystallina*, Kilmore, on old mossy wall; *H. nitidula*, Kilmore graveyard; *Arion ater, Limax maximus, Agriolimax agrestis*, in woods and shore of lake near Killykeen; *Helix rotundata*, a few only under fallen trees in Farnham demesne, and at Crossdoney and Killykeen; *H. hispida, H. rufescens*, almost everywhere; *H. nemoralis*, Killykeen; *H. nemoralis* var. *interrupta*, Farnham demesne; *H. aspersa*, Trinity Abbey; *Cochlicopa lubrica*, everywhere in damp moss and under stones, Kilmore; *Pupa cylindracea*, everywhere on old mossy walls and on Beech trunks near Derrywinny bog, some very light-coloured specimens; *Vertigo pygmæa*, on fallen leaves in old quarry near Crossdoney, plentiful; *V. antivertigo*, on lake-shore, Killykeen; *Clausilia laminata*, common on Beech trunks in Farnham woods; *C. bidentata*, damp walls and old trees almost everywhere; *Succinea putris*, on shore of Trinity Island, and fine large specimens on small island near Killykeen; *Carychium minimum*, lake-shore near Killykeen, a few; *Limnæa stagnalis*, a few on causeway at Trinity Abbey; *L. peregra*, Trinity Abbey, and on lake-shore near Killykeen, and Lough Cuttragh; *L. palustris*, a few in rejactamenta on Lough Oughter shore; *L. truncatula*, Lough Oughter, and in old quarry, Crossdoney; *Physa fontinalis*, locality not noted; *Planorbis vortex*, causeway at Trinity Abbey, very plentiful; *P. contortus, P. albus, P. fontanus*, Lough Cuttragh; *Bythinia tentaculata*, Trinity Island shore, and rejactamenta at Killykeen; *Valvata piscinalis*, Trinity Island shore, and rejactamenta at Killykeen; *Pisidium nitidum*, Trinity Island.

R. WELCH, Belfast.

FISHES.

The Shade Fish or Maigre (Sciæna aquila) on the Irish Coast.—Mr. Thornhill, of Castle Bellingham, recently obtained a specimen of this rare fish in the salmon-nets, near Annagassan, in Dundalk Bay. He sent it in the first place to Messrs. Williams & Son, of Dame-street, to have it mounted for himself, but, at their suggestion, he has kindly presented it to the Dublin Museum, as there was no specimen of the species in the Natural History collection. It may be of interest to note that this is only the second record of this fish having been observed on the Irish coasts, a specimen having been once caught in the harbour of Cork. *Maigre*, the French name of the fish, is sometimes applied to it, and refers to the bloodless appearance of its flesh. It is a large fish, somewhat like a huge perch, and of great strength, the present specimen measuring over three feet in length, and weighing about 30 lbs. Its stomach, Mr. Williams tells me, was full of flat-fish.

The genus *Sciæna* has a very wide distribution, and though most of the species are marine, some of them inhabit the lakes and rivers of the United States. The fish known to Americans by the name of the Drum or Thunder-pumper on account of the peculiar noise it makes, is one of these. The Shade-fish has of all the species of *Sciæna* the widest range, since it has occurred at the Cape of Good Hope and on the south coast of Australia.

R. F. SCHARFF, Dublin.

BIRDS.

Quail In Co. Dublin.—In the early part of June, this year, a Quail's nest was found in a meadow near Dundrum by some farm boys, who unfortunately managed to break all the eggs (ten in number) except one, which they gave to me. Messrs. Watkins and Doncaster identified the egg.

H. BULLOCK, Dundrum.

The Wood-Sandpiper (Totanus glareola) in the Co. Wicklow.—While out shooting on Calary bog (which is at least some half dozen miles from the sea) on the first of August, my dog sprang three birds of the sand-snipe appearance; not recognizing what they were, I emptied my choke barrel on one of them, and got him—the others were so wild that I could not mark them. On more careful examination I found the bird obtained to be the Wood-sandpiper, a bird as far as I can make out only once before recorded to have been shot in Ireland. Sunday being the following day I could not of course look out for the others, but was up on the spot at dawn on Monday morning, and had the luck to see and obtain another, which was by itself, its mate probably being shot in the interval, and doing service for a snipe to some fellow sportsman. The two birds are being preserved by Mr. Williams of Dame-street. If any reader could give me information of the distribution of this bird in Ireland I should feel much obliged.

ERNEST BLAKE KNOX, Bray.

Occurrence of the Night Heron in County Cork.—During a visit to my brother this summer, who was stationed near Kilworth for the manœuvres, I made the acquaintance of a gentleman who kindly presented me with the skin of an immature Night Heron (*Nycticorax griseus*). I regret to say he did not ascertain the sex after he had skinned it. It was obtained by him in March, 1894, not far from the town of Fermoy, as it was feeding in company with a Common Heron on the River Blackwater. My friend did not know what it was, and it was quite a chance that he had taken the trouble to preserve it.

C. B. HORSBRUGH.

GEOLOGY.

Caves in Co. Leitrim.—I have received from Mr. O. B. Maffett a description of a cave recently explored in Co. Leitrim. The cave is known as Phoula-Dingdong, and is situated on the slope of a hill "considerably above the level of Lough Gill, which is about half a mile away." The entrance, a passage thirty feet long, leads to a drop of forty feet, at the bottom of which is a talus of boulders and a small pool; from this chamber another passage runs for 300 feet. No invertebrates of any kind were observed by Mr. Maffett, but numerous bones of sheep and dogs, and the skeletons of a cow and a horse were found, and also part of a human skeleton which was supposed to be that of a woman who disappeared about 70 years ago.

Mr. Maffett informs me that there are unexplored caves at Glenaniff near Lough Melvin, and also at Ballinturbeck, near Bundoran.

H. LYSTER JAMESON, Killencoole.

The alleged Eurite of Lisnamandra, Co. Cavan.—In the *Irish Naturalist* for August, 1896, pp. 195 and 197, I am responsible for the statement that a grey eurite occurs in juxtaposition to the Carboniferous series at Lisnamandra. My notes were sent to Mr. Praeger from the country, in the absence of the specimens which had been collected. On unpacking the latter, the "eurite" at once proves to be merely a compact grey limestone, perhaps baked by the igneous intrusion in the neighbourhood. So little of the rock, however, was exposed in the field, that it may be questioned if the mass is truly in place. Its relation to the sandstones certainly suggests a fault. I much regret the erroneous statement to which our hurried work in the field gave rise.

GRENVILLE A. J. COLE, Dublin.

The Longest Cave in the British Isles.—John Naughton, of Harrogate, writes as follows :—"At a village within three and a-half miles of Westport, called Aglemore, there is a cave which is said to exceed two miles. This surpasses Mitchelstown cave. The Aglemore cave is well known in that part of Ireland. I cannot personally vouch for the accuracy of the length, but this I can at least say, that it is a most wonderful cave and well worth a visit."—*The Friend*, 24th July, 1896.

[Can any reader of the *I.N.* favour us with information ?—EDS.]

THE BOTANY OF A SCHOOL PLAYGROUND IN THE HEART OF DUBLIN.

BY REV. THOMAS B. GIBSON, A.M.

PERHAPS no spot of earth could be considered less likely to interest the botanist than the playground of a boys' school in the heart of a city. And yet I have there found material for study in my leisure moments; so that, after eighteen years observations, I am disposed to show that even the most unlikely hunting-grounds may afford pleasure to the enthusiastic lover of nature's own process of carpeting. The school I speak of is that of the King's Hospital, more commonly known as the Bluecoat; and when I say that the playground lies midway between Guinness's brewery and Jameson's distillery, and is adjacent to the Royal Barracks, besides being bounded on all sides by high walls, I think I have said enough to show that, at any rate, this plot of ground has no unusual capabilities for the reception, or perfection, of floral treasures. It may be that some few of the plants I shall mention have been introduced through my own agency; for it has been my custom, whilst enjoying my summer holidays in the country, to gather the seeds of such wild flowers as pleased me, and to scatter these seeds in the playground, on my return. No attempt has ever been made, however, to *assist* any growth by cultivation or protection; and, therefore, though everything there may not be indigenous, everything is in a sense natural, or at any rate uncultivated. Of course, under the circumstances, there have been in these eighteen years changes of flora, and fluctuations of prosperity even in the plants that are permanent, but, all things considered, there is not much appreciable difference in the *general* character of the flora now to what it was in 1878. Therefore, I think I am justified in assuming that the careful observer will find it worth while to scrutinize even the waste spaces of the city, when he has no opportunity of going out into the country.

A

I might of course begin by an enumeration of the most plentiful species, and from that descend to notice the less numerous and robust inhabitants; but, for purposes of classification, if not, indeed, as an aid to memory—writing as I do now, at a distance—it is, I think, well to follow the regular order of arrangement.

First then, of the Buttercup family there are to be found in more or less quantity *Ranunculus bulbosus*, *R. repens*, and *R. acris*, that is the Bulbous, Creeping, and Meadow Buttercups. I have also found *R. hirsutus*, but for the past two years it has not flowered, to my knowledge; though, of course, it may have done so in my absence. The Green Hellebore (*H. viridis*) and *H. fœtidus* are to be found there too; but these I believe to have sprung from seed scattered there by myself. The Winter Aconite (*Eranthis hyemalis*) I planted; but after two or three years it was crowded out, as I gave it no assistance. Columbine (*Aquilegia vulgaris*), of course, grows here and there; but the garden being near, it may be recruited from that source; and, indeed, it is, I think, doubtful if this be ever, in truth, a *wild* flower. The Common Poppy (*Papaver Rhœas*), is also to be found there; and, for a couple of years, the Horned Poppy (*Glaucium flavum*), seeds of which I brought from Wicklow, maintained a precarious existence, without flowering. The Greater Celandine (*Chelidonium majus*) too, I introduced from the Zoological Gardens; but its properties were too soon discovered by my pupils, who managed to get new boys to rub their eyes, after having besmeared their fingers with its juice, and thus brought about its banishment. The Fumitory, with its beautiful flowers, rose-coloured and tipped with purple, occasionally shows its head, especially if there be any waste top-dressing thrown out of the garden. Of *Cruciferæ* it is always hard to say what is stray and what is indigenous; but there is certainly no room for doubt that Shepherd's Purse (*Capsella Bursa-pastoris*) is of the latter character; for it is here, there, and everywhere, encroaching even upon the cricket crease to the despair of those who nurse that spot carefully. The Ladies' Smock or Cuckoo Flower (*Cardamine pratensis*) is but an occasional visitor in plenty, and yet there have been few years that one flower stalk, at least, is not to be found; but the

Hairy Bitter Cress (*C. hirsuta*) is more common, and less welcomed. The Common Hedge Mustard (*Sisymbrium officinale*) is there in force; and there, too, is the Garlic Mustard (*S. Alliaria*); though, on account of the dry nature of the soil, its leaves are seldom luxuriant. The White Mustard (*Sinapis alba*) and the Wild Mustard or Cherlock (*S. arvensis*) are always in evidence, as well as Rape (*Brassica Rapa*); but this may be from the refuse thrown out of my aviaries rather than that the plants are regular inhabitants. Of the Rocket family, *Reseda lutea* was introduced by me and still maintains an existence; though, unfortunately for its dispersal, it flowers *before* the summer holidays commence. The Dog-violet (*Viola sylvatica*) may now and then be seen to rear its head, though not for long; and three times have I found *V. arvensis* or Field Pansy; but alas, that I did show it. The Common Milkwort (*Polygala vulgaris*), too, is not unknown; and Soapwort (*Saponaria officinalis*), which I brought from the Dargle Road, has found a home in one of the corners, where it not only lives but also thrives. The Bladder Campion (*Silene inflata*) and the Sea Campion (*S. maritima*), though sometimes to be seen are, alas, only to be botanically denominated "common"; but the tiny Procumbent Pearl-wort (*Sagina procumbens*) is to be found on every wall, as well as infesting every path. Chickweed (*Stellaria media*) is to be found in every shady corner, I am thankful to say; for my birds never tire of it; and, though I have once, only, noticed a plant of Cathartic Flax (*Linum catharticum*), it then appeared at home and not a visitor. With regard to this I may say that I have never been in the place from the middle of June till the middle of August; and, so, many plants may have escaped my notice. I introduced the Common, Dwarf and Musk Mallows (*Malva sylvestris, M. rotundifolia, M. moschata*); and, with the exception of the last, they have indeed increased and multiplied exceedingly; so much so that were it not for the fact that the seeds are eaten by the pupils under the name of cheeses, nothing else would have room to grow at one side of the playground. Two species of St. John's-wort grow and flower; but the Tutsan (*Hypericum Androsæmum*) has not succeeded there, though I have sowed it more than once, and even introduced a plant. *Geranium sanguineum* and the *Erodium*, or Stork's-bill, bloom profusely, having been introduced; but Herb Robert (*G. Robertianum*) and the Dove's Foot (*G. molle*) are older inhabitants than myself, while everywhere, even on the paths, the Common Balsam finds a home, till flowering time. The Wood-Sorrel (*Oxalis Acetosella*) grows, but only where I planted it. Trefoils and Medick (*Medicago lupulina*), however, abound on the sloping banks, with which the playground is surrounded; and Rest-Harrow (*Ononis arvensis*) has lately obtained a footing, through planting a root which had chanced to come up in gathering a spray on one of our Field Naturalists' excursions. I brought seeds of the Spotted Medick (*M. maculata*) from Bray, and of the White Melilot (*Melilotus alba*) from Wicklow; and these have at once located themselves and spread. The Purple and White Clovers (*Trifolium pratense* and *T. repens*), but especially the latter, grow luxuriantly; and the fact that we always have one or more nests of Wild Bees in the playground may have something to do with this luxuriance. *Lotus corniculatus*, too, spreads along the slopes, and one or two of the vetches, but, except during the holidays, no legumes ever show. The Silver-weed, or Goose-grass (*Potentilla Anserina*) is everywhere, though its fleshy roots are eaten with relish; and the Creeping Cinque-foil (*P. reptans*), as well as the Strawberry-leaved Cinque-foil (*P. fragariastrum*), can be discovered. Here also you can see the Common Tormentil (*P. Tormentilla*), and in a corner the Blackberry sometimes preserves its fruit till it is quite *green*. The Agrimony (*Agrimonia Eupatoria*) I have only once seen; though it grows quite freely on the esplanade ground of the Royal Barracks adjacent. Of Willow-herbs there are no less than three kinds; and the Evening Primrose (*Œnothera biennis*), though, of course, a garden escape, is quite a weed; while Enchanter's Nightshade (*Circæa lutetiana*) is a terrible nuisance, though not so much so as Knot-grass, which ousts even the grass from the middle of the playground, especially where an old fly-pole once stood. The *Cotyledon Umbilicus* has lately located itself in a corner, though how, or why, I know not, for I did not bring it there; but stone-crop has been near that same corner for many years. I planted some London Pride (*Saxifraga umbrosa*) around the tennis pavilion some years ago, and, though the pavilion is gone, the *Saxifraga* remains, endeavouring to push its head between the Alexanders (*Smyrnium*), which love to congregate about a ruin. Here, too, a plant of Hemlock (*Conium maculatum*) grew this year, plainly distinguishable (though young) by its smooth and spotted stem; while Wild Parsley (*Anthriscus sylvestris*) and Gout-weed (*Ægopodium Podagraria*), known as Bishop-weed, from the difficulty of uprooting it, are more plentiful than is desirable. Fool's Parsley (*Æthusa Cynapium*), too, with its peculiar bracts, abounds; and the Common Fennel (*Fœniculum officinale*), grown from seed, is now domesticated. A few plants of the Cow-Parsnip (*Heraclium Sphondylium*) and Wild Carrot (*Daucus Carota*)—remarkable for the sheathing-base of the leaves in the one, and for the central purple flower in the other—have been allowed, by me, to grow, though I have no desire that the stock should increase. The Golden Elder grows luxuriantly; but it, of course, I have planted, as an ornament to the playground, and I only refer to it as being a specimen of an order which could not otherwise have been represented. Ladies' Bed-straw (*Galium verum*) survives, because of its flowering-time, and *Galium Aparine* has an attachment to the place quite distinct from that with which it favours a pedestrian's trousers; but Sweet Woodruff (*Asperula odorata*) can scarcely be said to thrive, although there are, at least, two plants. Field Madder (*Sherardia arvensis*) I planted some years ago; and, though scarcely spreading, it is, at least, not declining. The Red Valerian (*Centranthus ruber*) grows upon a wall. Corn Salad (*Valerianella olitoria*) is certainly indigenous, for, in my garden, it is by no means encouraged, and yet it spreads amazingly. Both the Field and Small Scabious (*Scabiosa arvensis* and *S. succisa*) sometimes show; and a plant of *Jasione montana* has not only established itself but started a colony. Of the Chicory group I introduced the Yellow Goat's-beard (*Tragopogon pratensis*), Salsafy (*T. porrifolius*), and Wild Succory (*Cichorium Intybus*); and these have propagated themselves, unaided, for several years. But this *Compositæ* group is so involved, with Hawk-bits, Hawk's-beards and Hawk-weeds, that I shall not even attempt an enumeration, except to say that we have many different species and all of them in a flourishing condition. The Dandelion (*Leontodon Taraxacum*) and Knapweed (*Centauria nigra*) are, of course, ubiquitous; and the Bur-dock (*Arctium*), with the hooked scales of its involucre, affords infinite amusement when a boy with back-hair sufficiently long can be pounced upon unobserved. There are four species of Thistle, besides the Sow-thistle; but I have not studied the class very closely, and shall not specify. The Tansy (*Tanacetum officinale*), the Common Wormwood (*Artemisia Absinthium*) and Mugwort (*A. vulgaris*) are all to be found, especially the last, while even of the Common Cudweed (*Filago germanica*) I found a plant growing on the foot-paths. *Petasites fragrans* I introduced; and it has so grown that it is now nearly as plentiful as the *Tussilago*, which needed no introduction. The Groundsel (*Senecio vulgaris*) is naturally common; and we have four plants of Ragwort (*S. Jacobæa*), which seem to supply food for numerous broods of caterpillars of the Cinnabar Moth, as we are never without a swarm of these during the summer. Indeed with regard to Lepidoptera, I may mention in passing that the Ghost Moth, the Yellow Underwing, the Herald Moth, and the Grey Arches are very plentiful, while I have even caught the Humming-bird Hawk and Convolvulus Hawk Moths: and, on one occasion, viz., 11th February, 1885, I found such myriads of the Caterpillar of *Aplecta nebulosa*, that they had to be swept out of the yards and thrown on the ash-heap. Of Daisies we have, in plenty, not only the Common Daisy (*Bellis perennis*), but the White and Yellow Ox-eye (*Chrysanthemum Leucanthemum* and *C. segetum*), and a few plants of the Common Feverfew (*Matricaria inodora*), while Yarrow (*Achillæa Millefolium*) is rampant throughout, and the Sneezewort (*Pulicaria dysenterica*) effecting an entrance. Both species of Periwinkle (*Vinca major* and *V. minor*) grow, having probably been planted or thrown out of the garden; and there are two species of Convolvulus, viz., *C. arvensis* and *C. sepium*, growing plentifully, besides another which has dark rose stripes down the petal. There is a plant of Comfrey (*Symphytum officinale*), a few of Borage (*Borago officinalis*), and two of Hound's-tongue (*Cynoglossum officinale*); but all these have grown from seed which I scattered, and may no more be counted natives than the small Bugloss (*Lycopsis arvensis*), which sprung up on a heap of waste earth and died off in a year or so. A plant of the Common Bittersweet (*Solanum Dulcamara*) has found a home against one of the walls; and, for several years back, in one corner, the Black Nightshade (*S. nigrum*) has grown up, seeded, and died. Henbane (*Hyoscyamus niger*) I tried to introduce, but it never survived the winter, though why I know not, as I have found it growing in an old stable-yard near Kilkenny.

The Ivy-leaved Toad-flax (*Linaria Cymbalaria*) grows on every wall, and the Knotted Figwort (*Scrophularia nodosa*) perfumes every corner; but Yellow-rattle (*Rhinanthis Cristagalli*), Eye-bright (*Euphrasia officinalis*), and *Bartsia Odontites* barely survive, though long ago naturalized. The little Wall Speedwell (*Veronica arvensis*) and the Germander Speedwell (*V. Chamædrys*) are, however, plentiful, as is also the Great Mullein (*Verbascum Thapsus*), which springs up everywhere, though seldom allowed to flower, as boys love the flannel-like feel of the leaves. The Hemp Nettle (*Galeopsis Tetrahit*) and Self-Heal (*Prunella vulgaris*) are scattered all over the place, and Ground Ivy (*Glechoma hederacea*) grows in one corner. I brought a plant of Vervain (*Verbena officinalis*) from Bective Abbey some years ago; but it has never flowered and is growing smaller every day, though, as it grows plentifully at Old Connaught cross-roads, I don't see why it fails to grow. The Primrose (*Primula vulgaris*) is an introduction, but the tiny Scarlet Pimpernel (*Anagallis arvensis*) seems to flourish in being trampled on, for its petals expand, every fine day, along the very paths and walls. Of Plantains we have the Greater and Ribwort species (*Plantago major* and *P. lanceolata*), and each too abundantly; for, always and ever, they come up before the grass, after our winter games, and spoil the appearance of the cricket creases. The Goose-foot (*Chenopodium album*) and the *Atriplex* (Orache) have found a footing in the untrodden corners, while Docks, and Sorrel (*Rumex Acetosa*) and Knot-Grass (*Polygonum aviculare*) abound, as well as the Spotted Persicaria (*P. Persicaria*), and *P. Convolvolus* is only too plentiful. Of the genus *Euphorbia*, the Caper Spurge (*E. Lathyris*), having been sown in the garden, has spread to the playground, but the Sun-Spurge (*E. Helioscopia*) is everywhere, despite of its being so often crushed to show the " milk." As for Dog's Mercury (*Mercurialis annua*) it springs up in every shady corner, and the Nettle is not unknown. The Wall Pellitory (*Parietaria officinalis*) too, with its curiously elastic filaments, causes great amusement; and one or two Orchids, now and then, appear spontaneously; though of those I have transplanted there scarcely one has ever flowered, whilst preserving life enough to throw up leaves. A few Wild Hyacinths (*Endymion nutans*) and Cuckoo Pints (*Arum maculatum*) have survived, out of many which I planted; but the flowers of the former grow less every year, and the latter have never flowered at all. Thus after many years observation I find that some specimens of nearly all the great Natural Orders spring up spontaneously, in most unlikely places, while others can be domiciled without any trouble; and even of those that require care to make them bloom profusely, it is possible to preserve the life, without unduly interfering to assist; for to do this would, I contend, remove them from the category of wild flowers altogether. If these remarks, from which all mention of grasses is excluded, induce anyone to take more interest in the plant-life—though it be but of the commonest—around him, I shall be satisfied.

NEW BOOKS ON BRITISH ZOOLOGY.

The Collector's Manual of British Land and Freshwater Shells. By LIONEL E. ADAMS. 2nd Edition; pp. 214; pls. x.; 8vo. Leeds: Taylor Bros., 1891. Price, 8s. (with coloured plates, 10s.)

The aim of Mr. Adams' little book is to give a critical treatise on the British Land and Freshwater Mollusca, with concise descriptions and with an account of their habits. It contains also hints on the preservation and arrangement of shells, and, as stated on the title-page, it purports to furnish us with the names and descriptions of all the varieties and with synoptical tables showing the differences of species difficult of identification.

The only work with which this can at all be compared is that by Lovell Reeve published in 1863, and now out of print, and though it shows a very considerable advance on it in some respects, it falls short of it in others. For instance, there is hardly any synonymy given by Mr. Adams, nor is there any mention of the distribution of the British land and freshwater mollusca outside the British Islands. Then why should *Paludestrina ulvæ*, *Otina otis*, and the genera *Melampus* and *Alexia* be omitted, whilst *Paludestrina similis* and *P. ventrosa* are described in the work? They are all more or less brackish forms, and all their nearest relations are typical freshwater species.

It is to be regretted that Mr. Adams should have adopted the absurd custom of attaching Latin names to mere normal variations, whilst the system of bestowing varietal names should be carried out strictly in accordance to the law of priority. The variety *roseolabiata* of *Helix nemoralis* was described and named by Dr. Kobelt long before Mr. Taylor attached his name to it.

In many other cases foreign authorities have not been sufficiently consulted. Dr. Böttger, the highest authority on *Clausilia*, has pointed out that the so-called varieties *Everetti* (Miller) and *tumidula* (Jeffr.) of *Clausilia bidentata* are type forms of that species, whilst all British forms of the latter may be grouped under the three varieties, *gracilior*, *septemtrionalis*, and *exigua*, only one of which is referred to by our author. *Helix costata* and *Hyalinia contracta* are now almost universally looked upon as distinct species, and not as varieties of *H. pulchella* and *H. crystallina*. Of *Helix sericea*, which was identified as such from Yorkshire specimens sent by us to Drs. Böttger and Westerlund, there is no mention at all. The latter, moreover, thinks it very doubtful if the *Helix itala* of Linné (p. 83) can really be referred to *H. ericetorum*, and before making such a sweeping change in a well-known old name, the opinion of the great modern Swedish conchological authority should be carefully considered. Even if we should not all agree with the propriety of Dr. Westerlund's applying the name of a distinct species (*H. lampra*) to the Aran Island form of *H. cricetorum*, some reference to it might have been made.

Although some of the figures, such as that of *Limnæa involuta*, are poor, they are on the whole satisfactory, and no one can help admiring the beautiful plate X. containing the *Pisidia*, a genus which is a sore trouble to the conchologist. It would have been well to place the figures of the shells of *Testacella haliotidea* and *T. Maugei* on plate II., instead of moving them to plate VII., where they are apt to be overlooked.

In speaking of the size of slugs (p. 2) it is misleading in the highest degree to say that they measure so many millimetres "*from the nose to the extremity of the keel*," since if slugs have an organ of smell at all, it certainly is not at the extreme anterior end of their body, whilst only few possess what may be called a keel.

Mr. Adams has in many ways made it easier for students to identify the British species of slugs, but it is doubtful whether any one could distinguish *Arion ater* from *A. minimus*, after reading the description on page 27. The latter cannot be at once identified, as Mr. Adams says it can, by its lateral bands, since it is more often without than with such; and *Arion ater* is certainly not without bands; during its youth, banded forms are the rule and bandless ones exceedingly rare.

Before we conclude our criticism of Mr. Adams' work, we should like to say a few words on the list of the "authenticated" records of the distribution of British land and freshwater mollusca given at the end. It appears that records are "authenticated" if the specimens have been seen by one out of the three following conchologists, viz., Mr. Taylor, Mr. Roebuck, and the late Mr. Ashford. Apparently such records as even those of the late Dr. Jeffreys would be rejected as *not authenticated*. The great merit of this system of authentication is supposed to lie in the uniformity of value which it gives to the records, but it is certain that there are many conchologists in the British Islands who are just as capable of identifying most of the British species as the gentlemen above mentioned. Would it not be a better plan in order to quickly arrive at the distribution of land and freshwater mollusca throughout the British Islands to enlarge the body of referees, and ask them to select a few of the critical species which should always be submitted to specialists before entering them as authenticated records?

A few defects and deficiencies in special parts of this work cannot, however, seriously detract from its value and importance. The print is excellent, and the book may be confidently recommended as the best existing collector's manual on the British land and freshwater mollusca.

R. F. S.

British Butterflies, being a popular Handbook for young Students and Collectors. By J. W. TUTT, F.E.S. London: George Gill and Sons, 1896. Pp. 469, plates 11, and 45 figures in text. Price 5s.

This work is an attempt to supply beginners in the study of our native butterflies with an introduction to the subject, which shall give due regard to recent work in morphology and classification. It cannot be denied that the books on British lepidoptera which issue in rapid succession from the press are, as a rule, too stereotyped in treatment, and too conservative in arrangement. Entomologists who wish to see the advance of their favourite science in these countries will be grateful to Mr. Tutt for having produced the present volume.

The author confesses in the preface that the book is "utterly inadequate as a finished manual." Nevertheless the beginner will find in it enough information to serve as a foundation for his studies. It is a pity that there is nothing of the nature of a bibliography to direct the student to original sources for more advanced study. There are chapters on egg-laying and eggs, caterpillars and how to obtain them, and chrysalids, which give a good general idea of lepidopterous development. We are glad to see that in writing of caterpillars, Mr. Tutt abandons the old, incorrect method of reckoning the head as a single segment and numbering the body-segments two, three, &c.; he adopts a nomenclature that shows the correspondence of the segments in the larval and perfect stages. It is a pity however that he should write "the horny biting jaws of the caterpillar give place to the spiral sucking tongue of the butterfly," in a connection which might lead the student to regard the two sets of organs as homologous; especially as he elsewhere states the correct homology of the sucking-tube of the imagine with the rudimentary maxillæ of the larva. In describing the pupa, Mr. Tutt naturally draws largely on the recent important researches of Dr. Chapman, pointing out that, as development proceeds from lower lepidopterous families to higher, a greater number of pupal segments tend to become fused. We are surprised however that no acknowledgment to Dr. Chapman is to be found either in the text or in the preface. The paragraph on p. 47, in which the temperature-experiments, presumably of such investigators as Weismann, Merrifield and Standfuss, are referred to, seems to show that Mr. Tutt is apt to state too positively his opinions on points still under discussion.

There are short chapters on hybernation and æstivation, and on variation, but in the systematic part of the work much space is devoted to the description and naming of varieties and aberrations. There are the usual chapters on catching, setting, and preserving insects; we wish that Mr. Tutt had seen his way to recommend the abandonment of curved setting-boards. Very valuable is the chapter inculcating the careful labelling and recording of insects, and we hope Mr. Tutt's readers will take it to heart.

In the chapter on names and classification, Mr. Tutt makes the astonishing statement that "butterflies in common with all other insects have two names by which they are known all over the world." How devoutly soever we may wish this were true, it would perhaps be as correct to say that no two entomologists use the same two names for any species! Mr. Tutt, doubtless quite correctly, has followed Continental and American writers in breaking up several of our old genera, such as *Vanessa*, *Lycæna*, and *Thecla*; as he points out, it is wrong to continue to "lump" species—however few—under the same generic name when they really deserve separation. But alas for uniformity in nomenclature! Mr. W. F. Kirby[1] has recently published a popular book dealing with the same question, and here is a comparison of the nomenclatures of the British Lycænidæ as given by these two authorities:—

TUTT.	KIRBY.
Chrysophanus.	*Lycæna.*
dispar.	*dispar.*
phlæas.	*phlæas.*
Lycæna.	*Nomiades.*
arion.	*arion.*
Nomiades.	
semiargus	*semiargus.*
Cupido.	*Zizera.*
minima.	*minima.*
Polyommatus.	*Polyommatus.*
corydon.	*corydon.*
bellargus.	*thetis.*
icarus.	*icarus.*
astrarche.	*alexis*
Plebeius.	*Plebeius.*
ægon.	*argus.*
Everes.	*Cupido.*
argiades.	*argiades.*
Cyaniris.	*Cyaniris.*
argiolus.	*argiolus.*
Lampides.	*Lampides.*
bætica.	*bæticus.*
Callophrys.	*Callophrys.*
rubi.	*rubi.*
Zephyrus.	*Zephyrus.*
quercus.	*quercus.*
betulæ.	*betulæ.*
Thecla.	*Thecla.*
w-album.	*w-album.*
pruni.	*pruni.*

[1] A Handbook to the Order Lepidoptera (Allen's Naturalists' Library.)

It will be seen that out of the eighteen British species in this family Messrs. Kirby and Tutt are in agreement only as to the names of ten. Whether *Lycæna* belongs to the "Large Copper" or the "Large Blue" is a matter of perfect indifference; but this uncertainty in nomenclature will be used as an excuse by many conservatively-disposed naturalists for holding to the old familiar names. It is the more deplorable since, except in one instance, the two authorities are in entire agreement as to the generic divisions.

In the systematic part of the work, Mr. Tutt arranges the families in a somewhat new sequence. The *Hesperiidæ*—undoubtedly the lowest group—naturally come first, and the *Satyridæ* are placed at the top. The *Lycænidæ* which, in Bates' scheme, come between the *Pieridæ* and *Lemonidæ* on account of the normal development of all three pairs of legs, are inserted by Mr. Tutt immediately after the *Hesperiidæ*, so that the *Nymphalidæ* may follow the *Pieridæ*, these two last families showing much similarity in pupal structure. It is doubtful if Mr. Tutt's removal of *Apatura iris* from the *Nymphalidæ* to the *Satyridæ* will meet with general acceptance. He points out that the caterpillar shows satyrid affinities, but it must be remembered that the larval stage in all lepidoptera must have undergone much adaptive modification.

In spite of a tirade against the use of English names for species, Mr. Tutt heads his chapters with such titles as "Coppers, Blues, and Hair-streaks," "Swallow-tails, Whites, and Clouded Yellows." A decided flaw in these descriptive chapters is the want in several instances of definite diagnoses of the genera; the fact that many of the genera used are new to most British lepidopterists should have made their justification specially desirable. We could better have spared the long lists of named aberrations and varieties; and with respect to these, nothing but confusion to the student can result from Mr. Tutt's frequent plan of giving a list of several varietal forms, and then, after a paragraph of general remarks, another list with a new series of numbers. The treatment of *Colias edusa* on p. 259 is a case in point.

The egg, larva, and pupa of each species are described in detail. Irish naturalists will be glad to know that one of their most isolated brethren, Mr. J. J. Wolfe, of Skibbereen, has been able to supply Mr. Tutt with valuable information on the transformation of several species of butterfly. The time of appearance of each insect is, of course, given, and a set of valuable tables indicate the months occupied by the various stages of the life-cycle of each species, together with the food-plants and method of pupation. The distributional notes are in many cases imperfect. We miss such recent Irish records as Mr. Dillon's captures of *Argynnis adippe* and *Polyommatus astrarche* var. *artaxerxes* at Clonbrock. And the statement that *Vanessa polychloros* haunts the "outskirts of woods" will not help the student who wishes to trace its British range.

We can heartily endorse the author's praise of the plates drawn by Mr. W. A. Pearce, and excellently reproduced. The figures are far more life-like than many coloured representations of insects. It is irritating to find eight pages of press-notices of Mr. Tutt's other works on natural history inserted between the explanation of the plates and the plates themselves. We hope that a new edition of the book will speedily be called for, when these advertisements may be relegated to their proper place at the extreme end of the volume.

G. H. C.

A Handbook of British Lepidoptera. By EDWARD MEYRICK, B.A., F.Z.S., F.E.S. Pp. 843. London: Macmillan & Co., 1895. Price 10s. nett.

Pressure on our space has prevented earlier notice of this book, which, like Mr. Tutt's, presents the British lepidoptera to the student in a new light. But, instead of being confined to the butterflies only, it deals with all the British species of the order, and consequently comes before us as a claimant to the place on our bookshelves long occupied by Stainton's time-honoured "Manual."

That the arrangement adopted by Mr. Meyrick is revolutionary will be inferred when we state that he places the *Arctiidæ*, or Tiger-moths, at the head of the series, and inserts the butterflies in the middle of his system, between the *Lasiocampidæ*, or Eggar-moths, and the Pyralids The families of the old "Bombyces"—such as the cossids, hepialids, sesiids, &c., which are now well known to be closely related to the so-called "Microlepidoptera"—are, as might be expected, to be found in the place required by their true affinities. It seems to us, however, that the removal of the butterflies from the headship of the lepidoptera is not warranted, when we consider the very great specialisation of their most elaborated members; while other eminent students of the order do not consider the *Arctiidæ* an extremely highly developed family.

The families, genera, and species are differentiated by the help of tables, and there are phylogenies of the tribes, genera, and families. Though quite in sympathy with Mr. Meyrick's desire to present the subject in the light of the doctrine of descent, we question the wisdom of genealogies which seem to indicate that existing genera of insects are the direct descendants of other existing genera.

In his definition of genera Mr. Meyrick is inclined to rely too exclusively on isolated characters, especially those drawn from wing-neuration, and the result is often a cumbersome assembly of species. We believe, however, that wing-neuration, being probably little affected by adaptive modification, is a safe guide to family relationships. The separation of the Coppers and Blues by Mr. Meyrick into only two genera, on the character of the eyes being hairy or glabrous, results in a most curious division of the insects, and we should not envy the naturalist who endeavoured to apply this method to the classification of the *Lycænidæ* of the world. We much regret to see that in the nomenclature of his genera, Mr. Meyrick has disinterred a number of Hübner's names published without descriptions, and substituted them for names familiar to entomologists for the last half century. And the superseded names are not even given as synonyms; the student, for instance, will not find *Cidaria* or *Eupithecia* in the index.

The descriptions of the species are naturally very condensed, but most of them give the salient points of the insect. The references to caterpillars and pupæ are, as a rule, meagre. The range of each insect is briefly indicated, but, so far as regards Irish localities, we can only marvel exceedingly whence Mr. Meyrick derived his information. In the preface he tells us that the records were tabulated for him by a lady from "various entomological periodicals" and "reliable private correspondents." A few instances will suffice. *Hylophila bicolorana* is said to be found " E. and W. Ireland—not uncommon "; according to the recent list of Mr. Kane, who certainly knows the Irish moths better than any other living naturalist, the species is unknown in Ireland. *Halias prasinana* is given as " N. and E. Ireland—common"; it ranges into the extreme south-western county of Kerry. *Gnophria rubricollis* appears as "N. and W. Ireland—common"; it has not been found north of counties Dublin and Galway, and, though widespread, is certainly not common. *Lithosia complana*—" N. and E. Ireland—local "; ranges round the coast from Derry to Cork. Mr. R. E. Dillon's Clonbrock records are omitted, but Mr. Meyrick tells us in the preface that all omissions are intentional, and imply disbelief. We cannot think that such misstatements as we have instanced are also intentional, but errors in matters of fact, so easily verifiable, tend to shake confidence in Mr. Meyrick's opinions on other matters in which the difficulty in arriving at correct conclusions is much greater.

The only illustrations are good figures of the wing-neuration, more rarely of other structural characters, in the various genera. It is satisfactory that the attention of the student should be so largely directed to the structure of moths, for collectors of the lepidoptera are too prone to think only of comparing wing-patterns when identifying their insects. In spite of its defects, Mr. Meyrick's work will be welcomed as a real attempt to describe, in brief compass, the whole of our native lepidoptera in the light of modern knowledge.

G. H. C.

THE ISLAND-FLORA OF THE CONNEMARA LAKES.

BY R. LLOYD PRAEGER, B.E.

MANY of the Connemara lakes have in them rocky islets, and most of these are thickly covered with shrubs and stunted trees, in one or two spots undoubtedly planted, but usually indigenous—the only native arboreal vegetation, excepting an odd bush on the mountain-cliffs, that I have observed in Connemara. Lying between Roundstone and Clifden is an enormous stretch of bog and rock, so intersected with winding lakelets that without a map one might spend a day in trying to find one's way out of the labyrinth. Here, miles from any road, house, or field, the islands contain a strictly indigenous flora, not easy to investigate, as there are no boats. Wishing to see what plants grew on these islets, my friend Frank M'Cormick and I left Roundstone one grey, chilly August day, and drove to Craigga More Lough, long famous as the head-quarters of that very rare heath, *Erica Mackaiana*, Bab. Here it grows in great abundance. Last year it was in full flower when I visited the place on July 17; this year, a remarkably early season, it was still blossoming in great profusion on August 22, so that its flowering period does not appear to be very restricted. In Craigga More there are several islets, thickly covered with low, tangled scrub. The intervening water is not more than waist-deep, so in discarding our clothes we were able to retain our jackets, for the sake of warmth, while boots and stockings were also retained, to ward off brambles. These, with the addition of vasculum and stick, made a cool and business-like costume. We waded the lake, through reefs of rock, great boulders, and muddy patches, green with a luxuriant growth of *Eriocaulon* and *Lobelia*, and visited the islets. The vegetation was limited in variety, but interesting. The Yew was the prevailing species. With it grew the Mountain Ash, not more than three or four feet high, but spreading widely, and gloriously covered with scarlet berries. The Juniper was also present, and the Dwarf Gorse (*Ulex gallii*) in full bloom. Stunted Hollies grew here and there, and bushes of Bog Myrtle. The Bear-Berry (*Arctostaphylos Uva-ursi*) spread luxuriantly among the Heather and Ling, as did also the Ivy. In a sheltered nook *Erica Mackaiana* was gathered with stems three feet in length and abundance of flower. The Cow-wheat (*Melampyrum pratense*) grew among the tangle, and one bramble, its fruit already ripe. The Royal Fern, Broad Buckler Fern, and Common Polypody represented the order *Filices*.

From Craigga More we pushed southward several miles across the bog to Lough Bollard, following a very devious course, on account of the network of lakelets that intervene. Lough Bollard is a comparatively large lake—perhaps a mile across—and is very deep, with a number of high, rocky islets. This was a plain case of swimming, so, with a costume consisting of one vasculum between us, we explored island after island, with plenty of swimming between-times. The wind had risen, covering the surface of the lake with a nasty jabble, and it was raining heavily, so that we found the deep water to the lee of the islands the warmest and most comfortable place. The rocky sides, thoroughly glaciated, rose out of deep water so steeply and smoothly that landing was often impracticable. We found that the flora of these islands was almost exactly similar to that of the ones previously explored, with the addition of a few very common plants, including the Nettle, which does not often grow in a spot so thoroughly wild. The trees along the eastern margin rise to a height of 20 feet or more, and slope down almost to water-level on the exposed western side. A visit to an adjoining habitat of the Maidenhair, a tramp up a valley filled with the rare *Erica mediterranea*, now completely out of flower, and a climb over the mountain of Urrisbeg in thick, driving mist, brought us back to Roundstone, and concluded an interesting and particularly aqueous day.

ADDITIONS TO THE LIST OF IRISH ACULEATE HYMENOPTERA.

BY PERCY F. FREKE.

THE collecting season for Aculeate Hymenoptera being now practically over for this year, it may be well to sum up the results in a list supplementary to mine published last year. I regret that the records which have come to my knowledge are very few indeed.

Halictus punctatissimus, Schenck.—Borris, co. Carlow. Freke.
Andrena rosæ, Panz. (not var. *trimmerana*).—Borris, co. Carlow. Freke.
Megachile maritima, Kirby—Lambay and Killiney, co. Dublin. Cuthbert.
Cœlioxys acuminata, Nyl.—Armagh. Rev. W. F. Johnson.
Psithyrus quadricolor, Lep.—Borris, co. Carlow. Freke.
Bombus smithianus, White—Poyntzpass, co. Armagh. Rev. W. F. Johnson.
Bombus soroensis, Fabr.—Mullinure, co. Armagh. Rev. W. F. Johnson.

I have also taken here at Borris a female of *Bombus hortorum* agreeing in coloration with var. *subterraneus*, Auct., the only variation from the *hortorum* type that I have yet met with in Ireland.

PROCEEDINGS OF IRISH SOCIETIES.

ROYAL ZOOLOGICAL SOCIETY.

Recent donations include three Bleeding-heart Pigeons from J. F. D'Arcy, Esq.; a Badger from J. F. Shackleton, Esq.; three Japanese longtailed fowl, a goat, and three Spinning Mice from J. B. O'Callaghan, Esq.; a Parrot from D. P. C. Smyly; two Otters and a Gannet from W. R. Joynt, Esq.; four Guinea-pigs from Col. Plunkett; ten Guinea-pigs from Messrs. J. and W. Robertson. Four Lemurs, two Squirrel-monkeys, and a Capuchin have been purchased.

12,330 persons visited the Gardens in September.

Belfast Naturalists' Field Club.

SEPTEMBER 12.—The GEOLOGICAL SECTION on their last formal excursion for this season went to Kilroot, studying the sections of Trias with abundant veins of gypsum, relics of the great lakes whose rock-salt is so invaluable in the present day. A walk along the coast gave plenty of time to ransack the Cretaceous rocks about Whitehead, where abundant sponges and other characteristic fossils were obtained. An informal meeting was held after tea, during which it was suggested that at the monthly meetings in the museum small field excursions should from time to time be organised.

SEPTEMBER 30.—The GEOLOGICAL SECTION met. Mr. F. W. Lockwood in the chair. A small collection of fossils, recently gathered in a chalk-pit in Kent, were shown by the secretary. Boulder clay deposits at Dromore and on Black Mountain, recently visited by members of the section, were described, in each of which two clays, differing in colour and texture, as well as in the nature of their stony contents, were observed. At Dromore the usual red boulder clay overlies a very tough blue clay, which rests upon beautifully smoothed Ordovician rocks. At Black Mountain the lower stratum is brown, similarly overlaid with red clay. In both places the lower deposit is tough, and well filled with beautifully glaciated stones. A letter from Mr. Kilroe, of the Geological Survey, having been read, arrangements for the expedition to Marino on the 10th inst. terminated the meeting.

OCTOBER 10.—In spite of somewhat inclement weather, a small geological party visited the Triassic and Carboniferous beds at Cultra. After inspecting the well-known fault on the shore which has brought up the Carboniferous rocks on a level with Triassic beds, the ardour of the geologists was rewarded by the acquisition of some good specimens of *Modiola Macadami* and scales of *Holoptychius Portlockii*.

Dublin Naturalists' Field Club.

SEPTEMBER 26.—WOODLANDS.—The Club held the last excursion of the season. The 1.0 o'clock tram was taken to Lucan, and some hours were busily spent in collecting fungi. The larger sorts, such as agarics and *Boleti*, were almost over, but a good harvest was obtained among the smaller forms. Tea at Lucan was followed by an hour's exhibition of the specimens collected, and a demonstration by Mr. Greenwood Pim and Dr. E. J. M'Weeney, who will report in due course on the rarer species gathered.

NOTES.

BOTANY.

MUSCINEÆ.

Moss Exchange Club.—A proposal was made in *Science Gossip* for December, 1895, and in the *Irish Naturalist* and *Journal of Botany* for February, 1896, by Rev. C. H. Waddell to organise a Club on the lines of the Botanical and Watson Exchange Clubs, for the exchange of Mosses and Hepaticæ. The response proved that the want of such a Society was widely felt, and it has now been got into working order. Twenty-two members have joined, and the parcels sent in for the first distribution will soon be distributed. It has not been possible this term to do more than exchange the plants sent in. In future it is hoped to obtain the assistance of referees to name doubtful and difficult plants, also to publish lists and an annual Report. Its object is to help beginners in the study of these lowly but interesting forms of vegetation, as well as to prove a means of communication and help to more advanced students. In this way it may prove instrumental in preparing the way for the publication of a new edition of the London Catalogue of British Mosses and Hepaticæ, the want of which is a serious hindrance to the advance of Bryology in this country.

PHANEROGAMS.

Alchemilla vulgaris L. and its segregates.—Very little progress has been made as yet in our knowledge of the distribution of the *Alchemilla vulgaris* group in Ireland. The restricted form which is regarded as the type of this aggregate species extends in Great Britain from the south coast to the Orkneys, occurring in numerous counties; in Ireland the counties from which I have seen specimens are three, Westmeath, Clare, and Antrim. It appears to be very scarce in the latter county, where Mr. S. A. Stewart informs me the other two forms are frequent. The subglabrous plant *A. alpestris*, Schmidt, occurs in Antrim, and near L. Salt, Donegal; I have several notes of its occurrence in the former county; and it must be found in many others, since it ranges in Great Britain from Cardigan and Derby (not to mention Sussex, for fear of some mistake in the label of the specimen which professedly comes from that county) northwards to Inverness and Mull. The other British form, *A. filicaulis*, Buser, is known to me from Co. Waterford, Co. Cork (twice seen from Fermoy), Kerry, and Antrim. In Great Britain this has been noted for many counties from the south coast northwards to Perthshire. The distribution of *A. vulgaris* forms, it will be seen, is very imperfectly known as yet for Ireland; and I shall be pleased to have specimens sent me, on loan or otherwise, which may aid in extending the range of any of the segregates.

EDWARD F. LINTON, Crymlyn, Bournemouth.

Crithmum maritimum in County Down.—Until this year no station in the north-east of Ireland could be certainly assigned to the Samphire, though there have been several verbal reports of its occurrence. Most of these referred to *Salicornia*, which is often called Samphire, and none were based on actual specimens or other sufficient authority. Tate, in preface to "Flora Belfastiensis," referred to such reports and rejected them as unreliable, and Dr. Dickie, in "Flora of Ulster," could only cite Donegal localities. The authors of "Cybele Hibernica," in 1866, included this species amongst the plants of district 12, but inasmuch as no specific locality in Down, Antrim, or Derry was given, their reference was too vague to be accepted. It is a plant to be expected on the rocky coasts of Down and Antrim, but though these shores have been closely scrutinised from the time of Templeton until now, a period of over a century, it seems to have escaped detection. I have, therefore, much pleasure in recording its occurrence in Co. Down, having seen a specimen freshly gathered by Mr. Samuel Moore, a member of the Belfast Naturalists' Field Club. The locality is Kearney Point, in the Ards, the most easterly point in Ireland. Mr. Moore informs me that he saw only one clump of the Samphire. It was situated so low that at high water it must be almost submerged. Since writing the foregoing, Mr. P. F. Gulbransen, another member of the Belfast Naturalists' Field Club, has informed me of a second station for the Samphire in County Down. This has come still more as a surprise, the locality being not far from Bangor, on a shore which for botanical purposes was thought to be exhausted long since. Mr. Gulbransen stated that a few plants occur clustered together in one spot, and availing myself of his directions I have seen them in the place indicated. There is one little clump of about five roots growing with other maritime species in a crevice of the uptilted Lower Silurian Slates, and just about the high water mark of spring tides. A careful and protracted, but fruitless search proved that the plant has not spread beyond this one spot.　　　　　　　　　　S. A. STEWART, Belfast.

Stachys Betonica in Co. Antrim.—Rev. S. A. Brenan has sent me a specimen of this plant, gathered in July near Whitehall, Broughshane, Co. Antrim. He writes that the plant was growing on a roadside, no house near it, and had all the appearance of being native. The Betony is very rare in Ireland, and though previously recorded from Co. Antrim it has not been seen in the county for half a century, so that Mr. Brenan's find is important.　　　　　　　　R. LLOYD PRAEGER.

Limosella aquatica in Clare.—A few weeks ago, while searching for *Adiantum Capillus-Veneris* on the limestone pavements about four miles from Lisdoonvarna, I found this interesting plant growing in hollows in the rock in which mud had deposited. The only other note of its occurrence in Ireland is that of Mr. Levinge, who records it as found by Mr. O'Kelly in Inchiquin Lough, Co. Clare, and near Gort, Co. Galway (*Journ. Bot.*, xxxi. (1893), p. 309). The specimens, which were in full fruit, were kindly identified for me by Mr. Praeger.

　　　　　　　　　　GREENWOOD PIM, Monkstown, Dublin.

Donegal Plants.—In the *Journal of Botany* for September, Mr. H. C Hart records *Cuscuta Epithymum, Galium Mollugo,* and *Reseda suffruticulosa* from the vicinity of Rosapenna Hotel, and *Cochlearia grœnlandica* from several headlands of north-west Rossgull.

Medicago sylvestris in Scotland.—With reference to my paper in last number on the occurrence of this plant in Ireland, it is worth giving prominence to the fact that at a meeting of the Natural History Society of Glasgow, held on Sept. 30, specimens of *M. sylvestris* from Heads of Ayr, Maybole parish, were exhibited on behalf of Mr. Andrew Gilchrist and Rev. D. Landsborough, who found the plant growing there abundantly in August last. I have to thank Mr. A. Somerville, B.SC., for a copy of a local paper containing a report of the meeting.

R. LLOYD PRAEGER.

Matricaria discoidea DC. at Howth.—This curious rayless *Matricaria*, whose occurrence in several stations in Co. Dublin has lately been recorded by Mr. Colgan (*I. N.*, III., 215, 1894), has now made its appearance at Howth, where I observed it on Sept. 18 growing on waste ground by the new road between the police station and the chapel. *M. discoidea* has not yet been observed in any other Irish county: it is a native of North America, now naturalized in several countries of Northern Europe, though as yet very rare in Britain.

R. LLOYD PRAEGER.

ZOOLOGY.

HYDROZOA.

British Hydroids and Medusæ.—Readers of Mr. E. T. Browne's list of the Medusæ of Valentia harbour in the July number of the *Irish Naturalist* will turn with interest to his paper "On British Hydroids and Medusæ" in *Proc. Zool. Soc. Lond.* (pp. 459-500, pls. xvi., xvii.), in which several of the Irish forms are described in detail and figured.

CRUSTACEA.

Free-swimming Copepoda from the West Coast of Ireland.—Under this title, Mr. J. C. Thompson contributes to the *Trans. Biol. Soc. Liverpool* (vol. x., pp. 92-102) an account of the copepods collected at Valentia Island by Mr. E. T. Browne by tow-netting. Twenty-two species are recorded, of which the most noteworthy are *Metridia armata, Candace pectinata, Pseudocalanus armatus, Monstrilla rigida, Corycæus speciosus,* and *Oncæa mediterranea.* The two last are of special interest as distinctly southern forms. The *Oncæa* has occurred at Plymouth, but the *Corycæus* appear new to British waters. Mr. Thompson also gives a list of the copepods taken on the west coast of Ireland by Prof. Herdman in the "Argo" in 1890.

SPIDERS.

Spider carrying Snail-shell.—On the warren near the sea here, one day several years ago, an object attracted my attention; something white moving along rather quickly. Looking closely I found that the object was a small bleached snail-shell (*Helix virgata*) which a large spider was carrying along underneath its body; supporting it by means of some of its fore-legs at one side, and hind legs at the other as it went. For the purpose of closer examination I deprived it of its burden, and found that the shell was packed with what appeared to be spiders' eggs. On placing the shell on the ground again near the spider, it took it up and walked off as before; going at good speed considering the weight of its burden and the limited number of legs at its disposal for walking purposes. That some kinds of spiders carry their eggs about enclosed in soft silky cocoons is a well-known fact, but I have never heard of a shell being so used before.

FRANCES SARAH O'CONNOR, Ballycastle, Antrim.

BIRDS.

Birds of Connemara.—As I do not see the *Irish Naturalist* regularly, Mr. Palmer's note in the March number referring to my article on the Birds of Connemara in the January number was not read by me until a little while ago, when my attention was drawn to it. I must therefore apologise to Mr. Palmer for not having answered his questions before. With regard to Mr. Palmer's first point, viz. :—whether it was the Dunlin or the Ringed Plover which I saw on the islands of Lough Corrib, I may say that I am perfectly satisfied that the birds were Dunlin (*Tringa alpina*). I quote my diary:—" May 20, 1895. Saw a number of Dunlin and noticed that they sang really nicely. Very short, but somewhat like a lark." I don't remember seeing the Ringed Plover, and have no note of it, but I certainly could not have confounded the two birds as I know both of them perfectly; moreover they are not easily confounded.

With regard to the Black Guillemots nesting amongst the boulders, I felt sure at the time that this was the case, and I now find that several authorities mention it as a fact.

Mr. Palmer's third point refers to the nesting habits of the Oyster-catcher. Of course it is well known that Oyster-catchers will nest on turf and rock where no shingle can be found, but I have never before seen the eggs in such a position when there was plenty of shingle available. Mr. Palmer's suggestion as to the cause of this peculiar habit is interesting, and is, perhaps, the correct solution. He says that " West of Ireland Oyster-catchers may have found that it is not always safe to nest on the shingle within possible reach of an unusually high Atlantic wave."

HARRY F. WITHERBY, Blackheath, Kent.

Quail in Co. Down.—A correspondent of the *Field* (Sept. 8th) records he nesting of the Quail at Seaford, co. Down.

FIELD CLUB NEWS.

We have to congratulate Rev. C. H. Waddell, Vice-President of the Belfast Club, on his successful establishment of an Exchange Club for British mosses and hepatics, some particulars respecting which will be found in our Botanical Notes.

The Belfast Club was recently honoured with a visit from its founder in 1863, Ralph Tate, then a science teacher under the South Kensington Department, now Professor of Natural History in the University of Adelaide, Director of the Museum there, and the foremost naturalist in Australasia. He received a cordial welcome from the veteran members of the Club—S. A. Stewart, William Gray, William Swanston, W. H. Phillips, and others—and delighted them with the freshness of his recollections of the old days when they laid the foundation of the first Irish Field Club.

It is pleasant to note the interchange of courtesies by which members of the Metropolitan Field Club were invited to take part in the Belfast Club Conversazione on 27th October, and members of the northern and southern Clubs to take part in the conversazione of the Dublin Club on 10th November. A goodly party of members from Dublin attended the Belfast meeting, and no doubt the compliment will be returned at the forthcoming meeting in Dublin. Both will be reported in our next issue.

It is a good sign to find our younger Field Club members appreciating the value of a scientific training in natural history work. H. Lyster Jameson, of the Dublin Club, having gained a studentship in the Royal College of Science, has gone to London for a six months course of biological study. Miss Knowles, of the Belfast Club, has come to Dublin for a special course on Algæ under Prof. Johnson. H. J. Seymour, of the Dublin Naturalists' Field Club, who goes to Belfast to study engineering at Queen's College under Prof. Fitzgerald, will be an acquisition to the Geological Section of the Belfast Field Club.

We much regret to learn that the expedition organized by the Royal Society, under the leadership of Prof. Sollas, to make a deep boring into a coral atoll, has failed to fulfil its main object. The island of Funafuti was selected as the scene of work, and it was found that at about 70 feet below the surface further boring became impossible, as a material like quicksand, which choked the borehole, containing great boulders of coral-rock, was reached. So far as the reef was pierced it appeared to be "a vast coarse sponge of coral, with wide interstices either empty or sand-filled." Prof. Sollas and his companions however made numerous highly interesting and valuable hydrographical, ethnological, and biological observations, and though the failure to solve one of the most burning scientific problems of the day will cause general disappointment, it is satisfactory to know that our knowledge of man and nature has been largely increased by the labours of our Dublin professor and his colleagues.

ON THE FLORA OF THE OX MOUNTAINS, CO. SLIGO.

BY NATHANIEL COLGAN, M.R.I.A.

Towards the middle of July last, after a few days spent in botanizing along the cliffs of Ben Bulben, it occurred to my friend the Rev. C. F. d'Arcy and myself that the remainder of our holiday in Sligo might be most profitably given up to a survey of the Ox Mountains. Whether viewed across the bay from the plateau of Ben Bulben or studied in its representation on the one-inch Ordnance maps, this line of mountains appeared to us anything but promising. Its elevation was too small and its contours too gentle to warrant any strong hopes that it would prove rich in alpine species. But we knew that it was almost virgin soil to the botanist, and that however poor the flora might appear on close examination, it could hardly fail to afford materials for an interesting comparison with the exceptionally rich district we were about to leave behind us.

We broke up from our very pleasant quarters in a farmhouse by the waterfall in Glencar, on Monday, the 13th July, *en route* for the Ox Mountains. Sending on our baggage by road we took boat across Glencar lake, climbed the range forming the southern boundary of the glen, and descended to Sligo early the same evening. On our way we made a rather careful examination of this southern mountain flank of Glencar, as it appeared to us to lie outside the limits of the Ben Bulben district proper so thoroughly explored by Messrs. Barrington and Vowell in 1884 ([1]). Nameless on the Ordnance map, three of the prominent points in this range, with heights varying from 1,450 to 1,500 feet, we found to be locally known as Lug-na-Gall, Meenaphuill and Faughrey, the last being the most eastern and highest of the three. Along this line there is a considerable extent of limestone cliff with a due north exposure and reaching in some places to over 1,400 feet. The result of our examination of these cliffs was not altogether disappointing. We could find, indeed, no trace of what we most of all hoped to find, *Arenaria ciliata*

([1]) Report on the Flora of Ben Bulben, by R. M. Barrington and R. P. Vowell—*Proc. R.I.A.*, 1885.

in a new station; but we found the following alpines in profusion:—*Draba incana, Silene acaulis, Saxifraga oppositifolia, S. aizoides, Sedum Rhodiola, Oxyria reniformis, Asplenium viride,* and *Selaginella selaginoides.* Specially interesting was *Silene acaulis,* which in the Ben Bulben district north of Glencar is apparently restricted to the western extremity or Ben Bulben proper. On the summit of Lug-na-Gall, where the limestone rises into peculiar rounded knobs, unusual in this formation, the *Silene* studded the rocks with countless bright green cushions. Further eastward towards Faughrey it ceased abruptly, and, indeed, a vigorous stone-thrower could span its whole area here with a single cast. On the way up from Glencar lake *Lotus pilosus* and *Carex pendula* were gathered, and near the head of the lake *Carex paludosa,* all three in Leitrim and additions to District IX. of *Cybele Hibernica.* And finally before taking leave of the Ben Bulben district it may be mentioned that we discovered a single plant of the rare *Hypopithys Monotropa* in a new station on Lough Gill, a hazel copse at Dooney Rock at the opposite side of the lake to Hazelwood, where the plant was found by Miss Wynne some twenty-five years ago.

Four days in all were spent in our survey of the Ox Mountains. The first day, July 14th, was given up to the ascent of Knockacree, which is easily accessible from Sligo by the Ballina mail-car. On Wednesday, the 15th, we moved our quarters some twenty miles westward from Sligo to Dromore West on the Ballina mail-car route, where we found an excellent little hotel; and here the day was spent examining the limestone tracts along the shore. On Thursday, the 16th, we drove from Dromore to Lough Easky, and tramped over the mountains north-eastward to the head-waters of the Owenduff, in the glen known as Lugdoon, examining several of the high-lying loughs on the way. On Friday, the 17th, we drove *via* Lough Easky and the Mass Valley to Lough Talt, explored the shores of the latter lake and part of the surrounding mountain-slopes, and driving on to Tubbercurry station returned by rail to Sligo the same evening. The southern or inland slopes of the range and its western extremity where it crosses the Mayo border we left almost altogether untouched; and it need hardly be said that our four days of steady work were very far from exhausting the flora of the district. It enabled us, however, to safely draw some conclusions as to its general character and to add something to the existing knowledge of the county Sligo flora.

Before proceeding to sum up the results of our hasty survey a few words may be said on the physical features of the district. The Ox Mountains stretch in a roughly north-east and south-west direction for twenty-five miles, from Ballysodare in the north-east to Aclare in the extreme south-west of Sligo, and have an average breadth of about eight miles. From their culminating point, Knockacree, which reaches to a height of 1,778 feet, six miles due south of the coast of Aughris Head, a wide and featureless table-land, covered with very wet bog, stretches N.E. and S.W. for a distance of some five miles, maintaining a general elevation of 1,600 feet. Towards the extremities the elevation becomes lower, averaging hardly 1,000 feet for the five miles west from Ballysodare, and about 1,200 feet for the eight miles N.W. from the neighbourhood of Aclare. At either end the range is more broken than near the middle, and on the northern slope of the central table land, as under Knockacree, where the drainage of the upper bogs rushing down to Lough Achree has ploughed a deep gully in the mountain flank, and, again, farther west, near Lugdoon, some bold rock faces appear which, however, nowhere deserve the name of cliffs. In the south-west, where the Owenaher, one of the chief affluents of the Moy, passes through the deep depression known as the Mass Valley, and at Lough Talt, where the hills rise rapidly from the water's edge, the scenery becomes picturesque. Elsewhere the range is monotonous.

The great mass of the Ox Mountains is of non-calcareous rock, mica-schist, quartzite, and granite, which latter, in some places, as round the Cloonacool lakes, S.E. of Lough Easky, and in the hills above Lough Talt, exhibits the characteristic wavy foliations of gneiss. The limestone is confined to the lower levels from about 400 feet downwards. Lakes are numerous, especially towards the south-west; but with two exceptions, Lough Talt and Lough Easky, which somewhat exceed a mile in length, they are of small size. The bog which caps the central plateau as with a vast saturated sponge sends down innumerable small streams to the north and south, those to the north reaching Sligo Bay after a short course, those to the south uniting at one end to form the Moy river, which reaches the sea at Ballina, and at the other to form the Owenboy, which discharges at Ballysodare. Save for some thin native scrub of Oak and Hazel along the rocky flanks of the Mass Valley the range may be said to be bare of wood.

It is hard to define precisely the limits of the **Ox Mountains**, and we made no attempt to do so in our four days' survey. Our observations were carried on within the following boundaries: the sea-coast from Ballysodare to Dromore West, a line from that point south to Lough Talt, the high road thence to Tubbercurry, and the railway back to Ballysodare. Inside of these limits we gathered 366 species of flowering plants and higher cryptogams. Had our area been more strictly defined by taking for its northern boundary the high road from Ballysodare to Dromore West, and for the southern the high road from Lough Talt through Coolaney back to Ballysodare, the total of species would have sunk to about 350.

The flora of the district is undoubtedly a poor one. Out of the total of 366 species observed by us no less than 307, or fully $84\frac{1}{2}$ per cent., belong to Watson's British type plants, common and wide-spread in Ireland no less than in Great Britain; 22, or say 6 per cent., to the English type; 15, or 4 per cent., to the Scottish and Highland types taken together; and 7, or less than 2 per cent., to the Atlantic type. The neighbourhood of the Ben Bulben district lying not more than fifteen miles to the northward, and the fact that it has been so thoroughly explored by Messrs. Barrington and Vowell, at once invites comparison of its flora with that of the Ox Mountains.

This comparison brings out in the most glaring way the relative poverty of the latter district. But it must be borne in mind that as yet the Ox Mountains have been very imperfectly examined, and that the peculiar structure of Ben Bulben, with its miles of lofty flanking cliffs, make it, perhaps, unique in Ireland as a congenial home for a whole group of alpine species. No less than twenty-two of Watson's Highland type plants were observed in the Ben Bulben district by Messrs. Barrington and Vowell in 1884, and to this total my friend, Mr. D'Arcy, was fortunate enough to add *Vaccinium Vitis-Idæa*, which he discovered at about 1,950 feet on the north-west slope of Truskmore during our few days' ramble in the district.

Against this array of twenty-three alpines the Ox Mountains, so far as at present known, can only set the following five species of the same type : *Saxifraga aizoides, Hieracium iricum, Vaccinium Vitis-Idæa, Salix herbacea, Selaginella selaginoides;* and inadequate as our survey was, we have no reason to expect that further search would add anything to this meagre total.

In the Scottish type plants, which may be ranked next to the Highland type as imprinting a northern character on a flora, the contrast between the two districts is less glaring. Against a total of eighteen for Ben Bulben our lists show ten for the Ox Mountains, and in the latter total are included two species absent from Ben Bulben, *Prunus Padus* and *Lobelia Dortmanna*, to which may be added a third, *Equisetum variegatum*, if we hold this to be distinct from *E. Mackaii*. In types other than those indicating a northern or alpine character, the divergencies between the two floras are much less marked. The number of species observed by Messrs. Barrington and Vowell in the Ben Bulben district in 1884, is set down in their Report at 430. Adding to this some fifteen species, since observed, we have a total of 445, or an excess of 80 over our list for the Ox Mountains. But with this decided preponderance in favour of the limestone district, a large proportion of the Ox Mountains species, no less than 41, or fully 9 per cent., are apparently absent from Ben Bulben. These species are set forth at length in the following list :—

Ox Mountains species not recorded for Ben Bulben.

Fumaria confusa.
Viola arvensis.
V. tricolor.
Lepigonum neglectum.
Trifolium medium.
T. procumbens.
Lathyrus macrorrhizus.
Alchemilla arvensis.
Potentilla reptans.
Prunus Padus.
Scandix Pecten-Veneris.
Sambucus Ebulus.
Sherardia arvensis.
Gnaphalium sylvaticum.
Pulicaria dysenterica.
Lobelia Dortmanna.
Jasione montana.
Gentiana campestris.
G. Amarella.
Convolvulus arvensis.
Veronica Buxbaumii.
Anagallis arvensis.
Utricularia minor.
Nepeta Glechoma.
Teucrium Scorodonia.
Plantago Coronopus.
Polygonum Convolvulus.
Populus tremula.
Epipactis palustris.
Juncus obtusiflorus.
J. lamprocarpus.
Sparganium affine.
Typha latifolia.
Lemna minor.
Triglochin maritimum.
Eleocharis multicaulis.
Scirpus Savii.
Carex arenaria.
Asplenium marinum.
Lycopodium clavatum.
Equisetum variegatum.

A scrutiny of this list might fairly be expected to show that the majority of the Ox Mountains plants absent from Ben Bulben are calcifuge species, that is to say, species which shun the limestone, while they appear in full development on non-calcareous soils. But we find that this is by no means the fact; for out of the forty-one species just mentioned only two —*Lathyrus macrorrhizus* and *Jasione montana*—can be classed as decidedly calcifuge. When on the other hand we examine the catalogue of Ben Bulben plants we find the following twenty-two calcifuge species recorded for this eminently calcareous district :—

CALCIFUGE SPECIES FOUND IN BEN BULBEN DISTRICT.

Galium saxatile.	*Rumex Acetosella.*	*Carex pilulifera.*
Vaccinium Myrtillus.	*Empetrum nigrum.*	*C. binervis.*
Calluna vulgaris.	*Myrica Gale.*	*Aira flexuosa.*
Erica cinerea.	*Narthecium ossifragum.*	*Nardus stricta.*
E. Tetralix.	*Juncus supinus.*	*Lomaria Spicant.*
Digitalis purpurea.	*J. squarrosus.*	*Lastræa dilatata.*
Pedicularis sylvatica.	*Scirpus cæspitosus.*	*Athyrium Filix-fœmina.*
Polygonum Hydropiper.		

This full representation of the calcifuge group in a district where the formation is almost purely limestone, would appear at first sight to utterly discredit the classification of plants by their apparent affection for, or aversion to limestone soils. In reality, the constitution of the Ben Bulben flora furnishes no argument against the validity of this classification, which is the expression of a very well-grounded induction. The explanation of the apparent anomaly is not far to seek. Ben Bulben, in fact, even if we restrict the name to the great steep-scarped rock-mass lying between Glencar on the south, and Glenade and Gleniff on the north, so as to cut off all but the purely calcareous formations, is capped for some eight miles with a deep bed of peat; and in this peat-cap the calcifuge species find that neutral or non-calcareous soil which appears to be a necessary condition of their healthy development.

Having thus sketched the general features of the Ox Mountains flora a few details may be given as to the more interesting plants observed by us in our hasty survey.

Trifolium medium, Linn.—Frequent amongst Gorse, and in field borders and on banks near Skreen and Dromore West.

Prunus Padus, Linn.—A single tree, apparently native, on the rocky shores of Lough Achree.

Rubus saxatilis, Linn.—Sparingly on the northern slope of Knockacree and at the head of Lugdoon.

Potentilla reptans, Linn.—Roadside banks near the sea below Dromore West. A rare species in many parts of West Ireland.

Saxifraga aizoides, Linn.—Abundant on Knockacree from about 300 to 900 feet, but confined to the gully above Lough Acree and to the neighbouring rocks. First observed here by Miss Kinahan, in 1893.

Gnaphalium sylvaticum, Linn.—Gravelly places by the shore of Lough Easky, and luxuriant on dry banks in the Mass Valley.

Hieracium iricum, Fries.—Sparingly in rocky places above Lough Acree, at about 450 feet. The only Hawkweed observed in the district except the ubiquitous *H. Pilosella*.

Vaccinium Vitis-Idæa, Linn.—On Knockacree at 1,400 feet, and abundant round Cloonacool lough to 1,350 feet.

Salix herbacea, Linn.—At Lugdoon, at Cloonacool lough, and on the mountain east of Lough Easky, descending to 1,200 feet. Very stunted where it clings to the wavy foliations of the gneiss, but well-developed when growing in the grassy or mossy capping of the rocks.

Epipactis palustris, Crantz.—Abundant in one spot on the northern shore of Lough Talt.

Juncus obtusiflorus, Ehrh.—In a marsh below Dromore West, and sparingly near the margin of Lough Acree. Apparently a new record for District IX.

J. supinus var. **fluitans,** Lamk.—A characteristic plant of the lakes in this district, occurring in Lough Acree, Lough Easky, Lough Glendarragh, and Cloonacool lough, and also in many of the loughauns in the central plateau. The young shoots developed by this viviparous form in the deep water of these lakes are exquisite examples of extreme tenuity of leaf, and exhibit perhaps the nearest approach amongst the Irish phanerogams to truly capillary foliage. When detached from the parent and stranded on the lake shores the young plants are very puzzling, and easily mistaken for forms of *Scirpus acicularis*.

Sparganium affine, Schnzl.—In Lough Ramduff near Lough Easky, and again in Lough Glendarragh, where it covers a large surface and flowers and fruits freely at a height of 1,332 feet.

Osmunda regalis, Linn.—Appears to be very rare in the district. Only one large patch observed, by a stream near Croagh, north of Lough Easky.

Botrychium Lunaria, Sw.—In pastures near the old tower below Dromore West.

Adiantum Capillus-Veneris, Linn.—Specimens of this species gathered on limestone rocks by the river below Dromore West were sent me near the end of July last, by Mr. John Quirk, who informs me that it grows in this station in considerable quantity. The plant was reported from this locality by Mr. R. Warren, in 1891.

Equisetum variegatum var. **majus,** Syme.—Abundant on the stony shores of Lough Talt.

Lycopodium Selago, Linn.—This species, rarely met with in abundance in east Ireland, occurs in profusion in the high-lying wet bogs N.E. of Easky lough.

L. clavatum, Linn.—Sparingly on the grassy hill-slopes west of Lough Talt, at 600 feet.

I am indebted to Mr. Arthur Bennett for assistance in determining some of the critical species observed, and to Messrs. H. and J. Groves for naming a few specimens of *Chara* gathered. These latter all belong to the common species *C. fragilis* and *C. vulgaris* which occur in all twelve of the Irish botanical districts.

CORRESPONDENCE.

Prof. R. Tate's Visit to Belfast.

Allow me to correct an erroneous impression which is conveyed by the note in November number of the *Irish Naturalist* respecting Prof. Ralph Tate's recent visit to Belfast. Prof. Tate did not honour Belfast Naturalists' Field Club by a visit, or, to put it plainly, the Club did not seize the opportunity to honour itself by receiving its distinguished founder when he revisited Belfast. Prof. Tate was invited by a former President of the Club, Mr. John Anderson, J.P., F.G.S., one of the original members; but he had accepted the prior invitation of Mr. Joseph Wright, F.G.S., and was the guest of the latter gentleman during his stay here. To quote the words of the Professor, the visit was intended for * * * "those who helped to make my sojourn at Belfast the most pleasant episode of my life." For the benefit of the younger members of the Belfast Club it may be well to mention that Prof. Tate's work in the Secondary rocks of Ireland, done over thirty years ago, gave us the most complete exposition of those rocks which has yet appeared. Subsequently appointed Professor of Geology and Natural History in Adelaide University, he has done an immense amount of work in South Australia, not only as a palæontologist, but also as a conchologist and a botanist, and has risen to the foremost place amongst Australasian naturalists. He has occupied the position of President of the Royal Society of South Australia, and of the Adelaide Naturalists' Field Club, of which he also was founder. There has been much said of late as to inter-communication of naturalists, and it is not creditable to the Belfast Club that no advantage was taken of this, the final visit of its foremost member.

S. A. Stewart, Belfast.

NOTES ON SOME CASUALS IN COUNTY ANTRIM.
BY J. H. DAVIES.

GALIUM MOLLUGO, Linn.—The usual English habitat for this plant is "hedges and thickets," whereas in Ireland it is principally "grassy lawns," which is exceedingly suggestive of the species having been introduced here with seed. It occurs in a large field at Glenmore, where there are several conspicuous patches of it, and where it is thoroughly well established, but although the field has not been disturbed for a long period of years, there would appear to be a possibility of its being an introduction. Mr. Stewart informs me that he has this year found it at Whitewell, Glengormley, in County Antrim. In this country it is decidedly rare, being absent from by far the larger portion of the island, and in the north, though it occurs in Down, Antrim, Derry and Armagh, it has not been observed in any of the other counties. There seems, however, to be some ground for regarding this Bedstraw as a casual, but it may be indigenous. At Glenarm it has certainly held its place for about half a century.

SOLANUM NIGRUM, Linn.—The Black Nightshade, which is of rare occurrence in Ireland, having been found in only four of the twelve districts of *Cybele Hibernica*, has this year appeared as a weed in cultivated ground at Glenmore, near Lisburn. It seems to be a very capricious plant and without permanence in any of its Irish localities. Like *Hyoscyamus niger*, which has also been seen at Glenmore, and is now lost, it springs up for one season, or it may be for two or three seasons in succession, and is not afterwards seen in the same place. In the Copeland Islands, and in the neighbourhood of Donaghadee, where it is recorded to have been noticed by Campbell, it has since been sought for by several observers, but cannot now be found. Rev. S. A. Brenan, who noticed it for five consecutive years, 1867 to 1871, near Cushendun, informs me that it has not subsequently been observed there. Mr. Richard Hanna met with it together with a goodly number of other out-of-the-way casuals on rubbish heaps near some of the Belfast distilleries and flour-mills, as noted in the remarkable list of plants supplied by him to the Supplement to the

"Flora N. E. of Ireland" (p. 141), but all these casuals were known to have been introduced with imported grain, and it is not to be seen there now.

In the Glenmore locality the plant did not appear until late in June, and its pretty white flowers, which close in the afternoon, were first seen in the latter part of July. The fruit of the earliest flowers attains its full growth by the end of August, but does not begin to assume the blackness characteristic of its maturity until about the first week in October. Of the enormous number of berries produced, only comparatively few have time to ripen before the plant dies; but when it is considered that a single berry contains upwards of sixty seeds (more than three times as many as there are in a berry of its congener *S. Dulcamara*), it seems remarkable that, with this possibility of reproduction, the Black Nightshade should be so fitful and inconstant in all its localities. The lower branches are procumbent (rooting at many of the joints), and those of one plant cover a space of about three square yards. A branch bearing the first flowers, that was cut off in July, and placed in a jar of water kept in the open air very soon threw out numerous strong roots, produced fully formed fruit, continued to grow and flourish, and to put forth its flowers until the end of September. Notwithstanding this, it is rather a tender annual, and its leaves, which begin to fade early in October, are killed by the first frost.

POLYGONUM SACHALINENSE, Schmidt.—This plant, an herbaceous perennial, native only in the Sachalin Islands,[1] and not previously recorded as occurring in Ireland, grows at Lisburn, in waste ground in an extensive enclosure between the old mill-race and the Lagan, where the river and canal are joined, and where there is an old dry dock which is used for the repairing of lighters that ply on the Lagan canal. The dock is mentioned, because, as will afterwards be seen, it seems not unlikely that it may have some bearing on the introduction of the plant to this place, where it is in some abundance, and though with every appearance of having been there for a long time, it was only first recognised at the end of September of the present year. It was found amongst a mass of tall-growing nettles (*Urtica dioica*) from which at a short

---

[1] "*Polygonum sachalinense*, F. Schmidt, ex Maxim. Prim. Fl. Amur. 233.—Ins. Sachalin." *Index Kewensis*.

distance it was hardly distinguishable, but from its overtopping the surrounding growth my attention was specially attracted. A gentleman, one of the owners of the land, who was present on the occasion, when asked how it came to be planted there replied, "Planted? Oh, no! it was not planted; it grows wild here." A Yorkshire botanist, Mr. William Foggitt, an old and valued friend, and one of my most frequent companions on botanical excursions so far back as the early fifties, in sending me a short time ago a collection of British casuals, sent also some dried specimens of this *Polygonum* as a plant, which, on account of its alleged economic value, was claiming the attention of North of England agriculturists. It would appear that the species was first brought into England, under the name of Sachalin, in 1869, as a forage plant. It was said that it yields from eighty to one hundred and twenty tons of green fodder to the acre, and that horses are especially fond of it. Mr. Foggitt informs me also that it was stated in the newspapers that the farmers of Wensleydale, in Yorkshire, were planting it on the bare oozy hillsides where no serviceable herbage will grow, but so far he is without information as to the result of the experiment. Its beauty seems to have recommended it to horticulturists, and it is now to be seen in many gardens in Yorkshire. A magnificent bushy plant, attaining a height of from eight to ten feet, with long branched racemes of delicate greenish-yellow flowers, springing from the axil of nearly every leaf, it is not to be wondered that it should be prized as an additional ornament for borders and shubberies. On noticing the plant at Lisburn, the dried specimens received from my friend were at once brought to mind, and on comparison they were found to be identical. The most probable explanation of the occurrence of the Sachalin here, seems to be that the seeds may have been brought by the lighters which carry, from Belfast to Lisburn, coal that has been shipped in the North of England; and that they have thus found their way to the ground near the canal dock which has been mentioned.

PLANTAGO MEDIA, Linn.—Several plants in a lawn near Lisburn. The grass of the lawn being usually kept closely shorn, there is little chance of the plant spreading from seed, and indeed I have only once seen it in flower at this place, but the leaves, lying flat on the ground, as is their habit, for the most part escape uninjured the knives of the lawn-mower, so that this fragrant and most beautiful of British Plantains may survive. Mr. Praeger some years ago met with it on the Curran of Larne, where it has since been sought for, but it seems entirely to have disappeared from that locality.

PROCEEDINGS OF IRISH SOCIETIES.

ROYAL ZOOLOGICAL SOCIETY.

Recent donations include five crocodiles, a lizard, and a tortoise from Dr. E. G. Fenton; a hawk from R. H. M. Orpen, Esq.; a pair of Japanese Doves from J. B. O'Callaghan, Esq.; a Muscovy Duck from Mrs. Harford; three Llamas from J. Nelson, Esq.; a Hedgehog from W. C. Pim-Evans, Esq.; an Otter from J. Clibborn, Esq.; and a pair of Fantail Pigeons from Miss O'Farrell.

7,623 persons visited the Gardens in October.

DUBLIN MICROSCOPICAL CLUB.

OCTOBER 15.—The Club met at the house of Dr. R. F. SCHARFF.

Prof. G. A. J. COLE exhibited sections, accompanied by specimens, of the junctions of diverse igneous rocks at Oritor Quarry, Co. Tyrone. Considerable mingling of highly silicated and basic rocks seems to have occurred, but it is difficult to determine what the original types were. The highly silicated rock consists, when found in clean veins, almost entirely of a felspar, sometimes showing microcline-twinning, and these veins graduate into a true granite.

Prof. T. JOHNSON exhibited preparations of *Prasiola stipitata*, Suhr., a green alga which is of interest in that it is generally regarded as a connecting link between the green algæ (*Ulvaceæ*, &c.) and the *Bangiaceæ*, a group of red algæ. Reference to the tetraspores, oospheres and spermatia of various authors was made. The material was gathered in March last, by a sea-weed party of the Dublin Naturalists' Field Club, at half-tide on the coast north of Skerries. The only previous record of the species as Irish is in Jessen's monograph of *Prasiola*:—'Specimina Hibernica nominis Ulvæ furfuraceæ inscripta in collectione Binderi asservantur.' The preparations and illustrations shown were due to Miss Knowles.

Mr. G. H. CARPENTER showed *Onesinda minutissima*, Cb., a spider of the family *Theridiidæ*, discovered at Ardara, Co. Donegal, by Rev. W. J. Johnson, and new to the Irish fauna. It does not seem to have yet been observed out of the British Islands, but has occurred both in England (Dorset), and in Scotland (Balmoral). It is perhaps the smallest spider known, measuring only one mm. in length. In structure it is remarkable by the great convexity of the sternum. The palp of the female bears a claw; this character separates it from the *Erigoninæ*, according to Rev. O. P. Cambridge its true position is near *Pholcomma*.

Dr. McWEENEY showed the germinated sclerotia of *Peziza sclerotiorum*, also known as *P. postuma* (Berk.). This lives parasitically on potatoes in Ireland, especially along the Western seaboard, and causes a dangerous disease. The sclerotia were gathered in full germination in Co. Donegal last July. He also showed sclerotia artificially produced from the ascospores of the *Peziza* by planting them on sterilised half cylinders of potato in test-tubes. Reference was also made to a smaller, more adherent form of sclerotium, resembling mouse's excrement, also found on the plants affected by *P. sclerotiorum*. This smaller form did not produce a *Peziza*—only a conidial fruitification known as *Botrytis*. The potatoes suffering from *Peziza* disease were generally affected with *Botrytis* disease also; but there appeared to be no essential connection between the two maladies.

Mr. A. VAUGHAN JENNINGS showed preparations of the peach-coloured Bacterium, *Chromatium Okenii*. This form is specially interesting on account of its large size, its distinctive colouring, and its habit of living in water containing sulphuretted hydrogen. Sulphur is liberated by the organism, and deposited in granules in the protoplasm, and the sulphuretted hydrogen is regarded as due to its power of breaking up the sulphates of lime and soda in solution. Apart from this physiological interest, the form is of value as illustrating the pleomorphism of the Schizomycetes. The motile flagellate type which, nearly half a century ago was named by Ehrenberg *Monas Okenii*, is only a stage in a varied life-history. Other stages are the 'sperillum' form known as *Ophidomonas sanguineum*, the filamentous form *Beggiatoa roseo-persicina*, and the aggregations of 'cocci' constituting the *Clathrocystis roseo-persicinus* of Cohn. The 'coccus' condition has been described as arising from the filamentous form; but the specimens exhibited indicate that after the motile forms have passed into the 'zooglæa' stage, they too may break up into aggregates of cocci like simple forms of "*Clathorcystis*."

Dr. C. HERBERT HURST showed a section of the cochlea of a Rabbit.

Prof. A. C. HADDON showed the *Phyllosoma* larva of the crustacean *Scyllarus arctus*.

BELFAST NATURALISTS' FIELD CLUB.

OCTOBER 27.—The winter session was inaugurated by a social meeting in the Exhibition Hall. The company was a large one, filling the available space in the main hall, and comprising a good representation of the membership of the Club, with many friends. There was an interesting exhibition arranged in the hall, comprising botanical, conchological, geological, and entomological collections; photographs, seals, and microscopic specimens. In the minor hall displays of the X-rays were given by W. J. Walker. The side hall was devoted to the lantern exhibition of a series of slides depicting botanical, geological, and archæological subjects, the photographs shown being the work of F. C. Bigger, Professor Cole, W. J. Fennell, W. Gray, A. R. Hogg, Dr. MacWeeney, J. St. J. Phillips, and R. J. Welch. A collection of photos of wild flowers in their natural habitat by that capable artist, R. J. Welch, was much admired. The exhibits of the botanical section comprised British and exotic ferns, illustrated by fresh-cut fronds and growing plants, supplied by W. H. Phillips (honorary treasurer) and Charles M'Kimm (curator of Botanic Gardens Park); and recent additions to the Irish flora by R. Lloyd Praeger. Professor MacWeeney, of Dublin, exhibited some bacterial cultures and slides, and a select series of Irish fungi, including some that cause disease of the potato plant. A compact collection under the departmental title of "Marine Life" comprised a number of books illustrative of marine life, lent by the Free Library, and some models of marine life, lent by the Queen's College. Henry Hanna, A.M., showed a collection of invertebrates and a series of slides, for which the Club's prize had been awarded, while seaweeds collected on last season's dredging excursions were exhibited by Prof. Johnston and Miss Hensman. Prof. A. C. Haddon contributed some examples of commensalism and symbiosis from the marine fauna of Ireland and other countries; and Mrs. J. T. Tatlow had a collection of seaweeds from Roundstone, Connemara, and a series of shells collected on Magilligan Strand, County Derry. The conchological section comprised the above, and a collection of land shells by R. J. Welch. A. G. Wilson, Hon. Sec., displayed rocks and miscellaneous objects of interest, including specimens of Irish fresh-water pearls and the pearl mussel (*Unio margaritifera*), and some primitive forms of lamps. The geological exhibits comprised photographs of features of the high Alps, by the late W. F. Donkin, from the geological department of the Royal College of Science, Dublin (Prof. Grenville A. J. Cole, President of the Dublin Field Club); crush conglomerates (with microscopic section) from the Isle of Man, Tertiary dykes from County Down (Miss M. K. Andrews); opal and chalcedony from the rhyolitic area of County Antrim, rhyolites from Kirkinriola and Cloughwater (Mr. Robert Bell); fossil wood perforated by insects, from the Gault of Ventnor, Isle of Wight (Mr. J. O. Campbell); microscopic sections of rocks and fossils (Mr. William Gray); rocks collected on Field Club excursion to County Cavan, rocks of Slieve Gallion, County Derry (Alec G. Wilson); junction of granite and Ordovician from the new waterworks tunnel at Newcastle (Leo M. Bell); microscopic section of riebeckite granophyre from Isle of Skye (J. St. J. Phillips); Lias and Greensand fossils (George M'Clean); banded and altered shale from waterworks, Newcastle (Robert Young); fossils from Cretaceous rocks of Kent, Rhætic fossils from Bath; specimens from lead mines, Foxdale, Isle of Man (Miss S. M. Thompson). To the microscopic section the following contributed:—Rev. John Andrew (President of section), Henry Hanna, A. R. Hogg, W. S. M'Kee, Joseph Wright, Dr. Lorrain Smith, Dr. Cecil Shaw.

In the entomological department J. T. Tatlow showed a collection of butterflies from the Austrian Tyrol. Among the miscellaneous attractions, the great seals of England, exhibited by John Vinycomb, formed a distinctive feature.

At eight o'clock the President, Lavens W. Ewart, took the chair. The President, who was received with applause, said—I have to offer a welcome on behalf of the Club to our visitors, and hope they may have an enjoyable and profitable evening, and I have especially to express our thanks to those who have come to help us in the business of the present meeting. Many of them have come from afar, and we are grateful to all from far and near. I should like to say a few words on a subject of much importance at the present time, that of the Giant's Causeway, and it is surely a subject which concerns the Club. As most of those present must be aware, a few speculators have banded themselves together to endeavour to exclude the public from free access to this truly gigantic creation in order to make money out of it for themselves, and they have invoked the Court of Chancery to establish them in this undertaking. Three gentlemen, of whom, unfortunately, I am one, have been served with writs in respect of so-called trespass, and the battle has begun. A committee had already been formed to protect the rights of the public, and they are defending the action. Owing to the fact that the Causeway Syndicate is a public company they cannot be required to give security for costs, and as their capital consists of, I am informed, but £7, whether we win or lose we—that is to say, the Causeway defence committee—will have to pay our own costs. Our solicitors, Messrs. Greer and Hamilton, of Ballymoney, estimate that the costs may amount to £400, and this sum at least we must raise. We ask for help in the matter of collecting subscriptions, and collecting lists will be supplied to all who will take them. We earnestly ask all those who value liberty to take lists, and get their friends to take them, so that practical interest may be aroused on all sides in asserting the independence of the public. Large subscriptions, as a rule, are not asked for, but small sums given by the many, for it is a matter which concerns the many. Evidence is also wanted from those who have known of the Causeway as a public resort for forty or fifty years or more. I shall not occupy your time longer, but direct your attention to the different exhibits mentioned in the programme.

The remainder of the evening passed quickly over.

OCTOBER 31.—BOTANICAL SECTION. A pleasing and interesting feature was the presentation of a set of mounted *Hieracia* to Mr. S. A. Stewart. This collection is being issued in four fascicles of twenty-five specimens each, by Messrs. E. F. and W. R. Linton. Rev. C. H. WADDELL, in presenting the first fascicle to Mr. Stewart on behalf of the subscribers, read the following inscription:—"Set of British *Hieracia* presented to Samuel Alexander Stewart, F.B.S.E., in recognition of his valuable services to Irish Botany, and especially in this genus, and as a mark of their affection and esteem by Members of the Botanical Section of the Belfast Naturalists' Field Club and other friends." Messrs. C. H. Waddell, J. H. Davies, and others, spoke of Mr. Stewart's great services to Irish Botany, and of the value of his "Flora of N.E. Ireland," and testified how willing he always was to place his wide experience and accurate knowledge at the service of any who were really interested in the science. Mr. Stewart replied, and said it would afford him much pleasure to help any of the members in their study of the *Hieracia* or in any way he could. Some recent additions to the local flora were then discussed, including *Solanum nigrum* which has been found near Lambeg, probably only as a casual. The rest of the time was given to the examination and description of *Compositæ*, and especially the genus *Hieracium*.

DUBLIN NATURALISTS' FIELD CLUB.

NOVEMBER 10.—The Winter Session was opened by a Conversazione at the Royal Irish Academy, which was largely attended. The President (Prof. G. A. J. COLE) opened the meeting at 8 o'clock. In the name of the Club, he welcomed the representatives of the Belfast and Cork Field Clubs who were present, and also the many local visitors. At 8.15 and at 9.15 lantern displays were given in the lecture hall. The subjects illustrated included Prehistoric Remains of Co. Antrim, by Prof. Haddon and G. Coffey; rare Fungi, by Greenwood Pim; Sea-birds and their nests on Lambay Island, by R. Welch and Greenwood Pim; the Field Club Union Excursion to Cavan, by R. Welch; and Wild Flowers in their homes, by R. Welch. The scientific exhibits which covered the tables were as follows:—

Prof. G. A. J. Cole (President)—Forms of Silica in Rocks, illustrated by specimens and microscopic sections; G. H. Carpenter—1. Some Curious Insect Larvæ; 2. New Irish Spiders; Hon. R. E. Dillon—Irish Lepidoptera, illustrating protective coloration, &c.; A. H. Foord—Specimens of Rocks from the Lava-flows and Geysers of Iceland; W. Gray (B.N.F.C.)—A fine Zeolite from Co. Antrim; Mrs. W. S. Green—Sea-weeds collected in Co. Kerry, 1896; Prof. A. C. Haddon—Animal Partnerships: Examples of Commensalism and Symbiosis; J. N. Halbert —Water Insects; Dr. C. Herbert Hurst—Microscopic Preparations, illustrating the structure of the Heads of Insects; A. Vaughan Jennings—Flowering Plants and Fungi from the Eastern Alps; Prof. T. Johnson—Irish Marine Algæ collected with the collaboration of Miss Knowles and Miss Hensman in 1896; Miss M. C. Knowles—Flowering Plants from Co. Tyrone, 1896; D. M'Ardle—Some rare Mosses and Hepatics; A. R. Nichols—Marine Shells collected on the Waterford Coast, 1896; Greenwood Pim—Restrepia striata and Ceropegia elegans in flower; W. H. Phillips (B.N.F.C.)—Varieties of British Ferns, illustrated by fresh and dried fronds; R. Lloyd Praeger—Additions to the List of Irish Flowering Plants, 1894-96; Dr. R. F. Scharff—New Crustacea from the West Coast of Ireland; Mrs. J. T. Tatlow—1. Sea-weeds collected at Roundstone, 1896; 2. Dried Specimens of alpine and other Plants grown at Dundrum, 1896; J. T. Tatlow—Butterflies from the Austrian Tyrol, 1896; Miss S. M. Thompson (B.N.F.C.)—1. Scotch Erratics from Boulder-clays of Belfast District; 2. Microscopic Sections of Riebeckite Eurite from Ailsa Craig and Skye; R. Welch (B.N.F.C.)—1. Irish Land and Fresh-water Mollusca; 2. Photographs of Wild Flowers, etc

CORK NATURALISTS' FIELD CLUB.

AUGUST 22.—The month's excursion took place, a good party going to the Waterfall station and walking thence to Ballinhassig Glen, taking on the way some bogs, which yielded amongst other plants the Lesser Skull-cap (*Scutellaria minor*), Sneeze-wort (*Achillea Ptarmica*), Branched Bur-reed (*Sparganium ramosum*), Bog Pimpernel (*Anagallis tenella*), Bog Asphodel (*Narthecium ossifragum*), Pale Butterwort (*Pinguicula lusitanica*), in flower, and *Pinguicula grandiflora*.

Large tracts of moor were crossed which were a magnificent sight, with the gorse and heather in full bloom.

Mr. J. Porter, B.E., Bandon, who acted as guide, explained the geology of the district. Waterfall and Ballinhassig stations, on the Cork, Bandon, and South Coast Railway, are on the northern and southern sides respectively of one of the main east and west anticlinal hill-ranges. The core of the arching fold is formed of the Dingle Beds, which have been laid bare on the broad summit of the range, while the Carboniferous rocks cover the flanks.

SEPTEMBER 5.—The last excursion of the season came off, when the Club visited Rock Close, Blarney, by kind permission of Sir George Colthurst, and after exploring the curious rocks, &c., walked to St. Ann's Hydropathic, where tea was provided.

NOTES.

ZOOLOGY.

INSECTS.

Abundance of Acherontia atropos.—From the British entomological magazines it appears that caterpillars of the Death's-head moth have been more common than usual in England and Scotland this year. A similar visitation appears to have prevailed in Ireland, as during the summer months I received a number of specimens from different parts of the country—Cos. Dublin, Meath, and Wexford.

GEO. H. CARPENTER.

Asteroscopus sphinx in Co. Dublin.—As Mr. W. F. de V. Kane in his recent list of Irish Moths, gives but two localities, Galway and Westmeath, for *Asteroscopus sphinx*, it may be of interest to note that my brother and I took a few specimens of this moth here in Co. Dublin, at light, early in November, 1893 and 1894; and this year, on November 2nd, two specimens, one flying round ivy and the other at light. In every instance they were males.

G. P. FARRAN, Templeogue.

[We have recently heard of the capture of this moth at Dundrum, also in Co. Dublin, by Mr. George Low, and in Co. Waterford by Rev. W. W. Flemyng.—EDS.]

Mixodia palustrana in Co. Wicklow.—On Whit Monday, May 25th (this year) while ascending Lugnaquilla, Co. Wicklow, I took a few specimens of a tortrix, which turns out to be *Mixodia palustrana*. I cannot find any previous report of its occurrence in Ireland. *M. schulziana* was on the wing at the same time and place.

GEORGE V. HART, Howth.

Clifton Nonpareil (Catocala fraxini) at Londonderry.—A specimen of this very rare moth came into Mr. R. B. Thompson's house, Marlborough Street, Derry, by an open window during the night. The date was about 10th September last. Mr. Thompson brought the insect to me for examination.

D. C. CAMPBELL, Londonderry.

MOLLUSCS.

Helix arbustorum in Co. Derry.—It is interesting to find this shell turning up again so soon in another new locality. Mr. Robert Bell, a member of the B.N.F.C., while fossil-hunting in an old quarry at Tamlaght, on the borders of the county (near Coagh, Co. Tyrone), found it fairly plentiful, and brought me a few specimens.

R. WELCH, Belfast.

Helix fusca.—I have searched carefully for this rare shell for year, in likely places—mountain glens and damp woods—but without success till lately, when I got one specimen on river-bank at Newcastle, Co. Down, on rejectamenta after flood, and four specimens this month in the ravine of Glenariff, Co. Antrim. Professor R. Tate found it many years ago common in winter in certain damp woods near Belfast, usually on the Wood-rush (*Luzula sylvatica*), and it has also been recorded from several mountain glens in the same district. Dr. Scharff noted it on Beech trees this summer at Clonbrock, Co. Galway.

R. WELCH, Belfast.

Slugs of Ireland.—Wanted living examples of the following species:—*Limax marginatus*, *Agriolimax lævis*, *Amalia gagates*, *Arion intermedius*, and *Geomalacus maculosus*.

WALTER E. COLLINGE, F.Z.S., Mason College, Birmingham.

BIRDS.

Kingfisher in Co. Dublin.—When travelling on the D.W. and W. Railway last September I noticed a Kingfisher flying over the water between Williamstown and Booterstown. Some years ago I have seen them where the Blackrock People's Park is now, but till the occasion mentioned, I have not seen one for a long time.

GREENWOOD PIM, Monkstown, Dublin.

A White Swallow.—Having shot a perfectly white Swallow or Swift on my lands at Camass near Bruff, Co. Limerick, on the 25th inst. I should be glad if any of your readers could inform me if they ever have seen one. The common Swallows were hunting this bird as if they did not like it.

J. V. BEVAN. [In *Limerick Chronicle*, August 28.]

[Mr. Williams reports that this specimen is a Swallow (*Hirundo rustica*) and a genuine albino, having pink eyes. He has received this year two other white Swallows, which, however, had eyes of the normal colour, and also an albino Sand martin (*Cotyle riparia*) from other Irish localities. —EDS.]

Birds of Connemara.—Referring to Mr. Witherby's statement that he has met with the Dunlin, as Mr. Palmer has the Ringed Plover, in the breeding season on Lough Corrib, I beg to say that no one need be suprised at either, for both species have a wide breeding-range on the Irish inland lakes.

I have a list of eighteen counties in which the Dunlin has either been found breeding or met with in June under circumstances denoting that it bred there. I have taken Dunlins' eggs in Londonderry, Donegal, and Westmeath, and seen it on many a lake in June, including the Shannon lakes and callows of the Shannon down to the Clare shores of Lough Derg.

I have found a Ringed Plover's nest on Lough Sheelin under a willow. That Oyster-catchers should prefer the tops of islands to the shingly beach is nothing unusual. On the Donegal coast last June I saw many nests, usually in crannies or hollows of the rocks, far up above the tide. On the Saltees they breed more frequently in hollows of the turfy sod on the top of the great hill, 290 feet high, than on the shingly beach. I saw one Oyster-catcher's nest there among the beans in a bean-field. They usually select spots on the hill where knobs of rock surround the nesting-hollow, but sometimes breed on the flat turf among short bracken.

In parts of Connemara, where there are no sea-cliffs, I should expect Black Guillemots to breed under the huge boulders, to be found in so many places, forming a chaos of rock. I have seen the birds there. At the Cliffs of Moher I saw none, but Black Guillemots were seen evidently breeding about a low limestone island off the little port of Fisherstreet, in the horizontal fissures of which they must have had their breeding nook. Fisherstreet is over a mile from the cliffs.

R. J. USSHER, Cappagh.

Carrion Crow (Corvus Corone) in Co. Antrim.—Whilst conchologising in the woods round Murlough Bay, during the early part of September last, my friend Mr. J. Ray Hardy picked up a recently dead specimen of this bird. It was a fully plumaged bird of the year and quite fresh. The incident would have passed without comment on our part, if a remark made by Mr. R. Welch (who was with us) to the effect that "the Crow is a rare bird in Ireland," had not led me to think that a record of the fact might interest Irish ornithologists. During the day we more than once heard the (to us) familiar cry of the Crow, and saw the birds themselves, either flying singly or associated with parties of Rooks and Jackdaws; and on a subsequent day we saw and recognised the cry of three individuals flying over the bog on the road between Ballycastle and Ballintoy. We have both been familiar with the Crow in England since boyhood, and Mr. Hardy has observed it frequently in various parts of Co. Kerry, and has now in his collection skins and eggs taken by himself in the woods in Gap of Dunloe—so there is no possibility of mistake.

R. STANDEN, Manchester Museum.

Fork-tailed Petrel (Oceanodroma leucorrhoa) near Londonderry.—About 20th October Mr. Buckle, of Culmore, near Londonderry, shot a specimen of this species on the shores of Lough Foyle.

D. C. CAMPBELL, Londonderry.

Bird Notes from Co. Cork.—A good specimen of the Squacco Heron (*Ardea ralloides*) was shot near Ballinacourty, County Waterford, on the 12th September, 1895 (no doubt the one referred to by Mr. E. Williams as having been shot in County Cork, see Vol. v., No. 2, *Irish Naturalist*), and a Ruff (*Machetes pugnax*) near Blarney, on the 20th February, 1896. The reports which I have received of Quail, *Coturnix communis*, from Co. Cork this year, show that the distribution has been pretty general over the county; in the locality of Midleton they appear to have been more numerous than elsewhere.

W. BENNETT BARRINGTON, Cork.

GEOLOGY.

Cave at Westport.—Referring to the note in the *Irish Naturalist* for October (page 276) as to the cave near Westport "called Aglemore," I believe that the place specified is evidently Ailemore, and the cave is nothing more than the underground passage of a mountain-stream. As far as I can understand, it has never been explored, and I doubt very much if a man could push his way through. I have thought of trying it, but the idea quite escaped my memory when the season was most favourable. All the same, the place is well worth a visit; and, though tourists will be disappointed of a three and a half miles walk underground, and though the Aile caves do not surpass those of Mitchelstown, a very pleasant day can be spent in the vicinity. The entrance to the underground passage is at the base of a limestone cliff of about thirty feet high, and concave in shape, formed of stratified limestone, which falls occasionally from the roof in huge square blocks.

JOSEPH M. M'BRIDE, Westport.

www.ingramcontent.com/pod-product-compliance
Lightning Source LLC
Chambersburg PA
CBHW031858220426
43663CB00006B/674